MW01199652

Seneca's Tragedies and the Aesthetics of Pantomime

Also Available from Bloomsbury

Polybius and Roman Imperialism by Donald Walter Baronowski
HB: 9780715639429
PB: 9781472504500

Emotion, Genre and Gender in Classical Antiquity by Dana Munteanu
HB: 9780715638958
PB: 9781472504487

Seneca: Select Letters edited by W.C. Summers
PB: 9780862921200

Seneca's Tragedies and the Aesthetics of Pantomime

Alessandra Zanobi

Bloomsbury Academic
An imprint of Bloomsbury Publishing Plc

B L O O M S B U R Y
LONDON · NEW DELHI · NEW YORK · SYDNEY

Bloomsbury Academic

An imprint of Bloomsbury Publishing Plc

50 Bedford Square
London
WC1B 3DP
UK

1385 Broadway
New York
NY 10018
USA

www.bloomsbury.com

**BLOOMSBURY and the Diana logo are trademarks of B
loomsbury Publishing Plc**

First published 2014
Paperback edition first published 2015

© Alessandra Zanobi, 2014

Alessandra Zanobi has asserted her right under the Copyright, Designs and Patents Act,
1988, to be identified as Author of this work.

All rights reserved. No part of this publication may be reproduced or transmitted in any form
or by any means, electronic or mechanical, including photocopying, recording, or any
information storage or retrieval system, without prior permission in writing
from the publishers.

No responsibility for loss caused to any individual or organization acting on or refraining
from action as a result of the material in this publication can be accepted by
Bloomsbury or the author.

British Library Cataloguing-in-Publication Data
A catalogue record for this book is available from the British Library.

ISBN: HB: 978-1-4725-1188-1
PB: 978-1-4742-4899-0
ePDF: 978-1-4725-1263-5
ePUB: 978-1-4725-0608-5

Library of Congress Cataloging-in-Publication Data
Zanobi, Alessandra, author.
Seneca's tragedies and the aesthetics of pantomime/Alessandra Zanobi.
pages cm
Includes bibliographical references and index.
ISBN 978-1-4725-1188-1 (hardback)—ISBN 978-1-4725-0608-5 (epub)—ISBN 978-1-4725-
1263-5 (epdf) 1. Seneca, Lucius Annaeus, approximately 4 b.c.–65 a.d.—Dramatic works.
2. Pantomime—History and criticism. I. Title.
PA6685.Z26 2014
872'.01—dc23
2013034324

Typeset by RefineCatch Limited, Bungay, Suffolk

Table of Contents

Introduction
The *Vexata Quaestio* of the Dramaturgy of Seneca's Tragedies   vii

1 Pantomime in the Ancient World   1
  Introduction   1
  Pantomime as a Genre   2
  Pantomime in Roman Culture   17

2 Pantomime and the Structure of Seneca's Tragedies   53
  Introduction   53
  Systematic Analysis of Seneca's Tragedies   53

3 Pantomime and Descriptive Running Commentaries   89
  Introduction: The Role of Descriptions in Seneca's Tragedies   89
  General Features of Running Commentaries of Onstage Actions   91
  General Features of Running Commentaries of Offstage Actions   111

4 Monologues of Self-analysis   129
  Introduction   129
  Phaedra (99–144; 177–94): Phaedra's Self-analysis   133
  Agamemnon (131–44): Clytemnestra's Self-analysis   135
  Medea (926–8; 937–44; 951–3): Medea's Self-analysis   136
  Thyestes (434–9; 496–505; 920–69): Thyestes' Self-analysis   137
  Trojan Women (642–62): Andromache's Self-analysis   143

5 Pantomime and Descriptive Narrative Set-pieces of Seneca's
    Tragedies   147
  Introduction: General Features of Narrative Set-pieces   147
  Analysis of the Narrative Set-pieces   154

Conclusion 201

Notes 205

References 255

Index of Ancient Authors 273

General Index 279

Introduction

The *Vexata Quaestio* of the Dramaturgy of Seneca's Tragedies

That Seneca's tragedies exhibit numerous features that set them apart from the theatrical conventions of fifth-century Greek tragedy and do not conform to the classical model, as defined for this genre by Aristotle, developed by Hellenistic critics, and accepted in Rome by Horace, is a fact well observed by most Senecan scholars;[1] among these peculiar characteristics of Seneca's tragic *corpus*, the most striking ones are the pronounced structural looseness, the freedom in the handling of the chorus, the showing of death onstage, and the presence of lengthy descriptive narratives. This has caused some scholars to consider them unstageable and to argue that Seneca was not interested in composing theatrical scripts to be performed onstage; rather they claimed Seneca wrote them to be recited by one or more voices.[2] The hypothesis of recitation was not only considered apt to solve the staging difficulties the tragedies presented, but also apparently fitted with the lack of positive evidence for full-length performances of tragedies from Imperial times onwards. However, since incontrovertible evidence is missing, the question about the intended destination of Seneca's tragedies is still open and debated by scholars.[3]

A major problem in the interpretation of the controversial features of Seneca's tragedies is due to the total loss of complete tragic play texts between Euripides and Seneca; in fact, since no complete tragedy survives from the Hellenistic, Republican, or Augustan period, the fifth-century Greek plays are necessarily the only extant models available with which Senecan tragedies can be compared. A direct comparison shows that Seneca's tragedy 'deviates in many ways from the dramatic technique of fifth-century Greek tragedy and that some Senecan scenes would be difficult or even impossible to stage within classical Greek conventions'.[4] If this is certainly true, it must be also observed that, since theatrical conventions underwent noticeable changes in the long span of time intervening between Euripides and Seneca, the comparison between fifth-century Greek tragedies and those of Seneca lacks a methodological basis and cannot be considered as absolutely reliable to postulate definitive conclusions.

The solution of this methodological problem has been rightly perceived by Senecan scholars as fundamental to the achievement of a better and fuller understanding of his dramatic art. Despite the exiguity of extant evidence, several attempts have been made to put Seneca's tragic *corpus* in its proper historical and literary context.[5] Tarrant's pivotal article focuses specifically on the antecedents of Senecan drama. He traces several features of Senecan theatre such as the lack of organic coherence, the free handling of the chorus, the large use of entrance monologues and asides back to the post-classical theatrical tradition.[6] Kelly's article, instead, offers a detailed account of the different kinds of theatrical performances attested in Seneca's time such as *tragoedia agenda* or *recitanda* (regular tragedies that could be staged or declaimed), *tragoedia saltata* (pantomime), and *citharoedia* or *tragoedia cantata* (concert tragedies). Kelly's survey demonstrates how complex and articulate the Roman stage in Seneca's time was, and his suggestion that genres such as *tragoedia saltata* and *cantata* may have influenced Seneca when composing his tragic *corpus* seems plausible. It is worth underlining that an interpretation similar to Kelly's had been already suggested by Herrmann early in the twentieth century as he observed that the tragedies had a pronounced 'mixed character';[7] Herrmann's definition implied that Seneca adopted technical devices that were typical of other genres popular in his time such as tragic singing, mime, and pantomime. For instance, several lyric monodies that seem removable from their context within the plays, such as the one at *Medea* (lines 740–848), which is sung by one actor and not strictly connected with the developing action, stand as bravura passages and can be compared to operatic arias.[8]

Seneca's adoption of different theatrical genres then would be in keeping with the attested contemporary practice of the Roman stage to combine different types of theatrical shows.[9] One genre, however, seems to have been of particular interest to Seneca, i.e. pantomime. Pantomime was an extremely popular type of performance in Seneca's time and he was well aware of this popularity; his appreciation for the pantomimic art is attested in his *Epistles* (121, 6): *Mirari solemus saltandi peritos quod in omnem significationem rerum et adfectuum parata illorum est manus et verborum velocitatem gestus adsequitur.*[10] The strict generic affiliations between tragedy and pantomime may have easily prompted the generic enrichment of tragedy through elements of pantomime.[11] Wagenvoort, who, to my knowledge, was the first scholar to claim the influence of pantomime on Seneca's tragedies, has argued that 'it is easily understandable that pantomime, once it became an established genre, must have exercised a strong influence on tragedy. In fact, if tragedy did not want to lose its popularity, it had to compete with pantomime, especially in the hunt for pathos.'[12]

The presence of pantomimic elements in Seneca's tragedies may in part due to his attempt to make them suitable to the taste of his audience. Seneca's sensitivity to and awareness of the taste of his contemporaries is consistent with Tacitus' description, which portrays him as a man endowed with a brilliant mind well suited to the taste of his age (*Annales* 13, 3: *fuit illi viro ingenium amoenum et temporis eius auribus accommodatum*).

But there are two additional reasons, arguably more interesting, for Seneca's interest in the techniques and aesthetics of pantomime. First of all, this theatrical medium, which expressed its art through movements and gestures, was the most suitable one, thanks to its effectiveness in expressing many different *affectus*, to display the effects of passions, whose treatment has a central place both in Seneca's tragic and philosophical works. In Seneca's philosophical view, individual identity is control over instinct and passion. The loss of control turns a person into one of a series of possible stereotyped masks of an archetypical behaviour. Although philosophically and morally unacceptable, the consequence of the loss of control can, however, be spectacular and worthy of artistic representation. Pantomime with its instances of stylization is the art most suited for representing extreme mental states associated with the tragic loss of control.

Second, experimental attitude and freedom in the handling of the models, which are, more generally, typical features of post-classical Roman writers, are two important and well-recognized Senecan characteristics. In this regard, Boyle's statement about Seneca's interest in 'dramatic experimentation even perhaps innovation' as well as his definition of Senecan tragedy as 'formally diverse tragedy' are particularly relevant.[13]

Thus, the pronounced hybrid form of Seneca's tragedies, produced by a blend of dramatic and narrative elements that do not traditionally belong together, may be a sign that Seneca has implanted formal features typical of the pantomimic genre in the tragic frame. To use Harrison's terminology, tragedy would stand as the 'host' genre while pantomime is the 'guest' one.[14] That the nature of the phenomenon of generic enrichment may have been suitable to Seneca's literary experimental attitude is suggested by a passage in one of his epistles in which Seneca claims that his dialogue with tradition accommodates original and personal invention (80, 1: *Non ergo sequor priores? facio, sed permitto mihi et invenire aliquid et mutare et relinquere; non servio illis, sed assentior*). Furthermore, Seneca's claim that many of Publilius' mimic verses are suitable to be included in tragedy may suggestively hint at Seneca's own keenness on appropriating elements from sub-literary genres.[15]

It is important to mention here that, among the generic affiliations of pantomime, rhetoric constitutes a major generic strand as attested by Lucian (35;

65). Rhetoric and pantomime share a common ground since both deal with impersonation, which is especially cultivated by rhetoricians in declamations, and the display of *êthos* and *pathos*. In considering the relationship between pantomime and rhetoric, Leo's analysis of Seneca's plays can be appreciated in a new light. He defined them as rhetorical tragedies (*tragoedia rhetorica*), namely dramatized rhetorical declamations, and claimed that Seneca created a new genre: 'A new genre has been created: rhetorical tragedy, whose nature can be briefly described as follows: there is no ethos in it, only pathos' and later on: 'These are not tragedies at all, but declamations composed in the form of tragedies and divided into acts; and if in them something were expressed beautifully or brilliantly, or described in a flowery and figurative manner, or narrated learnedly, the audience would have clapped and the art would have been fulfilled.'[16] Therefore, such features that Leo attributed to the influence of rhetoric can also be ascribed to that of pantomime;[17] such plausibility resides indeed in the above-mentioned generic contiguity in matter of themes and moods between tragedy and pantomime.

The original nature of Seneca's work can be seen as the result of generic enrichment, which was sought after by most of writers belonging to Nero's literary circle, such as Petronius and Lucan. Seneca's embracing of such a literary attitude may have been thus prompted by his being part of the same Imperial literary *entourage*. In relation to this, it is relevant to quote Tacitus' testimony relating that Seneca began to write his poetic compositions since Nero developed a passion for poetry;[18] if this is the case, it is highly plausible that the inclusion of pantomimic elements may have particularly pleased the emperor whose passion for these theatrical performances was such that he himself became a performer and would have danced Virgil's Turnus if he had survived the military overthrow that made an end to his reign.[19]

Moreover, that the literary activity in the age of Nero was probably inspired by the emperor's own interest in dramatic forms, pantomime and mime, and that such genres must have been conspicuously in the forefront of contemporary literary productions is also suggested by the pervasive mimic spirit of Petronius' *Satyricon* as well as by the notice found in Vacca's life that Lucan composed fourteen *salticae fabulae*; thus, Seneca, Petronius, and Lucan, the three leading figures of Nero's literary circle, all seem to have been attuned to the dominant interest of Nero the *artifex*.[20]

In a cultural climate craving for novelty, pantomime offered a fertile ground for brilliant writers to display their abilities in adapting well-known literary materials (attesting their familiarity and knowledge of the literary tradition) to a new and fashionable performative medium. In a sense, pantomime can be seen as an additional rhetorical exercise, in which the writer was challenged to cleverly find metaphors, metonymies, and similes meant to function as verbal analogues to the movements of the dancer.

The aim of the present work is to focus on the relationship between Seneca's dramas and pantomime. A close scrutiny of Seneca's tragic *corpus* with pantomime in mind is worth undertaking, especially because the hypothesis of this influence has been suggested by several scholars but never investigated on a systematic basis; in fact, Wagenvoort's contribution did not open the way to further investigations of the possible influence of the aesthetics of pantomime on Seneca's tragedies and only more recently Zimmermann and Erasmo have recast the point at issue.[21]

Even more importantly, the scrutiny of the influence of the aesthetics of pantomime addresses the compelling issue of Senecan modern criticism, which aims at delineating the historical development of dramatic genres and conventions as a fundamental instrument to assess Seneca's tragic work more accurately and in relation to its cultural context. If we take into account the most common features of pantomimic performances when reading Seneca's tragedies, some of the controversial features of the plays, which do not have a parallel in fifth-century Greek tragic conventions, can possibly be explained and better understood.

The thesis consists of five chapters. In the first chapter, after a preliminary outline of the general features of pantomime as a genre, I will show that the influence of sub-literary genres such as pantomime and mime, the sister art of pantomime, can be traced in several Roman writers whose literary production was antecedent or contemporary with Seneca's; this chapter is thus meant to provide the general background for the more specific exploration of the influence of the aesthetics of pantomime on Seneca's tragedies. The thesis will then continue with the systematic attempt to identify and analyse specific features of Seneca's tragedies, whose peculiar shape and handling can be attributed to the influence of the aesthetics of pantomime. These features are the peculiar loose dramatic structure, the presence of 'running commentaries' (minute descriptions of characters undergoing emotional strains or performing specific actions), of monologues of self-analysis, and of narrative set-pieces. The general features contributing to the loose dramatic structure of Seneca's tragedies will be discussed in Chapter 2; the occurrence and nature of 'running commentaries' will be discussed in Chapter 3, that of monologues of self-analysis in Chapter 4, and that of narrative set-pieces will be discussed in Chapter 5.

1

Pantomime in the Ancient World

Introduction

This chapter consists of two parts. The first one offers a preliminary outline of the general features of pantomime as a genre. The second shows that the influence of sub-literary genres such as pantomime and mime, the two most popular forms of drama in the late Republic and Imperial times, can be traced in several Roman writers whose literary production was antecedent or contemporary with Seneca's; this section of the chapter is thus meant to provide the general background for the more specific exploration of the influence of the aesthetics of pantomime on Seneca's tragedies. I deal here with both the influence of mime and pantomime since these two theatrical genres were closely related and ancient writers make no sharp distinction between the two of them.[1] Such affinity was due to the fact that both mime and pantomime relied on gestures and body movements as a preferred means to portray characters or narrate stories. The major difference between these two otherwise very akin genres was thematic. Mime tended to deal with comic, realistic, and low-life themes, pantomime, instead, with tragic and mythological ones; however, these are generalizations, since mime could present mythological themes (burlesques) and a comic type of pantomime also existed. Moreover, it is attested that some themes, as, for instance, that of adultery, featured in both genres. Finally, the section is also meant to show that, as Fantham has argued, mime and pantomime constitute the 'missing link in Roman literary history' and that an assessment of their influence on higher literary genres would contribute to a better understanding of the various facets of Roman culture.[2]

Pantomime as a Genre

Origins and Development of Pantomime

The origins and development of pantomime are shrouded in obscurity and hence debated. Pantomime had its roots in the tradition of mimetic dancing that was practised and, most probably independently developed, by geographically and culturally separated peoples such as the Etruscans, the Greeks, and the Egyptians. Scholars have alternatively assigned the origins of this genre to Egypt, Greece, or Italy.[3] Jory has maintained that the different scholarly theories about the origins of pantomime are not 'mutually exclusive'.[4] Greek forerunners of pantomime are to be found in the sort of performance described by Xenophon in his *Symposium* (9, 43), in an epigram by Dioscorides (about 250 BC) about the victory of a certain Aristagoras who danced a Gallos, and in an inscription from Priene (80 BC) recording the activity of a pantomime named Plutogenes.[5] Italian antecedents of pantomime are to be found in the *Ludus talarius* and in the mime, of which dancing constituted an integral element.[6] Indeed, as Garton has stressed, mime was the type of performance with which pantomime was most closely associated; this association is attested by the undifferentiated terminology with which ancient writers refer to mime and pantomime, confirming that these theatrical genres were perceived as sister arts closely related to each other and that no sharp distinction between the two of them actually existed.[7]

The pivotal role of dance in the mime is then attested already in the first recorded presence of a mimic actor on the Roman stage (211 BC). The story transmitted by Festus (436–38 L) and Servius (*ad Aen.* VIII, 110) says that the mimic actor Pomponius kept dancing to the flute in order to preserve the ritual, despite the fact that his fellow citizens were compelled to leave the theatre at the news of Hannibal's approach to the city. The episode originated the well-known anecdote *salva res est, saltat senex*. Movement, gesticulation, and facial expressions constituted the quintessential feature of mime and this is the reason why it was considered the most mimetic among the performative genres.[8] The practice of barefoot performance, which originated the epithet *planipedes* that was often applied to mimic performers, indicates their necessity to be able to move freely.[9] An inscription from Rome dated to the Imperial period in praise of an actor seems to attest the existence of a type of mime in which dancing featured so prominently that it was named 'dancing mime': *Lau]datus populo, solitus mandata referre,/Adl]ectus scaenae, Parasitus Apollinis idem,/Quar]tarum in mimis saltantibus utilis actor*.[10] Moreover, the thematic repertoire of mime and pantomime apparently dealt with the same subjects as, for instance, that of adultery which constituted one of the most preferred motifs in both mimic and pantomimic performances. Furthermore, mime reached the apex of its popularity in the first century BC in connection with the productions of the mimographers Laberius and Publilius Syrus, who added a literary dimension and thus transformed the rather crude genre which mime once must have been.

Tracing the development of pantomime in Rome is a difficult task because of the dearth of extant evidence; still, ancient writers provide accounts of when pantomime was introduced at Rome, and of the names of the two pantomimic dancers to whom the creation of the genre is ascribed, i.e. Pylades from Cilicia or Bathyllus of Alexandria.[11] Athenaeus records that Bathyllus introduced the pantomimic dance in Rome and, relying on the authority of the Alexandrian grammarian Aristonicus, that he and Pylades developed the 'Italian style of dancing' which was a combination of the dances found in tragedy (*emmeleia*), in comedy (*cordax*) and in the satyr play (*sicinnis*).[12] Suetonius' account names only Pylades, to whom he ascribes not the introduction or invention of the genre, but its transformation consisting in the introduction of the accompaniment by a chorus and a pipe player;[13] that Pylades transformed a genre already in existence seems to be confirmed by a passage in Macrobius where Pylades is said to have brought revolutionary changes by adding 'the sound of the flutes and pipes and the murmur of men'.[14]

Concerning the time at which the pantomimic dance made its first appearance in Rome, Macrobius provides the information that Pylades flourished in the age of Augustus;[15] this dating is confirmed also by Lucian and the Byzantine historian Zosimus.[16] The year 22 BC was the date at which Jerome asserted that pantomime was introduced to Rome, but it is most likely that the year 23 BC was actually the one in which pantomime made its official entry in the city, being included in the games of Marcellus, Augustus' nephew.[17] As argued by Jory, if pantomime was included in the games, it must have arrived in Rome before the date reported by Jerome; the year 22 BC was most probably fixed by ancient writers out of their general concern for origins and dates of foundation in order to provide a date for the introduction of pantomime in Rome.[18] The new genre was actually perfected under the emperor Augustus, but its introduction in Rome must have taken place before that date as it is possibly attested by two passages in Horace (*Satires*, I, 5, 63 dated to 37 BC: *Pastorem saltaret uti Cyclopa rogabat*; *Epistulae*, II, 2, 124–5: *ludentis speciem dabit et torquebitur, ut qui/nunc Satyrum, nunc agrestem Cyclopa movetur*).[19] Furthermore, a Varronian fragment written around 60 BC, which most probably refers to a pantomimic performance of the story of Actaeon, would attest the presence of pantomime already in the first half of the first century BC (fr. 513 = 515 Cèbe from the *Synephebus* in Nonius 5, 355): *crede mihi, plures dominos servi comederunt quam canes. quod si Actaeon occupasset et ipse prius suos canes comedisset, non nugas* **saltatoribus** *in theatro fieret;* that Varro is referring to pantomime is corroborated by Lucian's statement (41) that the story of Actaeon featured as a theme in pantomimic performances.[20]

Augustus was the first patron of pantomime and Pylades, the original innovator of the pantomimic genre, is said to have been on terms of familiarity with him by Macrobius;[21] moreover, Cassius Dio and Macrobius also report that Pylades could afford to reply fearlessly to Augustus' rebuke about the quarrels between him and his rivals (either Bathyllus or Hylas); thus Pylades is said to have given to Augustus the daring answer that such disputes among famous performers were advantageous for the emperor because people's minds were kept off politics by them.[22]

As Beacham has argued, Augustus supported pantomime because he saw in it 'a useful medium both for mass entertainment and for embodying and popularizing the classical mythology and traditional beliefs so central to the ideology of the principate'.[23] On a similar line of thought, Garelli has claimed that since pantomime was an 'ecumenical' type of performance, which could cross the linguistic boundaries and ethnic divisions of the Empire, it was well suited to embody Augustus' ideology of a world unified and pacified under his reign.[24] It is not coincidence then that pantomime was at first introduced at festivals celebrating the Imperial cult such as the *Augustalia* in Rome and the Sebasta games in Naples, which were instituted in honour of Augustus in 2 AD (Dio 55, 10, 9; Strabo 5, 246) and in which pantomime was introduced in 18 AD.[25] Moreover, archeological findings at Aphrodisias, which under Augustus received a number of privileges among which was direct imperial patronage, have shown that the frieze of the propylon of the Sebasteion was decorated with masks which can be attributed to pantomime, since they present the typical closed-mouth of the pantomimic masks.[26] Jory has remarked that the presence of pantomimic masks on the frieze at Aphrodisias could be a form of homage paid by the Aphrodisian founders of the Sebasteion to 'Augustus' own tastes' in matter of theatrical performances.[27] The 'pantomania' grew enormously during Augustus' reign to the point that Tiberius, his successor, had to face the riots that broke out among the factions supporting rival pantomimic dancers. At the beginning, because of the popularity the dancers had attained in all the strands of the populace and unwilling to change Augustus' decision in matter of the treatment of misbehaving performers, Tiberius chose to act against such disturbances with restrictive measures applied to the pay of the pantomimic dancers, by permitting their performances only inside the theatre, and by forbidding performers to receive senators in their homes or to be accompanied in public by members of the equestrian order.[28] However, in 23 AD he was compelled to ban pantomimic dancers from Rome.[29]

Caligula (37–41 AD) recalled the artists as soon as he became emperor and indulged openly in the company of one of them, Mnester, whom he shamelessly treated as his favourite.[30] Claudius (41–54 AD) kept protecting pantomimic dancers because of Messalina, his wife, who is said to have had a love affair with the dancer Mnester; right after Messalina's disgrace, the performer was immediately sentenced to death by Claudius.[31] It is well known that Nero (54–68 AD) enjoyed theatrical and dancing performances and was also a performer himself;[32] it seems that he was primarily interested in singing, but ancient writers also hint at the artistic attempts he made as a pantomimic performer. Suetonius mentions Nero's intention to dance Virgil's Turnus and affirms that the artistic rivalry he felt for the famous and initially favourite dancer Paris caused the latter's execution;[33] Dio (63, 18, 1), referring to the same event, says, instead, that Paris was condemned because Nero 'had wished to learn dancing from him, but lacked the talent' (τί γὰρ δεῖ λέγειν ὅτι καὶ τὸν Πάριν τὸν ὀρχηστὴν ἀποθανεῖν ἐκέλευσεν, ὅτι ὀρχεῖσθαι παρ᾽ αὐτῷ μαθεῖν ἐθελήσας οὐκ ἠδυνήθη).[34]

Founders of the Genre

According to Plutarch and Athenaeus, Pylades of Cilicia and Bathyllus of Alexandria were the founders of the pantomimic genre in its two diverse forms: the tragic pantomime and the comic pantomime.[35] Athenaeus attributes to Pylades the invention of tragic pantomime, while to Bathyllus the invention of the more comic and light-hearted type. In fact, while Pylades' dancing was 'solemn, expressing passion and variety of character' (ἦν δὲ ἡ Πυλάδου ὄρχησις ὀγκώδης παθητική τε καὶ πολυπρόσωπος), Bathyllus' one was more 'jolly' (ἱλαρωτέρα).[36]

Both artists had a relationship with the Imperial house and the cultural elite around it; in fact we know that Pylades was a freedman of Augustus, while Bathyllus was a freedman of Maecenas.[37] That Pylades and Bathyllus were felt to be the founders of the pantomimic genre in antiquity is attested by the fact that their names were assumed by successive generations of dancers as professional names; we know of at least five dancers named Pylades and two named

Bathyllus.[38] Seneca reports that both Pylades and Bathyllus opened their own schools in Rome.[39] One of Pylades' most famous pupils, Hylas, is remembered by several ancient writers, who stress the public disorder caused by the rivalry of the two claques supporting the pupil and the former teacher respectively, to the point that Augustus was compelled to banish both of them from the city of Rome in 18 BC.[40]

Macrobius relates two episodes of Pylades' dissatisfaction and hypercritical attitude towards Hylas' performances.[41] In the first case, Pylades criticised Hylas for his dancing of the words *'great Agamemnon'*; Pylades claimed that Hylas was making the king of the Greeks just tall instead of great; on another occasion he reproached his pupil because, in portraying the blind Oedipus, he was badly pretending not to use his eyes, whereas he clearly was.

The Pantomimic Show

In its most traditional and widespread form, pantomime was a solo mute dance performance based on a tragic libretto sung by a chorus or a soloist. The dancer neither spoke nor sang, but interpreted by means of his dancing a story usually based on a mythological theme. Lucian (66) reports that the dancer danced all the roles in succession and the fact that the performer could use up to five masks within a performance seems to suggest that with the changing of the mask a change of character or scene took place as well. A typical constituent of pantomime performances was the representation of a character in an altered state of mind: anger, sorrow, grief, pain, or frenzy. The 'tragic' dancer aimed precisely at portraying characters as they underwent emotional strain, such as being in love, being mad, or being consumed with grief; Lucian (67), speaking in more general terms, states that:

Τὸ δὲ ὅλον ἤθη καὶ πάθη δείξειν καὶ ὑποκρινεῖσθαι ἡ ὄρχησις ἐπαγγέλλεται, νῦν μὲν ἐρῶντα, νῦν δὲ ὀργιζόμενόν τινα εἰσάγουσα, καὶ ἄλλον μεμηνότα καὶ ἄλλον λελυπημένον, καὶ ἅπαντα ταῦτα μεμετρημένως. τὸ γοῦν παραδοξότατον, τῆς αὐτῆς ἡμέρας ἄρτι μὲν Ἀθάμας μεμηνώς, ἄρτι δὲ Ἰνὼ φοβουμένη δείκνυται, καὶ ἄλλοτε Ἀτρεὺς ὁ αὐτός, καὶ μετὰ μικρὸν Θυέστης, εἶτα Αἴγισθος ἢ Ἀερόπη· καὶ πάντα ταῦτα εἰς ἄνθρωπός ἐστιν.

Cassiodorus gives a similar account:[42]

Idem corpus Herculem designat et Venerem, feminam praesentat in mare, regem facit et militem, senem reddit et iuvenem: ut in uno credas esse multos tam varia imitatione discretos.

Thus, one of the main appeals of the genre was the virtuoso ability of the pantomime actor to become a vast range of different characters in rapid succession.[43] The shift from one character to the other did not always strictly require a change of mask and the dancer could suggest persons who supposedly stood by, but were in fact absent as it seems to be implied in a passage in Libanius (113):

καὶ τὸ μὲν Ἀθηνᾶς δεικνυμένης Ἀθηνᾶν ἐννοεῖν καί Ποσειδῶνος Ποσειδῶ καὶ Ἡφαίστου γε ῞Ηφαιστου οὔπω πάμμεγα, τὸ δὲ δι᾽ Ἀθηνᾶς μὲν τὸν Ποσειδῶ, διὰ δὲ Ἡφαίστου τὴν Ἀθηνᾶν, διὰ δὲ Ἄρεος ῞Ηφαιστον, διὰ δὲ Γανυμήδους Δία, διὰ δὲ Ἀχιλλέως Πάριν, ταῦτα ποίων οὐ γρίφων ἱκανώτερα ψυχὴν ἀκονᾶν.

Similarly, the dancer was able to suggest physical surroundings that did not feature onstage (Libanius 116; Plutarch *Quaest. Conv.* B IX, 15, 2) and he could portray inanimate objects such as flames, trees, rivers, and bodies of water (Lucian 19).[44] According to Lucian (19), the dancer could imitate even 'the liquidity of water, the sharpness of fire in the liveliness of its movements, the fierceness of a lion, the rage of a leopard, and the quivering of a tree'.[45] To convey the idea of inanimate objects such as fire, flora, and water, the dancer, we can infer, embodied an intrinsic quality of the object represented; for instance, in the case of water, liquidity may have been the quality represented through a wave-like movement; if the object represented was fire, the mobile quality or the variety of colours of the flame could have been used to convey the idea of fire through, in the first case, shivering and trembling movements, in the second, through a change in the intensity of the movements themselves; if this was the case, the dancer must have heavily relied on visual analogues to convey the inanimate objects represented. Because of this, we can reasonably suppose that the portrayal of such elements was of a more allusive than strictly denotative nature and thus imagistic in essence. Because of this ability to portray imaginary objects via allusive gestures, the scenic space in pantomimic performances was more open than in more conventional theatrical performances and was less bound to the physical and material constraints of the actual setting. For instance, imaginary landscapes and unreal creatures could be suggested by the allusive art of the dancer. Thus, the phantasmagoric landscape of the Underworld with its infernal creatures is attested to have been one of the favourite subjects in pantomimic performances.[46]

The Pantomimic Cast

The pantomimic cast seems normally to have consisted of a solo dancer accompanied by singers and musicians; nonetheless, there are two passages in Lucian that mention the presence of an actor in a pantomimic troupe. In the first passage (68), Lucian provides an account of the equipment of the dancer in which he includes the presence of the actor:

> ὁ δὲ ὀρχηστὴς τὰ πάντα ἔχει συλλαβών, καὶ ἔνεστιν ποικίλην καὶ παμμιγῆ τὴν παρασκευὴν αὐτοῦ ἰδεῖν, αὐλόν, σύριγγα, ποδῶν κτύπον, κυμβάλου ψόφον, ὑποκριτοῦ εὐφωνίαν, ἀδόντων ὁμοφωνίαν.

What was exactly the role of the actor? There are two possible explanations of the role of the actor according to the evidence provided by ancient writers. The first one is that the actor had the function of the prologue speaker (*praeco*). The presence of the prologue speaker seems to be confirmed by two passages, one in Augustine and the other in Isidore of Seville. Augustine affirms that in the earliest period there was a *praeco* telling the story the dancer was going to dance:

> histriones quosdam in theatro fabulas sine verbis saltando plerumque aperiunt et exponunt. primis temporibus saltante pantomimo praeco pronuntiabat populis Carthaginis quod saltator vellet intelligi. Quod adhuc multi meminerunt senes, quorum relatu haec solemus audire.[47]

Similarly, Isidore speaks in more general terms of the presence of an actor who would speak the prologue: *mimi sunt dicti Graeca appellatione quod rerum humanarum sint imitatores; nam habebant suum auctorem, qui antequam mimum agerent, fabulam pronuntiare[n]t.*[48] Another possibility is that the actor supported the pantomimic dancer by playing the secondary roles. This would find support in a passage in Quintilian in which he reports that a dancer (*saltator*) and an interrupter (*interpellator*) mimed a dialogue with gestures: *Nam et finitione usus est Augustus de pantomimis duobus qui alternis gestibus contendebant, cum eorum alterum saltatorem dixit, alterum interpellatorem.*[49] Lucian (83) provides strong evidence which confirms that the role of the actor was essentially that of playing secondary roles; in fact, in a discussion of a pantomimic performance that dramatized the madness of Ajax, Lucian mentions the presence of an actor playing the secondary role of Odysseus together with the dancer impersonating Ajax.[50] Further support for the possibility that in some cases an actor could be present and support the dancer comes from a passage in Plutarch (*Quaestiones*

Conviviales 711e), which both attests that the Pyladic type of pantomime at times required a large cast and clarifies the main reason why this type of performance was not suitable for private parties.[51]

The Pantomimic Instruments

The pantomimic action, performed either by the dancer alone or with an actor, was accompanied by an orchestra as well as a chorus or a soloist who sang the words of the libretto. According to one source, the orchestra was made up of a variety of musical instruments including flutes, pipes, lyres, castanets, cymbals, tympana, and even a water-organ could be present (Lucian 26, 68, 72). The rhythm was maintained by the *scabellum*, a wooden clapper attached to the foot of one of the musicians.

The Pantomimic Mask and Costume

The pantomimic dancer wore a mask that differed from that of the tragic actor. Perhaps, because the dancer did not speak, he wore a mask with a closed mouth (Lucian 29). As is shown by the archaeological findings, the pantomimic masks have, besides a closed mouth, elaborate hair, and large holes for the eyes.[52]

The pronounced dimension of the eye holes of the masks strongly suggests that through them it was possible to see the expression of the dancer's eyes. That the eyes of an actor could remain visible through the mask is attested by a passage in Cicero, who states that the eyes of the actor seemed to gleam from behind the mask (*Saepe ipse vidi, ut ex persona mihi* **ardere** *oculi hominis histrionis viderentur*).[53] Cicero is probably referring to the performance of a tragic actor, but if the eyes were indeed visible through a tragic mask, this would have been even more the case for the pantomimic mask. It is not a coincidence then that ancient writers repeatedly praise the expressiveness of the dancers' eyes. For example, Apuleius claims that the dancer 'would dance with her eyes alone' (*nonnunquam saltare solis oculis*) and similarly Augustine affirms that the dancers 'almost talk with their eyes' (*cum oculis quasi fabulantur*).[54]

The costume commonly worn by the pantomimic dancer was a light silk tunic (Lucian 63) reaching down to the ankles; the light and silky fabric of the tunic was designed to follow and emphasise the movements of the dancer's body. The dancer wore also a *pallium* which, according to Fronto, was used as an expressive and versatile prop to represent successively the tail of a swan, the long hair of the goddess Venus, and the scourge of the Fury.[55]

The Pantomimic Training

Ancient writers repeatedly insist on the existence of an almost standard physical type required to become a dancer. According to Libanius (103), the aspiring dancer needed to undergo a test made by trainers who would establish whether he possessed the right physique for the profession. This scrutiny was meant to establish whether the body of the young pupil was going to conform to the requirements needed by the art: a moderate height and weight, a straight neck, and well-formed fingers. Lucian (75) similarly affirms that the dancer must be well proportioned and thus neither too tall nor too short, too fat nor too thin. Ideally, Lucian claims, the body of the dancer should conform to the canon of Polyclitus. Libanius' account mentioned above also points out that the physical training was demanding and began at an early age. This is confirmed by two inscriptions dedicated to two young dancers who died at an early age.[56] According to Libanius, the training was characterized by progressive steps meant to achieve first bodily qualities and control of the body in general and then technical skills and knowledge of the various routines required. Concerning the bodily qualities, the dancer needed to achieve strength, suppleness, and elasticity of limbs; after this stage was accomplished, the capability to move the limbs in isolation (Libanius 104) was the next step of the training; finally the dancers had to learn and memorize the schemes of the dance (105). The process described by Libanius seems to imply that as soon as the training was accomplished, the movements and the schemes were basically ingrained and rooted in the body of the dancer thus becoming a sort of language the dancers were able to use without the need to think consciously about each movement.

From a more technical point of view, the dancer relied on gesture and on hand language (cheironomy), through which he described the story sung by the chorus; the artist used the movement of the fingers to express the words of the libretto or to convey the emotions experienced by the characters portrayed. In fact, ancient writers do not only put a lot of emphasis on the speaking hands of pantomime dancers (Lucian 63; 69; Libanius 103; Sen. *Epist.* 121.6), but Libanius (103) also states that well-formed fingers were an essential bodily requirement to become a professional.

In addition to the movement of the hands, the dancer also performed acrobatic figures such as turns, leaps, circles, and backward bends (Lucian 71;

Libanius 68–69). A typical technical feature of the dance was the rapid alternation between swift movements and static poses as described by Libanius (118):

πότερον δὲ ἄν τις ἀγασθείη μειζόνως τὴν τῆς περιφορᾶς ἐν πλήθει συνέχειαν ἢ τὴν ἐξαίφνης ἐπὶ τούτῳ πάγιον στάσιν ἢ τὸν ἐν τῇ στάσει τηρούμενον τύπον; ὡς μὲν γὰρ ὑπόπτεροι περιάγονται, τελευτῶσι δὲ εἰς ἀκίνητον στάσιν ὥσπερ κεκολλημένοι, μετὰ δὲ τῆς στάσεως ἡ εἰκὼν ἀπαντᾷ. πόνος δὲ μείζων ἕτερος συγκαταλῦσαι τῷ ᾄσματι. τοσοῦτος τοῦ μέτρου λόγος ἐν ὀρχησταῖς.

Libanius' account is worth comparing with the description of the art of the dancer found in a Latin epigram (lines 5–7): *Nam cum grata chorus diffundit cantica dulcis,/Quae resonat cantor, motibus ipse probat./Pugnat ludit amat bacchatur vertitur adstat.*[57] As Ruth Webb has argued, the epigram describes an 'increasing pitch of intensity in the movements enacted until the final dramatic stop (*pugnat, ludit, amat, bacchatur, vertitur,* **adstat**)'.[58]

The dance also required a good rhythmical coordination and synchronization of the movements of hands and feet. Thus the elder Seneca complains about the dancer Nomio whose hands move slower than his feet.[59] The ability of moving all the limbs harmoniously was such a distinctive and charming characteristic of the pantomimic dancer that it even enchanted the severe Augustine who recommended it to his Christian fellows as an inspiring model to attain harmony of behaviour: *facite vos congruentia morum quod faciunt saltatores motu membrorum. Intus hoc agite; mores consonant.*[60]

Dance Vocabulary

The long training undergone by the aspiring dancer was needed both to acquire the necessary bodily requirements and to learn the *schemata*, the standard repertoire of dance steps and sequences. As Habinek has suggested, Lucian's claim that the dancer's knowledge must span from Chaos to contemporary history implies that the dancer 'must know all the *schemes* from Chaos to knowledge'.[61] That such routines were somehow fixed and established in relation to the story told and that a 'very significant amount of stylization in the bodily enactment of particular motifs or types or stories' featured in pantomime can be inferred from a passage in Lucian (80), in which he says that a dancer depicting the tecnophagy of Cronus turned it into that of Thyestes;[62] the mistake made by the dancer was probably due to the fact that 'tecnophagy was conveyed by a set choreographic pattern, making it quite easy for a pantomime to confuse the stories of Cronus and Thyestes'.[63] As Beacham has suggested, the most prominent roles enacted in pantomimic performances had a conventional nature.[64]

The Pantomimic Thematic Repertoire

The main source for our knowledge of the thematic repertoire of pantomime is Lucian, who provides in his treatise (37–61) a long catalogue of themes arranged along geographical lines.[65] He prefaces his list with the general statement that the dancer needs to have knowledge of everything that happened from the creation of the world to the times of Cleopatra (36). He then rounds off the section by stating that the pantomimic reservoir adapts the stories told by the best epic writers, dramatists, and poets of the past at large (61). Libanius also provides information about pantomimic themes and some others are recorded by Greek and Latin writers.

Generally speaking, pantomime tended to prefer emotionally charged themes. For instance, Lucian (67) states that pantomimic performances dealt primarily with the portrayal of characters undergoing emotional strain, being in love, being mad, or being consumed with grief.[66] Such emphasis on emotionality was directly linked with a preference for stories dealing with intense and extreme situations producing intoxicating passions. The *furor* of love in all its different aspects actually constituted the bread and butter of pantomimic performances; Lucian (9) even claims that a natural interconnectedness exists between dance and love since dance came into being and made its first appearance together with the cosmogonic Love (Eros) and Ovid compares the enervating effects produced by pantomimic performances portraying lovers (*ficti amantes*) to those caused by love poetry (*Remedia*, 751–8):[67]

> At tanti tibi sit non indulgere theatris,
> > Dum bene de vacuo pectore cedat amor.
> Enervant animos citharae lotosque lyraeque
> > Et vox et numeris bracchia mota suis.
> Illic adsidue ficti saltantur amantes:　　　　　　　　　　755
> > Quod caveas actor, quam iuvet, arte docet.
> Eloquar invitus: teneros ne tange poetas!
> > Summoveo dotes impius ipse meas.

The prominent erotic component of pantomimic performances also underwrites a passage in the *Amores* (2, 4, 29–32), where Ovid humorously claims that the sensuality of a dancing girl would be able even to bend the misogynist Hippolytus and transform him into a Priapus:

> illa placet gestu numerosaque bracchia ducit
>> et tenerum molli torquet ab arte latus
> ut taceam de me, qui causa tangor ab omni,
>> illic Hippolytum pone, Priapus erit![68]

The *furor* of love was possibly the passion which, with its intoxicating effects, featured most prominently as the focus of pantomime; together with this, the *furor* produced by grief, divine inspiration, madness, thirst of revenge and the like were favoured subjects in this type of performance. Also, ancient writers attest that violence and death were a central focus of pantomimic performances, listing violent actions such as dismemberment, tecnophagy, killings, and both self-mutilation and mutilation of others as recurring topics of pantomimic performances. For instance, Lucian attests the wide popularity of the theme of dismemberment listing that of Iacchus (39), Orpheus (51), Apsyrtus (53); Pentheus and Actaeon (41);[69] and the fate of Hippolytus (40). Closely related to dismemberment, the theme of tecnophagy such as that of Cronus, Procne, and especially Thyestes, is frequently mentioned by ancient writers as preferred subjects of pantomimic performances (Lucian 80; Sidonius Apollinaris, *Carmina* 23, 277–99). Similar to dismemberment and tecnophagy, self-mutilation was also a major attraction; for instance Attis' self-castration perpetrated in an attack of divine madness and Oedipus' self blinding in retribution of his incestuous guilt fulfilled the pantomimic need for spectacular and emotionally charged effects. Also very popular were those plots that included attacks of madness leading to killings of kindred as in the case of Hercules' and Athamas' killings of their family (Lucian 41). Apuleius and Lucian attest to the popularity of plots dealing with angered women cruelly punishing their husbands such as Clytemnestra's murder of Agamemnon (Lucian 43), Medea's killing of her sons, and Deianira's murder of Hercules through the poisonous robe (Lucian 50). In general, the visual representation of death, violence, grief, and *furor* at large constituted the core of the pantomimic spectacle. Lada-Richards has remarked that the pantomimic trend towards violence brought to the front stage the violent and intense actions which in tragedy were usually relegated to offstage scenes.[70] Such a tendency is attested, for instance, by Lucian's description of a pantomimic performance adapting the tragic plot of Ajax's madness (83–4); if in Sophocles' *Ajax* the slaughter of the army's cattle takes place offstage and is then reported through narration, in the case of the pantomimic enactment of the same story,

Ajax's madness is the very action around which the performance revolves. A similar case is to be found in a passage from Macrobius' *Saturnalia* (II, 7, 16), in which the pantomimic performance described enacts the dramatization of Hercules' madness and killing of his family.[71]

To sum up, the classical and timeless 'eros and *thanatos*' motif well summarizes the two most favoured themes of the pantomimic repertoire.

The Pantomimic Libretto

It is not easy to understand what a pantomimic libretto looked like since, as it is generally assumed, that none has survived.[72] We know that these scripts usually had mythological themes and they presented the most sensational moments of the given myth. The libretti could be both adapted from epic and tragic poets or could be original compositions. Ancient writers attest that pantomimic libretti were adapted from Virgil, and Ovid reports such appropriations for his own works (*Tristia* 2, 519–20: *et mea sunt populo saltata poemata saepe*).[73] In the case of original compositions, we know that authors such as Silo, Statius, and Lucan composed pantomimic libretti.[74] A passage in Juvenal, for example, attests that Statius composed a libretto entitled *Agave* for the famous dancer Paris.

To try to grasp what a libretto may have looked like, it is important to point out first that pantomime was a very 'hybrid mode' of representation which made use of two strands of performance: that of the chorus/soloist singing the libretto and that of the dancer embodying the text.[75] In this framework, pantomime needed various modes of presentation, one more dramatic and another more narrative, since the dancer dramatically enacted the story which, in turn, was descriptively mirrored by the singing voice of the chorus or the soloist. We may describe pantomimic libretti as compositions in between epic and tragedy; that this was the case is possibly suggested by Lucian's statement (61) that pantomimic libretti 'were adapted from the best epic and tragic poets of the past' (συνελόντι δὲ εἰπεῖν, οὐδὲν τῶν ὑπὸ τοῦ Ὁμήρου καὶ Ἡσιόδου καὶ τῶν ἀρίστων ποιητῶν καὶ μάλιστα τῆς τραγῳδίας λεγομένων ἀγνοήσει). Lucian links pantomime directly to tragedy, which, as a performative genre, provided pantomime not only with themes and situations but also a *corpus* of dramatic conventions amenable to be adapted and modified according to the specific structural and stylistic necessities of the pantomimic genre. In addition to tragedy, epic is the other genre which Lucian explicitly mentions in connection with the thematic reservoir of pantomime. I would suggest that epic must have provided, in addition to themes, the descriptive mode of narration. Thus, it is likely that pantomimic libretti featured a hybrid mixture of narrative and dramatic technique of presentation. The singing voice in charge of delivering the narrative possibly performed the function of a sort of external narrator rather than a character involved in the action, with the advantage of avoiding the difficulty of portraying complicated interactions between several characters and the consequent need for the story to be told in the first person. Moreover, the vehicle of narration was better suited to interpret more articulately and explicitly the motifs or actions of a character than a strictly dramatic narration in which the same elements were meant to emerge somehow implicitly from the words of the characters themselves as in tragedy or comedy. The very displacement of the verbal action from the mute dancer to the singer allowed indeed the possibility for the story to be told explicitly. Furthermore, it is likely that pantomimic libretti contained descriptive sections devoted to set and evoke the scenario and atmosphere in which the movements of the dancer took place or act as a commentary to his gestures.[76] This interpretation is corroborated by a passage in Libanius (64, 116) in which he praises the art of the dancer who, by means of his gestures, can even portray a landscape:

ποία γὰρ γραφή, τίς λειμὼν ἥδιον ὀρχήσεως καὶ ὀρχηστοῦ θέαμα περιάγοντος εἰς ἄλση τὸν θεατὴν καὶ κατακοιμίζοντος ὑπὸ τοῖς δένδρεσιν ἀγέλας βοῶν, αἰπόλια, ποίμνια καὶ τοὺς νομέας ἱστῶντος ἐπὶ φρουρᾷ τῶν θρεμμάτων τοὺς μὲν σύριγγι χρωμένους, τοὺς δὲ αὐλοῦντας ἄλλον ἐν ἄλλοις ἔργοις.

Now, we can infer that the text accompanying such a performance must have contained a descriptive presentation of the landscape of herds and trees, actually an *ecphrasis topou* mirroring the mute gestures of the dancer. That the libretto entailed a 'pictorial dramaturgy' seems confirmed by several comparisons made between the figurative arts at large and pantomime (Lucian 35 and Libanius 64, 116);[77] for instance, in the epitaph to the dancer Panarete, Aristaenetus compares the dancing girl to a painter (Aristaenetus 26, 9). More generally, in a passage from Nonnus, the language of the figurative arts is metaphorically employed to describe the art of the dancer (*Dionysiaca* 5, 104–7):

καὶ παλάμας ἐλέλιζε Πολύμνια, μαῖα χορείης,
μιμηλὴν δ᾽ ἐχάραξεν ἀναυδέος εἰκόνα φωνῆς,
φθεγγομένη παλάμῃσι σοφὸν τύπον ἔμφρονι σιγῇ,
ὄμματα δινεύουσα.

Now, if the dancer's movements in the space of the stage (*schemata*) were comparable to the drawings of the painter on a canvas, then the words of the libretto must have provided the impressionistic colours and the more minute details of the picture as a whole. In contrast to painting and sculpture, pantomime also had a dynamic dimension. The figures, which in painting and sculpture were presented as frozen in a fixed position, appeared in movement in this performative genre; thus, pantomime dancing could be defined as a transient pictorial dramaturgy.[78]

Lucian (63–4) hints at an additional feature of the libretto, namely that pantomime relied on a codified repertoire of 'bodily attitudes and configurations', which constituted a sort of 'formulaic dance vocabulary';[79] possibly such stylization was matched in the libretto through the adoption of a mirroring 'formulaic' vocabulary. This feature of the libretti may have been one of the reasons why they have not come down to us; at least in most of the cases, they were probably not works of high literary value as they were not composed for literary purposes but in view of their sheer performative function. In any case, the role of the libretti was secondary to the skilful danced enactment of a preferably well-known and famous story and to the impact of the musical accompaniment which constituted the real attractions of the genre.

As to the structure of the tragic libretto, Lucian's (67) and Libanius' accounts (67) suggest that it did not present the whole development of the myth but only its most emotionally climactic and spectacular moments. That the solo dancer could change up to five masks within a performance seems to indicate that with the changing of the mask a change of character or scene took place as well with each scene being dramaturgically only loosely connected to the others. Each scene was a sort of single tableau representing a relevant part of the mythological whole. Lucian (67), for example, describes a pantomimic performance as follows:

τὸ γοῦν παραδοξότατον, τῆς αὐτῆς ἡμέρας ἄρτι μὲν Ἀθάμας μεμηνώς, ἄρτι δὲ Ἰνὼ φοβουμένη δείκνυται, καὶ ἄλλοτε Ἀτρεὺς ὁ αὐτός, καὶ μετὰ μικρὸν Θυέστης, εἶτα Αἴγισθος ἢ Ἀερόπη·

There is a similar description in Libanius (67): εἶδε Δηιάνειραν τὸ θέατρον, ἀλλὰ καὶ τὸν Οἰνέα καὶ τὸν Ἀχελῷον καὶ τὸν Ἡρακλέα καὶ Νέσσον.

Libanius' account is particularly interesting; the pantomimic performance he describes is concerned with the final segment of the saga of Heracles and its thematic unity resides in the fact that all the characters have a strict relation with the hero; but, since the episodes related to each character did neither happen at the same time nor in the same place, we have to infer that the transitions between single episodes of the myth were not subjected to a logical development. Rather, each episode was somehow performed in a pictorial-tableau and not in a proper dramatic sequence so that the show consisted of a sequence of juxtaposed danced monologues. Such quality seems to be mirrored in the titles chosen for pantomimic performances such as 'Niobe turned to stone' (*rigidam Nioben*) or 'the Trojan woman in tears' (*flentem Troada*).[80]

Pantomime in Roman Culture

Affiliations between Rhetoric and Pantomime

> Omnis enim motus animi suum quemdam a natura habet vultum et sonum et gestum; totumque corpus hominis et eius omnis vultus omnesque voces, ut nervi in fidibus, ita sonant ut a motu animi quoque sunt pulsae.
>
> (Cicero, *De oratore* 3, 216)

> Quippe non manus solum sed nutus etiam declarant nostram voluntatem, et in mutis pro sermone sunt, et saltatio frequenter sine voce intellegitur atque adficit, et ex vultu ingressuque perspicitur habitus animorum ...
>
> (Quintilian, *Institutio Oratoria* 11, 3, 66).[81]

The above quotations from Cicero and Quintilian attest to the intimate connection perceived in Roman culture between emotions and the way such emotions found their physical expression in gestures, movements, tone of voice, and bodily attitudes at large.[82] The oratorical *actio*, which Cicero defines as *quasi sermo corporis* (*De oratore* 3, 222) and *quasi corporis quaedam eloquentia* (*Orator* 55), constituted one of the five parts of rhetoric and concerned the delivery of a speech; the verbal delivery had to be accompanied by gestures, which had the function of conveying and thus arousing emotions in the audience. Because of this, the systematic study of bodily movement had a central position in rhetorical training. In this respect, the bodily language of the oratorical *actio* had obviously many affinities with that employed by actors onstage. It is well known that Cicero observed with interest the performances of the comic actor Roscius and the tragic actor Aesopus, in order to take inspiration from them for the delivery of his own speeches.[83] Macrobius also reports that Roscius wrote a book in which he compared the art of the public speaker and that of the actor.[84]

Despite the intrinsic affinity of the oratorical and theatrical *actio*, the gesturing of a good orator had to avoid an overtly theatrical mimicry; in fact, elite Romans anxiously policed the divide between the two social categories of orators and actors. In several passages of the *De Oratore*, Cicero cautions against excessive mimicry and especially in indulging in the acting style of mimes; in dealing with the topic of how to use humour in oratorical speeches, Cicero again prescribes moderation in order for the orator not to resemble the vulgar grimacing mime:

(2, 239):
Est etiam deformitatis et corporis vitiorum satis bella materies ad iocandum; sed quaerimus idem, quod in ceteris rebus maxime quaerendum est, quatenus. In quo non modo illud praecipitur, ne quid insulse, sed etiam, si quid perridicule possis, vitandum est oratori utrumque, ne aut scurrilis iocus sit aut mimicus.

(2, 251):
Atque hoc etiam animadvertendum est, non esse omnia ridicula faceta. Quid enim potest esse tam ridiculum, quam sannio est? Sed ore, vultu, imitandis moribus, voce, denique corpore ridetur ipso. Salsum hunc possum dicere, atque ita, non ut eiusmodi oratorem esse velim, sed ut mimum.[85]

That such a restrained appropriation of theatrical rhetoric, which Cicero warmly and repeatedly recommends, ran counter to a tendency towards exaggeration in his days is attested by a further passage in the *De oratore* (3, 214), where Cicero complains that *histriones* have taken the place of the good orators of the past:

Haec ideo dico pluribus, quod genus hoc totum oratores, qui sunt veritatis ipsius actores, reliquerunt, imitatores autem veritatis, histriones, occupaverunt.

Even the much praised orator Hortensius was censured for excessive mimicry because his gesturing resembled too closely that of an actor. Once, he was even mockingly nicknamed as 'Dionysia', a famous dancing-girl (*saltatricula*) of the period.[86] Similarly, the languishing and effeminate gestures of the orator Sextus Titius resulted in a dance that came into vogue after him, being named the 'Titius'.[87]

A century later, Quintilian echoes Cicero's precepts. The Roman rhetorician also admits that the aspiring orator should master the art of the comic actor, as far as he needs to be educated in the ways of dramatic delivery (1, 11, 1: *Dandum aliquid comoedo quoque, dum eatenus qua pronuntiandi scientiam futurus orator desiderat*).[88] Quintilian then sets up the restrictions with which histrionic gestures and movements ought to be appropriated: the orator needs to employ gestures and movements with moderation and he needs to avoid overtly theatrical facial expressions, gesticulation, and moving around.[89] Like Cicero, Quintilian complains about contemporary orators whose increasing appropriation of theatrical style has corrupted oratory. It is possible that the similarities between actors and orators may have become more pronounced over time.[90]

Quintilian himself proclaimed that the style of delivery practised in his time was more animated than that of earlier generations, and his concern that oratory and acting were becoming too similar may thus reflect a genuine trend toward theatricality on the part of the orators.[91] It may have been partly the practice of set exercises (*declamationes*), *suasoriae* and *controversiae* (the former on deliberative topics, the latter on law-court themes), which the young students of rhetoric had to practise in order to achieve proficiency in the art of oratory, that dangerously reduced the distinction between orators and theatrical performers, since such exercises had a marked dramatic nature and, in a sense, they were 'embryonic drama'.[92] *Suasoriae* and *controversiae* alike involved the exercise of impersonating and the art of depicting characters (*ethologia* or *characterismon*). In the case of *suasoriae*, the student had to impersonate the role of a mythological or historical character confronted with a dramatic choice; in the case of *controversiae*, the student had to play the role of the appellant, legal defendant or opponent in a given trial. In relation to this, Lucian's statement (35, 65) that rhetoric and pantomime share a common ground since both deal with impersonation, and the display of *êthos* and *pathos* is worthy to be considered closer:

Lucian (35):
οὐ μὴν οὐδὲ ῥητορικῆς ἀφέστηκεν, ἀλλὰ καὶ ταύτης μετέχει, καθ᾽ ὅσον ἤθους τε καὶ πάθους ἐπιδεικτική ἐστιν, ὧν καὶ οἱ ῥήτορες γλίχονται.

Lucian (65):
Ἡ δὲ πλείστη διατριβὴ καὶ ὁ σκοπὸς τῆς ὀρχηστικῆς ἡ ὑπόκρισίς ἐστιν, ὡς ἔφην, κατὰ τὰ αὐτὰ καὶ τοῖς ῥήτορσιν ἐπιτηδευομένη, καὶ μάλιστα τοῖς τὰς καλουμένας ταύτας μελέτας διεξιοῦσιν· οὐδὲν γοῦν καὶ ἐν ἐκείνοις μᾶλλον ἐπαινοῦμεν ἢ τὸ ἐοικέναι τοῖς ὑποκειμένοις προσώποις καὶ μὴ ἀπῳδὰ εἶναι τὰ λεγόμενα τῶν εἰσαγομένων ἀριστέων ἢ τυραννοκτόνων ἢ πενήτων ἢ γεωργῶν, ἀλλ᾽ ἐν ἑκάστῳ τούτων τὸ ἴδιον καὶ τὸ ἐξαίρετον δείκνυσθαι.

It is worth reading the Lucianic passage against the one in which Quintilian (11, 1, 55) warns against the danger hidden in the practice of fictional and emotionally charged declamations:

Quod praecipue declamantibus [...] custodiendum est, quo plures in schola
finguntur adfectus, quos non ut advocati sed ut passi subimus: cum etiam
hoc genus simulari litium soleat, cum ius mortis a senatu quidam vel ob
aliquam magnam infelicitatem vel etiam paenitentiam petunt: in quibus non
solum cantare, quod vitium pervasit, aut lascivire, sed ne argumentari
quidem nisi mixtis, et quidem ita ut ipsa probatione magis emineant,
adfectibus decet. Nam qui intermittere in agendo dolorem potest, videtur
posse etiam deponere.

The danger, as Quintilian puts it, is passivity to the emotions. In a sense, the
decline of rhetoric and the rise of pantomime seem to have concided in this very
trend towards an emasculated emotionality. It is no by chance that declamations
and pantomimic performances amply favoured themes that were naturally
charged with an emotional excitement of their own, such as the supernatural, the
miraculous, the horrifying, and the violent, which attests that both arts were not
so much interested in the ideas or situations in themselves but in their potential
to generate emotions.

In the part of the *Institutio Oratoria* concerning the delivery of speeches in
general, and the *actio* more precisely, Quintilian states that the orator should be
as different from a pantomimic dancer as possible and thus expresses an anxiety
that hints at the practice of appropriating the gestural language of the stage.[93]
Moreover, he considers overtly theatrical (and thus inappropriate for the orators)
the habit of mirroring the words with gestures, which is indeed what the practice
of the dancer was; the orator's motion should, instead, reflect the thoughts
expressed (11, 3, 88):

Et hi quidem de quibus sum locutus, cum ipsis vocibus naturaliter exeunt
gestus: alii sunt qui res imitatione significant, ut si aegrum temptantis venas
medici similitudine aut citharoedum formatis ad modum percutientis
nervos manibus ostendas, quod est genus quam longissime in actione
fugiendum.[94]

Quintilian's concern is echoed by Tacitus who reports a proverb in circulation
in his days according to which orators speak softly while dancers dance
eloquently.[95]

The trend towards emotionality did not only affect the rhetorical *actio*, but
also the oratorical style itself. The frequent injunctions already hinted at by
Cicero against the habit of composing excessively rhythmic orations (*De orat.* 1,
151; 3, 188; *Orat.* 57, 175, 229) are more forcefully reiterated by Quintilian (11, 3,

57–60) because of their overtly histrionic character.[96] Quintilian (9, 4, 142) blames the fact that the word-arrangement (*compositio*) of contemporary orations actually dances:

> In universum autem, si sit necesse, duram potius atque asperam compositionem malim esse quam effeminatam et enervem, qualis apud multos, et cotidie magis, lascivissimis syntonorum modis saltat.

If injunctions point to widespread preferences, Cicero's and Quintilian's considerable efforts to keep apart the art of the orator and that of the theatrical performer suggest that the interface between the two was indeed rather slippery.[97]

The Influence of Sub-literary Genres (Mime and Pantomime) on Roman Writers

As early as 1924, Kroll argued that Latin literature after the third century BC was characterized by a phenomenon he called '*Die Kreuzung der Gattungen*' ('The Crossing of Genres'), which consisted in the appropriation and consequent inclusion of technical and thematic features typical of one genre into another.[98] This 'creative confrontation of different literary genres' may have developed as an attempt to overcome the problem of generic exhaustion and renewal of literary genres through the process of cross-fertilization and the resulting creation of new hybrids.[99] In his influential *Arte Allusiva* (1942), Giorgio Pasquali addressed the issue of the role of poetic allusion in Latin texts and interpreted it as a means strategically employed by authors to evoke a poetic memory; thus the poetic allusion had to resonate for the reader and prompt the interpretation of the 'hidden' meaning that the allusion generated.[100] Taking inspiration from Pasquali's interpretation of poetic allusion and developing Kroll's too mechanical notion of the crossing of genres, Gian Biagio Conte adapted the techniques of semiotics to the interpretation of the role of poetic allusion.[101] Very recently, Harrison has proposed a synthesis of Kroll's and Conte's positions and has coined the notion of 'generic enrichment', i.e. 'the way in which generically identifiable texts gain literary depth and texture from detailed confrontation with, and consequent inclusion of elements from, texts which appear to belong to other literary genres.'[102] Harrison's formula of generic enrichment thus comprises both the expansion of the range of genres through cross-breeding and the process of poetic allusions as interpreted by Conte. Still, the reciprocal appropriation of formal and thematic features between sub-literary and literary genres has not been fully investigated as part of the same process. This neglect is perhaps partly due to the difficulty posed by the scanty survival of mimic *canovacci* and pantomimic libretti. In addition to this, there is an ingrained tendency to believe that sub-literary genres are not likely to have provided thematic or stylistic material for higher literature, which is caused by the prejudicial conviction that the hallmark of such genres was vulgarity, baseness, and an overall lack of positive artistic value. Indeed, this opinion is not wholly accurate. Several ancient writers attest the erudition of many mimographers. Thus, Seneca praises the learned verses of the mimographer Publilius Syrus twice in his prose works (*Epistles* 8, 8; *De Tranquillitate animi* 11, 8);[103] Horace gives a complimentary judgement on Laberius' mimes in his *Satires* (I, 10, 5–6). Similarly, Lucian (35; 36) claims that pantomime is an art that requires a great deal of erudition to be fulfilled in a proper way and that the dancer must be learned and endowed with excellent memory.

In fact, the divide or dialogue between 'high' and 'low' forms of literature was more dynamic than is generally assumed. As Fantham has remarked, mime is a 'missing link in Roman literary history' and another one is pantomime.[104] More generally, there is much evidence for 'osmosis and continuity' between the so-called high and low genres, to borrow Andreassi's definition.[105] An important element in the influential role played by the mimic and pantomimic languages resides in the fact that they constituted a commonly shared idiom in the ancient world, which can be traced in several ancient authors who adopted thematic or formal features peculiar to these genres.

The complex system of interactions between literary and sub-literary genres can be described as a two-directional flow: sub-literary genres drew motifs well established in the literary tradition and literary genres adopted thematic and stylistic features that belonged to the realm of sub-literary ones. For example, the *Charition*-mime, dated to the first or second century AD, takes its name from the protagonist of the skit, a young Greek woman, who is to be sacrificed by the king of the barbarian country whose power she is in;[106] her brother arrives just in time to rescue her from the hands of the king by making him and his fellows drunk. The mime is clearly a parody of the Euripidean *Iphigenia in Tauris*, where Charition is Iphigenia, the brother Orestes, the fool Pylades, the king Thoas. As in the *Iphigenia in Tauris*, we find the theme of the theft of the goddess' image (which is in the mime substituted by the goddess' property). The detail of the means of escape is, instead, reminiscent of the Euripidean *Cyclops*. The prominence of farcical and vulgar elements renders it rather removed in tone from its tragic model. Nonetheless, it is evident that the composer of the

Charition-mime relied on the audience's knowledge of the tragic models, otherwise the parodic twist given to them, which constitutes the very source of the fun of the skit, would have been lost.

As discussed above, high literature also adopts themes and features drawn from the sub-literary tradition. A good example of this is to be found in one episode narrated in Book ten of Apuleius' *Metamorphoses* (X, 2–12). The episode deals with the story of a stepmother's love for his stepson who rejects her. Having been dismissed, the cruel stepmother makes an attempt at poisoning him with the help of her compliant slave, but, by mistake, she poisons her own son. She charges his stepson with the murder who is eventually saved by a physician serving as judge in the trial, while the stepmother is sent into exile and her accomplice slave is crucified. As to the literary sources of the Apuleian story, the episode is inspired by a tragic model reminiscent as it is of the story of Hippolytus and Phaedra; Apuleius himself acknowledges, though deceptively, that the story he is about to narrate comes from tragedy (*iam ergo, lector optime, scito te tragoediam, non fabulam, legere et a socco ad cothurnum ascendere*).

Nonetheless, the major model of inspiration is that type of adultery mime that involved a sexual attempt of a mistress on her slave who does not reciprocate. Apuleius' indebtedness to a mimic plot has been claimed by Wiemken and more recently by Steinmetz, who believe that Apuleius' story of the incestuous stepmother is indeed the equivalent, in narrative form, of one of the types of the adultery-mime, whose plot is best represented to us by the Adulteress-mime.[107] It seems then that Apuleius crossed the Phaedra tragic plot with the Adulteress-mime plot and created a hybrid overtly reminiscent of its two models. It is difficult to establish whether Apuleius' generic fusion can be accounted as original on Apuleius' part, since a fragment by Laberius seems to have involved the love of a stepmother for her stepson (*Belonistria: domina nostra privignum suum/amat efflictim*); unfortunately, it is not possible to reconstruct the plot of Laberius' *Belonistria* because only few fragments survive. The Apuleian description of the disruptive effects of the stepmother's love for her stepson (*Met.* X, 2) is particularly interesting in relation to the two-directional process existing between literary and sub-literary genres:

> At ubi, completis igne vesano totis praecordiis, immodice bacchatus Amor exaestuabat, saevienti deo iam succubuit, et languore simulato vulnus animi mentitur in corporis valetudine. Iam cetera salutis vultusque detrimenta et aegris et amantibus examussim convenire nemo qui nesciat: pallor deformis, marcentes oculi, lassa genua, quies turbida, et suspiritus cruciatus tarditate vehementior. Crederes et illam fluctuare tantum vaporibus febrium, nisi

> quod et flebat. Heu medicorum ignarae mentes, quid venae pulsus, quid
> coloris intemperantia, quid fatigatus anhelitus et utrimquesecus iactatae
> crebriter laterum mutuae vicissitudines!

The Apuleian description shows an intricate fabric of allusions to several sources;
however, it seems that the major source of Apuleius here is the Senecan portrayal
of tragic heroines taken in the grip of passion at large, and, more specifically that
of Phaedra (362–83).[108] It is true that such catalogues of love symptoms became
formulaic from Hellenistic love poetry onwards, but the extended length as well
as the sort of 'clinical' character of Apuleius' description differentiates it from its
antecedents, although the allusions to the literary predecessors are often overt.

Moreover, since the situation portrayed by Apuleius has its model in mime, it
is possible that the description of the lovesick *noverca* is modelled on the way
the role was actually performed onstage; the description would thus translate
into narrative form the gestures and attitudes typical of the character. There is
one formulation in particular that strongly suggests that the Apuleian description,
although employing the literary *topoi* of the symptoms of love, is mimic in
essence; that is the reference to the physician who is unable to recognize the
symptoms of love (*Heu medicorum ignarae mentes*); Apuleius' blame of the
doctor patently echoes the Virgilian *heu vatum ignarae mentes* with which
the famous description of lovesick Dido begins (4, 65).

The farcical twist given by Apuleius to the Virgilian allusion works via the
substitution of the seers (*vatuum*) with doctors (*medicorum*). In relation to this,
in a passage of the *Institutio Oratoria*, in which Quintilian warns the orator
against too descriptive a use of mimicry (which he sees as the hallmark of mimic
and pantomimic actors), he gives as an example of imitation to avoid the way of
suggesting the illness of someone by mimicking a doctor feeling the pulse;[109]
since Quintilian's warning explicitly links such an imitation to the repertoire of
the mimic and pantomimic actors, it is possible to infer that in their performances
such a device was employed. Going back to the Apuleian passage, it seems that
the substitution of the Virgilian seers with the doctors would acquire an even
more farcical tone if the doctors hinted at by Apuleius were typical figures of
mimic performances.[110] The grafting and transference of an allusion to the
Virgilian epic onto a mimic situation would be fitting and in keeping with the
overall mimic nature of the episode. However, the Apuleian episode, no matter
whether an original Apuleian creation or not, attests to the ongoing and two-
directional process of generic enrichment between literary and sub-literary
genres.

In the following sections, examples will be provided of the presence of elements belonging to sub-literary genres in writers such as Catullus, Cicero, the elegists, Seneca, and Petronius.

Pantomime in Catullus' Attis (Poem 63)

Poem 63 describes Attis' self-castration, his participation in the ritual procession of Cybele and, at the end, his contrition and regret for what he has done; the poem is in galliambics and it is structurally arranged as an alternation between narrative and direct speech. Poem 63 stands out in Catullus' lyric *corpus* in several respects: genre, originality, and metre (galliambics). As to genre, scholars have long debated to which literary genre the poem should be assigned; several ones have been proposed ranging from epyllion and hymn to tragedy and pantomime.[111] The major difficulty in assigning the poem to a specific genre, as Morisi has remarked, is due to its irreducibility to a codified set of literary norms and conventions.[112] As to its originality, the debate has not been less tantalizing. Generally speaking, several scholars have suggested that poem 63 was indebted to a popular Hellenistic genre (i.e. hymns in galliambics addressed to Cybele) and thus modelled on lost Hellenistic poems. This interpretation was based on the alleged evidence found in the Greek metrician Hephaestion who, in the section of his synopsis of metrical theory devoted to ionic metre, affirmed that the galliambic was the metrical pattern in which poems to the mother of the gods were composed.[113] A gloss on this passage provided the additional information that Callimachus also used this metre.[114] Wilamowitz-Möllendorff, relying on the evidence found in Hephaestion's passage and the *scholium*, identified Catullus' model in a lost poem by Callimachus, of which 63 was either a translation or a close imitation.[115] More recently, the generally accepted scholarly view has been that Hellenistic poems in galliambics existed and that Catullus may have drawn some elements from them, but the extent of such a debt is impossible to establish since the designated models are now lost to us.[116] In addition to this, Catullus' originality in the composition of 63 seems to find support in the fact that the poem does not consistently belong to any known literary genre, but adopts features and stylistic qualities that can be ascribed to different ones.[117] In this respect, Morisi's claim that the poem cannot be with confidence ascribed to any given genre and that, as an overall characteristic, the arrangement of the poem is eminently dramatic in content and style with its tendency to translate actions and emotions into emphatic scenic gestures seems to be the best possible interpretation given the status of the evidence.[118] In relation to the dramatic texture of 63, Guillemin's definition of the poem as conceived as a tragedy in three acts deserves a closer scrutiny.[119] She divides the poem as follows:

I act (1–38):
Arrival of Attis at Cybele's Phrygian homeland, self-castration, and frenzied ascent to Mount Ida followed by his companions, the *Gallae*.

II act (39–73):
Awakening on the day after and Attis' regret at the self-mutilation; lament and melancholic remembrance of his past life in front of the sea.

III act (74–90):
Cybele sends one of her lions to re-kindle Attis' devotion.[120]

Several elements closely recall the tragic genre such as the choice to begin the poem *in medias res*, the dramatic use of speeches in place of narratives, the emphasis on Attis' inner turmoil as well as interest in portraying the psychological effects of a sweeping passion as well as stylistic features of diction.[121] Nonetheless, the poem cannot be properly ascribed to the tragic genre, since it lacks the required length and development of the plot. In light of this, Newman's proposal to ascribe poem 63 to a tragic pantomime seems very suggestive and fitting.[122] Three elements can be used as corroborating evidence, namely theme, stylistic features, and metre.

As to theme, that the story of Attis featured in pantomimic performances is attested by literary and archaeological evidence.[123] As to literary ones, it suffices to say that an epigram by Dioscorides (*AP* 11, 195), written as early as the middle of the third century BC, attests that a certain Aristagoras danced the role of a Gallus.[124] As to archaeological ones, the popularity of the subject in pantomimic performances is attested by the many *oscilla* featuring a mask of Attis, although they belong to a later period.[125] In addition to this, the theme of Attis' frenzied act of self-castration is in itself eminently suitable for pantomime which favoured the representations of characters undergoing emotional turmoil.[126] Indeed, the poem is an exploration of the workings produced by a maddening passion.[127] Furthermore, the play with the feminine and the interchange of sexual roles is also a common feature in pantomime as can be inferred from the popularity of stories such as that of Hercules and Omphale or that of Achilles in Scyros.[128] As Lada-Richards has remarked, 'the transcendence of gender boundaries' is one of the key elements of pantomimic performance and possibly the most dangerous one as perceived by ancient authors, since it 'blurred all notions of sexual distinction'.[129]

In relation to stylistic features, the preponderance of verbs of activity, the paratactic syntax (where past participles are preferred to subordinate clauses), the construction of the verse κατα στίχον, the absence of enjambement and of carry-over of a main clause into the following line (both these features occur only once: lines 51–2; lines 87–9), and the rhetorical devices employed (repetition, anaphora, geminatio, questions, self-address) underline the performative nature of the poem.[130] Such a nature is further emphasized by the metrical pattern adopted: the galliambic verse. The galliambic verse was the metre used in the actual rites of the Galli in honour of the Great Mother and took its name from the self-castrating priests of the goddess Cybele whose ritual included processions with music and dance of orgiastic intonation in which a re-enacting of the salient moments of the myth itself took place.[131] This ionic metre, which is characterized by a preponderance of short syllables over long ones producing a frenzied rhythm, perfectly matches the excited and ecstatic movements characteristic of the dance of the Galli.[132] Kirby has remarked that 'in view of the ritual origin of the meter . . . Catullus' choice of the galliambic was with a clear view toward its performance'; he has further added that 'the poem's success depends on its actualization in some kind of performance . . . since the poem needs to be read aloud in order to achieve its poetic effect'.[133] In addition, there is one more remark that needs to be made about this metre in relation to its association with the sotadean, another metre of ionic origin.[134] The sotadean, just as the galliambic, was rarely used by Latin writers.[135] The association of galliambics and sotadeans was due to metrical and rhythmical similarities (the weakness and effeminacy of the two are repeatedly insisted upon by ancient authors), as is attested, for example, by Martial (*Ep.* 2, 86, 1–5).[136] The association was not then confined to metrical issues, but included thematic ones too; as the galliambics were linked with the *galli*, the sotadeans were linked with the *cinaedi*, these figures being, as it were, perceived as identical.[137] That *galli* were frequently identified with *cinaedi* (especially in satirical portrayals) is attested by the fact that the two terms were used as synonyms.[138] Additionally, the *galli/cinaedi* were also associated with the pantomimic dancers; according to Nonius (5, 16), the word *cinaedus* was actually an appellative for the *saltator* and *pantomimus* (*cinaedi dicti sunt apud veteres saltatores vel pantomimi*).[139] Thus, the *galli*, *cinaedi*, and pantomimic dancers all fell in the same category.[140] This association is not difficult to understand since all these characters shared similar characteristics, the most conspicuous one being the ambiguity of their gender. In fact, *galli* and *cinaedi* were usually said to be *semiviri*, something in between a male and a female, while the pantomimic dancers, even though not marked by the actual physical mutilation that characterized both *galli* and *cinaedi*, also possessed a dubious sexual identity, since their art required them to impersonate female and male roles;[141] as Lada-Richards has remarked, 'the perceived link between effeminacy and pantomime' is so strong that pantomimes or dancing-masters are constantly associated with *cinaedi*.[142] Having set the general context, it is worth looking at a poem in sotadeans in Petronius' *Satyricon* in relation to the generic nature of Catullus 63. In the Quartilla episode, a *cinaedus* and his troupe, probably hired for the special occasion, entertain the guests with singing and dancing; the song sung by the *cinaedus* is in ionics, more specifically in sotadenas (23, 3):

> Intrat cinaedus, homo omnium insulsissimus et plane illa domo dignus, qui
> ut infractis manibus congemuit, eiusmodi carmina effudit:
> 'Huc huc [cito] convenite nunc, spatalocinaedi,
> pede tendite, cursum addite, convolate planta,
> femoreque facili, clune agili et manu procaces,
> molles, veteres, Deliaci manu recisi'.

The Petronian cinaedus' summons to his fellows (*spatalocinaedi*) recalls closely the Catullan Attis' invitation to the *Gallae* to launch into dances; the only (though considerable) difference being in the satirical mood of the Petronian passage, which is totally absent in the Catullan one (11–26):

> canere haec suis adortast tremebunda comitibus:
> 'agite ite ad alta, Gallae, Cybeles nemora simul,
> simul ite, Dindymenae dominae vaga pecora,
> aliena quae petentes velut exules loca
> sectam meam exsecutae duce me mihi comites   15
> rapidum salum tulistis truculentaque pelagi,
> et corpus evirastis Veneris nimio odio,
> hilarate erae citatis erroribus animum.
> mora tarda mente cedat; simul ite, sequimini
> Phrygiam ad domum Cybebes, Phrygia ad nemora deae,   20
> ubi cymbalum sonat vox, ubi tympana reboant,
> tibicen ubi canit Phryx curvo grave calamo,
> ubi capita Maenades vi iaciunt hederigerae,
> ubi sacra sancta acutis ululatibus agitant,
> ubi suevit illa divae volitare vaga cohors: 25
> quo nos decet citatis celerare tripudiis'.

Although the intonation of the two passages is different, nonetheless the two poems seem to stand as flip sides of the same coin; thus, they could paradigmatically represent the two types of pantomime as described by ancient writers who credited Pylades with the development of the tragic and serious one, and Bathyllus with the more comic and light-hearted type.[143]

Mime in Cicero's Pro Caelio

Katrine Geffcken has shown that in the *Pro Caelio* Cicero relied on elements borrowed from the comic stage to construct his argument in defence of Caelius.[144] I would like to highlight here those elements specifically borrowed from mime. Such elements are particularly eminent in the characterization of Clodia and in the episode in the baths. The inclusion of comic elements was also prompted by the period during which the trial was held (3–4 April 56 BC), that is during the *Ludi Megalenses*. Cicero's speech was delivered on the 4th of April, the very opening day of the festivities.[145] Since trials were not supposed to be held during such festivities, Cicero stresses that someone could think that the charges against the accused were extremely serious to violate this custom. To show that this is not the case, Cicero immediately states that all charges against Caelius are imaginary and have been prompted by a single cause, that is the passion of a woman (*muliebrem libidinem*) who, through the means provided by her wealth (*opibus meretriciis*), is trying to take a personal revenge on the accused. From the very beginning of his speech, Cicero has thus already brought up the equation of Clodia with a *meretrix* driven by her uncontrollable *libido*.[146] In what follows, Cicero keeps emphatically insisting on the fact that Clodia's behaviour is that of a *meretrix*.[147] Clodia's loose sexual behaviour must have prompted in the mind of the jury an association with a *mima*; in fact, *mimae* and *meretrices* were perceived basically as one and the same in the Roman mind.[148] Additionally, the transformation of a *matrona* into a *meretrix* was a familiar one in mime since Laberius (*Compitalia* frg. 3: *quo quidem/me a matronali pudore prolubium meretricium/progredi coegit*) and Publilius (in Petronius *Sat.* 55: *An ut matrona ornata phaleris pelagiis/tollat pedes indomita in strato extraneo?*).[149] Later on in the speech, Cicero discusses at length the fifth charge against Caelius (61–9), that is his alleged attempt at poisoning Clodia (*de veneno in Clodiam parato*); the entire story is said to have taken place in the baths where Licinus, a young friend of Caelius, had to hand over a box of poison (*pyxis*) to Clodia's slaves who were supposed to be Caelius' accomplices, but eventually betrayed him and informed Clodia of Caelius' murderous intentions.[150] The attempt at poisoning is overtly and strategically equated by Cicero to an illogical and badly constructed plot of a mime; even more interestingly, Cicero claims that Clodia herself is the author of such a plot, a poetaster setting in motion *fabellae* or *mimi* that have no coherent plot (63–4):

> O magna vis veritatis, quae contra hominum ingenia, calliditatem, sollertiam contraque fictas omnium insidias facile se per se ipsa defendat! Velut haec tota fabella veteris et plurimarum fabularum poetriae quam est sine argumento, quam nullum invenire exitum potest!

Such an equation is hinted at when Cicero begins the discussion of the last charge against Caelius; Cicero already states here that he can find neither the origin nor the end (56: *reliquum est igitur crimen de veneno; cuius ego nec principium invenire neque evolvere exitum possum*). Even the alleged escape of Licinus from Clodia's friends, incredible in its incoherence as it is, is connected with the typical finale of the mimes, in which the development of the action is brought to a sudden and incongruous end by the escape of someone from somebody's hands (65–6):

> Tempore igitur ipso se ostenderunt, cum Licinius venisset, pyxidem expediret, manum porrigeret, venenum traderet. Mimi ergo est iam exitus, non fabulae; in quo cum clausula non invenitur, fugit aliquis e manibus, deinde scabilla concrepant, aulaeum tollitur. Quaero enim, cur Licinium titubantem, haesitantem, cedentem, fugere conantem mulieraria manus ista de manibus amiserit, cur non comprenderint, cur non ipsius confessione, multorum oculis, facinoris denique voce tanti sceleris crimen expresserint.

A moment later, Cicero strikes again a 'malicious allusion' to the finale of one of the most popular mimic plots, the adultery-mime, when he asks (and imagines the possible answer) about where exactly Clodia's friends would have been hidden in the Senian baths (67):

> ex quibus requiram, quem ad modum latuerint aut ubi, alveusne ille an equus Troianus fuerit, qui tot invictos viros muliebre bellum gerentes tulerit ac texerit.

Wiseman has suggestively connected the bathtub/*alveus ille* with the chest/*arca* (Horace, *Satires* II, 7, 59), the basket/*cista* (Juvenal, *Satires* 6, 44), and the jar/*dolium* (Apuleius, *Met.* IX, 23, 26) of the adultery-mime; in such hiding places, the lover of the adulterous woman usually had to hide because of the sudden and unexpected return of the husband.[151] Thus Clodia, the crafty lady (62: *mulier ingeniosa*), just like the cunning *moecha* of the mimes intent at plotting against her husband or rivals in love, is very well acquainted with tricks and subterfuges. In addition to this, the fact that mimes often involved poisonings (*veneficiae*) would have provided a very apt scenario in which to insert Clodia's charge; in fact, the link between Caelius' attempt at poisoning Clodia and the popular mimic scenario would have clearly evoked in the jury the idea that the episode in the baths ought to be considered a mimic trick purposely faked up by Clodia.[152] Thus Clodia, whom at the beginning of the speech Cicero compares to tragic Medea, undergoes a progressive degradation to the character of the *moecha* of the mimic stage.[153] As Wiseman has remarked, the association of Clodia with theatrical performances must have been a means to attack the luxurious and, especially, Hellenized lifestyle of both Clodia and her brother Clodius, indulging as they did in theatrical performances and being performers themselves.

In the *Pro Sestio* (54, 116) Cicero attacks brother and sister thus: [Clodius] *ipse ille maxime ludius, non solum spectator, sed actor et acroama, qui omnia sororis embolia novit, qui in coetum mulierum pro psaltria adducitur.* It is not clear whether Cicero meant that Clodia used to perform in balletic interludes (*embolia*) as a dancer (during aristocratic dinner parties) or that she was the composer of balletic interludes.[154] Perhaps, Cicero is hinting here at the common ground between Roman high society and the popular stage, as attested, for example, by the funerary inscription for the dancer Eucharis, a freedwoman of Licina's household of the late-Republican period:

> ... Docta erudita paene Musarum manu,
> quae modo nobilium ludos decoravi choro
> et Graeca in scaena prima populo apparui ...[155]

The fact that Eucharis performed in the *ludos nobilium* must mean either that she danced in private exhibitions held in noble houses or during votive and funerary games (*ludi votivi* and *ludi funebres*) rather than in the public dramatic festivals, which would have been rather called *ludi deorum immortalium*. Such private games were often a means for the politician to advertise himself and gain popular approval. It is possible that Cicero's emphasis in associating the Claudii with the theatre may contain also the allusion that their interest in it was not just of an aesthetic kind but rather for demagogic political exploitation. According to Macrobius, Clodius asked the mimographer Laberius to compose a mime for him, but the Roman knight refused.[156] As Wiseman has remarked, the memorability of the story lies in the fact that Laberius dared to refuse.[157]

The Adultery-mime in the Elegiac Poets

The adultery-mime is by far the best known type of mime. It consisted basically of a love-story in which three main characters featured: a jealous husband (the *stupidus*), an adulterous wife, and a lover. The basic plot consisted in the deception of the husband by his wife and her lover. The popularity and longevity of the adultery-mime is attested by references in ancient authors over a long span of time (from the first century BC to the sixth AD).[158] The first trace of a mime dealing with adultery appears in a fragment of the *Compitalia* by Laberius (*quo quidem/me a matronali pudore prolubium meretricium progredi coegit*).[159] Ovid provides a basic description of what the plot of the adultery-mime looked like (*Tristia* 2, 497–500, 505–6):

> quid, si scripsissem mimos obscena iocantes,
> > qui semper vetiti crimen amoris habent:
> in quibus assidue cultus procedit adulter,
> > verbaque dat stulto callida nupta viro?   500
>
> . . .
>
> cumque fefellit amans aliqua novitate maritum   505
> > plauditur et magno palma favore datur.

The rhetorician Choricius of Gaza (sixth century AD), who wrote a defence of the mimes, attests the existence of a variant on the type: the lover and the wife are caught by the husband and prosecuted in a trial where judges threaten punishment.[160]

A situation similar to that described by Ovid is found in Juvenal (6, 41–4):

> quid fieri non posse putes, si iungitur ulla
> Ursidio? si moechorum notissimus olim
> stulta maritali iam porrigit ora capistro,
> quem totiens texit periturum cista Latini?

The presence of Latinus, a famous archimimus during Domitian's reign, proves that Juvenal is here drawing on a well-known mimic scenario.[161] Suggestively, the situation outlined by Juvenal is already present in Horace (*Satires* I, 2, 127–34; II, 7, 58–61):

> nec vereor ne, dum futuo, vir rure recurrat,
> ianua frangatur, latret canis, undique magno
> pulsa domus strepitu resonet, vepallida lecto
> desiliat mulier, miseram se conscia clamet,   130
> cruribus haec metuat, doti deprensa, egomet mi.
> discincta tunica fugiendum est et pede nudo,

ne nummi pereant aut puga aut denique fama.
deprendi miserum est: Fabio vel iudice vincam.

quid refert, uri virgis ferroque necari
auctoratus eas, an turpi clausus in arca,
quo te demisit peccati conscia erilis,   60
contractum genibus tangas caput?

Lines II, 59–61 in particular (... *an turpi clausus in arca/quo te demisit peccati conscia erilis,/contractum genibus tangas caput*) matches the situation described by the *scholium* at Juvenal (6, 41–4) *superveniente marito sub cista celatus est, ut in mimo*.

An analogous scenario is found also in Propertius (2, 23, 9–10: *cernere uti possis vultum custodis amari,/captus et immunda saepe latere casa?* and 19–20: *nec dicet 'timeo, propera iam surgere, quaeso:/infelix, hodie vir mihi rure venit'*); Propertius (4, 8) shows even 'more fundamental links with the Adultery-mime'.[162] The elegist varies the usual scheme of the plot, inverting the usual roles of deceived husband and adulterous wife, since it is the woman (Cynthia) who returns from Lavinium and finds her man (Propertius) with two girls of questionable reputation. The inversion of roles itself has also mimic (and pantomimic) overtones and there are several instances that recall mimic situations where a jealous wife takes the role of the more commonly jealous husband.[163] The jealous mistress theme seems to lie also behind Propertius 3, 15. The poem deals with Cynthia's jealousy of Lycinna. In the poem, the triangular relationship between Cynthia–Propertius–Lycinna is paralleled to the mythical triangle Dirce–Lycus–Antiope; strangely, Antiope is said to be Dirce's slave (*famulam* 15), but no extant version of the myth makes her Dirce's servant. According to Yardley, it is possible that Propertius 'altered the relationship between the characters of the myth to suit the purposes of the poem';[164] the mythical parallel suggests thus that Lycinna is actually Cynthia's slave and Cynthia's jealousy resembles closely that of the jealous mimic mistress (44: *nescit vestra ruens ira referre pedem*).[165]

Ovid exploits the theme of adultery at *Amores* (3, 4) in a way reminiscent of the love-triangle of the Adultery-mime. McKeown has remarked that the high percentage of the occurrence of the word *adulter/a* in the elegy is a conscious strategy devised to remind his audience of the connection with the popular Adultery-mime.[166]

That the theme of adultery was borrowed from mime is suggested by the fact that the two literary genres that are usually considered to have provided material for Augustan elegy, Hellenistic erotic epigram and comedy, do not feature the theme of adultery in the way the Augustan elegists present it. In fact, in Hellenistic erotic epigrams women usually tend to be prostitutes, while in comedy they are either prostitutes or unmarried girls.[167]

The theme of adultery was popular also in pantomime, as is attested by Lucian (60, 63); in 60 Lucian relates that above all other themes, the pantomimic dancer must know, in order to enact them, all the (adulterous) loves and metamorphoses of Zeus;[168] in 63, in relating how the dancer Paris convinced Demetrius the Cynic of the worthiness of his art, Lucian describes the dancer enacting the love of Ares and Aphrodite, Hephaestus' discovery of the adultery, and the shame of the two lovers caught in the flagrant act.[169]

Suggestively enough, the same mythical episode features in Ovid's *Metamorphoses* (4, 171–89) and it is couched in a linguistic register very reminiscent of the adultery-mime: first of all, the love of Mars and Venus is emphatically called *adulterium* at the very opening of the story (171–2: *primus adulterium Veneris cum Marte putatur/hic vidisse deus*); then, the emphasis on the adulterous nature of the relationship is reiterated by the terminology employed to describe the three protagonists, since Vulcanus is called husband (*marito*), Venus wife (*coniunx*), and Mars paramour (*adulter*).

Mime and Pantomime in Ovid

Ovid's compositions are particularly rich in mimic and pantomimic overtones.[170] It has been discussed in the preceding paragraph that the mimic and pantomimic theme of adultery was adapted by Ovid (*Amores* 3, 4; *Met.* 4, 171–89). A passage in the *Tristia*, where Ovid states that his poems have been danced several times even before Augustus himself (2, 519–20: *et mea sunt populo saltata poemata saepe/saepe oculos etiam detinuere tuos*), has opened a tantalizing debate among scholars on whether Ovid purposely composed pieces for the pantomimic stage or whether his poems were adapted for the theatre. The phrasing seems to imply that some of his poetic compositions were adapted for the stage rather than written for it on purpose. This interpretation finds support in another passage in the *Tristia* where Ovid claims that he never composed anything for the stage (5, 7, 27–8: *nil equidem feci (tu scis hoc ipse) theatris/musa nec in plausus ambitiosa mea est*). However, this last statement contrasts with the evidence that his tragedy *Medea* was most likely written for the theatre. Generally speaking, scholars have interpreted the Ovidian passages as evidence against composition for the stage. An exception is Cunningham who claimed that Ovid purposely wrote one of his poetic compositions (i.e. the *Heroides*) for the pantomimic stage.[171] To solve the difficulty posed by *Tristia* 5, 27–8, Cunningham argued that Ovid's words are not to be taken literally and proposed to interpret and translate the lines as 'I never wrote for the gallery, nor have I gone out of my way to win applause'. Cunningham's thesis was based on three elements, namely Ovid's statement at *Tristia* (2, 519–20), the novelty of the *Heroides* as a literary genre, and internal evidence.

The novelty of the *Heroides*, which Ovid himself claimed not to belong to any previously known literary genre, lies for Cunningham in the fact that 'they present Latin erotic elegy in a form adapted to a new type of theatrical performance which was first introduced at Rome when Ovid was a young man'.[172] For this reason, Cunningham felt confident to recognize in these poems the most plausible candidate for pieces written for the pantomimic stage. Cunningham brought forward internal evidence to support his thesis such as the monologic unfolding and the subjective mood of the epistle, which gave room to explore different and conflicting emotions, as well as the fact that the addressee of the letter was often completely forgotten because of the monologue's shifting into soliloquy. In 1996, Cunningham's seminal idea was taken up by Sargent who tried to elaborate further and expand upon Cunningham by comparing the similarities between certain features of pantomime and similar ones found in the *Heroides*.[173] Nonetheless, Cunningham's hypothesis remained isolated and scholars dismissed the idea of an Ovidian poetic collection written for the stage and focused instead on trying to establish which of Ovid's poetic compositions were most suitable to be adapted as pantomimic pieces. Owen identified the *saltata poemata* of the *Tristia* as portions of the *Ars Amatoria*;[174] Galinsky, instead, underlined some analogies between the *Metamorphoses* and pantomime, namely 'the emphasis on the single scenes, the narrator's bravura performance, his sophistication, the constant shifts and changes, and the graphic, visual appeal of many scenes'.[175] More recently, Ingleheart has signalled three episodes in the *Metamorphoses* (Apollo and Daphne 1, 452–567; Althaea and Meleager 8, 445–546; Iphis 9, 666–796) whose features may have been extremely palatable for pantomimic adaptations.[176] Setting aside the issue of identifying which of Ovid's works is the most suitable to have received performance in pantomime, it seems more compelling to try to establish whether the aesthetics of pantomime and mime at large can be spotted in Ovid's poetic works. This does not mean that Ovid wrote for the popular stage, but that he appropriated and reshaped elements typical of it. In relation to this, Horsfall has proposed that the episode of the Calydonian boar-hunt (*Met.* 8, 260 ff.) shows clear signs of the influence of mime, which are recognizable in the characteristic parodist twisting of epic elements into burlesque.[177] The possibility of the existence of mimes with mythological themes has been much disputed by scholars (especially by Crusius in 1910), but we know that Laberius wrote a mime entitled *Anna Perenna* (an archaic Roman deity) and Varro mentions mimes about Liber and the Nymphs.[178] In addition to this, Tertullian and Minucius Felix attest the existence of a skit on the loves of Cybele in which a young Attis rejects the favours of an ageing and decrepit Mother Goddess.[179] Suggestively, an extant fragment by Laberius (frag. 176: *quid properas? ecquid praecurris Calidoniam?*) seems to refer to the myth of the Calydonian boar-hunt; the myth is also attested as a theme popular in pantomime since both Lucian (50) and Libanius (67) name the story of Meleager and Atalanta as being a theme of pantomimic performances. On the same line of thought, Fantham has proposed that at least in four episodes contained in the *Fasti* (2, 303–56; 1, 393–440; 6, 321–44; 3, 677–96) the ancestry of mime or pantomime can be detected.[180] The four episodes all oddly deal with stories of sexual frustration, an awkward theme in the context of the *Fasti*;[181] in addition to this, for three of the four episodes there is no known Hellenistic or Roman source. Fantham thus suggested that Ovid borrowed the themes from mimic or pantomimic representations.

Fasti 2, 303–56 narrates the story of the encounter of Hercules, Omphale, and Faunus and comes in the section concerned with this old Roman deity (Pan's counterpart in the Greek world). The story falls into three sections: the first one opens with Hercules and Omphale walking into the wood where they are seen by Faunus who is suddenly burnt with desire for the Lydian princess and resolves to assault her as soon as possible. The second section describes at length the exchange of garments between Hercules and Omphale (probably representing the preliminary period of chastity before initiation to Bacchus).[182] Then Hercules and his mistress reach a grotto where they lie down in separate beds. The third section is devoted to the farcical description of Faunus' misdirected assault (due to the exchange of garments between Hercules and Omphale) and his subsequent frustration. The story is closed by the narrator's remark that the reason why Faunus' worshippers are naked is due to the fact that since Faunus was deceived by garments, he does not love them.[183] Fantham claims that 'this passage of *Fasti* describes a sequence of events that could be fully understood as pantomime by the onlookers' and remarks that the story is more suitable to pantomime since dialogue (of which mime made full use) is not really required to represent the story; Fantham then explicitly makes clear that Ovid 'did not compose the story for pantomime, but that he derived it from pantomime'.[184]

The story of Anna Perenna (*Fasti* 3, 677–96) is again a tale of sexual frustration. Anna, an old goddess, is asked by Mars to intercede for him with Minerva with whom he is in love. Anna agrees but then starts delaying the encounter up to the moment in which Mars is not keen to accept any more delays. Thus Anna takes Minerva's place, covers up her own face with a veil, and presents herself to Mars, who, almost deceived and ready to kiss her, finally recognizes the old goddess. Giancotti and Bömer claimed that Ovid derived the story from a mime by Laberius entitled *Anna Perenna* of which some fragments survive; one of them (frag. 10: *conlabella osculum*) seems to be echoed in line 691 (*oscula sumpturus subito Mars aspicit Annam*).[185] Furthermore, that Ovid was probably inspired by a pantomimic situation seems to be also supported by the context of the passage (*Fasti* 3, 535–8), that is, in the description of the plebs gathered to celebrate the festivity of Anna Perenna:

> illic et cantant, quicquid didicere theatris,
>> et iactant faciles ad sua verba manus
> et ducunt posito duras cratere choreas,
>> cultaque diffusis saltat amica comis.

The verses make use of a terminology particularly linked with pantomimic representations; in fact the expression *iactare manus* is the technical term and the verb *saltare* is the *vox propria* used to describe pantomime.[186] Giancotti has also argued that in Ovid's treatment of Anna's life before becoming a deity (i.e. as sister of Dido *Fasti* 2, 543 ff.) there are other elements reminiscent of a mimic situation, such as Lavinia's jealousy of Anna and Anna's night-time escape half-dressed from Aeneas' palace after the appearance of her sister Dido in a dream who compelled her to leave.[187] Both jealous mistress and sudden escapes (especially from a window) were, in fact, basic ingredients of the mimes.[188]

Finally, there are two more stories of sexual frustration in the *Fasti*, in which Priapus is firstly aroused by Lotis and then by Vesta (*Fasti* 1, 393–440; 6, 321–44).[189] The figure of Priapus itself is well suited to mimes, as we know from Augustine (*De Civitate Dei* 6, 7: *numquid Priapo mimi, non etiam sacerdotes enormia pudenda fecerunt? an aliter stat adorandus in locis sacris, quam procedit ridendus in theatris?*).

The story of Priapus and Lotis ends with Priapus being discovered and laughed at by all participants, while in the story of Priapus and Vesta, the god manages to escape from the hands of the other gods. The finale (here as in the case of the story of Faunus) is closely reminiscent of what Cicero describes to be the typical ending of the mimes where the villain's escape brings to an abrupt but easy end the not-craftily-constructed mimic representation.[190] Furthermore, Barchiesi has remarked that the four comic episodes in the *Fasti* make explicit reference to the theatre so that the language itself signals 'the relationship between the story and stage traditions'.[191] In addition, there are two other elements that overtly hint at the fact that the episodes are 'based on a sort of theatrical code', namely the 'promise of a good jest' (*Fasti* 2, 304; 3, 738; 6, 319) and the 'laughter as seal of approval' (*Fasti* 1, 438; 2, 355, 377; 3, 343, 693; 5, 691).[192]

As to the reason why Ovid may have adapted and included mimic and pantomimic elements in the *Fasti*, Barchiesi's suggestion that the adoption of such elements may be the sign of a search on Ovid's part 'for a literary language that is able to recuperate the "popular" element in the cultivated literature of the Augustan age', is perfectly fitting with Ovid's innovative and unconventional literary attitude.[193]

Mime in Seneca's Apocolocyntosis

Seneca's *Apocolocyntosis* is a Menippean satire which was probably written shortly after Claudius' death in 54 A D and may have been presented at the *Saturnalia* of the same year.[194] Indeed, the satire has a pronounced performative character as has been pointed out by scholars such as Eden, who noticed that the satire strongly 'invites recitation before a select audience'.[195] Weinreich had already remarked that the *recitatio* of the *Apocolocyntosis* would give ample scope to display acting abilities and it could easily develop into a *mimus*.[196] In agreement with Weinreich's line of thought, Fantham and Purcell have advanced the hypothesis that the *Apocolocyntosis* may have been originally conceived as a mime and subsequently reshaped when written down. More precisely, Fantham has further suggested that Seneca 'has reworked in the narrative form of Menippean satire his own original libretto, written for intimate staging at Nero's *Saturnalia* as a mime in four scenes'.[197] The division of the scenes could have been as follows:

1) Prologue: on earth (1–4).
   Claudius is shown on his deathbed while Mercury scolds the fates for prolonging his life.
2) The council of the gods: in Heaven (5–11).
   Claudius finally dies and is brought by Mercury to heaven where his deification is discussed.
3) The funeral: on earth (12).
   After the denial of the deification, Mercury escorts Claudius back to earth, where he assists to his funeral.

4) The trial: in the Underworld (13).

Claudius is lead into the Underworld and he is judged by Aeacus.

Kehoe has argued for the existence of mimes constituted by more than a single scene and involving a conspicuous number of characters.[198] He has shown that in several cases, it is possible to reconstruct mimes with four scenes, which matches Fantham's division of the scenes of the *Apocolocyntosis*. Purcell has suggested that the *Apocolocyntosis* may have been 'part of the text performed by whichever *mimus* appeared at Claudius' funeral'.[199] Purcell's hypothesis relies on the evidence of the existence of the practice of funerary mimes, but it is not possible to establish what degree of comic hostility was allowed.[200] It remains a matter for debate as to whether the *Apocolocyntosis* was first conceived as a mime; nonetheless, it is worth pointing out that several mimic elements can be detected in the satire with a good degree of confidence. For instance, Claudius' depiction, with the emphasis on his physical and mental deformities, seems much indebted to mime, which made heavy use of such grotesque characterizations; this type of representation is attested by several statuettes, representing mimic actors, which present grotesquely and emphatically distorted facial and bodily features.[201] As to Claudius' mental and physical defects: the emperor is lame (I, 11: *non passibus aequis*; V, 6: *pedem dextrum trahere*; V, 14: *insolitum incessum*); his utterances are unintelligible since he stammers (V, 7–9 *respondisse nescio quid perturbato sono et voce confusa; non intellegere se linguam eius*; V, 14–16: *ut vidit novi generis faciem, insolitum incessum, vocem nullius terrestris animalis sed qualis esse marinis beluis solet, raucam et implicatam*; VI, 12: *quid diceret nemo intellegebat*); he shakes his head and his hands at all times (V, 6: *nescio quid illum minari, assidue enim caput movere*; VI, 13: *illo gestu solutae manus, et ad hoc unum satis firmae*); he is irascible by nature (VI, 11–12: *excandescit hoc loco Claudius et quanto potest murmure irascitur*); overall, his outward appearance is more that of a monster than of a human (V, 16–17: *diligentius intuenti visus est quasi homo*), so much so that Hercules himself is at first sight scared (V, 12–13: *tum Hercules primo aspectu sane perturbatus est, ut qui etiam non omnia monstra timuerit*).

Seneca clearly casts Claudius in the mimic role of the fool from the very opening of the satire, where he is presented as a 'born fool' (I, 5–7: *ille, qui verum proverbium fecerat, aut regem aut fatuum nasci oportere*). Stupidity was the distinguishing feature of one of the most popular of mimic characters, the *stupidus/ μωρός*. References to Claudius' dullness are insisted upon in the satire over and over again: Hercules bids him to stop playing the fool (VII, 1: *tu desine fatuari*) and he fears that Claudius may have in reserve for him the blow of a fool (VII, 19: μωροῦ πληγήν; VIII, 3). The names of the two companions chosen by Clotho to keep company to Claudius in death, Augurinus and Baba, seem to be selected because they were typically associated with fools; a passage in Seneca's epistles attests that the name Baba proverbially had such a connotation (15, 9: *quam tu nunc vitam dici existimas stultam? Babae et Isionis?*);[202] scholars have remarked that the names appear in alphabetical order and seem thus to paradigmatically signify that Augurinus, Baba, and Claudius are the ABC of foolishness;[203] Claudius' life itself is said to be *stolida* (IV, 2: *abrupit stolidae regalia tempora vitae*); the climax of Claudius' foolishness is then represented by him having impersonated the *Saturnalicius princeps* all his life (VIII, 7–8: *cuius mensem toto anno celebravit Saturnalicius princeps*); here Seneca not only emphasizes that Claudius always behaved like a clown prince, but he also hints at the fact that the reversal of roles was a constant feature of his reign. Thus, similar to the reversal of roles enacted in mimes, in which the cunning slave dexterously deceives his master and the adulterous wife her husband, so the *princeps* Claudius has always been deceived by his canny freedmen and wives.[204] The mention of the *pantomimus* Mnester in the satire (XIII, 4) can be interpreted in this light. Mnester was for many years Messalina's lover and all the populace in Rome was well aware of this, apart, it seems, from Claudius who, compelled by his treacherous wife, even commanded Mnester to obey Messalina's bidding. He was then put to death by Claudius shortly after Messalina's disgrace. Seneca's characterization of Claudius as the popular mimic fool may have been prompted by the fact that Claudius' dullness had become proverbial, as is attested by a satirical pamphlet about Claudius entitled the 'Elevation of the Fool' (μωρῶν ἐπανάστασις) circulating in Rome during the emperor's lifetime.[205] According to Suetonius, Claudius' widespread reputation of foolishness was perpetuated even after his death by Nero, who never ceased to make jokes about his predecessor's stupidity (*Nero*, 33, 1: *nam et **morari** eum desisse inter homines producta prima syllaba iocabatur . . .*).[206]

Furthermore, the title itself of the satire, *Apocolocyntosis*, is to be connected with stupidity.[207] In fact, the most probable meaning of the word *apocolocyntosis* is 'metamorphosis into a gourd' or 'gourdification', and it is made up in analogy to '*apotheosis*', transformation into a god, deification. Thus, as human beings enacting high and almost divine values are transformed into gods, in a similar, though opposite, process, Claudius, whose intrinsic and distinguishing quality is stupidity, is transformed into the very symbol of it, a gourd.[208] That the gourd is associated with foolishness and vacuity is attested by two passages, one in Petronius and the other in Apuleius.[209] As Coffey has aptly remarked, Seneca 'chose the pumpkin as the means of ridiculing Claudius' divinity on the grounds that it would be difficult to think of anything more lacking in positive characteristics than a pumpkin'.[210] Moreover, that the satire stands as a mimic travesty of deification is explicitly stated by the contrast made between deification and the farcical imitation of it as presented in the *fabam mimum* (IX, 12–13: *magna res erat deum fieri: iam Fabam mimum fecisti*).[211] The *fabam mimum* is just mentioned here and by Cicero (*Ad Att.* I, 16, 13) and it is not clearly known what the 'Bean' mime was about; nonetheless, since in both the Senecan and Ciceronian passages the 'Bean' mime is contrasted with apotheosis, it is plausible to infer that the 'Bean' mime dealt with the 'meanest and most risible form of survival after death'.[212]

As to thematic influences, motifs such as the trial and the descent to the Underworld are attested in mimes and may well be derived from them. Several ancient writers provide evidence that trials were a very popular subject in mimes;[213] in relation to this, a funerary inscription found in the *columbarium* in the Vigna Codini in Rome and dedicated most probably to a mimic actor (*lusor mutus*) bears evidence that the role of barrister (*causidicus*) is not only attested in mimes, but also that such a character was one of the most important in the genre; in fact, the deceased performer of Villa Codini is remembered and praised for having discovered how to imitate barristers:

Caesaris lusor
mutus et argutus imitator
Ti. Caesaris Augusti qui
primus invenit causidicos imitari.[214]

The theme of the descent to the Underworld is also a favourite one in mimic performances and two mimes of Laberius seem to have dealt with the topic (*Necyomantia* and *Lacus Avernus*). In the *Apocolocyntosis*, the trial-scene is set in Aeacus' tribunal in the Underworld (XIV, 1: *ducit illum ad tribunal Aeaci*); Pedo Pomponius acts as the prosecutor and Publilius Petronius as the defence counsel, to whom Aeacus does not grant a word, since, just after having heard the prosecution, he condemns Claudius straightaway. Claudius is condemned to play dice using a dice-box with a hole in it (XIV, 19–20: *tum Aeacus iubet illum alea ludere pertuso fritillo*).

Suddenly, Gaius Caligula appears and claims Claudius as his runaway slave; he produces witnesses who testify to having seen Claudius being beaten by Gaius with whips, canes, and fisticuffs (XV, 10: *producit testes, qui illum viderant ab illo flagris, ferulis, colaphis vapulantem*); on the basis of this evidence, Aeacus hands Claudius over to his master who employs him as secretary for petitions.

Even the conclusion has a pronounced mimic quality since Claudius is presented as a runaway slave and the reference to beating and slapping, one of the most common and trivial ingredient of mimes, is an indisputable mark that Seneca chose to represent Claudius, both in life and death, as a character of the mimes.

Mime in Petronius' Satyricon

The most remarkable feature of the *Satyricon* is its pronounced composite nature; it is made up of a generic mixture and is irreducible to a single and prominent genre. Petronius drew the material for its novel form from several different genres such as Menippean Satire, Milesian tale, and the mime.[215] As to the influence of mime, the prominence of mimic elements in Petronius' *Satyricon* was first underlined by the Christian apologist Marius Mercator (late fourth-early fifth century AD) who, in his attack against the emperor Julian, compared the mimic licentiousness of his verses to those, among others, of Petronius:

> Erubesce, infelicissime, in tanta linguae scurrilis, vel potius mimicae obscenitate. Vulgares tu dignus audire acclamationes: unus tu, unus Philistion, unus Latinorum Lentulus, unus tibi Marullus comparandus; namque Martialis et Petronii solus ingenia superasti.[216]

In the twelfth century, John of Salisbury (*Polycraticus* 3, 8) summarized the very essence of Petronius' *Satyricon* with the statement that *fere totus mundus ex Arbitri nostri sententia mimum videtur implere* and *fere totus mundus, iuxta Petronium, exerceat histrionem*. In more recent times, the presence of elements borrowed from the mimic and pantomimic stage in Petronius has been established since Collignon's seminal work on the *Satyricon*.[217] Despite the general agreement in relation to the influence of mime in the *Satyricon*, scholars give different evaluations of the extent of it; these range from considering the mime as the primary 'formative' genre to arguing that mime was one, among others, of the constitutive genres of Petronius' *Satyricon*.[218] According to Sandy, elements such as the 'fondness for certain stock-characters', the 'treatment of sex with *nova simplicitas*', the 'inclusion of literary parody and the depreciation of elevated poetry' are clearly mimic; in addition to this, stylistic features such as the mingling of prose and verse and the unparalleled range of tone, subject, and speech can be ascribed to mime.[219] Moreover, the reason that sets in motion the novel is the wrath of the god Priapus, a figure prominent in the mimes (obviously, the theme of the wrath of a divinity is an overt parody of an epic commonplace).[220]

The novel is actually constituted by a number of episodes loosely connected one to the other and most of them present situations that are clearly derived from the mime. What follows is a tentative list.

(1) The Quartilla-mime (16. 1–26.6): a Priapus-mime?

As Sandy has remarked, the Quartilla episode is 'unusually rich in mimic associations, most notably in the clause: *omnia mimico risu exsonuerant* (19.1)'.[221] Panayotakis has argued that the episode can be read as the narrative equivalent of a three-scene mimic stage-piece according to the different rooms which serve as setting: 1) the *cella* in the *deversorium* (16–21); 2) the *triclinium* (21.5–26.3); 3) the *cubiculum* (26.3–26.6).[222] The piece's eminently mimic character is provided by the presence of songs and dance, studied gesturing and flamboyant laughter, sex and slapstick (as in the episode of the Syrian thieves who attempt to steal valuables while the guests are asleep).

Quartilla, the alleged priestess of Priapus, basically acts as the *archimima* whose instructions make the skit unfold. Quartilla is presented as performing a ritual in honour of the god Priapus (*sacrum*), which Encolpius, Giton, and Aschyltos are accused of having disrupted, as Quartilla's veiled maid let them know (16). As the episode develops, it becomes clear that the protagonists of the novel are not witnessing any religious ceremony, but have simply got involved in an orgy. Then the veiled Quartilla theatrically enters the room (*intravit ipsa* 17), bursts into carefully arranged tears, and claims that she is worried that the three men may reveal to the profane the religious and secret devotions they saw in the chapel of Priapus. After being reassured that they will keep silent, Quartilla and her maids suddenly change their attitude and begin their sexual 'exorcism' (19–20). To provide additional pleasure to the guests, Quartilla offers to them the services of her *cinaedi*, who first sing some obscene songs and then make themselves sexually available to the guests.[223]

The last act of the episode stages the mock-marriage between 7-year-old Pannychis and 16-year-old Giton (25–6). The mock-marriage is explicitly defined as *mimicae nuptiae*; the pseudo-marriage motif seems to have been a stock theme in mimes; a mime by Laberius and an Atellan farce by Pomponius were entitled *Nuptiae*.[224]

(2) The Cena Trimalchionis (26)

The theatricality of the *Cena Trimalchionis* has long since been underlined by scholars;[225] in fact, the *Cena* basically develops as a spectacle constituted by a succession of different performances acted by professionals of the stage (the *scissor/essedarius* 36: *processit statim scissor et ad symphoniam gesticulatus ita laceravit obsonium, ut putares essedarium hydraule cantante pugnare; Petauristarii* 53; *Homeristae* 59; the *comoedi* recite a medley of Atellan farce and Virgilian epic 68; 79), the household slaves (*puer Alexandrinus* 68; Habinnas' slave 68; Massa 69; the cook Daedalus 70), and finally by Trimalchio himself (he sings a *canticum* from the *Laserpiciarius* mime 35: *atque ipse etiam taeterrima voce de Laserpiciario mimo canticum extorsit*). Trimalchio sings the songs of Menecrates (73); he recites verses of the mimographer Publilius Syrus (55) and imitates the mimic actor himself (52).[226] The *cena* is framed by continuous musical accompaniment;[227] the slaves sing while attending to their duties (31: *Ac ne in hoc quidem tam molesto tacebant officio, sed obiter cantabant . . . Paratissimus puer non minus me acido cantico excepit, et quisquis aliquid rogatus erat ut daret . . .*). This gives the impression to Encolpius that the whole affair resembles more an actor's dance than a gentleman's dining-room (31: *pantomimi chorum, non patris familiae triclinium crederes*). Trimalchio theatrically enters to music (32: *. . . cum ipse Trimalchio ad symphoniam allatus est*); the different courses are introduced or taken away as well to musical accompaniment (33: *accessere continuo duo servi et symphonia strepente scrutari paleam coeperunt*; 34: *cum subito signum symphonia datur et gustatoria pariter a choro cantante rapiuntur*; 36: *Haec ut dixit, ad symphoniam quattuor tripudiantes procurrerunt superioremque partem repositorii abstulerunt*). Sandy has argued that 'the *Cena Trimalchionis* simply cannot be accounted for in the traditions of Menippean satire' and has claimed that mime, instead, 'may have provided the germ of a burlesque *convivium* replete with brummagem and bungled erudition'.[228] For what concerns *cenae* as a common theme in Roman satire by which Petronius could have been inspired, Sandy has convincingly argued that features such as the 'extended dramatization and exuberance of character and incident that distinguish it' are lacking in the satirical *cenae*, while these very elements seem to appear eminently mimic.[229] As to the sources of mimic *cenae*, Pliny and Jerome possibly provide evidence to support that the banquet featured in mimes.[230] The passage in Jerome (*Ep.* 52, 8, 3) deals with a quotation of a lost speech of Cicero in which the orator blames the credulity of uneducated people who uncritically believe what they see onstage. To illustrate this, Cicero gives the example of the overt anachronism of a theatrical piece entitled *Convivia poetarum ac philosophorum*, which stages a discussion between the non-contemporary Euripides and Menander, Socrates and Epicurus. Cicero does not specify what sort of performance he is referring to, but the hypothesis that the *convivia* was a mimic performance is suggested by the fact that the performance is described as unsophisticated; a passage in Pliny (*Naturalis Historia*, VIII, 209) seems to provide further evidence for the presence of the theme in mime:

> Hinc censoriarum legum paginae, interdictaque cenis abdomina, glandia, testiculi, vulvae, sincipita verrina, ut tamen Publili mimorum poetae cena, postquam servitutem exuerat, nulla memoretur sine abdomine, etiam vocabulo suminis ab eo inposito.

Pliny states that in every dinner (*cena*) given by the mimographer Publilius the belly of a sow always features among the dishes he offered and to which he gave the name of *sumen* (sow or hog).[231] Skutsch has interpreted *cena* as a staged mime by Publilius, possibly entitled *Sumen*, and not as a reference to the mimographer's private life. Additional evidence of *mimic convivia* is to be found in a passage by Choricius (*Apologia mimorum*, 110), in which he reports that the host and his guest as well as banqueters more generally were mimic roles.

(3) *The sea trip and shipwreck on the way to Croton*[232]

The adventures on board Licha's ship experienced by Encolpius, Giton, and Eumolpus present two motifs which are derived from the mime; the first one, the motif of sea adventures, which was a recurring one in almost all of the surviving Greek romances, was also popular in the mimes.[233] Gellius attests that one of the character in Laberius' *Anna Peranna* was a *gubernius* (steersman);[234] in his reconstruction of the plot of Laberius' *Anna Peranna*, Giancotti has suggested that the mime may have included a sea trip; he based this assumption on the account found in Ovid's *Fasti* (III, 544) which narrates a sea trip undergone by Anna Peranna to escape Iarbas' invasion of Carthage (565–6: *nacta ratem comitesque fugae pede labitur aequo/moenia respiciens, dulce sororis opus*); the presence of a steersman (586: *navita*; 589: *pugnante magistro*; 593–4: *nec iam moderator habenis/utitur*) also in Ovid's account reasonably corroborates Giancotti's reconstruction of the plot of the *Anna Peranna*.[235] A passage in Seneca's *De ira* (2, 2, 4–5) also illustrates the popularity of the sea trip as a theme in the mimes:

> Quae non sunt irae, non magis quam tristitia est, quae ad conspectum mimici naufragii contrahit frontem, non magis quam timor, qui Hannibale post Cannas moenia circumsidente lectorum percurrit animos . . .

Moreover, in the Charition-mime (second century AD), a sea trip is featured (105–7) which, as in the case of Anna Peranna, is a means to escape enemies.

The second motif is that of the trial (106–7). A trial scene features in the second mime of Herodas, in which a pimp has to defend himself in a court. Panayotakis has suggested that a court scene may have featured in the Laureolus-mime (usually dated to the age of Caligula), which could have taken place before the crucifixion of the brigand.[236] Apuleius describes a trial scene in an episode of his *Metamorphoses*, which is overtly indebted to the mime (10, 2–12).[237] Choricius of Gaza attests that a trial constituted the finale of the Adultery-mime at least in his age (*Apologia Mimorum*, 30).

(4) The Fugitive Millionaire-mime (117): 'Quid ergo', inquit Eumolpus, 'cessamus mimum componere?'[238]

After having been shipwrecked in an unknown location, Encolpius and his friends finally come to know from an old man that the city they see on the top of the mountain is Croton. They then question the farm-bailiff about how people earn their leaving in such an old and famous city; the old man replies with a monologue full of blame in which he informs our heroes of the contemporary practice at Croton where the means of one's support is earned by a single activity: legacy-hunting (*sed quoscunque homines in hac urbe videritis, scitote in duas partes esse divisos. Nam aut captantur aut captant*).[239] Because of this, Eumolpus has the brilliant idea of constructing a mime, in which he plays the part of the rich man at the point of death and his friends act as his assistants. Eumolpus casts himself as the *dominus gregis* (*facite ergo me dominum*) and instructs his troupe about the plot of the skit and the roles everyone is going to play: Encolpius and Giton will be the *mimi calvi*, and Corax the buffoon slave. The alleged mimic troupe acts out the script so well and the legacy-hunters in the city are so convinced by their performance that among the legacy-hunters a harsh competition starts to win Eumolpus' favour and his legacy.[240]

Although several generic strands form the *Satyricon*, the motif that life is a *theatrum mundi* lies at the heart of this work and the *mimicus risus*, as Panayotakis puts it, is indeed the leitmotif of the novel.[241]

The Pantomime of the Judgement of Paris in Apuleius (Met. 10, 30–4)

Apuleius' description of the pantomime of the judgement of Paris is an extremely important source for our knowledge of this genre since it is the only description of a pantomimic performance transmitted to us. Unfortunately, it is difficult to establish whether Apuleius' account faithfully records the real proceedings of pantomimic performances or whether his narration is a free adaptation of them.

Scholars have argued that Apuleius' 'Judgement of Paris' is not a straight translation of pantomime into narrative form since there are many deviances from what the pantomimic norm seems to have been and because of the authorial interventions present in the text.[242]

If we compare Apuleius' description with the information found in other sources referring to pantomime, some discrepancies arise. The first one is that pantomime is said to be a solo performance, while in the Apuleian version we find five principal dancers and a large number of extras. This divergence from the norm, if a norm existed at all, is explicable since the existence of pantomimic performances entailing a larger cast is attested by Plutarch (*Quaest. Conviv.* 711e) and Lucian (83).[243]

A major issue arises also in relation to the use of masks attested in pantomimic performances, since in Apuleius' description no explicit mention of the use of masks by the dancers is made and the text seems to describe facial expressions of the characters (30: *vultu honesta*); therefore, it has been inferred that the dancers are actually unmasked.[244] Moreover, the pantomime described seems also to lack the usual accompanying libretto. In relation to this, I would suggest that the verbal description of the performance made by the author actually works as a substitute for the libretto. It mirrors the typical features of the libretto and, at the same time, distances itself through authorial intrusions emphasizing the artificiality of the performance. The insistence upon the fictional nature of the spectacle could also in itself be meant to reflect, through a deliberately exaggerated mirroring, the overtly fictional character of pantomimic performances.[245] Several features contained in Apuleius' description are clearly attested as typical of the pantomimic genre. For instance, the charming beauty of the performance is in keeping with the enchanting nature of pantomimic performances as described by ancient writers.[246]

The narration focuses on a segment of the story of the judgement of Paris, namely the contest of Juno, Minerva, and Venus. The background motivation of the story is not mentioned; basically, the performance enacts a reduced and simplified version of the plot which focuses around its climactic moment. Moreover, the real interest of the performance resides in the artful gesticulations and movements of the dancers rather than the content of the story itself. The characters played by the dancers are recognized by means of costuming and props; the character of Paris is identified through the tiara and the short cloak (30: *aurea tiara contecto capite; barbaricis amiculis umeris def[l]uentibus*); Mercury through the wings, the caduceus, and the virgula (30: *et inter comas eius aureae pinnulae cognatione simili sociatae prominebant; quem caduceum et virgula Mercurium indicabant*); Juno by a diadem and a sceptre (30: *nam et caput stringebat diadema candida, ferebat et sceptrum*); Minerva by a helmet topped with an olive wreath, a shield, and a spear (30: *caput contecta fulgenti galea, et oleaginea corona tegebatur ipsa galea, clypeum attollens et hastam quatiens*); Venus by a light and luxurious silky tunic (31: *pallio bombycino*).

The stage-setting of the action is provided (30):

> Erat mons ligneus, ad instar incliti montis illius, quem vates Homerus Idaeum cecinit, sublimi[s] instructus fabrica, consitus virectis et vivis arboribus, summo cacumine, de manibus fabri fonte manante, fluvialis aquas eliquans.

The setting described implies an extraordinary structure representing Mount Ida planted with real trees (30: *summo cacumine, consitus virectis et vivis arboribus*) and a fountain pouring water (30: *de manibus fabri fonte manante, fluvialis aquas eliquans*) where goats are shown browsing the grass (30: *capellae pauculae tondebant herbulas*).

Now, it is attested that such ambitious structures could be staged, but they did not constitute 'a representational norm for the genre'.[247] In addition to this, the fact that the stage setting is actually mirrored through the conventional literary device of an *ecphrasis topou* of a *locus amoenus* seems to me a sign that, in most cases, the stage setting was primarily constituted by a verbal scenery conjured up by the words of the libretto. Moreover, the narrator's claim that Mount Ida represented is not the real one, but that described by Homer (30: *ad instar incliti montis illius, quem vates Homerus Idaeum cecinit*) and the use of epic phrasing (30: *summo cacumine; virectis; fonte manante*) seems to point in this direction.[248] It is hence possible to suggest that the verbal scenery evoked by the libretto may have employed famous and familiar descriptions of *loci amoeni* as well as *horridi* depending on the story enacted. Such an appropriation would have been a useful tool because of the familiarity of the audience with such descriptions; moreover, the fact that the landscape portrayed may have been more imaginary and thus evocative than strictly real is absolutely in keeping with the essence of pantomime itself whose charm consisted mainly in the allusive and evocative power of the dancer's movements.

After having provided the setting, five main characters appear onstage in succession: Paris, Mercury, Juno, Minerva, and Venus. Their swift entrances are stylistically marked by the initial position of the verbs introducing them: *adest* (Mercury); *insequitur* (Juno); *inrupit* (Minerva); *introcessit* (Venus); *influunt* (Graces and Hours); the verbs also indicate the characteristic ways in which the characters move: the epiphany-like appearance and disappearance of Mercury is illustrated by the verbs *adest/facessit*; his swift and elegant dance steps are indicated by *saltatorie procurrens* and *protinus gradum scitule referens*;[249] Minerva's impetuous gait is illustrated by *inrupit*; the flowing quality of the Graces and Houres by *influunt*.

The first character appearing onstage is the dancer playing the role of Paris, who pretends to be guarding his herd on Mount Ida. There, he is reached by Mercury who gives him the golden apple to be awarded to the most beautiful of the goddesses. Then, the three dancers playing the role of the three goddesses make their entrance and dance in turn accompanied by their own entourage (Juno by Castor and Pollux; Minerva by the personifications of Terror and Metus; Venus by Cupids, Hours, and the Graces).

The diverse quality of the dancing of the three performers is emphasized by explicit statements about the different types of gesticulation and movements adopted by each: Juno's movements are described as quiet and unaffected (31: *procedens quieta et inadfectata gesticulatione*); through lady-like nods she indicates to Paris what her reward would be if he would award her the prize (31: *nutibus honestis pastori pollicetur*);[250] Minerva's eye and head movements as well as gestures, instead, are quick and jerky (31: *inquieto capite; oculis in aspectu[m] minacibus; citato et intorto genere gesticulationis*). The two personifications accompanying the goddess, Terror and Metus, exhibit themselves in war-like leaps (31: *nudis insultantes gladiis*).

The dance steps of Venus are slow, languid, and undulating (32):

> ...longe suavior Venus placide commoveri cunctantique lente vestigio et leniter fluctuante spi[n]nula[s] et sensim adnutante capite coepit incedere, mollique tibiarum sono delicatis respondere gestibus, et nunc mite coniventibus, nunc acre comminantibus gestire pupulis, et nonnumquam saltare solis oculis.

Similarly, the movements of the Hours and Graces accompanying the goddess are fluid and flowing (32: *influunt*).[251] The dancer impersonating Venus concludes her solo by signifying the prize she will give to Paris through a motion of her arms (32: *nisu brachiorum polliceri videbatur*). After the prize has been awarded to Venus by Paris, the dancers playing the roles of Juno and Minerva show their bitterness and rage (34: *tristes et iratis similes; indignationem repulsae gestibus professae*), while the dancer impersonating Venus manifests her happiness by leaping around the stage (34: *Venus vero gaudens et hilaris laetitiam suam saltando toto cum choro professa est*).

The representation is ended by the splitting open of the earth and the sinking of the wooden mount into the abyss. The puzzling sinking of the scenery seems a spectacular way, both in its visual and aural impact, to end the piece. It is noticeable that Apuleius' description combines a detached and quite satirical attitude towards the performance, attained by his constant reminding of its artificiality and illusionary nature, with a portrayal of it that indulgingly emphasizes its beauty.[252]

This contradictory attitude seems to be the sign of a tension in Apuleius' vision (or Lucius') of the spectacle. In a way, the satirical stance seems constantly employed as a tool to maintain a detached and alert gaze; the need to constantly keep the gaze (and thus one's frame of mind) under control seems to be prompted by the need to prevent and avoid being absorbed by the charming and sweeping effect of the performance; therefore, even in this respect, Apuleius' description of the pantomimic enactment of the judgement of Paris is a faithful testimony of the almost ecstatic effect that this type of show could provoke and of its power to deeply affect the audience; that pantomime had this intoxicating quality is repeatedly hinted at by ancient writers at large and is even more forcefully revealed by the fierce opposition shown by the Church Fathers towards pantomimic and mimic performances.[253] Their violent hostility stands out as a clear reaction to performances whose sweeping power and popularity was such to provoke the need to attack them forcefully. Nonetheless, one case of appropriation of mimic elements by a Christian writer, the apostle Paul, unexpectedly features; given the hostility of the Church Fathers towards mimic and pantomimic performances, Paul's appropriation is not only baffling but also revealing in relation to the popularity of them and deserves thus a closer scrutiny. According to Windisch, in one of his letters to the Corinthians (2, 11–12), Paul presents and characterizes himself as the mimic fool so well known from the stage.[254] On Windisch's line of thought, Welborn has remarked that Paul, in his own portrait as a fool, has combined several types of fools, such as the 'leading slave' (11: 21b-23), the 'braggart warrior' (11: 24–7), the 'anxious old man' (11: 28–9), and 'the learned impostor' (12: 1b-4).[255] It is interesting to point out that, in doing so, Paul may have had as inspiration Seneca's characterization of Claudius as the mimic fool in the *Apocolocyntosis*.[256] It is perhaps no coincidence that Paul employs allusions to the mimic stage in the Letters addressed to the inhabitants of Corinth, the same city in which the wanderings of Apuleius' fictional character, Lucius, find a closure and the place where the many theatrical performances included in Apuleius' novel take place. Corinth was indeed known for its lascivious costumes and for its addiction to gladiatorial contests and theatrical performances of mimes and pantomimes.[257] Because of this, Paul's adoption of the mimic language only in his epistles addressed to the Corinthians can be interpreted as a strategic choice directly linked with the suitability of such a language for its inhabitants. Leaving aside the consideration of Paul's agenda in presenting himself as the mimic fool, which do not concern us here, it is, instead, important to underline that his adoption of the popular theatre as a familiar background to convey his message provides evidence for the popularity of such a *milieu*. Even more importantly, the somehow paradoxical presence of such an idiom in a Christian writer shows the extent to which the idiom of sub-literary genres constituted a common cultural currency in the ancient world.

Pantomime and the Structure of
Seneca's Tragedies

Introduction

Several features of Seneca's plays contribute to what scholars unanimously observe to be a remarkably loose dramatic structure: the independence of individual scenes at the expense of the dramatic coherence of the whole;[1] the diversity of the episodes; the severe suspension of dramatic time produced by lengthy descriptions that do not advance the action of the main plot; conversely, the extreme acceleration of dramatic time due to the concentration of several actions in a brief span of time; the fluidity of setting; the abandonment of the unifying handling of the chorus; the lack of consistent indications of the characters' entrances and exits or, more generally, the relative scarcity of dramatic information; the prominence of monologues rather than dialogues. Regenbogen has aptly defined the result of this process as 'dissolution of the dramatic structure'.[2]

This chapter takes a detailed look at these controversial elements of Seneca's tragedies (all of which diverge from classical norms) and tries to provide support to the thesis that they may reflect Seneca's adoption of the aesthetics of pantomime, as defined in the previous chapter. After an overview of the structure of each play, I shall return in more detail to the above-mentioned characteristics.

Systematic Analysis of Seneca's Tragedies[3]

Hercules Furens

Act 1 (1–124): Juno.

place: in front of the royal palace of Thebes (134–5).

Juno is angered because of the presence in heaven of many illicit sons of Jupiter. She fears now that Hercules, the most detested of her stepsons, having successfully concluded the last task she has imposed on him, will attack heaven.

Transition: the entrance of the chorus is un-cued.

Chorus I (125–204): Dawn song.

Transition: the chorus announces the entrance of Megara and Amphitryon (202–4).

Act 2 (205–523): Amphitryon, Megara, Lycus.

Scene 1 (205–331): Amphitryon, Megara.

Amphitryon and Megara hope Hercules will soon return and save them from the threats of the usurper Lycus.

Transition (329–31): Lycus' entrance is announced by Megara.

Scene 2 (332–523): Lycus, Megara, Amphitryon.

Lycus, wanting to legitimize his status as king of Thebes, intends to marry Megara, but she refuses his marriage offer. Having been rejected, Lycus sentences Hercules' whole family to death.

Chorus II (524–91): Hercules' labours.

Transition: Hercules' entrance is announced by Amphitryon (521–3); Theseus' one is un-cued (his presence onstage is made explicit only later in the act by Hercules who addresses him just before his exit. Most probably, Theseus is meant to enter onstage with Hercules).

Act 3 (592–829):

Scene 1 (592–640): Hercules, Amphitryon, Theseus, Megara (mute).

Hercules returns with Theseus from the Underworld. He comes to learn of the situation in Thebes and immediately leaves to confront Lycus.

Transition: Hercules announces his exit (637–40).

Scene 2 (640–829): Theseus, Amphitryon, Megara (mute).

Amphitryon asks Theseus to narrate Hercules' descent to the Underworld.

Transition: the entrance of the chorus is announced by Theseus (827–9).

Chorus III (830–94): song of praise for Hercules speculating on the frailty of human life.

Transition: the chorus announces Hercules' entrance (893–4); we must infer that Amphitryon and Megara remain onstage during the choral song. As to Theseus, even though his exit is not cued, we must infer that he leaves the stage at some intervening point.

Act 4 (895–1053): Hercules, Amphitryon, Megara, chorus, sons of Hercules (mute), servants (mute).

Scene 1: Hercules, Amphitryon, Megara, chorus, sons of Hercules (mute), servants (mute).

Hercules returns from the killing of Lycus. He then prepares to make offerings to the gods. As he attends to the sacrifice, an attack of madness possesses him. Because of it, Hercules has hallucinatory experiences that make him confuse his own sons for Lycus' ones and his wife Megara for Juno, whom he kills one by one.

Transition: the entrance of the chorus is not announced.

Chorus IV (1054–1137): mourning song for Hercules

Transition: the entrance of Theseus is not cued

Act 5 (1138–1344): Hercules, Amphitryon, Theseus.

Scene 1: Hercules, Amphitryon, Theseus.

Having realised what he has done, Hercules threatens to commit suicide; the hero is restrained by the plea of his father Amphitryon and by Theseus who offers to take Hercules to Athens for purification from bloodguilt.

Trojan Women

Act 1 (1–163): Hecuba.

place: at Hector's tomb.

Scene 1 (1–66): Hecuba mourns over the fall of Troy.

Transition: no indication that the chorus has entered, but *lamenta cessant* (63) suggests that they have been moaning softly onstage.

Chorus I (67–164): Hecuba leads the chorus of Trojan women in a formal antiphonal lament for Troy, Hector, and Priam.

Transition: Talthybius' entrance is un-cued.

We have to infer that Hecuba exits at 164 and the chorus remains onstage.

Act 2 (164–370): Talthybius, chorus of Trojan women, Agamemnon, Pyrrhus, Chalcas.

place: at Hector's tomb; from 203 in the Greek camp.

Scene 1 (164–202): Talthybius, chorus of Trojan women.

Talthybius recounts to the chorus of Trojan women the appearance of Achilles' ghost, demanding that Polyxena be sacrificed to him.

Transition: Pyrrhus' and Agamemnon's entrances are un-cued.

Scene 2 (203–370): Pyrrhus, Agamemnon, Chalcas.

Pyrrhus and Agamemnon discuss Achilles' demand.

They afterwards summon Chalcas (351–2, appears 353) who proclaims that not only Polyxena but also Hector's son Astyanax must be killed before the Greeks can sail.

Transition: the intervention of the chorus is un-cued.

Chorus II (371–408): reflective ode on the afterlife.

Transition: Andromache's entrance is un-cued.

Act 3 (409–813): Andromache, old man, Astyanax, Ulysses.

place: at Hector's tomb.

Scene 1 (409–523): Andromache, old man, Astyanax (mute).

Andromache, warned by her dead husband Hector in a dream, hides her son Astyanax in Hector's tomb chamber.

Transition: Ulysses' entrance is cued; no information is provided of the movements of the old man.

Scene 2 (524–813): Andromache, Astyanax, Ulysses.

Ulysses arrives to fetch the boy; Andromache almost convinces him that the boy is dead, but her nervousness betrays her. Ulysses drags the boy away.

Transition: the intervention of the chorus is un-cued.

Chorus III (814–60): the chorus lists all the different cities and regions in Greece to which the Trojan women may be sent.

Transition: all entrances are un-cued apart from that of Pyrrhus (enters 999 and exits 1003).

Act 4 (861–1008):

place: near Sigeum (931); battlefield and Achilles' tomb (893–5)?

Scene 1 (861–1008): Helen, Andromache, Hecuba, Polyxena, Pyrrhus.

Helen is sent to collect Polyxena on the pretext of preparing her for marriage. Unable to maintain the pretence, she reveals the truth. Finally Pyrrhus enters and silently drags Polyxena away.

Transition: the intervention of the chorus is un-cued.

Chorus IV (1009–55): the chorus reflects on the nature of grief, which is more endurable when shared.

Transition: all entrances are un-cued.

Act 5 (1056–1179): Messenger, Hecuba, Andromache.

place: by the shore.

A messenger recounts at length the deaths of Astyanax and Polyxena.

Phoenissae

Act 1 (1–319): Oedipus, Antigone.

place: on or near Cithaeron.

Oedipus' longing for death is restrained by Antigone who tries to convince her father to intervene to stop the strife between his sons, Polynices and Eteocles.

Transition: the entrance of the *nuntius* is un-cued.

Act 2 (320–62): Nuntius, Oedipus.

A messenger, sent on behalf of the Thebans, asks Oedipus to halt the fraternal strife, but Oedipus not only refuses to do so, but also hopes that the brothers will attack each other.

Transition: the entrance of Jocasta and the *satelles* are un-cued. Antigone's movements are not indicated. Since a change of scene is required from the wildness of Cithaeron to the battlements of Thebes, Antigone should supposedly exit at some point and enters again to spur Jocasta to halt the fraternal strife (403–6).

Act 3 (363–442): Jocasta, *satelles*, Antigone.

place: on the battlements of Thebes; at 425–6 Jocasta moves to the battlefield.

Antigone and the *satelles* urge Jocasta on to go and reconcile the brothers.

Transition: the change of scene from the battlements to the battlefield, the setting of the next act, is described as it is taking place. The *satelles* describes Jocasta rushing down from the battlements and arriving at the battlefield where her sons are about to fight.

Act 4 (443–664): Jocasta, Polynices, Eteocles.

place: on the battlefield of Thebes.

Jocasta urges her sons to stop the fight or kill her. She then addresses the two of them in turn and asks Polynices to withdraw from the battle and avoid staining himself with the crime of attacking his own city. Polynices laments that in so doing Eteocles will not be punished for his crime, but Jocasta replies that being king of Thebes is a sufficient punishment. Eteocles closes the act with the statement that for him kingship is worth any price.

Medea

Act 1 (1–55): Medea.

place: in front of the palace of Corinth.

Scene 1 (1–55): Medea.

Medea, abandoned by Jason for Creusa, invokes the gods to assist her revenge.

Transition: the chorus' entrance is un-cued; Medea supposedly remains onstage since she hears the choral song (116: *occidimus: aures pepulit hymenaeus meas*).

Chorus I (56–115): hymn for Jason's marriage to Creusa sung by the women of Corinth.

Transition: the nurse's entrance is un-cued.

Act 2 (116–300): Medea, Nurse, Creon.

Scene 1 (116–49): Medea.

The hearing of the wedding song sharpens Medea's hatred; she is now resolved to destroy Creon who is guilty of having forced Jason, by means of his tyrannical power, to abandon her for Creusa.

Transition: the entrance of the nurse is un-cued.

Scene 2 (150–78): Medea, Nurse.

The nurse, scared by Medea's resolve to avenge herself, tries to restrain and convince her to bend to the circumstances.

Transition: Creon's entrance is announced by Medea (177–8: *Sed cuius ictu regius cardo strepit?/Ipse est Pelasgo tumidus imperio Creo*).

Scene 3 (179–300): Medea, Creon, Nurse (mute).

Creon faces Medea and bids her to leave his kingdom immediately; Medea prays him to grant her one more day to prepare for exile; Creon reluctantly concedes it and leaves in haste to assist with the marriage rites.

Transition: Creon announces his exit (299–300); the entrance of the chorus is un-cued.

Chorus II (301–79): first argonautic ode (anapaests); the chorus is impersonal (*nefas Argonauticum*)

Transition: the chorus provides no clue about the presence or absence of Medea and the nurse.

Act 3 (380–578): Nurse, Medea, Jason.

Scene 1 (380–430): Nurse, Medea.

The nurse tries again to calm Medea's *furor*, but Medea cannot be restrained.

Transition: Jason's entrance is un-cued.

Scene 2 (431–578): Jason, Medea.

Jason tries to justify and exculpate himself from Medea's accusations with the motivation that his new marriage is a means to protect their sons against Acastus. Medea, unable to convince Jason to flee again with her, feigns resignation.

Transition: Jason's exit is announced by Medea (560: *Discessit*); the intervention of the chorus is un-cued.

Chorus III (579–669): second argonautic ode.

Transition: the chorus provides no clues about the presence or absence of Medea and the nurse.

Act 4 (670–848): Nurse, Medea, children (mute).

place: inside Medea's house from line 675–6. (*Namque ut attonito gradu/ evasit et penetrale funestum attigit.*)

Scene 1 (670–739): Nurse.

The nurse describes at length Medea's preparation of the poisonous concoction through which she will cause Creusa's and Creon's death.

Scene 2 (740–848): Medea.

Medea invokes the gods of death and Hecate to assist her in the preparation of the poison.

Transition: the entrance (843–4) and exit (845–6) of the children is announced by Medea.

Scene 3 (817–48): Medea, Nurse (mute), children (mute).

Medea summons the nurse and orders her to bring in her children who have to deliver the poisonous robe to Creusa.

Transition: the intervention of the chorus is un-cued.

Chorus IV (849–78): Medea maenad.

Transition: the entrance of the messenger is un-cued.

Act 5 (879–1027): Messenger, chorus, Nurse, Medea, children (mute), Jason, soldiers (mute).

Scene 1 (879–90): Messenger and chorus.

The messenger reports that Creon and Creusa are dead and that the royal palace is on fire.

Transition: all entrances are un-cued.

Scene 2 (891–970): Nurse, Medea, children (mute).

The nurse compels Medea to escape; Medea kills one of her sons and, as soon as she hears Jason and the soldiers approaching, she climbs on the roof of the palace.

Transition: the entrance of Jason and the soldiers is announced by Medea (971–4).

Scene 3 (971–1027): Medea, Jason, children (mute), soldiers (mute).

Medea is on the roof where she kills her second son and from there throws the dead bodies of her children to Jason; she then escapes in a chariot drawn by dragons.

Phaedra

Act 1 (1–273): Hippolytus, huntsmen (mute), Phaedra, Nurse.

Scene 1 (1–84): Hippolytus, huntsmen.

place: Attica.

Hippolytus and his fellow hunters prepare for a hunt.

Transition: Phaedra's entrance is un-cued.

Scene 2 (85–128): Phaedra.

place: royal palace at Athens.

Phaedra soliloquizes about the fierce and shameful love she feels for her stepson Hippolytus.

Transition: the entrance of the nurse is un-cued.

Scene 3 (129–273): Phaedra, Nurse.

The nurse tries to bring Phaedra to her senses, but when she threatens suicide as the only possible solution, the nurse changes her attitude and promises to approach Hippolytus in order to soften the fierce mind of the young man.

Transition: the entrance of the chorus is un-cued.

Chorus I (274–359): ode on the universal sway of Love.

Transition: the chorus announce the return of the nurse (358–9).

Act 2 (360–735): chorus, Nurse, Phaedra, Hippolytus.

Scene 1 (360–405): chorus, Nurse, Phaedra.

Questioned by the chorus about Phaedra's condition, the nurse replies that the queen is in a pitiful state (360–83); as soon as Phaedra exits from the royal palace, her attitude reveals her frenzied state.

Scene 2 (406–30): Nurse.

The nurse prays to the virgin goddess Diana to favour her undertaking.

Scene 3 (431–588): Hippolytus, Nurse.

The nurse confronts and criticizes Hippolytus for his contempt of love and sex and tries to convince him to tame his wild nature (435–82); Hippolytus gives a lengthy reply asserting that his way of life is pure and innocent and that he does not want to change it (483–564).

Scene 4 (589–735): Phaedra, Hippolytus, Nurse.

An increasingly distraught Phaedra arrives and confesses to Hippolytus her love for him. Hippolytus is horrified by the revelation and almost ready to kill Phaedra with his sword. He then desists and runs away leaving his weapon behind him. The nurse resolves to accuse Hippolytus of rape and uses his sword as proof of his crime.

Transition: the intervention of the chorus is un-cued.

Chorus II (736–834): ode on beauty's brief span.

Transition: the entrance of Theseus is announced by the chorus (829–34).

Act 3 (835–958): Theseus, Nurse, Phaedra.

Scene 1: Theseus, Nurse, Phaedra.

Theseus returns to Athens from the Underworld and comes to know from the nurse about Phaedra's decision to die; he thus confronts his wife who confesses that her desire to die is caused because of Hippolytus' attempt at raping her. Having heard the news, Theseus curses his son with the last wish granted him by Neptune.

Transition: the entrance of the chorus is un-cued.

Chorus III (959–90): the orderly course of heavenly bodies is contrasted to the chaos of human life.

Transition: the chorus announce the messenger's entrance (989–90).

Act 4 (991–1122): messenger, Theseus.

The messenger provides a lengthy description of Hippolytus' death (991–1122).

Transition: the entrance of the chorus is un-cued.

Chorus IV (1123–55): ode on the fickleness of fortune, of which Theseus is an example (1123–53).

Transition: Phaedra's entrance is announced by the chorus (1154–5).

Act 5 (1156–1280): Phaedra, Theseus, chorus.

Phaedra confesses her guilt and commits suicide (*coram populo*); Theseus mourns over Hippolytus' mangled body.

Oedipus

Act 1 (1–109): Oedipus, Jocasta.

place: in front of the royal palace of Thebes.

Scene 1 (1–81): Oedipus.

Oedipus laments over the plague affecting Thebes. The king thinks that the fierce epidemics is a punishment Fate has disposed against him.

Transition: Jocasta's entrance is un-cued.

Scene 2 (82–109): Oedipus, Jocasta.

Jocasta spurs Oedipus to set aside the laments and think and act in accordance with his kingly status.

Transition: the entrance of the chorus is un-cued.

Chorus I (110–205): ode on the effects of the plague at Thebes.

Transition: Creon's entrance is announced by the chorus (201–5).

Act 2 (206–402): Oedipus, Creon, Manto, Tiresias.

Scene 1 (206–90): Oedipus, Creon.

Oedipus questions Creon about the response of the Delphic oracle about the causes of the plague which affects Thebes. The response of the oracle is that the plague is caused by the presence in the city of Laius' murderer, who must be discovered and leave the city.

Transition: the entrance of Tiresias and Manto is announced by Creon (288–90); Creon's presence onstage in the next scene is not made explicit from the text; nonetheless, he must be present at the necromancy of Laius since in the third act he will be in charge of delivering the response.

Scene 2 (291–402): Oedipus, Tiresias, Manto, Creon (mute).

Tiresias orders a divinatory sacrifice in order to name the murderer of Laius. The sacrifice proves ineffective and Tiresias decides to resort to the necromancy of Laius' ghost.

Transition: the intervention of the chorus is announced by Tiresias (401–2).

Chorus II (403–508): hymn in honor of Bacchus.

Act 3 (509–708): Oedipus, Creon, attendants (mute).

Scene 1: Oedipus, Creon, attendants (mute).

Creon narrates at length the necromancy of Laius' ghost which reveals that Oedipus is the murderer. After the revelation, Creon is imprisoned.

Transition: Creon's exit is cued by Oedipus' order to his attendants to lead Creon in prison (707–8); the intervention of the chorus is un-cued.

Chorus III (709–63): the chorus does not believe that Oedipus is guilty, but that the plague is caused by the longstanding hatred of the gods towards Thebes.

Transition: the entrance of Jocasta is unannounced. She is possibly onstage since the opening of Oedipus' speech who addresses her at 773–5.

Act 4 (764–881): Oedipus, Jocasta, old man from Corinth, the shepherd Phorbas.

Scene 1 (764–83): Oedipus, Jocasta.

Shaken by Creon's accusation against him, past and confused memories begin to surface in Oedipus' mind; he begs Jocasta to help him clarify his confusion.

Transition: the entrance of the old man is un-cued.

Scene 2 (784–844): Oedipus, old man from Corinth, Jocasta.

An old man from Corinth brings the news that Polybus, Oedipus' alleged father, has died and he is now called to the throne. Oedipus refuses the kingship because he is in dread of his mother Aerope; in order to dispel such fear, the old man reassures him that Aerope is not his true mother since he himself received the infant Oedipus from the hands of a shepherd.

Transition: the entrance of Phorbas is announced by Oedipus (838–40).

Scene 3 (845–81): Oedipus, Jocasta, old man from Corinth, the shepherd Phorbas.

The shepherd Phorbas mentioned by the old man happens to be present and is questioned about the truth of the old man's words which Phorbas confirms; finally Oedipus understands the truth.

Transition: the exit of Oedipus is announced by the character himself (880–1); all other exits are un-cued. The next brief intervention of the chorus is un-cued.

Chorus IV (882–914): the chorus praises a modest status in contrast with the dangers faced by a high status.

Transition: the entrance of the messenger is un-cued.

Act 5 (915–1061): messenger, chorus, Oedipus, Jocasta.[4]

Scene 1 (915–79): messenger.

A messenger narrates Oedipus' self-blinding.

Choral interval (980–96): the power of Fate.

Scene 2 (997–1009): Oedipus, chorus leader.

Oedipus bursts into a brief monologue of satisfaction for the self-punishment he has inflicted on himself in retribution for his guilt.

Transition: the chorus leader announces the entrance of Jocasta (1004–9).

Scene 3 (1010–61): Oedipus, chorus leader, Jocasta.

Jocasta kills herself (*coram populo*) and Oedipus goes into exile.

Agamemnon

Act 1 (1–56): Thyestes' ghost.

place: in front of the house of the Pelopids (6–7: *video paternos, immo fraternos lares./hoc est vetustum Pelopiae limen domus*).

Scene 1 (1–56): Thyestes' ghost.

Thyestes' ghost announces that Agamemnon will return to Mycenae and will die at the hands of Clytemnestra and Aegisthus.

Transition: the entrance of the chorus is un-cued.

Chorus I (57–107): Ode on the mutability of Fortune.

Transition: the entrance of Clytemnestra and the nurse is un-cued.

Act 2 (108–309): Clytemnestra, Nurse, Aegisthus.

Scene 1 (108–24): Clytemnestra.

Clytemnestra, torn between contrasting feelings of loyalty to her husband Agamemnon and desire of avenging Agamemnon's sacrifice of their daughter Iphigenia and his infidelities, soliloquizes.

Scene 2 (125–225): Clytemnestra, Nurse.

The nurse attempts to restrain Clytemnestra from her plans of revenge against her husband Agamemnon.

Transition: Aegisthus' entrance is un-cued.

Scene 3 (226–309): Aegisthus and Clytemnestra.

Aegisthus removes Clytemnestra's doubts and spurs her to prepare to act against Agamemnon.

Chorus II (310–91): the women of Argos sing a thanksgiving song to the gods for Agamemnon's victory at Troy.

Transition: Eurybates' entrance is announced by the chorus (388–91).

Act 3 (392–588): Eurybates, Clytemnestra.

Scene 1 (392–588): Eurybates, Clytemnestra.

The messenger narrates the shipwreck undergone by the Greek fleet on the way back to Greece.

Transition: Cassandra's and the Trojan women's entrance is announced by Clytemnestra (586–8).

Chorus III (589–658): The Trojan women lament over their destiny while recollecting their memories of the last day of Troy.

Act 4 (659–807): Cassandra, chorus, Agamemnon, Clytemnestra (mute).

Scene 1 (659–781): Cassandra, chorus of Trojan women.

While the Trojan women lament over their destiny, Cassandra has a first clairvoyant vision of Agamemnon's murder.

Transition: Agamemnon's and Clytemnestra's entrance is announced by the chorus (778–81).

Scene 2 (782–807): Agamemnon, Cassandra, Clytemnestra (mute), Trojan women (mute).

Agamemnon finally arrives and finds Cassandra in a faint. As she speaks, he thinks she is still under the effects of prophetic *furor* and fails to understand that Cassandra is predicting to him his death at the hands of Clytemnestra and her lover.

Transition: the intervention of the chorus of Argive women is un-cued.

Chorus IV (808–66): hymn to Hercules.

Transition: the exits of Agamemnon and Clytemnestra are un-cued.

Act 5 (867–1012): Cassandra, Electra, Orestes (mute), Strophius, Pylades (mute), Clytemnestra, Aegisthus.

Scene 1 (867–909): Cassandra.

Cassandra describes her clairvoyant vision of Agamemnon's murder, which takes place at the same moment the prophetess is having her vision.

Transition: all entrances are un-cued.

Scene 2 (910–52): Electra, Strophius, Orestes (mute), Pylades (mute).

After Agamemnon's murder, Electra fears for the life of his brother Orestes who she decides to entrust to Strophius.

Transition: Clytemnestra's entrance is announced by Electra (497–50); that of Aegisthus by Clytemnestra (978–80).

Scene 3 (953–1012): Electra, Clytemnestra, Aegisthus, Cassandra.

Electra refuses to reveal to Clytemnestra and Aegisthus the hiding place of Orestes. Electra is led to prison and Cassandra to execution.

Thyestes

Act 1 (1–121): Tantalus, Fury.[5]

place: in front of the royal palace of Argos.

The ghost of Tantalus is dragged out from the Underworld by a Fury in order to infect the royal house of Argos with its maddening influence.

Transition: the chorus enters unannounced.

Chorus 1 (122–75): the chorus prays that the gods will stop the evildoing among Tantalus' descendants.

Transition: the entrance of Atreus and the *satelles* are un-cued.

Act 2 (176–335): Atreus, *satelles*.

Atreus plans his revenge against his brother Thyestes by offering him a share in the throne; the *satelles* tries to convince Atreus to take a better course of action, but the king of Argos is unmovable in his thirst for revenge.

Transition: the intervention of the chorus is un-cued.

Chorus II (336–403): ode on true kingship and praise of simple life.

Transition: the entrance of Thyestes and his sons is un-cued.

Act 3 (404–545): Thyestes, Tantalus, Atreus (mute until 491).

Thyestes does not trust the alleged reconciliation offered by his brother Atreus and his son Tantalus has to convince him to continue his journey to Argos. As soon as they get to the city, Atreus welcomes his brother and falsely reassures him of his good intention.

Transition: the intervention of the chorus is un-cued.

Chorus III (546–622): ode on the mutability of Fortune.

Transition: the entrance of the messenger is un-cued.

Act 4 (623–788): messenger, chorus leader.

The messenger narrates Atreus' slaughter of Thyestes' sons, the cooking of their flesh, and Thyestes' banqueting on them.

Transition: the intervention of the chorus is un-cued.

Chorus IV (789–884): *conflagratio mundi*.

Transition: the entrance of Atreus is un-cued; the entrance of Thyestes is announced by Atreus (900 ff.).

Act 5 (885–1112): Atreus, Thyestes.

Atreus rejoices over his accomplished revenge; Thyestes, who is still ignorant of the truth, cannot dispel a feeling of foreboding; Atreus finally revels to Thyestes what he has done. Thyestes calls for the gods of revenge to whom he consigns for punishment his brother Atreus.

Detached Episodes rather than Dramatic Coherence and Lack of Plot Development

As has been observed above, one of the factors that produce the characteristic structural looseness of Seneca's plays is the independence of individual scenes, which are often juxtaposed without connecting passages or appropriate transitions and seem curiously 'freestanding'.[6] In so doing, Seneca overtly transgresses Aristotle's precept about the primary importance of a well-structured and coherent plot. All Senecan plays, to a greater or lesser extent, present such an emphasis upon episodes at the cost of sustained dramatic development.[7] As Owen has remarked, this neglect seems partly motivated by the fact that Seneca is substantially more interested in 'collapse' rather than development; hence, his actions basically consist of 'an amplification of *dénouement*'.[8] Such a reiteration of *dénouement* seems a strategic tool chosen by Seneca to exhibit as many melodramatic and pathetic situations as possible. This tendency is noticeable already in the prologues, which are not so much designed to set up the plot, but to 'create a portrait of violent and uncontrolled emotion'.[9] Medea's *ira* (*Med*), Oedipus' maniac sense of guilt (*Oed*), Juno's hatred (*Hf*), the infecting and maddening effects of Thyestes' and Tantalus' ghosts (in the *Ag* and *Thy* respectively), Phaedra's love (*Phae*), Hecuba's grief (*Tro*), Oedipus' longing for death (*Phoe*) are spasmodic already in the prologue.[10] The prologue of the *Hercules furens* well exemplifies this feature; the speech is delivered by Juno and consists of a monologue or rather a soliloquy since it is not addressed to an audience; it has no expository function, but it portrays a furious Juno enraged by Hercules' return from the Underworld which she presents as something already happened as she is speaking (50–63). This is in contrast with the development of the action as described in the following acts, in which Hercules' return from the Underworld takes place only at the closing of act two. Inconsistencies of this kind are not unusual in Seneca's plays; in the specific case of the *Hercules furens*, the inconsistency between the prologue and act two seems to be caused by Seneca's interest in exploiting the dramatic effects of Hercules' return from the Underworld in the prologue to provide immediacy to Juno's fears. Thus, the handling of the prologue of the *Hercules furens* provides an additional instance of Seneca's tendency to anticipate the *dénouement* of the action for emotional effects. A similar interpretation is prompted by the choice of Juno as prologue speaker. Even though the jealous wrath of Juno pursuing Hercules is a traditional motif, the goddess does not appear as *dramatis persona* in Euripides' *Heracles*, the Greek prototype of Seneca's *Hercules furens*. In Euripides, Iris and Lissa are sent on earth to carry out Juno's plans (822–74). In the choice of Juno as prologue speaker, Seneca was most probably inspired by the numerous depictions of Juno *irata* found in the epic tradition, where Juno's resentment against Jupiter's infidelities was a familiar literary *locus*.[11] However, the use of Juno gave Seneca 'an opportunity for a good recitation of her wrongs and plans of vengeance'.[12] More generally, such a handling has as a consequence that the action cannot really develop since, in a sense, the emotional intensity has peaked at the beginning of the play. In the acts, a similar tendency can be observed. Usually Seneca dwells on the portrayal of emotionally distraught characters who soliloquize about their obsessive passions or are described in their broken state of mind by other characters onstage rather than on plot development. This lack of plot development affects also the construction of dramatic suspense. In Greek tragedy, dramatic suspense is usually built up through a series of events that leads to the climactic moment of the final revelation; in Seneca, the presence of several climactic moments is actually built almost independently into each single episode of the play.[13]

Scholars have offered conflicting explanations of this peculiar feature of Seneca's tragedies. For Zwierlein, in his influential *Die Rezitationsdramen Senecas* (1966), the lack of organic structure provides strong evidence of a lack of interest in stage drama. Tarrant, approaching the issue from the perspective of dramatic history, reaches the conclusion that 'Seneca's neglect of classical norms of coherence' may be inherited from postclassical tragedy.[14] More recently, Erasmo has proposed that 'Seneca's concentration on episodes, rather than on the dramatic structure as a whole, may be due not only to the influence of epic, but also to the success of the episodic mime productions of Publilius Syrus and to the influence of pantomime'.[15]

My argument develops a similar hypothesis. The fact that Seneca sacrifices large-scale structure in order to privilege momentary effects and organizes the dramatic action around a series of theatrical high spots has suggestive affinities with the same trend in pantomimic entertainment which, as we have seen in Chapter 1, focused primarily on the most emotionally climactic and spectacular moments of the chosen myth and did not present the development of the myth as a whole. The story was presented more as a sequence of pictorial tableaux than as proper drama where one action causes the following one and the structure is coherent and unified. Similarly, Zwierlein has claimed that Seneca's tragedies are constituted by a 'juxtaposition of various independent and self-contained tableaux'.[16] For instance, the dramatic structure of Seneca's *Agamemnon* is extremely loose, more so, perhaps, than of any other of his tragedies. The play is thematically arranged in two parts: the first one unfolds around the plotting of Clytemnestra and Aegisthus against Agamemnon before his return; the second part is concerned with the return of Agamemnon and the destiny of the enslaved Trojan women. In this bipartite structure, Eurybates' long narration of the shipwreck of the Greek fleet returning after the fall of Troy, which spans over 157 lines and has all the features of a set-piece, occurs as the dividing line between the events that happened before and after Agamemnon's return.[17] A remarkable aspect of the play is also the lack of a central dominant figure; in fact, Agamemnon, who is supposed to be the title role, only delivers twenty lines and his role within the action of the play is not particularly significant; the focus of the play are rather the characters' reactions set in motion by the return of

Agamemnon from Troy. As a consequence, no character has a central role in the tragedy and Cassandra is the only figure who dominates two adjacent acts, thus establishing the major presence onstage. As to dramatic structure, the acts are constructed almost independently from one another and even scenes within the same act are often unconnected. The prologue is spoken by Thyestes' ghost and no transition is provided for the subsequent unfolding of the action. The second act is constituted by two unconnected scenes, the first one deals with Clytemnestra and the nurse and the second features a confrontation between Aegisthus and Clytemnestra. The third act features Eurybates and Clytemnestra and the long narration of the shipwreck of the Greek fleet returning after the fall of Troy. Eurybates' entrance is announced by the chorus and we have to infer that Clytemnestra remains onstage during the second choral ode. No notice is given about the movements of Aegisthus and the nurse; again, we have to infer that exits take place since they are not onstage during the next act. The third choral ode is a lamentation over the fall of Troy sung by the Trojan captives, which, although not specified, requires a subsidiary chorus, since the previous one, a hymn of thanksgiving to several gods for the victory of the Greeks over Troy, cannot be sung by the Trojan women but by the citizens of Argos. The fourth act is devoted to Cassandra, the actual protagonist of this section; she first dialogues with her fellow captives and then, as Agamemnon finally arrives, with the king, whose impending death she foreshadows in a first clairvoyant vision. The fifth act is peculiar in many respects; it is constituted by three unconnected scenes; the first scene revolves around Cassandra uttering, for the second time, a clairvoyant vision of Agamemnon's murder. The second one focuses on Electra who fears for the life of her little brother Orestes. The last one deals with the destinies of Electra and Cassandra, which are now in the hands of Clytemnestra and Aegisthus. Thus Cassandra appears in the first scene and foreshadows Agamemnon's murder, which actually takes place as she is having her vision; in fact, in the following scene, Electra has, in some unspecified way, come to know of Agamemnon's murder. No proper transition features between the Cassandra scene and the Electra one; moreover, Cassandra will reappear in the third scene of the act, but we have to infer that she leaves the stage during the Electra scene and comes back at some point. Tarrant thinks that the lack of unity between the scenes of this last act as well as the condensed nature of the second section, which contains five short scenes in the space of 100 lines, could be a sign that Seneca awkwardly conflated two different models.[18]

As to lack of plot development, the structure of the *Phoenissae*, which is unusual even within Seneca's tragic *corpus*, is particularly illustrative.[19] The play consists of two structurally unconnected sections, of which the first one deals with the story of Oedipus and Antigone in exile and the second deals with Jocasta attempting to halt the fraternal strife. The antecedent of the first section is Sophocles' *Oedipus at Colonus*, while Euripides' *Phoenician Women* is that of the second; most probably, Seneca originally combined together 'two strands of the legends into a unique drama'.[20] This tendency to combine in one play events that traditionally belong to different plays is evidence that Seneca was not so much interested in developing a tragic action in full, but rather in exploiting the climactic core provided by the single events. For instance, in the *Phoenissae*, no tragic action is really developed. The play actually works through a juxtaposition of the figures of the furious Oedipus and the grief-stricken Jocasta and their reactions to the same event, the strife of their sons. The fact that the play does not have a proper conclusion may be due to its incompleteness as well as to the fact that, since no proper tragic action is developed, no resolution can be sought.

Diversity of the Episodes and Doubling of Themes

Seneca tends to develop episodes unevenly; this disproportionate handling is produced by either excessive expansion or extreme concentration of single themes, episodes, or actions. Expansion and concentration heavily affects the flow of dramatic time, which becomes slowed down or almost suspended in the first case and extremely accelerated in the second. As a general tendency, episodes dealing with melodramatic, spectacular or emotionally charged themes are treated expansively, while actions relevant to the development of the plot are condensed.[21]

For instance, the fourth act of the *Medea* is entirely devoted to Medea's spectacular magic (670–842);[22] the episode, although relevant to the development of the dramatic action, is expanded well beyond what the conveying of dramatic information would require. Despite the fact that the preparation of the poisonous concoction is dealt with at length, the final phase of the scene is condensed in the exiguous space of five lines (843–8) in which, moreover, several actions that are crucially relevant for the subsequent development of the plot take place: Medea summons the nurse to bring the children; the children arrive; Medea orders them to deliver the deadly gift to Creusa.[23]

The fifth act of the *Agamemnon* presents an unprecedented concentration of events even by Senecan standards: Cassandra has a lengthy vision of Agamemnon's murder (867–909); no transition links this first scene to the following one in which Electra, somehow privy to Agamemnon's murder, tries to save her brother Orestes from the fury of Clytemnestra and Aegisthus (910–43); Strophius arrives at this point and agrees to shelter Orestes under his protection; then Clytemnestra arrives and threatens Electra to reveal where her brother is hidden, but the girl refuses and is taken to prison (944–1000); now Clytemnestra and Aegisthus turn to Cassandra who is taken to execution (1001–13).[24] In the fourth act of the same play, Cassandra's visions (659–774) occupy the major part of the act, while the first and last appearance of Agamemnon and his encounter with Clytemnestra, which could be accounted as one of the pivotal moments of the play, is dealt with in just few lines (782–806).[25]

In the *Oedipus*, large expansion is given to the treatment of the supernatural that forms the subject of the second (206–402) and third act of the play (509–708);[26] while the fourth act, which is devoted to the *anagnorisis* (764–881), is fairly short (117 lines). Despite the pivotal role of the recognition in the unfolding of the plot, this act is briefer in comparison to the second and third ones, which, from the point of view of development of the dramatic action, are not as centrally relevant.[27]

The tendency to develop expansively secondary episodes presents itself also in the form of doubling of themes and episodes which are recast not so much as to provide additional dramatic information, but for the spectacular possibilities they offer. For instance, the lengthy description of the macabre effects of the plague, which features in Oedipus' opening monologue, is doubled by the description of the epidemics narrated in the first choral ode (110–205). In the *Phaedra*, the presentation of the emotionally distraught Phaedra features in the first act and it is recast in the second one with little variations;[28] despite the fact that Phaedra's state of mind has already been described and thus does not serve to provide additional dramatic information, the disproportionate length of this act in comparison with the average length of the other acts of the play, is even more striking.[29] In the *Medea* too, Seneca seems so interested in exploiting the spectacular elements embedded in the episode of the magic that he casts them twice: the first time they are described by the more external stance of the nurse, which allows a more objective and detached narration; then they are described by Medea, the direct agent of the magic, thus providing a more emotional and subjective account.[30]

Un-cued Transitions, Entrances, and Exits

A characteristic feature of Seneca's tragedies is the lack of transitions between acts or even scenes in the same act as well as of consistent indication of entrances and exits of characters. All instances are listed in the outlines of the plays at the beginning of this chapter. Here, I again limit myself to pointing out some particularly striking instances of what is a pervasive phenomenon.

For instance, in the *Thyestes*, the dramatic movement from the prologue to the first act lacks an explicit transition; the prologue is spoken by the ghost of Tantalus and no indication is provided for Atreus' entrance in the following act. In the *Phaedra*, the prologue of the play is constituted by two unconnected scenes; the prologue is spoken by Hippolytus and the subsequent entrance of Phaedra is left unannounced. The prologue of the *Phaedra* is unusual within the Senecan *corpus*. In fact, the play opens with a first scene in anapaests, actually a lyric monody. The division of the first act in two scenes is also unusual; generally, the first act is constituted by a single scene followed by a choral song after which the dramatic action begins. The prologue has no expository function since no information concerning the action of the play is provided and we have to infer that the speaker is Hippolytus since the text provides no clue for the identification of the character; actually, Hippolytus is presented simply as a huntsman urging his fellow huntsmen to get ready for the hunt and it actually stands as a self-contained tableau portraying a hunting scene.[31] The connection between the prologue and the second scene is very weak. Scholars have tried to link them on the basis of psychological contrast, namely between Hippolytus' idyllic life and Phaedra's tormented love; but this kind of juxtaposition is hardly a device of dramatic cohesion. Basically, the prologue presents a self-contained tableau that does not provide information important for the development of the dramatic action. The fact that the prologue is a lyric monody reinforces the impression that it was written as a virtuoso song.

In the *Agamemnon*, there is no transition between the prologue and the second act, which features a distraught Clytemnestra whom the nurse attempts to restrain.[32] Neither Clytemnestra's nor the nurse's entrances are announced, so no indication is provided about when they enter onstage. Transition is also lacking between the two scenes that constitute the second act. In fact, the subsequent entrance of Aegisthus is again unannounced; he appears onstage and delivers an entrance monologue aside, which is followed by a dialogue between him and Clytemnestra. As Tarrant has remarked, the second act of the *Agamemnon* is constituted by two 'independent dramatic units', whose connection is just thematic.[33] Similarly, the connection between the two scenes constituting the second act of the *Trojan Women*, i.e. Talthybius' lengthy narration of the appearance of Achilles' ghost demanding the sacrifice of Polyxena and the *altercatio* between Agamemnon and Pyrrhus about this request, is just thematic, since an explicit transition is lacking. Here as in the *Agamemnon*, the two scenes are simply juxtaposed instead of linked together by appropriate connecting material.

In the cases in which transitions or information about the movements of the characters are provided, these tend to be awkwardly and implausibly crafted. The entrance of Chalcas in the *Agamemnon* (351–3), that of Medea's children in the *Medea* (843–5), or that of Pyrrhus in the *Trojan Women* (999–1003) are, among several other instances, good examples of how characters appear onstage at a moment's notice. In the same way, characters disappear with no notice. Zeitlin has employed the term 'dance-pattern' to describe the random and chaotic appearances and disappearances of characters in Petronius' *Satyricon*; the same term can be applied to the entrances and exits of Seneca's tragic characters, who often step onstage unannounced, give no reason for their coming or leaving, and whose movements are often difficult to trace.[34]

It is possible to argue that entrances and exits of characters in pantomime were similarly handled. In this type of performance in fact, a strictly logical and verisimilar handling of entrances and exits were not needed since pantomime did not rest on a linear development of plot or on a well-crafted structuring of the dramatic action. As discussed in Chapter 1, pantomime tended to portray single episodes in a tableau-like manner, which featured temporal and spatial leaps as well as characters leaping in and out without any further notice.

Fluidity of Setting

Seneca's tragedies are characterized by fluid settings.[35] In this respect, the *Trojan Women* presents the most severe case of lack of unified location, since the play is obviously not confined to a single setting. According to Fantham, the actions of the first, second, and third acts are meant to take place in front of Hector's tomb, but the second scene of act two has its setting in the Greek camp. The fourth act is set near Sigeum (931), the battlefield, and Achilles' tomb (893–5), and the fifth perhaps by the shore.[36] In the *Phaedra*, a change of setting from the wild in Attica to the royal palace of Athens between the first and the second scene of the first act is required.[37]

More generally, spatial location is often ambiguously handled. In the *Hercules furens, Thyestes, Medea, Phaedra*, and *Agamemnon*, scenes which are supposed to take place inside are handled as if happening onstage.[38] Moreover, Seneca handles space in a symbolic rather than realistic or concrete manner. For instance, the geographical apparatus displayed (1–30) in the prologue of the *Phaedra* is representative of this tendency. Even though Seneca is describing real Attic locations, the places are so far away one from the other that it is evident he is not aiming to provide a concrete setting for the hunt (just an example will suffice here: Parnetho in line 3 is a mountain range north of Athens, Marathon in line 16 is a town north-east of Athens, and Hymettus in line 21 is a mountain south-east of Athens; Seneca even includes the Riphaean mountains which were located in the extreme north, in Scythia 8). Thus, the landscape becomes more an imaginary one suited to recall in the audience very famous and well known areas within Attica. Similarly, in the *Hercules furens*, Juno's soliloquy opens with a long and detailed *ecphrasis* of the constellations in the night-sky (6–18), which she actually seems to be able to see since the presence of the adverbs *hinc* (repeated four times, lines 6, 8, 10, 12) and *illinc* (one occurrence, line 10) points to the position of the stars in the different regions of the sky. The opening *ecphrasis* of the *Hercules furens* is classified by Larson among the numerous descriptions found in Seneca's tragedies of transient aspects of the environment;[39] descriptions of such a kind outdo those of topography, which are, instead, heavily preponderant in Greek theatre, where they are purposely employed as a sort of stage-direction to convey to the audience the physical setting and the time of day of the action. Larson rightly states that while descriptions of topography are concrete and tend to make explicit the reality of the stage, descriptions of transient aspects of the environment tend to be necessarily more abstract and thus to substitute imagination for reality. Larson describes this tendency thus: 'the typical Senecan description invites the audience to ignore their present circumstances and those of the reciter(s) or actors to replace them with a world of imagination'.[40] Because of this, such descriptions set the mood and atmosphere of the play but they do not convey information about the physical reality of the setting of the stage. Seneca then is not interested in delimiting the space in which the action takes place, but, on the contrary, he strives to expand that space as much as he can; now, since this tendency is a pervasive mark of Senecan style, we have to infer that Seneca purposely aimed at this substitution of reality for imagination. This type of landscape, where places that are separated by a consistent distance are put together or transient aspects of environment are depicted, would certainly be fitting for a pantomimic performance where an imaginary and symbolic landscape would have provided a more appealing atmosphere than a strictly concrete one.

Prominence of Monologues over Dialogues

Monologues are a prominent feature of Seneca's tragedies. Five of the eight genuine plays have a monologic prologue (*Trojan Women* 1–163, *Phaedra* 1–84,

Medea 1–55, *Hercules furens* 1–124, *Agamemnon* 1–56); the prologue of the *Oedipus* comprises a long monologue spoken by Oedipus (1–81) and a brief concluding exchange between Oedipus and Jocasta (82–109), while the *Thyestes* (1–121) is the only play that has a prologue in true dialogic form. In itself, this would not necessarily be significant. After all, many classical Greek tragedies also begin with a monologue; Euripides, for instance, likes to employ a divinity to 'clue in' the audience before the action proper starts. Still, in Seneca the opening monologues are more than convenient introductions; rather, they set the tone for the rest of the play. Seneca favours monologues so much that his tragedies are all but built up of successive monologues, whereas the place of dialogues is much diminished;[41] for example, the first act of the *Phaedra* (85–273; 188 lines) contains two monologues of Phaedra (85–128; 177–94 for a total of 60 lines) interspersed with two of the nurse (129–77; 195–217 for a total of 70 lines), and only the last 55 lines feature a proper dialogue between the two. The last act of the same play features one long monologue by Phaedra (1159–200) preceded by a brief question asked by Theseus (1156–8) and one monologue by Theseus (1201–80) interrupted by one brief intervention of the chorus (1244–6). In the *Agamemnon*, the fourth act (659–807; 148 lines) features three speeches of Cassandra (659–63; 695–709; 720–74 in lyric metre) and three interventions of the chorus (664–94 in lyric metre; 710–19; 775–81). Only the first speech by Cassandra (659–63) is directly addressed to the chorus; similarly, the chorus does not engage in any kind of dialogue with Cassandra; only its first intervention is set up as a sort of reply to Cassandra's words at least initially, but quickly turns into a lyric monody that mourns the desperate fate of the house of Priam. The other two interventions of the chorus simply describe in the third person Cassandra's prophetic frenzy. The fourth act of the *Medea* is made up of two monologues (670–848): the first one is uttered by the nurse (670–739) and the second by Medea (a lyric monody 740–848). No dialogue features between the two, and Medea addresses the nurse, ordering her to bring the children to her, only at the very end of her long speech (843–8).

The fifth act of *Thyestes* features Atreus' revelation to Thyestes of his accomplished revenge on him perpetuated through Thyestes' eating of his own sons. The act is characterized by the predominance of monologic interventions, through which Atreus (885–919; 976–97; 1052–68) and Thyestes (920–69; 999–1004; 1006–21; 1035–51; 1068–96) confront each other. It is remarkable that even though the dialogic form would well suit the needs of the dramatic conflict at hand, Seneca has privileged the monologic form, which allows the characters to indulgently expand on their feelings: fulfilment over the accomplished revenge in the case of Atreus, grief and outrage for the bloodthirsty act in the case of Thyestes. In the *Phaedra*, the second act of the play features the confrontation between the nurse and Hippolytus; the handling of the dialogue between Hippolytus and the nurse shows again Seneca's preference for monologues over dialogues, since the debate of the two characters takes place through alternate monologues rather than proper dialogic exchanges.[42] This technique allows Seneca to make the characters expand on personal motifs that are tangential to the specific issue at hand. Thus, Hippolytus' long intervention (483–564) configures itself as a generalizing eulogy of the simple and natural life in the wild as compared with the corrupted life of the city, and, in a sense, it is a self-contained set piece.[43] In addition, the acts featuring narrative set-pieces also have substantially a monologic form. For instance, in act three of the *Agamemnon* the messenger's narration of the storm that shipwrecked the Greek fleet is a monologue. The speech is preceded by an introductory dialogue (392–420) between Clytemnestra and the messenger, but the proper narration of the storm (421–578, 157 lines) is delivered without any intervention of Clytemnestra at all. In act four of the *Phaedra*, the messenger's *rhesis* of Hippolytus' death is again introduced by a brief dialogue between him and Theseus (990–9) and then the messenger's narrative proceeds without any interruption for 114 lines (1000–114). Messenger reports are typical cases in which some degree of interaction with other characters onstage is supposed to occur. Examples are found in the *Hercules furens* or in the *Thyestes*. But even in most of these passages, the speech maintains a pronounced monologic texture. For example, in act three of the *Hercules furens*, Theseus' description of the Underworld (658–829, 171 lines) is preceded by a short introductory dialogue (645–57) in which Amphitryon compels Theseus to narrate Hercules' deeds in the Underworld. Theseus' speech is interrupted by brief questions asked by Amphitryon (five interventions of one or two lines: 697; 707–8; 727–9; 747–9; 760–1), which Seneca seems to have introduced mainly to avoid the necessity of providing linking transitions between the parts of the narrative; nonetheless, despite Amphitryon's brief interventions, Theseus' speech develops basically as a soliloquy. In a similar way, in the messenger's narration of Atreus' murder of Thyestes' sons to the chorus (act four of the *Thyestes* 641–788, i.e. 147 lines), which is the most advanced instance in the direction of dialogue, the seven interventions of the chorus (690; 716; 719; 730–1; 743; 745–6; 747–8) do not substantially alter the monologic character of the speech.[44]

A special category of monologues, which Tarrant has called 'entrance monologues', features as an innovative dramatic technique in Seneca's plays.[45] Entrance monologues are those in which a character enters onstage while the action is in progress and delivers a soliloquy without realizing the presence of other characters since he/she addresses them in the third person. They are placed at the beginning of each scene and delivered in a void since they are not addressed to any of the characters onstage and the impression produced is that of a character speaking out loud. The character's speech is thus totally isolated from the action that is taking place (*Hf* 329 ff. Lycus; *Tro* 861 ff. Helen; *Med* 179 ff. Creon; 431 ff. Jason; *Thy* 491 ff. Atreus; *Ag* 108 ff. Clytemnestra; 226 ff. Aegisthus). Tarrant has pointed out that 'the Senecan passages resemble each other so closely that one may justly speak of a new convention'.[46]

In Greek tragedy there is no precedent for this technique. In Aeschylus' *Agamemnon*, the herald's invocation (530 ff.) does not seem addressed to any character in particular and his speech produces the impression that he is thinking out loud. Aegisthus' speech (1577 ff.) shares the same features. Nonetheless, both the Aeschylean instances do not achieve the degree of isolation of the character and suspension of dramatic time found in Seneca. Closer instances can be found in Euripides (*Hecuba* 1109–13; *Trojan Women* 860 ff.; *Suppliants* 1034 ff.; *Orestes* 356 ff., 1554 ff.; *Phoenician Women* 261–77); the instance in the *Phoenician Women* is the closest one and looks forward to the Senecan entrance monologues: in Polynices' entrance monologue, the hero pours out his feelings without noticing the presence of the chorus onstage.

For what concerns a parallel technique in comedy, similar entrance monologues can be found in Aristophanes' *Plutus* (335 ff.) and in Menander's *Dyscolus* (153 ff.). In Roman comedy, there are instances in Plautus (*Trinummus* 843 ff.; *Stichus* 58–67 ff. 68–74; 75–87; *Amphitruo* 551 ff.). According to Tarrant, the prominence of monologue in New Comedy finds its explanation in the need to give more details in portraying characters' states of mind and feelings. Seneca could have pushed forward a technique already in existence in post-classical drama. Seneca's fondness for monologues is a conscious stylistic choice adopted to minutely portray the interior of the characters; in fact, such detached speeches delivered in a void allow an exploration of the character's flowing emotions; thus the function of the diffuse use of monologues in Seneca's plays can be accounted as a sort of stream of consciousness *ante litteram*. The preference for monologues over dialogues is not to be interpreted, in any way, as a sign of Seneca's poor expertise in dramatic composition, but rather as a deliberate adoption of a dramatic technique meant to exploit at its fullest the emotional effects offered by a monologue. Such a choice also has implications concerning the type of dramatic performance, other than conventional drama, that was in Seneca's mind when composing his tragedies.

Finally, even when a confrontation between characters occurs, the characters rarely engage in proper dialogues, but rather utter monologues in turn. The result is that characters are juxtaposed one to the other and thus they do not give the impression of interacting, but rather of speaking in isolation.[47] Proper dialogues feature rarely in Seneca's tragedies and they tend to assume the form of stichomythic exchanges in which the utterances of the characters feature often a moral maxim (*sententia*) in each line of the exchanges;[48] the passion-restraint scene between Clytemnestra and the nurse in the *Agamemnon* (145–58) and the *altercatio* between Medea and Creon in the *Medea* offer particularly representative examples of this technique:

Agamemnon (145–58):
Nutr. Caeca est temeritas quae petit casum ducem.
Clyt. Cui ultima est fortuna, quid dubiam timet?
Nutr. Tuta est latetque culpa, si pateris, tua.
Clyt. Perlucet omne regiae vitium domus.
Nutr. Piget prioris et novum crimen struis?
Clyt. Res est profecto stulta nequitiae modus.
Nutr. Quod metuit auget qui scelus scelere obruit.
Clyt. Et ferrum et ignis saepe medicinae loco est.
Nutr. Extrema primo nemo temptavit loco.
Clyt. Rapienda rebus in malis praeceps via est.
Nutr. At te reflectat coniugî nomen sacrum.
Clyt. Decem per annos vidua respiciam virum?
Nutr. Meminisse debes subolis ex illo tuae.
Clyt. Equidem et iugales filiae memini faces ...

Medea (192–201):
Med. Quod crimen aut quae culpa multatur fuga?
Cr.   Quae causa pellat, innocens mulier rogat.
Med. Si iudicas, cognosce; si regnas, iube.
Cr.   Aequum atque iniquum regis imperium feras.
Med. Iniqua numquam regna perpetuo manent.
Cr.   I, querere Colchis.
Med. Redeo: qui avexit, ferat.
Cr.   Vox constituto sera decreto venit.
Med. Qui statuit aliquid parte inaudita altera,
      aequum licet statuerit, haud aequus fuit.
Cr.   Auditus a te Pelia supplicium tulit?
      sed fare, causae detur egregiae locus.

Such a handling of dialogues does not aim at any kind of nuanced portrayal of individualized characters debating their personal situations, but of mouthpieces oddly and extensively employing general and universal truths in crucially dramatic moments.[49] This treatment of dialogues seems to be conceived as such as a means towards stylization, since it employs a sort of fixed linguistic repertoire, well intelligible and easily understood by everyone thanks to the gnomic nature of the *sententiae*; Seneca himself attests to this quality of *sententiae* by quoting some of Publilius (*Epistles* 108, 8, 11):

> Non vides quemadmodum theatra consonent, quotiens aliqua dicta sunt, quae publice adgnoscimus et consensu vera esse testamur?
> 'Desunt inopiae multa, avaritiae omnia'
> 'In nullum avarus bonus est, in se pessimus'
> Ad hos versus ille sordidissimus plaudit et vitiis suis fieri convicium gaudet . . .

> magis tamen feriuntur animi cum carmina eiusmodi dicta sunt:
> 'Is minimo eget mortalis qui minimum cupit'
> 'Quod vult, habet, qui velle, quod satis est, potest.'

In relation to this, it is interesting to consider a passage in Quintilian (6, 3, 65) that can be useful for understanding Seneca's peculiar handling of dialogues and connecting it with a device of pantomime: *Nam et finitione usus est Augustus de pantomimis duobus qui alternis gestibus contendebant, cum eorum alterum saltatorem dixit, alterum interpellatorem . . .*[50] Quintilian's passage implies that a gestural dialogue of some kind could be a feature in pantomime; the gestural dialogue of the dancers was accompanied by the matching verbal dialogue. It is conceivable that such a gestural dialogue was mimetic in essence and that the content of the verbal dialogue accompanying it must have verbally matched such mimicry. Weinreich ventured the hypothesis that the performance of the *saltator* and *interpellator* mentioned by Quintilian consisted of a sort of imitation fight ('Zeichendisput').[51]

Now, Seneca's dialogues basically appear in two categories, those contained in the passion-restraint scenes and those in which two characters confront themselves. The dialogues in the passion-restraint scenes basically consist of a sort of verbal duel which is fought between the passions of one character and the reasons offered by the other; similarly, the second category of dialogues presents a verbal duel between two opponents (Medea's and Creon's in the *Medea*; Medea's and Jason's in the *Medea*).[52] Therefore, the combination of *stichomythia*, rapid-fire responses, and *sententiae* (a codified system of set meanings easily understandable and universally applicable) could be a well-envisioned device to verbally reproduce the sort of mimetic fight hypothesized by Weinreich.

The Non-integration of the Chorus

Senecan choruses tend to be loosely connected or even unrelated to the preceding or following course of action. Quite often they stand as lyric interludes detached from the action (e.g. *Phae* 274–359; *Ag* 808–66; *Oed* 403–508). In addition to this, the choruses are often impersonal, since they lack an explicit identity;[53] the chorus' movements are not consistently cued and their presence onstage can be difficult to establish. Finally, they often ignore events that they are supposed to know, or, conversely, they know events that they are not supposed to be aware of. Some scholars have claimed that thematic consistency ensures the interlacing between action and choral interventions; it is true that thematic connections exist; but, as Tarrant has pointed out, thematic consistency by itself does not provide organic unity.[54] Moreover, scholars often desperate to establish a connection between chorus and dramatic action (and be it a thematic one) have resorted to what amounts to very tenuous arguments. For instance, the last chorus of the *Agamemnon* (808–66) deals with a description of Hercules' twelve labours; the very slight and almost irrelevant connection of the chorus with the action is that Hercules, like Agamemnon, is a conqueror of Troy. The verbal echoes between the choruses and the episodes are perhaps more a consequence of the fact that Seneca employs a rather repetitive vocabulary instead of evidence for the existence of a cogent thematic relationship. There are set phrases, descriptions, and themes that are recurrent in the whole *corpus*. Despite the fact that they do not perform the dramatic function fulfilled in Greek tragedy, Senecan choruses are nonetheless dramatically powerful. Their dramatic potential then is not the result of a strict relationship between the chorus and the action, but is intrinsic to the chorus itself. In a way, the dramatic power of the chorus is of a self-contained and self-sufficient nature. The dramatic quality of the choruses combined with their nature of lyric interludes, which stand as bravura solos, may have been conceived as such by Seneca in accordance with the contemporary practice of pantomime in which *cantica* were sung by the choir accompanying this form of performance.[55] Even more importantly, it is possible to evaluate the choruses as being in tune with the performance culture of Seneca's age if we view them (and the emphasis is indeed on viewing) as being influenced by mime and pantomime. Two recurrent features point in this direction: thematic affinities between Seneca's choral interludes and the mimic and pantomimic repertory; and the surprising frequency with which Seneca refers to specific body parts in some of his choral odes. As for the themes, in what follows, I am not arguing that Seneca derived the themes of his choral odes (such as the fickleness of fortune, the omnipotence of love, or the praise of Bacchus) from pantomime. They were the stock-in-trade of any genre at the time that dealt in moral philosophy (such as declamation, mime, pantomime, as well as Seneca's tragedies). Nevertheless, the clear parallels between the preoccupations of some of Seneca's choral odes and the thematic preferences of the mimic and pantomimic stage would seem to point to an intertextual (or rather inter-dramatic) relationship. Such an affinity exists, for instance, in the predilection for rehearsing the mutability of fortune, which Seneca shares with pantomime. Many of his choruses comment on the fickleness of Fortune;[56] and while this motif is of course very common in rhetorical declamations, it can also be said to constitute the essence of pantomime. As Manilius maintains, a dancer would impress in particular if he was able to assume every aspect of fortune's vicissitude.[57] The theme featured no less prominently in the mimes, the sister art of pantomime. Sudden changes of fortune constituted the very essence of the genre as attested by many of Publilius Syrus' *sententiae*, which were devoted to Fortune;[58] even in the prologue prefacing the mime presented by Laberius in the famous dramatic contest between him and Publilius Syrus, Fortune is blamed for having reserved a cruel blow to the aged Laberius (155–61; 167–70):[59]

Fortuna inmoderata in bono aeque atque in malo,	155
si tibi erat libitum litterarum laudibus	
florens cacumen nostrae famae frangere,	
cur cum vigebam membris praeviridantibus,	
satis facere populo et tali cum poteram viro	
non me flexibilem concurvasti ut carperes?	160
nuncine me deicis? quo? quid ad scaenam adfero?	
non possunt primi esse omnes omni in tempore,	167
summum ad gradum cum claritatis veneris,	
consistes aegre, et citius quam ascendas, cades.	
cecidi ego, cadet qui sequitur, laus est publica.	170

The second chorus of the *Oedipus* (403–508), a hymn in praise of Bacchus, has troubled scholars since the ode both serves no purpose in the dramatic progress of the action and its joyous character strikingly contrasts with the catastrophic situation at Thebes.[60] The theme and the stylistic features of the ode may be directly inspired by pantomimic performances in which Bacchic themes, as ancient authors attest, were remarkably popular; the lengthy portrayal of Bacchus (413–28) and of the Bacchic *thiasos* (Silenus and the Bacchants 420–43) with its detailed account of gestures and clothing gives the depiction a particularly vivid, pictorial, and dynamic dimension:[61]

> Te decet cingi comam floribus vernis,
>   te caput Tyria cohibere mitra
>   hederave mollem
>   bacifera religare frontem,   415
> spargere effusos sine lege crines,
> rursus adducto revocare nodo:[62]
> qualis iratam metuens novercam
> creveras falsos imitatus artus,
> crine flaventi simulata virgo,   420
> lutea vestem retinente zona.
> inde tam molles placuere cultus
> et sinus laxi fluidumque syrma.

Moreover, the description of Bacchus who wears a silky, flowing transparent dress, has long hair, shows a pronounced *mollitia* of behaviour, and disguises his male nature under a female appearance, seems actually to be the mythical progenitor of the pantomimic dancer. Also, the ode contains a high number of metamorphoses: the transformation of Ino and Melicertes into sea divinities, Leucothea and Palaemon respectively (445–8); the transformation of the sea into a meadow (449–56); the transformation of the Tyrrhenian pirates into dolphins (457–67); the transformation of nature wrought by Bacchus' presence (491–6); the transformation of Apollo; and Jupiter taking part in Bacchus' and Ariadne's marriage (448–503). This element makes it extremely suitable to a pantomimic rendition, where the protean ability of the dancer to metamorphose swiftly from one form to the other constituted the most paradigmatic and appealing feature of the genre.[63]

In the *Trojan Women*, the first chorus features the only lyric exchange between the character of Hecuba and the chorus and could well bear the sign of the influence of the aesthetics of pantomime. The chorus clearly echoes the parallel one in Euripides' *Trojan Women* (153 ff.); at the same time Euripides' chorus is 'less ritualistic and formal, focusing on the fates awaiting the Trojan women, not on the deaths of Hector and Priam or on Troy's tragic past'.[64] As Boyle has observed, the character of the chorus is not only ritualistic in content but also in form: the Trojan women perform wild gestures such as the beating and baring of their breasts and the tearing of their hair, which are the typical gestures of the lamentation for the dead; the expression *iusta Troiae facite* at line 65 confirms that the women are performing the prescribed acts of the dirge. The sacred effect of the lamentation, which in Euripides is in part dissipated by the inclusion of dramatic information, is in Seneca particularly emphasized.[65]

The heavy presence of gestures, which are required to perform the instructions given by Hecuba to the chorus, are interpreted by Fantham as necessary since 'Seneca's public sees no chorus but draws their ideas of the action from the poetry alone'.[66] Fantham's interpretation implies that Seneca's tragedies were not written for performance and thus extended descriptions were required to make the audience understand what they could not see. In the case of a performance, instead, such detailed descriptions would have had no point since the action was taking place in front of the audience. Even if this were the case, namely that Seneca did not write the tragedies for performance, which is, however, still a controversial question in the scholarly interpretation of the Senecan *corpus*, nonetheless Fantham's interpretation does not seem to take into account the strong spectacular and visual character of the passage. This particular passage seems to have been conceived by Seneca as a written paraphrase of a vivid image. In this regard, the display of the Trojan women in mourning was not only a favourite literary topic, but also a popular one in pantomimic performances.[67] That the portrayal of the Trojan women as a mournful crowd lamenting for their dead was a diffuse one seems to be confirmed by Hecuba's very words at lines 95–6: *placet hic habitus,/ placet: agnosco Troada turbam.*[68] These words, whose metatheatrical implications were rightly recognized by Boyle, could imply and refer both to the long literary tradition in which the Trojan women were typically represented in mourning and to the pantomimic tradition which exploited the performing possibilities of that representation.[69]

A remarkable stylistic feature of the choruses in the *Oedipus* and *Trojan Women* is the language of corporality used by Seneca. The ode in the *Oedipus* (403–508) contains a conspicuously high number of references to body parts: *comam; bracchia; palmis; caput; vultu; comam; caput; frontem; crines; artus; crine; tempora; pede; pectora; comam; latus; manu; artus; membra; facies; bracchia; utero; pectus; lateri; manus; humero; capillis.* So too the ode in the *Trojan Women* (67–163): *manum; crinem; colla; capilli; manus; lacertos; utero; artus; pectora; manus; crinem; coma; ora; umeris; latus; pectora; dextras; manus; pectus; dextra;*

lacertos; umeros; caput; dextera; ubera; palmis; umeris; truncus; cervice; colla; manus; terga; dextra.

This language of the body and its emphasis on physicality could have been employed with the function of mirroring the semiotic system of the body characteristic of the pantomimic genre. In this respect, Ovid already had made use of such language of the body and Seneca may have borrowed it from him;[70] however, the formulaic nature of the language of the body used by Seneca seems a feature connected or rather inspired by a fixed and stereotypical system of body signs, thus quite similar to the one which most probably constituted the body grammar of pantomime. Seneca's language of corporeality has nothing of the sophisticated, elusive, and complex character of Ovid's language of the body. However, it is possible to suggest that Ovid's use of the language of the body was a feature that made his poems suitable to be adapted in pantomime (*Tristia* 2, 519–20: *et mea sunt populo saltata poemata saepe*). Seneca's tendency to employ a somehow simplified and less poetically sophisticated version of Ovid's language of the body would seem to reflect his engagement with pantomime.

Pantomime and Descriptive Running Commentaries

Introduction: The Role of Descriptions in Seneca's Tragedies

Scholars have unanimously pointed out that Seneca's tragedies are highly descriptive. Descriptions can occur in the forms of broad narrative passages or briefer accounts of a character's behaviour. An example of the former is the storm description in the *Agamemnon*, which expands on the shipwreck of the Greek fleet (421–578, 157 lines); an example of the latter is the chorus describing Cassandra's frenzied movements produced by prophetic *furor*, again in the *Agamemnon* (710–19, 9 lines).

In general, the presence of narrative passages hinders the development of the plot since it results in a suspension of dramatic time and a 'freezing of the action'.[1] Extended descriptions are a conventional device of epic where they are widely employed as a means for visualization and picture-making. In fact, description has the power to bring the subject vividly before the mind's eye and to generate an emotional response in the audience (either of readers or listeners). Now, if descriptions have a natural place in epic, enabling the readers or listeners to appreciate the visual dimension of the tale, the same does not apply in tragedy, where the audience can actually see onstage what is happening. While descriptions are not totally absent in Greek tragedy, where they serve the function of overcoming difficulties of stage production or of describing concisely a character's attitude, they are usually brief and always pertinent to the action; for instance, the narration of past events strictly relevant to the advancement of the plot or events that cannot be presented onstage (such as killings and death). Because of their restrained character, descriptions in Greek theatre do not result in a suspension of the dramatic time and can be placed within the dramatic conventions.

Unlike descriptions found in Greek drama, descriptions in Seneca's tragedies heavily disrupt dramatic conventions, so that their presence has been interpreted by many scholars, starting with Leo in the late nineteenth century, as a mere means for rhetorical display and the narratives have been dismissively labelled as 'pieces of virtuoso entertainment'.[2] Furthermore, descriptions have also been used as evidence of Seneca's lack of interest in dramatic coherence and stage performance, since, in the case of a stage performance, extended descriptive narratives would have been redundant and out of place. Among recent scholars, Zwierlein was the one who most strongly considered the occurrence of descriptive narratives as evidence that Seneca wrote the tragedies for recitation instead of stage performance.[3] In this case, their presence would have the function of supplying information that can not be conveyed by means of stage production. On the same line of thought as Zwierlein, Larson, who devoted an extensive study to the role of descriptions in Seneca's tragedies, has also claimed that 'the predilection for description in Senecan tragedy is indicative of a lack of concern for dramatic effect'; she further argues that 'its presence represents the *importation of an alien technique*, which properly belongs to the narrative mode, into drama'.[4] Thus, what Larson defines as the 'hybrid mixture of narrative technique with dramatic genre' is interpreted as a tool employed by Seneca to achieve an 'authorial control over the audience's understanding and interpretation of the drama'.[5] I would suggest, instead, that the alien technique imported into drama derives from the penetration into Seneca's tragic texts of the stylistic technique of composition of pantomimic libretti, which adopted features typical of both epic and tragedy. Pantomimic libretti, so the evidence suggests, featured a similar hybrid mixture of narrative technique with dramatic genre attributed by Larson to Seneca's tragedies.[6] It is likely that pantomimic libretti were made up of narratives, where the character in charge of delivering the narrative acquired the stance of an external narrator rather than a character involved in the action, this being due to the difficulty of portraying complicated interaction between several characters and the consequent need for the story to be told somehow explicitly. Furthermore, it is likely that pantomimic libretti employed descriptions to set and evoke the scenario and atmosphere in which the movements of the dancer took place or to act as a commentary on his gestures. If this is right, we may describe pantomimic libretti as compositions in between epic and tragedy.[7] This is possibly supported by Lucian's statement (61) that pantomimic libretti 'were adapted from the best epic and tragic poets of the past'. Several ancient writers attest that pantomimic libretti were adapted from Virgil, and Ovid himself claims that his poems were adapted in pantomimic performances (*Tristia*, 2, 519: *et mea sunt populo saltata poemata saepe*).[8]

It is now appropriate to examine in more detail the narrative parts of Seneca's tragedies in the attempt to define more precisely their connection with pantomime.

General Features of Running Commentaries of Onstage Actions

Running commentaries are those passages of Seneca's tragedies in which the emotions, actions, or physical appearance of a character are described by the chorus or by another actor in the third person; usually, the character described remains mute and does not hear or react to the words spoken about him. Running commentaries can describe actions that are taking place onstage or offstage.[9] Running commentaries thus consist of a speaking actor describing a mute performance by a silent one. Such a technique does not feature in Greek theatre, where emotions are portrayed instead by means of very brief and simple physical descriptions or are usually 'conveyed implicitly rather than explicitly described';[10] furthermore, the observations of an actor's behaviour are usually addressed to him and in turn trigger a response.

Running commentaries can either portray a character undergoing emotional strain (Medea driven by anger, Phaedra by love, Cassandra by prophetic madness) or describe various actions performed by characters, such as Astyanax's supplication, Medea's preparation of the poison, or Hercules' killing of his family. Senecan tragedies contain the following running commentaries, which can be divided into two groups on the basis of their occurrence onstage or offstage:

1) Onstage running commentaries:

- *Medea* 380–96; 849–78: nurse and chorus on Medea
- *Agamemnon* 710–19: chorus on Cassandra
- *Hercules furens* 895–1053: Amphitryon on Hercules
- *Trojan Women* 705–35: Andromache on Astyanax
- *Trojan Women* 883–5; 845–8; 925–6; 965–8: Helen and Andromache on Polyxena

2) Offstage running commentaries:

- *Phaedra* 362–83: nurse on Phaedra
- *Oedipus* 915–79: messenger on Oedipus
- *Hercules Oetaeus* 233–53: nurse on Deianira

- *Agamemnon* 867–909: Cassandra on Agamemnon
- *Medea* 670–751: nurse on Medea
- *Phoenissae* 427–42: messenger on Jocasta

The presence of descriptions of the character's movements has played an important role in the evaluation of Seneca as a dramatist. Zwierlein defined these descriptive parts as a 'mute performance' ('stummes Spiel') and did not like the result: 'The audience must receive the impression that he is witness to a pantomime described in a troublesome and pedantic way by a third person, as if the audience were blind'.[11] The fact that the action is described by a third person makes Zwierlein think that the tragedies were meant for recitation because, if they were staged, there would have been no need to describe the action, as it would have been before the eyes of the audience. More recently, Bernard Zimmermann, however, reconsidered the widespread descriptive scenes present in the tragedies.[12] He argues that they can be easily explained as pantomimic elements and suggests that three different types of pantomime scenes can be found in Seneca's tragedies: 'regelrechte Pantomimen' (actual pantomimes) is the one in which the chorus describes the action of a character (*Med* 849–78; *Ag* 710–19; *Hf* 1082–93); the second type is the one in which an actor describes the action of another actor (*Med* 380–96); the third type, 'pantomimische Kurzkommentare' (short pantomimic commentaries), is the one in which the chorus or an actor announces the entrance or the exit of another actor, giving a brief description of the character's movements (*Phae* 583–6; 728; 829–34; *Tro* 615–17; *Med* 186; *Ag* 775–81). Zimmermann gives some examples for each of the three types, but his analysis is not exhaustive. In what follows, I wish to build on Zimmermann's insight through a systematic analysis of all the running commentaries featuring in the plays and by investigating the reasons why Seneca might have found this technique so attractive. More specifically, I propose that the influence of the aesthetics of pantomime in Seneca's running commentaries dealing with descriptions of emotions is apparent in three aspects: content, distinctive stylistic features, and construction of the verse.

Running commentaries deal with descriptions of characters under the effects of harmful emotions such as erotic passion, *furor*, anger, madness, and pain. For instance, Phaedra, Medea, Deianira, Cassandra are all characters who experience extreme emotional states. The representation of a character in a mental state of extreme intensity by means of a highly sophisticated allusive gesturing was typical of pantomimic performances.[13] Seneca's interest in the potential offered by absorbing techniques from this emotive theatrical medium may, therefore, have been aroused by a perception that pantomime was exceptionally suited to display the effects of passions. Indeed, Seneca tells us in his own words that his appreciation for pantomime was due to the dancer's ability to portray emotions (*Epistulae*, 121, 6): *Mirari solemus saltandi peritos quod in omnem significationem rerum et adfectuum parata illorum est manus et verborum velocitatem gestus adsequitur.*[14]

In the tragedies, it is noticeable how Seneca tends to describe emotions or states of mind in terms of the bodily symptoms and physical sensations that they produce, perhaps to stress the loss of dignity and composure produced by uncontrolled passion. This technique seems intentionally employed to achieve a physical externalization of passions and a visualization of the outward manifestation of an inner state of mind. The extensive presence of body parts contained in the passages is strongly suggestive of a poet producing verse with gestural and choreographic accompaniment in mind: the special emphasis on the movements of the eyes recalls the similar emphasis ancient writers gave to the highly expressive and fundamental role of the dancer's gaze (in particular Apuleius' statement that the pantomimic performer could dance with his very eyes alone). For instance, in the passage dealing with Cassandra's prophetic frenzy, eye movements are described at length.[15] The eye movements may have been suggested by emphatic movements of the head to which a vivid expression of the eyes may have provided emotional intensity and the words of the libretto more specific explanatory or descriptive information. Philosophically, the emphasis on the eyes seems to point to the belief that the eyes are windows to one's internal condition and recalls Quintilian's statement about the relevance of the gaze for the orator (*Inst.* 11, 3, 75: *Sed in ipso vultu plurimum valent oculi, per quos maxime animus elucet*).

The descriptions of emotions and states of minds in the running commentaries are heavily stereotyped to the point that Seneca employs the same or very similar formulas and attributes to portray each characteristic passion, such as anger, love, or grief. If we compare the descriptions discussed above, the recurrences of similar patterns of behaviour are evident: the characters all move with hasty or agitated movements and are affected by a constant change of attitude (*Med 385: talis recursat huc et huc motu effero*; 862: *huc fert pedes et illuc*; HO 247: *incurrit, errat*; *Phae 372–3: semper impatiens sui/mutatur habitus*; HO 250: *nec unus habitus durat*); their eyes are flashing and turning (*Phae 364: erumpit oculis ignis*; 380: *oculi nihil gentile nec patrium micant*; *Oed 958: ardent minaces igne truculento genae*; *Ag 714–15: incerta nutant lumina et versi retro/torquentur oculi, rursus immoti rigent*); the colour of their faces is in a state of constant change

(*Phae* 376: *non ora tinguens nitida purpureus rubor*; *Med* 387: *flammata facies*; *Med* 858–61: *Flagrant genae rubentes,/pallor fugat ruborem./nullum vagante forma/servat diu colorem*; *HO* 251–2: *nunc inardescunt genae/pallor ruborem pellit*; *Ag* 710–11: *pallor genas . . . possidet*); they cry and groan (*Phae* 370: *noctem querelis ducit*; 381–2: *lacrimae cadunt per ora et assiduo genae/rore irrigantur*; *Med* 388: *oculos uberi fletu rigat*; 390: *queritur gemit*; *Oed* 922: *gemitus et altum murmur*; *HO* 249: *fletus insequitur minas*; 253: *queritur implorat gemit*).

Even the range of comparison used in the descriptions is limited and recurs especially in the adoption of a set of similar epic similes: comparison with a wild animal (*Med* 863–5: *ut tigris orba natis/cursu furente lustrat/Gangeticum nemus*; *Oed* 919–20: *qualis per arva Libycus insanit leo,/fulvam minaci fronte concutiens iubam*; *HO* 241–2: *feta ut Armenia iacens/sub rupe tigris hoste conspecto exilit*). Another pattern recurs in comparisons with a maenad: (*Med* 382–3: *Incerta qualis entheos gressus tulit/cum iam recepto maenas insanit deo/Pindi nivalis vertice aut Nysae iugis*; 849–51: *Quonam cruenta maenas/praeceps amore saevo/rapitur*; *HO* 243–4: *aut iussa thyrsum quatere conceptum ferens/Maenas Lyaeum dubia quo gressus agat*; *Ag* 719: *maenas impatiens dei*).

The use, therefore, of the same standard repertoire of either behaviour or expressions used in the descriptions seems to suggest that Seneca did not aim at variation or nuanced portrayal of different emotions and characters; on the contrary, running commentaries seem to offer standardized and rather predictable descriptions of stock exhibitions of emotional disturbance by the characters. Moreover, the same apparatus of gestures, attitudes, and symptoms is expressed by a sort of formulaic vocabulary constituted by a set repertoire of imagery (especially similes). It is tempting to suppose that this formulaic vocabulary reflects the parallel formulaic vocabulary of movements and gestures that most probably constituted the alphabet of the dancers.[16]

Because of this stylized characterization, Seneca's characters appear to be types or even archetypes rather than individuals.[17] Schlegel defined them as 'gigantic puppets' and, similarly, T.S. Eliot claimed that Seneca's 'characters all seem to speak with the same voice and at the top of it'.[18] Such an impression of stylization is further enhanced by the fact that Seneca's characters are invariably presented at the acme of emotional intensity, which makes them appear much larger than life in the intensity of their feelings. For example, Clytemnestra affirms that her conflicting emotions (love for Aegisthus, outrage for Agamemnon's infidelities) are so enormous that she cannot endure delays (*Ag* 131: *Maiora cruciant quam ut moras possim pati*); Oedipus claims that he has made the heaven sinful and that all of him is guilty (*Oed* 36: *fecimus caelum nocens; Phoe* 158: *totus nocens sum*); usually, the enormity of the characters' passions are measured against their sinful family background (generally mythical predecessors) or their past actions, which are regularly outdone by the fierceness of the present emotional condition: for instance, Phaedra's love for Hippolytus is said to outdo Pasiphae's love for the bull (*Phae* 142–3: ... *quid domum infamem aggravas/superasque matrem? maius est monstro nefas*); Medea's rage is said to grow monstrously, renew its past violence, and prepare a monstrosity bigger than the past ones she has committed (*Med* 671–2: *immane quantum augescit et semet dolor/accendit ipse vimque praeteritam integrat*; 674–5: ... *maius his, maius parat/Medea monstrum*); Clytemnestra's betrayal of her husband Agamemnon must be an outrage greater than that of Helen against Menelaus (*Ag* 123–4: *quid timida loqueris furta et exilium et fugas?/soror ista fecit; te decet maius nefas*). The climax in the outdoing of predecessors or past actions is to be found in the *Thyestes*, in which Atreus' thirst for revenge moves on a cosmic scale and it is said even to transcend human limits (*Thy* 267–70: *Nescioquid animo maius et solito amplius/supraque fines moris humani tumet/instatque pigris manibus. haud quid sit scio,/sed grande quiddam est!*).[19]

The excessive nature of Seneca's characters may be a further sign of the influence of the aesthetics of pantomime. As Lada-Richards has put it, pantomimic *personae* were primarily 'emotional landscapes, whose innermost recesses his dancing sought to illuminate'; arguably, an emphatic and often excessive emotionalism was an outstanding feature of pantomimic performances.[20]

In the following sections, I will provide an analysis of the features of running commentaries that I have singled out as belonging to pantomime in this introduction.

Medea (380–96): Nurse on Medea

In Seneca's *Medea* we can identify two onstage running commentaries. The first occurs at lines 380–96 (iambic trimeters) where the nurse describes Medea; the second at lines 849–78 (anacreontics with three interspersed galliambics) where the chorus describes the protagonist again.

> (Lines 380–96):
> Alumna, celerem quo rapis tectis pedem?   380
> resiste et iras comprime ac retine impetum.
> Incerta qualis entheos gressus tulit
> cum iam recepto maenas insanit deo

Pindi nivalis vertice aut Nysae iugis,
talis recursat huc et huc motu effero,   385
furoris ore signa lymphati gerens.
flammata facies, spiritum ex alto citat,
proclamat, oculos uberi fletu rigat,
renidet; omnis specimen affectus capit.
haeret minatur aestuat queritur gemit.   390
quo pondus animi verget? ubi ponet minas?
ubi se iste fluctus franget? exundat furor.
non facile secum versat aut medium scelus:
se vincet. irae novimus veteris notas.
magnum aliquid instat, efferum immane impium.   395
vultum Furoris cerno. di fallant metum!

The nurse's description of Medea opens the third act of the play; the nurse addresses the protagonist in the first two lines and provides the clue that Medea is coming out from the house in a hurry (380: *Alumna, celerem quo rapis tectis pedem?*); the following part of the speech delivered by the nurse describes Medea in the third person and is an account of the symptoms produced by the anger with which Medea is seized: Medea keeps moving here and there (385: *talis recursat huc et huc motu effero*) and the nurse compares this attitude with that of a frenzied maenad (382: *Incerta qualis entheos gressus tulit/cum iam recepto maenas insanit deo/Pindi nivalis vertice aut Nysae iugis*);[21] it is worth noting that Seneca uses two vivid expressions *recursat huc et huc motu effero* and *entheos gressus tulit* (taking erratic steps) to convey the image of Medea rushing around. Medea bears in her expression the signs of frenzied rage (386: *furoris ore signa lymphati gerens*); her face is blazing (387: *flammata facies*); she draws deep breaths (387: *spiritum ex alto citat*); she shouts (388: *proclamat*); she wets her eyes with tears (388: *oculos uberi fletu rigat*); she beams with joy (389: *renidet*); she shows evidence of each emotion (389: *omnis specimen affectus capit*); she hesitates (390: *haeret*); she threatens (390: *minatur*); she rages (390: *aestuat*); she laments (390: *queritur*); she groans (390: *gemit*). Then the nurse asks herself where the weight of Medea's mind will come down (391: *quo pondus animi verget?*), where she will place her threats (391: *ubi ponet minas?*), and where the wave of her anger will break (392: *ubi se iste fluctus franget?*); she then goes back to Medea and concludes the section with the image of Medea's rage overflowing (392: *exundat furor*). It is remarkable that each emotion is described as an active agent with almost an independent life of its own which, in turn, possesses Medea's body. The metaphor of the wave of emotion begins at line 392 (*ubi se iste fluctus franget*) and reaches its climax in the same line with the image of rage that pours out and implies an externalizing movement of the feeling from the inside to the outside.[22]

It is worth noting that the passage features a small amount of connectives and it articulates itself paratactically. Subordination is used only in the simile. Line 390, with five verbs in asyndeton, is the extreme example of this tendency. The syntax seems to rhythmically match Medea's hasty movements.[23] At no point is there any suggestion of Medea's awareness of the nurse or her discourse.

Both content and style of the description point to the influence of pantomime. Thematically, the description of the enraged Medea matches the depictions of women wronged by their husbands such as Medea, Philomela, and Clytemnestra, which are attested to have been very popular in pantomime.[24] Stylistically, the original 'psychoplastic' nature of the description may have been conceived as such by Seneca because of the influence of the language of corporeality of pantomime.[25]

Medea (849–78): Chorus on Medea Maenad

Quonam cruenta maenas	
praeceps amore saevo	850
rapitur? quod impotenti	
facinus parat furore?	
vultus citatus ira	
riget, et caput feroci	
quatiens superba motu	855
regi minatur ultro.	
quis credat exulem?	
Flagrant genae rubentes,	
pallor fugat ruborem.	
nullum vagante forma	860
servat diu colorem.	
huc fert pedes et illuc,	
ut tigris orba natis	
cursu furente lustrat	
Gangeticum nemus.	865

Frenare nescit iras
Medea, non amores;
nunc ira amorque causam
iunxere: quid sequetur?
quando efferet Pelasgis   870
nefanda Colchis arvis
gressum, metuque solvet
regnum simulque reges?
Nunc, Phoebe, mitte currus
nullo morante loro,   875
nox condat alma lucem,
mergat diem timendum
    dux noctis Hesperus.

The fourth chorus of the play deals with a second description of Medea's frenzied
behaviour and recasts the symptoms previously described by the nurse. Medea is
here compared to a maenad driven by a savage love (849–51: *Quonam cruenta
maenas/praeceps amore saevo/rapitur?*). The account then moves on to describing
the physical symptoms produced by anger: first there is a striking juxtaposition
between violent movement (853: *citatus*) and immobility (854: *riget*): her face
driven by anger sets (853–4: *vultus citatus ira/riget*); then she tosses her hair with
violent movements and she threatens the king (854–6: *et caput feroci/quatiens
superba motu/regi minatur ultro*). After that, the chorus describes at length
Medea's burning face and emphasizes the swift alternation between red and pale
complexion, which was interpreted as a common sign of distress: her reddened
cheeks are inflamed, but pallor displaces redness (858–9: *Flagrant genae
rubentes,/pallor fugat ruborem*), and she does not keep any colour for long in her
shifting appearance (860–1: *nullum vagante forma/servat diu colorem*).[26] Lines
862–5 recast the comparison of Medea with a maenad pacing to and fro (*huc fert
pedes et illuc,/ut tigris orba natis/cursu furente lustrat/Gangeticum nemus*), which
had been already employed in the opening of the chorus and reiterates with
slight variations the similar comparison between Medea and a maenad made by
the nurse in the previous passage (382–5: *Incerta qualis entheos gressus tulit/cum
iam recepto maenas insanit deo/ . . . talis recursat huc et huc motu effero*).[27] The
chorus then states that Medea is unable to rein in her feelings either of love or
anger and provides the image of the protagonist pulled in different directions by
these two opposite emotions (866–7: *Frenare nescit iras/Medea, non amores*). The
chorus concludes its song with an invocation to Phoebus to let the night come
and hide Medea's evil projects.

The fourth chorus of the *Medea* has a peculiar metrical pattern. Scholars have long debated the issue and reached different conclusions. Costa and Zwierlein interpret the metrical structure of the chorus as a system of catalectic iambic dimeters with three lines one syllable shorter: 857, 865, 878.[28] The difficulty in regarding the lines as iambics is the atypical and consistent presence of a short syllable in the fifth element of the foot.[29] Leo already felt the difficulty and considered the lines as anacreontics with sporadic substitutions of the two short syllables with a long one and interspersed with catalectic clauses.[30] More recently, Bruno Häuptli has suggested that this choral part is composed by anacreontics interspersed with three galliambics; more specifically the galliambics would be line 856–7: *regi minatur ultro./quis credat exulem,* line 864–5: *cursu furente lustrat/ Gangeticum nemus* and line 877–8: *mergat diem timendum/dux noctis Hesperus.*[31]

This metrical structure, with the presence of ionic meters, is inferred on the basis of the analogy with line 73 of Catullus poem 63: *iam iam dolet, quod egi,/ iam iamque paenitet.* While solving the metrical problems of the chorus, Häuptli's proposal also opens a new question as to the reasons for such a singular metrical choice and prompts us to wonder about the special dramatic and scenic effect Seneca was trying to obtain. Now, ionic verses have an 'oriental' character and they are usually linked to a Dionysiac context. In fact we find them very predominantly in Aeschylus' *Persians* (694–6; 700–2) as well as in Euripides' *Bacchae* (parodos 64–169, first 370–401 and second *stasimon* 519–71 are extensively ionic). For instance, in the parodos of the *Bacchae* the oriental character of the procession of worshippers is emphasized by the fact that 'asiatic associations are repeatedly stressed', 'the cult of Dionysus is linked with those of Cybele', and the singers play the *tympanum* (tambourine) which, together with the *aulos* (flute), was the characteristic instruments of orgiastic cults.[32]

The metrician Terenzianus Maurus links the rhythm of the ionic verse to another orgiastic and oriental context, that of the *Galli*, who were the priests of the Goddess Cybele and who practised ritual emasculation.[33] For instance, galliambics feature in one of Varro's Menippean satires, the *Eumenides* (of which 49 fragments survive), which contains a Cybele episode.[34]

The ionic metre was a traditional cult metre used in the songs sung during the orgiastic ritual ceremonies of Dionysus and Cybele, whose cults were often associated with one another.[35] For example, the Greek metrician Hephaestion explicitly affirms that the galliambic metre was used for hymns to Cybele.[36] As Häuptli also underlines, the metrical structure of the ionic verse, especially of galliambics, is particularly suitable for the orgiastic intonation of several short syllables in close sequence; the rhythm of the short syllables in close sequence suggests, in a very appropriate mimetic way, the cadence of the tambourine (*tympanum*) accompanying convulsive movements of the *Galli* reaching in procession the temple of Cybele.[37]

In poem 63, Catullus describes Attis' self-castration, his participation in the ritual procession and, at the end, his contrition for what he has done. The ionic verse is apparently used in specific relationship to the theme (the ritual ceremony of the cult of Cybele); this would also explain why many attempts to assign poem 63 to other codified genres have been so unsatisfactory. Although the apparent lack of relation to any recognized metrical and poetic form leaves the question still open, it has been suggested by Morisi that the poem has a well-recognizable dramatic structure because the story is not told and experienced by a narrator or in the third person, but it is told by the protagonist himself, who translates his feelings and his actions in scenic gesture.[38] Newman ascribes poem 63 to tragic pantomime;[39] he argues that Catullus, relying on an Alexandrian model, could have been influenced by it in composing 63. Newman's interpretation is supported by the fact that Attis' self-castration was a very popular subject in pantomimic performances, as demonstrated by the many *oscilla* featuring an Attis mask, although belonging to a later period.[40] Catullus' Attis has been analysed in detail in Chapter 1;[41] here it is enough to underline the dramatic texture of the poem, which is interesting in relation to the metrical parallels of it found in the *Medea*. Overall, then, it seems likely that the fourth chorus of *Medea*, in which the chorus sings its song describing Medea's gesture at the acme of her *furor*, has strong affiliation with tragic pantomime.

Agamemnon (710–19): Chorus on Cassandra

Silet repente Phoebas et pallor genas   710
creberque totum possidet corpus tremor;
stetere vittae, mollis horrescit coma,
anhela corda murmure incluso fremunt,
incerta nutant lumina et versi retro
torquentur oculi, rursus immoti rigent.   715
nunc levat in auras altior solito caput
graditurque celsa, nunc reluctantes parat
reserare fauces, verba nunc clauso male
custodit ore, maenas impatiens dei.

The fourth act of the *Agamemnon* features a confrontation between Cassandra and the chorus, which, from a dramaturgical point of view, does not involve a significant advancement of the plot. Basically, the act is given to Cassandra, who either describes the approach of her prophetic state with her own words or is described by the chorus in the third person. Thus, in the act, there are several sudden shifts from third-person description to first-person speech.

Cassandra's prophetic *furor* is described by the chorus step by step and has its climax in her mute performance at lines 710–19. The portrayal of Cassandra's behaviour starts with the ripping of the bands (693: *Sed cur sacratas deripis capiti infulas?*), increases with her acting as a maenad possessed by the god (710–19), and culminates with her clairvoyant speech (720–74; the striving for tension is confirmed by the shift from the iambic trimeter to the iambic dimeter within Cassandra's speech). Cassandra's tense speech ends with her fainting, described again by the chorus (775–8).

The running commentary made by the chorus at lines 710–19 describes the outward symptoms of Cassandra's prophetic frenzy and is heavily modelled on Virgil's description of the Cumean Sybil, even though Seneca adds some new details (as, for example, the emphasis on the movement of Cassandra's eyes): she is suddenly silent (710: *Silet repente Phoebas*); pallor spreads over her cheeks (710–11: *pallor genas ... possidet*);[42] two signs of fear are then described: a continual tremble that takes hold of her whole body (711: *creberque totum possidet corpus tremor*), the standing out of her holy ribbons, and of her hair (712: *stetere vittae, mollis horrescit coma*). It is then the turn of the signs of possession: her panting breasts resound with an enclosed murmur (713: *anhela corda murmure incluso fremunt*);[43] her eyes are unsteady, roll backwards, and then become fixed and rigid again (714–15: *incerta nutant lumina et versi retro/ torquentur oculi, rursus immoti rigent*);[44] she raises her head higher than usual and walks tall (716–17: *nunc levat in auras altior solito caput/graditurque celsa*);[45] after that, Cassandra is described as caught in the struggle between two contrasting forces: on the one hand, she is ready to open her reluctant mouth, but, on the other, she tries in vain to hold her words behind her closed mouth (717–19: *nunc reluctantes parat/reserare fauces, verba nunc clauso male/custodit ore*); the description is closed by the comparison of Cassandra with a maenad (719: *maenas impatiens dei*) and recalls closely Virgil's *at Phoebi nondum patiens* (6, 77). The word *maenas* was generally applied to any woman who behaved as possessed; in Euripides' *Trojan Women* (173) Cassandra is so called. It is interesting that Seneca stresses Cassandra's similitude with a maenad, although adapting closely a Virgilian passage in which the maenad simile is not present. It is remarkable that, in running commentaries, the comparison with a maenad is a favoured one which Seneca widely employs.[46] In the already mentioned anonymous epigram in praise of the art of the pantomimic dancer, the maenad performing frenzied movements (*bacchatur*) is among the most performed pantomimic shows.

In terms of verse construction, it is helpful to explore what the influence of the aesthetics of pantomime might have had on a conventional type of scene when turned into a Senecan "running commentary". This can be done by looking more closely at the description of Cassandra delivered by the chorus in the *Agamemnon* and by comparing it with its literary model, the description of the effects of the prophetic frenzy on the Cumean Sybil in the *Aeneid*:

Seneca, *Agamemnon* (710–19)	Virgil, *Aeneid* (6, 46–51)
Silet repente Phoebas et pallor **genas**	…cui talia fanti
creberque totum possidet **corpus** tremor;	ante fores subito non **vultus**,
	non color unus,
stetere vittae, mollis horrescit **coma**,	non comptae mansere
	comae; sed **pectus** anhelum,
anhela **corda** murmure incluso fremunt,	et rabie fera **corda** tument,
	maiorque videri
incerta nutant **lumina** et versi retro	nec mortale sonans, adflata
	est numine quando
torquentur **oculi**, rursus immoti rigent.	iam propiore dei.
nunc levat in auras altior solito **caput**	
graditurque celsa, nunc reluctantes parat	
reserare **fauces**, verba nunc clauso male	
custodit **ore**, maenas impatiens dei.	

Stylistically, the Senecan passage adopts a staccato mode, which sharply contrasts with the flowing mode of the Virgilian description. Seneca thus tends to present the image of Cassandra in clipped segments rather than as a continuous sequence, so that a single image is self-contained within a line or two. The staccato mode is achieved by a heavy use of end-stopped lines and a sparing use of enjambement, which usually runs just over two lines. In fact, in the Senecan passage end-stopped lines are interspersed with enjambed lines, while the Virgilian one is heavily enjambed. The presence of end-stopped lines creates breaks and pauses in the flow of the rhythm of the verse. Furthermore, the syntax of the passage also moves predominantly in staccato phrases; connectives are used seldom, the style is mostly paratactic, asyndetic constructions are favoured, and there are few subordinate clauses. This syntactical device lends the passage a restless rhythm that matches the feverish inner state of the protagonist. The visualization of the actions performed is facilitated by the use of parallel statements, which describe the character's movements in a very simple and arguably unpoetic way. In conclusion, these stylistic devices combine to produce an image that would be not only easy to visualize, but also to convey physically, by means of gestures.

As to the metrical patterns of running commentaries, we have seen that they can occur in connection with dialogue or lyric metre; therefore the metrical shift may claim a different musical accompaniment; otherwise, the portrayal of specific emotions may be related to the peculiar metrical pattern employed; concerning this point, the application of the principle, according to which 'certain meters can convey certain attitudes', can provide a deeper insight into the meaning implied in Seneca's dramatic technique.[47] Finally, the different metrical patterns may be a sign of the necessity of a different range of movements and gestures.

Hercules Furens (895–1053): Amphitryon on Hercules

Hercules' attack of insanity is described by Amphitryon in a lengthy running commentary. Fitch has noticed that 'basically, act IV represents a translation into stage action of the Euripidean messenger-speech describing Hercules' madness and the murder of his family'.[48] He has also remarked that 'this is quite in keeping with Seneca's tendency to dramatise rather than narrate tragic violence'.[49] As to Seneca's sources, Fitch believes that Seneca borrowed the dramatization of Hercules' madness from an unknown drama where the scene was enacted onstage. Since there is no evidence of a play of such a kind, I would suggest, instead, that Seneca's dramatization of Hercules' madness betokens the influence of pantomime; in fact, there is evidence from Lucian (41) and Macrobius (*Saturnalia* 2,7,16) that Hercules' madness featured in pantomimic performance.[50]

It is worth analysing how this dramatization takes place. The scene, as described by the dialogue, is quite confusing; as a consequence, scholars have given rather different interpretations of it.

At line 987 Hercules sees one of his sons (whom he believes to be Lycus' son) trying to hide and kills him with an arrow; Amphitryon describes Hercules' action (991–5): *Quo se caecus impegit furor?/vastum coactis flexit arcum cornibus/pharetramque solvit, stridet emissa impetu/harundo; medio spiculum collo fugit/vulnere relicto.*

Immediately after Amphitryon's intervention, we hear again Hercules who wants to 'drag out' the whole of Lycus' offspring and 'tear open' their hiding places; Amphitryon describes how Hercules attacks the palace, breaks down the doors (999–1001: *huc eat et illuc valva deiecto obice/rumpatque postes; columen impulsum labet./perlucet omnis regia*), and sees one of his own sons who is hidden there (1001–2: *hic video abditum/ natum scelesti patris*). He thus enters the palace and kills the second son. Again, the killing is described by Amphitryon (1002–7): *En blandas manus/ad genua tendens voce miseranda rogat./scelus nefandum, triste et aspectu horridum!/dextra precantem rapuit et circa furens/bis ter rotatum misit; ast illi caput/sonuit, cerebro tecta disperso madent.* Immediately afterward, Amphitryon describes Megara escaping from her hiding place with the third child (1008–9: *at misera, parvum protegens natum sinu,/Megara furenti similis e latebris fugit*). Where was Megara hiding before rushing out? In the palace? If so, she runs out from the palace and comes onstage. Hercules follows her (1010–11: *Licet Tonantis profuga condaris sinu,/petet undecumque temet haec dextra et feret*); Megara implores Hercules to recognize that she is his wife and not Juno and that the small child who stretches his hands towards him is his. Hercules cannot be persuaded by Megara's words and spurs her to follow him (1018: *sequere*); does this verb imply that they go offstage again? Once more, we come to know from Amphitryon's words that Hercules is actually killing his third son and his wife (1022–6): *pavefactus infans igneo vultu patris/perit ante vulnus, spiritum eripuit timor./in coniugem nunc clava libratur gravis:/perfregit ossa, corpori trunco caput/abest nec usquam est.*

Now that the murders are accomplished, Hercules' father calls for his son's rage to strike him as well. Hercules does not reply to Amphitryon's plea, so we have to infer that he is still offstage and comes back only at line 1035 where he expresses his satisfaction at the accomplishment of the murderous deed (*Bene habet, pudendi regis excisa est domus*). Amphitryon offers himself again as the final victim remaining to be killed, but Hercules just faints, and his father's words describe the coma into which he falls (1142–8).

Fitch and Sutton envisage the scene as such:

1) Killing of the first son: Fitch proposes that Hercules may exit at 990 f. to make the shot or, if he is onstage, he 'may shoot from the stage at a target unseen by the audience'; Sutton thinks, instead, that the first child is killed onstage.
2) Killing of the second son: Hercules enters the palace at 1001–2 and kills the second son;
3) Killing of Megara and the third son: after the killing of the second son, Megara rushes onstage from the palace, pursued by Hercules (1008–9). Hercules catches and spurs her to follow him. They exit again (1018: *sequere*) and Hercules kills his wife and his son offstage.

4) Hercules re-enters onstage at line 1035 and there collapses (as can be inferred by lines 1143 ff.).

Then, since Amphitryon describes the killings, Fitch and Sutton suggest that he can see them through the ruined doorway. Mackay, instead, proposes that the whole scene takes place offstage but that the audience, through the open door, 'catches glimpses' of the actions taking place there, while the rest, i.e. the action that could not plausibly be performed, is described by Amphitryon's words.[51]

From the above analysis, it is clear that the different interpretations of the scene are due to the ambiguity of the dialogue, which does not render the course of the action incontrovertibly evident; the stage directions implied in the character's words do not allow us to establish, for example, if the first child is killed onstage or offstage; even the setting of the scene is rather fluid.

In addition to this, if it is true that Hercules' madness is dramatized onstage and the whole scene strives for visual effects, why then, does Amphitryon describe Hercules' action in the third person instead of addressing his son directly or, even more importantly, why does he not try to stop him? From the point of view of concern for dramatic illusion, Amphitryon's objective and detached description in such a situation of crisis is quite implausible; we have to imagine that while he witnesses the killings of his own nephews he narrates the terrible events to the audience instead of making an attempt at stopping Hercules. In my opinion, the implausibility can only be explained if we take into account that a sort of dramatic convention is at play here. To put it more clearly, it seems that Seneca could handle the scene so implausibly, because such a handling had became conventional. Amphitryon assumes in this scene a similar function to that which the messengers have in Seneca's tragedies; he becomes a sort of external narrator much like the 'speaking voice' to which a pantomime dancer danced and which remained aloof from the action.

Trojan Women (705–35): Andromache on Astyanax

The third act of the *Trojan Women* is devoted to Andromache's attempt to conceal her little child in a safe place as suggested in a dream by her husband Hector who warned her of the danger Astyanax was about to incur because of the Greeks. The act is divided into three scenes: the first scene features a long dialogue between Andromache and an old man about the need to hide the child and the choice of Hector's tomb as the hiding place. The second one features Andromache's confrontation with Ulysses who came to collect the little child who has been sentenced to death. Andromache tries to convince Ulysses that the child is dead, but Ulysses discovers she is deceiving him and finds the child. The act ends with Andromache's lyric monody in which she begs and makes her son beg for pity and life. Andromache's lyric monologue (705–35) is the climax of her desperate attempt to rescue her child and is achieved by the building up of a progressive and increasing crescendo, which starts at lines 672–5:

> . . . qualis Argolicas ferox
> turmas Amazon stravit, aut qualis deo
> percussa Maenas entheo silvas gradu
> armata thyrso terret atque expers sui   675
> vulnus dedit nec sensit, in medios ruam
> tumuloque cineris socia defenso cadam.

The simile that compares Andromache to a maenad (which recalls directly *Medea* 382–6 where the nurse describes the protagonist thus) is used to underline that desperation and anger are driving her mad and furious. The shifting into madness continues at lines 683–5 where she has a vision of Hector brandishing his arms: *arma concussit manu,/iaculatur ignes! cernitis, Danai, Hectorem?/an sola video?*; Fantham parallels this passage with *Medea* (961–2) and *Agamemnon* (765) where Medea and Cassandra respectively undergo a similar kind of hallucinatory experience.[52]

Andromache's excited state of mind is visually conveyed, as suggested by Calder, by the fact that she strikes her breast (681: *Me, me sternite hic ferro prius*) and seems to reach its end when she falls at Ulysses' knees (691–3: *Ad genua accido/supplex, Ulixe, quamque nullius pedes/novere dextram pedibus admoveo tuis*).[53] Afterwards she delivers ten lines in iambics (694–704) where she more calmly tries to move Ulysses to pity; once she realizes that her attempts are void, she breaks through in a lyric monody (705–35) in anapaests. The peculiar feature of this lyric monody, which one would expect to be a surrendering lament of a mother in front of the cruel destiny of her son and thus characterized by a sorrowful and intimate tone, is its descriptiveness. Actually, Andromache's words describe the mute performance of Astyanax who acts out a supplication. Fantham argues that 'by composing these lines as an anapaestic monody, Seneca marks the movement of the child's surrender and raises Andromache's appeal above the emotional level of the dialogue surrounding it in a way without parallel in his other tragedies.'[54] The emotional tone of the passage is conveyed by the metrical patterns adopted, which underline and emphasize the acts performed by the child. In relation to this, a preliminary discussion of the controversial colometry of the passage, which diverges in the two main families of the manuscript tradition (E and A), is necessary. The manuscripts of the A family write a sequence of anapaestic dimeters closed by a trimeter (line 734–5), while the *Etruscus* writes a sequence of anapaestic dimeters closed by a monometer.[55] I give below the two different colometry arrangements of lines 705–35 as given by Zwierlein and Fitch respectively:

(Zwierlein, 1986)   (Fitch, 2002–2004)

Huc e latebris procede tuis,   Huc e latebris procede tuis,
flebile matris furtum miserae.   flebile matris furtum miserae.
Hic est, hic est terror, Vlixe,   Hic est, hic est terror, Ulixe,
mille carinis.   **mille carinis.**
Submitte manus dominique pedes   **Summitte manus,**
supplice dextra stratus adora   **dominique pedes**
nec turpe puta quidquid miseros   supplice dextra stratus adora,
Fortuna iubet.   **nec turpe puta**
pone ex animo reges atauos   quidquid miseros Fortuna iubet.
magnique senis iura per omnis   pone ex animo reges atavos
incluta terras, excidat Hector,   **magnique senis**
gere captiuum positoque genu-   iura per omnes inclita terras,
si tua nondum funera sentis-   excidat Hector, gere captivum,
matris fletus imitare tuae.   **positoque genu-**
Vidit pueri regis lacrimas   si tua nondum funera sentis-
et Troia prior, paruusque minas   matris fletus imitare tuae.
trucis Alcidae flexit Priamus.   Vidit pueri regis lacrimas
Ille, ille ferox, cuius uastis   **et Troia prior,**
uiribus omnes cessere ferae,   parvusque minas trucis Alcidae
qui perfracto limine Ditis   **flexit Priamus.**
caecum retro patefecit iter,   Ille, ille ferox,
hostis parui uictus lacrimis   cuius vastis viribus omnes
'suscipe' dixit 'rector habenas   **cessere ferae,**
patrioque sede celsus solio;   qui perfracto limine Ditis
sed sceptra fide meliore tene':   caecum retro patefecit iter,
hoc fuit illo uictore capi.   hostis parvi victus lacrimis

Discite mites Herculis iras-
an sola placent Herculis arma?
iacet ante pedes non minor illo
supplice supplex uitam petit-
regnum Troiae quocumque uolet
Fortuna ferat.

'suscipe' dixit 'rector habenas,
patrioque sede celsus solio;
sed sceptra fide meliore tene'.
hoc fuit illo victore capi.
discite mites Herculis iras-
an sola placent Herculis arma?
iacet ante pedes
non minor illo supplice supplex
vitamque petit;
regnum Troiae quocumque volet
Fortuna ferat.

Fitch's colometry, which has been developed on a statistical analysis based on Richter's principle of sense-correspondence, identifies more monometers than Zwierlein.[56] From a general point of view, Fitch explains that 'monometers coincide with heightened emotion, marked by apostrophe' and their occurrence creates a broken rhythm which is in contrast with the more controlled rhythm created by the sequence of dimeters; in the specific case of Andromache's monody, he affirms that the 'frequent monometers match the pathos of her address to Astyanax, but give way to consecutive dimeters in a more objective passage expounding the *exemplum* of Hercules' clemency'.[57] If we consider the visual impact, Fitch's arrangement is the one that underlines more vividly Astyanax's movements. Since Andromache's apostrophes imply Astyanax's movements, Fitch's arrangement of colometry restores the coinciding of the occurrence of monometer and movement, the latter being then emphasized by the metrical structure and possibly by the related musical accompaniment. Of the twelve monometers written by Fitch, six of them imply movements: *summitte manus* (hold out your arms); *dominique pedes* (at your master's feet); *positoque genu* (on bended knee); *flexit Priamus* (Priam turned aside);[58] *iacet ante pedes* (there lies at your feet); *vitamque petit* (asking for life).

The broken rhythm created by monometers slows down the flow of the anapaests and creates pauses required by the kinds of movements implied by the words: Astyanax holds out his arms, bends at Ulysses' feet and touches them asking for life.

Later on in the act, Astyanax, who is mute until now, speaks his only line in the whole tragedy (792: *Miserere, mater*), which is the emotional response to Andromache's pathetic farewell (790–1: *Troia te expectat tua:/i, vade liber, liberos Troas vide*); right afterwards Andromache's words (in iambics this time) describe again the child's gesture at lines 793–4 (*Quid meos retines sinus/manusque matris, cassa praesidia, occupas?*). The farewell scene between mother and son, which begins at line 793 and ends at line 812, shows to what extent Seneca exploited this highly melodramatic moment of the parting of the two. Andromache's lyric monody, then, calls for performance; its sophisticated interplay of metre, music, and description of movement would be lost in the recitation of a single voice and the composition of such a passage would not make any sense but with performance in mind.

Trojan Women (883–5; 845–8; 925–6; 965–8): Helen and Andromache on Polyxena

In the fourth act of the *Trojan Women* there are three speaking characters (Helen, Andromache, and Hecuba) and two mute ones (Polyxena and Pyrrhus). This act presents the description of various mute performances (occurring here in iambics rather than in lyric metres) played by Polyxena (lines 883–5; 925–6; 945–8; 965–8), Hecuba (lines 949–54), and Pyrrhus (lines 999–1003 where he enters onstage at the end of the act, performs his mute role and exits with the young Trojan girl).[59] The mute role played by Polyxena, which is described by various speaking characters, is central to the act in the same way as the mute role of Astyanax in the previous one. Fitch observed that Astyanax's and Polyxena's destiny provides the structural framework and constitutes the unifying factor of the play itself;[60] in fact, in the second act the destiny of the two Trojan captives is announced; in the third one Astyanax's capture is displayed and in the fourth Polyxena's; the last act features the deaths of both of them. This being the case, it is absolutely remarkable that both Astyanax and Polyxena just have a mute role in the play. If the silent role of Astyanax can possibly be explained by his very young age, Polyxena's muteness is more striking. Yet, as Boyle suggests, 'the silence of Polyxena throughout this act is a major aspect of the act's dramatic power'.[61]

The first appearance of Polyxena occurs at lines 883–5 when Helen addresses and spurs her on to abandon her sad state of mind, wear festive clothes, and comb her hair (*depone cultus squalidos, festos cape,/dedisce captam; deprime horrentes comas,/crinemque docta patere distingui manu*). That Polyxena is reluctant to do what Helen suggests is made clear by Helen's apostrophe calling for Andromache's attempt to convince Polyxena at lines 924–5 (*Nunc hanc luctibus paulum tuis,/Andromacha, omissis flecte*).

As Andromache unveils the reason behind Polyxena's treacherous wedding with Pyrrhus, the young girl's attitude finally changes; she is now eager to wear the bridal gown because she knows she is about to die. This change is described by the words of Andromache at lines 945–8:

> Vide ut animus ingens laetus audierit necem.
> cultus decoros regiae vestis petit
> et admoveri crinibus patitur manum.

Afterwards Polyxena undergoes, if the controversial lines in question refer to her and not Hecuba, another change of mind, described at lines 965–8;[62] she now grieves for her cruel destiny: *Inrigat fletus genas/imberque victo subitus e vultu cadit/ Laetare, gaude, nata. quam vellet tuos/Cassandra thalamos, vellet Andromache tuos!*

A similar mute performance is played by Hecuba and described by Andromache's words at lines 949–54:

> At misera luctu mater audito stupet;
> labefacta mens succubuit. assurge, alleva   950
> animum et cadentem, misera, firma spiritum.
> quam tenuis anima vinculo pendet levi!
> minimum est quod Hecubam facere felicem potest.
> spirat, revixit. prima mors miseros fugit.

It remains to take into account Pyrrhus' mute entrance to drag Polyxena off at lines 999–1003:

> Sed incitato Pyrrhus accurrit gradu
> vultuque torvo. Pyrrhe, quid cessas? age   1000
> reclude ferro pectus et Achillis tui
> coniunge soceros. perge, mactator senum,
> et hic decet te sanguis.-abreptam trahit.

Fantham defines his entrance as 'unparalleled in stage drama and theatrically gratuitous, since Helen, who came to fetch Polyxena, could very well have led her away'.[63] If Fantham is right in pointing out that Pyrrhus' entrance does not have dramaturgic coherence, on the other hand it is not necessarily gratuitous, since the dramatic effect would not be the same if Helen were to lead Polyxena away; from the point of view of dramaturgic coherence, Helen would seem the best candidate to lead the girl away if Seneca's aim had been to achieve a fluid transition from this act to the next one, where she is not onstage. But Seneca had different priorities and operated within a different aesthetics, creating as he did a silent tableau that features the two partners in a wedding of death.

General Features of Running Commentaries of Offstage Actions

In Senecan tragedies there are several instances of running commentaries of offstage actions which describe either the symptoms of emotions experienced or the actions performed by different characters. All these running commentaries share, as a peculiar common feature, an extremely fluid handling of time and space; in fact, they usually are supposed to be subsequent reports of events that already happened, but they turn out to describe events as if they took place simultaneously with the narration of them (Oedipus' self-blinding described by the messenger in the *Oedipus* 915–79; the incantation scene in the *Medea* described by the nurse 670–751); in other cases, they are supposed to describe actions taking place offstage simultaneously with the narration, so that the narrator onstage is meant to see what he describes as he sees it; the narrator usually does not provide information regarding how he is able to see offstage actions (the description of love-sick Phaedra made by the nurse in the *Phaedra* 362–83 and the murder scene in the *Agamemnon* described by Cassandra 867–909).

Such a handling of interior scenes is unusual. A similar dramatic device does not feature in Greek tragedy, even though its development can be traced back to the messenger's *rhesis* reporting facts and actions that occur offstage. The main points of difference between the messenger's *rhesis* and the Senecan interior scenes are the following:

1) the messenger's *rhesis* in Greek tragedy relates facts and actions that happened in the past; in the Senecan interior scene the time at which the actions are taking place is ambiguous (as in the case of the *Phaedra*);
2) the messenger's *rhesis* relates facts and actions necessary for the plot to advance; in the Senecan interior scene the actions described are often tangential to the advancement of the plot;
3) the messenger's *rhesis* relates facts and actions in a dramatically condensed way, while in the Senecan interior scenes actions of characters are described in detail and at length.

This peculiar handling must then be regarded as an innovative feature of Seneca's dramatic technique, whose function and meaning is worth investigating.

Apart from these, the offstage running commentaries are similar in tone, content, and stylistic features to the onstage running commentaries. I list them as follows:

- *Phaedra* (362–83): nurse on Phaedra;
- *Oedipus* (915–79): messenger on Oedipus;
- *Hercules Oetaeus* (233–53): nurse on Deianira;
- *Agamemnon* (867–909): Cassandra on Agamemnon;
- *Medea* (670–751): nurse on Medea;
- *Phoenissae* (427–42): messenger on Jocasta;

Phaedra (362–83): Nurse on Phaedra

torretur aestu tacito et inclusus quoque,	
quamvis tegatur, proditur vultu furor;	
erumpit oculis ignis et lassae genae	
lucem recusant; nil idem dubiae placet,	365
artusque varie iactat incertus dolor:	
nunc ut soluto labitur marcens gradu	
et vix labante sustinet collo caput,	
nunc se quieti reddit et, somni immemor,	
noctem querelis ducit; attolli iubet	370
iterumque poni corpus et solvi comas	
rursusque fingi; semper impatiens sui	
mutatur habitus. nulla iam Cereris subit	
cura aut salutis. vadit incerto pede,	
iam viribus defecta: non idem vigor,	375
non ora tinguens nitida purpureus rubor;	
[populatur artus cura, iam gressus tremunt,	
tenerque nitidi corporis cecidit decor]	
et qui ferebant signa Phoebeae facis	
oculi nihil gentile nec patrium micant.	380
lacrimae cadunt per ora et assiduo genae	
rore irrigantur, qualiter Tauri iugis	
tepido madescunt imbre percussae nives.	

The second act of the play opens with a long description made by the nurse of Phaedra who is tormented by the fierce love she feels for her stepson. The nurse's description of Phaedra comes in reply to the chorus, who asks how the queen feels and whether her passion has found rest. It is remarkable that, from the point of view of dramatic action, the description made by the nurse is superfluous and repetitive, since it does not provide any additional information about

Phaedra's mental and physical condition. For already in the first act, Phaedra herself gives a detailed self-analysis of the fierce symptoms of love she is experiencing (99–112).

What is then the function of the lengthy description? First of all, the actions performed by Phaedra and described by the nurse take place inside the royal palace; in fact, at the end of her speech, the nurse says that the door of the palace opens and Phaedra comes out reclining on a couch (384–6: *Sed en, patescunt regiae fastigia:/reclinis ipsa sedis auratae toro/solitos amictus mente non sana abnuit*). It is not then clear whether the nurse is describing Phaedra's behaviour as she sees her in that precise moment or whether she is just relating to the chorus the symptoms that are affecting Phaedra without the implication that she is actually giving an eye-witness account.[64]

In the specific case of the *Phaedra*, the description made by the nurse recalls closely in style and content the descriptions of Medea made by the nurse (380–96) and the chorus in the *Medea* (849–78); in both cases Seneca offers a detailed portrayal of the bodily symptoms produced by destructive feelings (of love in the case of Phaedra and of *furor* in that of Medea); the descriptions of Phaedra and Medea clearly belong to the same category and very plausibly share the same function. Now, since I suggested that the description of Medea bears the sign of the influence of pantomime, I would argue that the description of Phaedra can be interpreted in the same way. The only difference between them is that Phaedra's actions take place offstage, while Medea's ones are performed onstage. The fact that Phaedra's actions are performed inside and thus are not visible is a difficulty if we envisage the passage as a pantomimic insertion (the difficulty would persist even in the case of a more traditional staging of the play); but since the description of Phaedra's behaviour provides a very realistic examination of the symptoms of Phaedra's passion, it seems that its visual dimension calls strongly for performance; the effects of love are minutely described thus: her madness is betrayed in her face and the fire of love bursts out from her eyes (363: *proditur vultu furor*; 364: *erumpit oculis ignis*); her eyes cannot bear the daylight (364–5: *lassae genae/lucem recusant*); pain shakes restlessly her limbs (366: *artusque varie iactat incertus dolor*); she collapses and cannot support her head on her neck (367–8: *nunc ut soluto labitur marcens* **gradu**/*et vix labante sustinet* **collo caput**); she can neither sleep nor eat (369–70: *somni immemor/noctem querelis ducit*; 373–4: *nulla iam Cereris subit/cura aut salutis*); she is restless and constantly changing attitude and condition (372–3: *semper impatiens sui/mutatur habitus*). She walks with uncertain steps since she has lost all her strength (374–5: *vadit incerto pede,/iam viribus defecta*); she is weak and pale (375–6: *non idem vigor,/non ora tinguens nitida purpureus rubor*); she cries continuously and abundantly (381–2: *lacrimae cadunt per ora et assiduo genae/rore irrigantur*).

Since the case of Phaedra, as previously discussed, is not isolated in the Senecan *corpus*, I would suggest that in pantomimic performances it was an accepted dramatic convention to perform in front of the audience scenes that were meant to happen indoors; in fact, the strict constraints of dramatic illusion necessary in a traditional play would not have been necessary in the more versatile performative genre which pantomime was. From a stylistic point of view, the syntax of the passage moves predominantly in staccato phrases; connectives are seldom used, the style is mostly paratactic, and subordination is sparsely used. This choice of syntax gives to the passage a restless rhythm which matches the feverish inner state of the protagonist. The visualization of the actions performed is made easy by the use of parallel statements describing in a very simple and unpoeticized way Phaedra's movements. As to content, the depiction of love-sick Phaedra contains all the traditional elements found in the description of the effects of love, but it is interesting to consider how Seneca reworked and adapted them. Virgil's description of Dido consumed by love for Aeneas (*Aen.* 4, 1–5; 66–9; 74–89) is heavily echoed in the Senecan passage. Fantham has pointed out the elements borrowed from Virgil: 'the flames, the unspoken anguish, the frenzy all repeat elements of *Aen.* 4, 66–9. The account of restless change (365–8) and sleepless night (368–9) match the range of *Aen.* 4, 74–89'.[65] The imagery of fire as a metaphor of the passion of love borrowed from Virgil is appropriated and reshaped, while lines 362–3 echo Ovid (*Met.* 4, 64: *quoque magis tegitur, tectus magis aestuat ignis*).

In the Senecan passage, abstract notions such as *furor* (363) or *dolor* (366) are personified and become overwhelming forces, which have acquired a life of their own. If Dido is wasted with the fire of love, in Seneca it is *furor* itself that burns Phaedra. We could say that in the Senecan passage the passion is so strong that it overcomes the individuality of the speaker. In addition to this, the language used by Seneca is simple and almost prosaic; compare, for instance, the concrete way of presenting Phaedra's restlessness *artusque varie iactat incertus dolor* with the Virgilian poetic one *uritur infelix Dido totaque vagatur/urbe furens* (*Aen.* 4, 68–69). In this respect, the sudden change in stylistic register from the preceding tone with the insertion of an epic-sounding simile, which rounds off the description, is notable: *qualiter Tauri iugis/tepido madescunt imbre percussae nives* (382–3). The simile recalls the Catullan *tristique imbre madere genae* (68, 56), and is also reminiscent of two Ovidian passages (*Met.* 2, 852–3: *quippe color nivis est, quam nec vestigia duri/calcavere pedis nec solvit aquaticus auster*; and *Am.* 1, 7, 57–8: *suspensaeque diu lacrimae fluxere per ora,/qualiter abiecta de nive manat aqua*); the Senecan simile is simple and easy to visualize, the linguistic register is not particularly elevated (with the exception of the inchoative verb *madescere* used in a metaphorical sense). Furthermore, the insertion of the simile is abrupt and seems to have no other function than to expand on the preceding line. The presence of the verb *iactare* (366: *artusque varie iactat incertus dolor*), which is *vox propria* for pantomime, may be an additional sign of the pantomimic nature of the description.[66]

Love-sick Phaedra was no doubt a very palatable character for the pantomimic dancer; similar to Dido, whose unfortunate love story is attested by Macrobius to have been very popular in pantomimic performances, Phaedra and her burning passion held sway on the pantomimic stage. Lucian (2) attests that the portrayal of love-sick heroines such as Phaedra, Parthenope and Rhodope constituted one of the essential ingredients of pantomime.[67]

Oedipus (915–79): Messenger on Oedipus

A running commentary presenting a handling of an interior scene similar to that found in the *Phaedra* (which involves the description of a past event narrated as taking place at the same time as the narration) also features in the *Oedipus*. Oedipus' self-blinding is clearly reported by a messenger's speech as an event that happened offstage (inside the royal palace): at lines 917–18 the messenger states that Oedipus headed to and entered the palace (*regiam infestus petens/ invisa propero tecta penetravit gradu*).[68]

As in the case of the *Phaedra*, the impression of an event taking place conterminously with the messenger's narration is caused by the shift from the past tense, used just at the very beginning of the narration (916: *deprendit*; 917: *damnavit*; 918: *penetravit*), to the present (which is then used all the way through, with the exception of 935: *haec fatus*, but right after the present *aptat* is used; *dixit* 957 where again the present is immediately resumed with *furit*; the three perfects *gemuit* 961; *torsit* 962; *steterunt* 963 depict an instantaneous action).[69] In the Sophoclean model (1237–85), where the messenger's *rhesis* narrates both Jocasta's suicide and Oedipus' self-inflicted punishment, the past tense is used all the way through.

In addition to this, the impression of immediacy is further strengthened, as the messenger reports extended passages in direct speech, which produces a sort of alternation between the messenger's voice and that of Oedipus:

(915–26): the messenger describes Oedipus stricken by pain;

(926–34): Oedipus' self-exhortation;

(935–6): the messenger describes Oedipus drawing his sword;

(936–56): Oedipus' second self-exhortation including a description of himself in the third person;

(957–5): the messenger describes the self-blinding;

(975–7): Oedipus' supplication to spare his fatherland;

(978–9): the messenger describes Oedipus weeping.

The first description of Oedipus made by the messenger (915–26) depicts the protagonist stricken by pain and is similar in content and style to the descriptions of Phaedra and Medea:

> qualis per arva Libycus insanit leo,
> fulvam minaci fronte concutiens iubam.   920
> vultus furore torvus atque oculi truces,
> gemitus et altum murmur, et gelidus volat
> sudor per artus, spumat et volvit minas
> ac **mersus** alte magnus **exundat** dolor.
> secum ipse saevus grande nescioquid parat   925
> suisque fatis simile.

The description begins with a simile comparing Oedipus to a lion (919–20) and then continues with a list of bodily symptoms produced by the emotions: his face is wild with fury (921: *vultus furore torvus*); his eyes are savage (921: *oculi truces*); he groans and mutters (922: *gemitus et altum murmur*); cold sweat runs over his limbs (922–3: *et gelidus volat/sudor per artus*); he foams from his mouth and spills threats (923: *spumat et volvit minas*); a great pain buried within pours out (924: *ac mersus alte magnus exundat dolor*). The juxtaposition of *mersus* and *exundat* remarkably describes a movement through which the emotion is externalized (in the *Phaedra* there is a similar description of an emotion moving from the inside to the outside 362–3: *inclusus . . . proditur vultu furor*).

The description is followed by Oedipus' self-exhortation not to delay punishment; he then asks himself which kind of punishment will come and destroy his *pectus* (927–8: *hoc scelestum pectus aut ferro petat/aut fervido aliquis igne vel saxo domet*) and compels his *animus* not to fear death (933: *anime, quid mortem times?*).

The messenger briefly describes Oedipus drawing his sword (935–6): *haec fatus aptat impiam capulo manum/ensemque ducit*. The following direct speech of Oedipus contains a long tirade in which the protagonist disputes whether death is a suitable punishment for his crime and a description of himself in the third person (952–7):[70]

>   ... subitus en vultus gravat
>   profusus imber ac rigat fletu genas-
>   et flere satis est? hactenus fundent levem
>   oculi liquorem: sedibus pulsi suis   955
>   lacrimas sequantur. hi maritales statim
>   fodiantur oculi!

Then the messenger resumes his narration and describes Oedipus' self-blinding in the most detailed and graphic way possible (957–75):[71]

>   Dixit atque ira furit:
>   ardent minaces igne truculento genae
>   oculique vix se sedibus retinent suis;
>   violentus audax vultus, iratus ferox   960
>   iamiam eruentis. gemuit et dirum fremens
>   manus in ora torsit; at contra truces
>   oculi steterunt et suam intenti manum
>   ultro insequuntur, vulneri occurrunt suo.
>   scrutatur avidus manibus uncis lumina,   965
>   radice ab ima funditus vulsos simul
>   evolvit orbes; haeret in vacuo manus
>   et fixa penitus unguibus lacerat cavos
>   alte recessus luminum et inanes sinus,
>   saevitque frustra plusque quam satis est furit: 970
>   tantum est periclum lucis. attollit caput
>   cavisque lustrans orbibus caeli plagas
>   noctem experitur. quidquid effossis male
>   dependet oculis rumpit, et victor deos
>   conclamat omnes ...   975

A few lines later the messenger concludes his report with a final description of Oedipus weeping and bleeding from his head (978–9):

>   rigat ora foedus imber, et lacerum caput
>   largum revulsis sanguinem venis vomit.

Seneca's description of the self-blinding is striking in regard to the amount of gruesome and graphic details included. The description owes very little to the

Sophoclean model (1238 ff.); rather the chief inspiring model here is probably Ovid (*Met.* 13, 561–4 the scene between Hecuba and Polymestor): *et digitos in perfida lumina condit/expellitque genis oculos (facit ira potentem)/immergitque manus foedataque sanguine sonti/non lumen (neque enim superest), loca luminis haurit.*

By comparison with his model, it is remarkable that Seneca uses a plethora of different names for eyes as *radix ima, orbes, cavos recessus luminum*, and *inanes sinus*, whereas Ovid has just *lumina* and *oculi*. The use of the verbs is also more graphic in Seneca than in Ovid: *scrutari, vellere, evolvere*, and *lacerare*, whereas Ovid has *condere, expellere, immergere*, and *haurire*. Seneca concludes the description of the self-blinding with a pleonastic amplification (968–9: *cavos/ alte recessus ... inanes sinus*).[72]

As examined in the preceding analysis, Seneca's description of Oedipus' self-blinding is stylistically innovative in the amount of language of corporeality employed; this feature can easily be connected with pantomime in which the language of the body was the means of communication *par excellence*. Such an interpretation is also supported by the fact that the story of Oedipus was a very popular subject in pantomimic performances.[73] For instance, Macrobius (*Saturnalia*, 2, 7, 12 ff.) reports that Hylas danced, not very skilfully according to his master Pylades, the blind Oedipus. Such a climactic moment of the story of Oedipus was understandably well suited to pantomime's preference for emotionally charged themes. Suetonius (*Nero* 21) says that the 'Blinding of Oedipus' was one of the favourite *arias* of Nero's singing repertoire and it is easily conceivable that such arias could actually function as a background to pantomime.[74]

Hercules Oetaeus (233–53): Nurse on Deianira[75]

The second act of the *Hercules Oetaeus* begins with a long description of Deianira in the grip of jealousy made by the nurse (233–53).

O quam cruentus feminas stimulat furor,	
cum patuit una paelici et nuptae domus!	
Scylla et Charybdis Sicula contorquens freta	235
minus est timenda, nulla non melior fera est.	
namque ut reluxit paelicis captae decus	
et fulsit Iole qualis innubis dies	
purisve clarum noctibus sidus micat,	
stetit furenti similis ac torvum intuens	240

Herculea coniunx, feta ut Armenia iacens
sub rupe tigris hoste conspecto exilit,
aut iussa thyrsum quatere conceptum ferens
Maenas Lyaeum dubia quo gressus agat
haesit parumper. tum per Herculeos lares   245
attonita fertur, tota vix satis est domus;[76]
incurrit, errat, sistit, in vultus dolor
processit omnis, pectori paene intimo
nihil est relictum; fletus insequitur minas.
nec unus habitus durat aut uno furit   250
contenta vultu: nunc inardescunt genae,
pallor ruborem pellit et formas dolor
errat per omnes; queritur, implorat, gemit.

Such a violent portrayal of Deianira is lacking in Sophocles' *Women of Trachis*, the antecedent on which the Senecan play is modelled. While Sophocles stresses the destructive force of uncontrolled passion in connection with Hercules' seizure of Iole, the author of the *Oetaeus* transfers it to Deianira.[77] Her *furor* resembles thus very closely that of Medea and Phaedra on one hand, and that of Juno on the other.

As Watson has remarked, Deianira assumes the role of Juno and thus becomes a second Juno; in doing so, she also takes on the role of *noverca*, recalling closely the portrayal of the jealous Juno enraged by the accomplishments of her stepson Hercules in the prologue of the *Hercules furens*. This novel characterization of Deianira, which combines stereotypical characteristics of women swept away by fierce erotic passions and jealous women at large (either heroines betrayed by their husbands or cruel stepmothers), seems prompted by the popularity of the theme of jealousy and adultery in mime and pantomime.[78] For what concerns pantomime, Lucian (50) attests that Deianira's jealousy (Δηϊανείρας ζηλοτυπίαν) and its outcome, Hercules' death on Oeta, was a common subject in pantomimic performances.[79] Lucian's emphasis on Deianira's jealousy seems suggestively to match the portrayal of the jealous Deianira we find in the *Oetaeus* and which is not so prominent in Sophocles' *Women of Trachis*. Even more importantly, Lucian's phrasing seems to hint at the fact that Deianira's jealousy constituted the most important element in the pantomimic adaptation of this myth.

Different from the cases discussed in the *Phaedra* and in the *Oedipus*, where the character's actions take place offstage, in the case of the *Hercules Oetaeus* the action takes place in part onstage and in part offstage. In fact, the nurse, after having described Deianira's onstage actions, remarks that the queen enters into the palace (245–6: *tum per Herculeos lares/attonita fertur*). The most extended and detailed part of the description of Deianira takes place offstage, while in the previous lines, the nurse just expresses some generalizing thoughts about the threat jealous women can be (233–5) and compares Deianira's behaviour to that of a tiger and a maenad (241–5). In relation to the time at which Deianira's actions take place, we find the same ambiguity observed in the *Phaedra* and in the *Oedipus*. The nurse begins her speech in the past (237: *namque ut reluxit*; 238: *fulsit*; 240: *stetit*) and then switches to the present (the simile is all in the present apart from 245: *haesit* and 248: *processit*, which are instantaneous perfect; 246: *fertur*; 247: *incurrit, errat, sistit*; 249: *est, insequitur*; 250: *durat, furit*; 251: *inardescunt*; 252: *pellit*; 252: *errat, queritur, implorat, gemit*).[80]

Deianira's attack of jealousy is provoked by the view of Hercules' new mistress, Iole. Deianira sees Iole in all her beauty and is overwhelmed by *furor*, which makes her freeze (240: *stetit*) and glare savagely (240: *torvum intuens*); after the sudden halt, Deianira bursts into undirected movements that are compared to those of a tiger's cub scared by a foe (241–2: *feta ut Armenia iacens/sub rupe tigris hoste conspecto exilit*) and those of an excited maenad who does not know where to direct her steps (243–5: *aut iussa thyrsum quatere conceptum ferens/Maenas Lyaeum dubia quo gressus agat/haesit parumper*); she then rushes into the house and there she charges forward (247: *incurrit*), she roams (247: *errat*), she stops (247: *sistit*); all her pain is in her face (247–8: *in vultus dolor/processit omnis*); almost nothing is left hidden in her breast (248–9: *pectori paene intimo/nihil est relictum*); then the nurse describes how her attitude is unstable and constantly changing: tears follow threats (249: *fletus insequitur minas*), a single attitude does not last long (250: *nec unus habitus durat*); the mental changes are paralleled by the alternation of her complexion between pallor and redness: her cheeks are inflamed (251: *nunc inardescunt genae*), pallor expels redness (252: *pallor ruborem pellit*); her pain roams through every possible form (252–3: *formas dolor/errat per omnes*); she laments (253: *queritur*), she begs (253: *implorat*), she groans (253: *gemit*). The last three verbs are used in asyndeton as at line 247 (*incurrit, errat, sistit*); this construction is recurrently employed in running commentaries, since it conveys the impression of speed and immediacy.[81]

Agamemnon (867–909): Cassandra on Agamemnon

The fourth act of Seneca's *Agamemnon* opens with Cassandra's foreshadowing of Agamemnon's murder at the hands of Clytemnestra and Aegisthus (867–908). The prophetess relates in a detailed and graphic descriptive monologue the clairvoyant vision she is having. It is worth looking at her monologue more closely (867–909) since the handling of the scene as described by her words presents some ambiguities in relation to spatial and temporal location.[82]

As to spatial location, Cassandra's words seem to imply that the vision of Agamemnon's murder takes place inside her mind: *Res agitur intus magna* (867); the word *intus* seems to indicate so and this would seem confirmed by the following lines 868–9 (*anime, consurge et cape/pretium furoris*) and 872–4 (*tam clara numquam providae mentis furor/ostendit oculis: video et intersum et fruor;/ imago visus dubia non fallit meos*). Yet, there is then an obstacle to this interpretation caused by Cassandra's following exclamation at line 875: *spectemus!*

As Boyle has remarked, the verb *spectare* has a specifically theatrical connotation, for it is properly used for the viewing of theatrical entertainments by an audience. In addition to this, the *vox propria* usually used to indicate prophetic visions is *cerno*.[83] Because of this, it is not clear whether Cassandra is seeing something going on in her vision, or she is seeing something actually taking place. Tarrant has advanced the hypothesis that Cassandra might be peering through the door of the palace, but he does not find tragic parallels for such an action and only one case in New Comedy, in which, however, the character peering from the door is offstage and only later relates to the characters onstage what he has seen.[84] Apart from the difficulty of finding a tragic parallel, Tarrant observes that peering through a door is an action suitable for a comic character, but it would be quite ludicrous for a tragic character and even more so for Cassandra, who has the gift of prophecy.

As to temporal location, Cassandra is seeing a vision in her mind which has its fulfilment at the very moment she is having it; the two actions happen simultaneously. This is confirmed by the fact that right after the conclusion of Cassandra's speech, Electra addresses to her brother Orestes words that imply that Agamemnon has been murdered (910: *Fuge, o paternae mortis auxilium unicum*).

The simultaneous narration of actions taking place inside has no antecedents in Greek tragedy; the only parallel handling of such a scene is to be found in a papyrus fragment of postclassical tragedy, which involves an account delivered by Cassandra on the wall of Troy about the confrontation between Achilles and Hector.[85] However, there is no parallel for the peculiar ambiguity provided by the Senecan passage that fits the prophetic vision of the killing with the actual killing itself. If this is the case, we can move a step further and propose that Cassandra is actually viewing the performance of the killing, a fact that is strongly suggested by the presence of the word *spectemus* (875); in a way, Cassandra acquires the stance of an external narrator who describes the actions as they unfold.

Noticeable is also the detailed and graphic nature of Cassandra's description, especially if we think that the vision is supposed to happen in her mind; the graphic quality of the passage under discussion emerges even more strikingly when compared with the first clairvoyant vision of Agamemnon's killing that Cassandra has in the previous act; in fact, in this case, even though the killing of the Greek leader is foreseen, it is hinted at only briefly and in a very allusive and metaphoric way, which stylistically matches the clairvoyant nature of the vision (lines 734–40):

> Quid ista vecors tela feminea manu
> destricta praefert? quem petit dextra virum   735
> Lacaena cultu, ferrum Amazonium gerens?
> quae versat oculos alia nunc facies meos?
> victor ferarum colla summissus iacet
> ignobili sub dente Marmarici lupi,
> morsus cruentos passus audacis leae.   740

In contrast, in the second occurrence, Cassandra describes realistically the whole setting and every single step of the action in detail; the description moves from the depiction of the royal hall in which a banquet has been prepared for Agamemnon (875: *epulae regia instructae domo*), the portrayal of the king reclining on a red couch dressed with Priam's robe (877–80: *ostro lectus Iliaco nitet/merumque in auro veteris Assaraci trahunt./et ipse picta veste sublimis iacet,/ Priami superbas corpore exuvias gerens*), the removal of the enemy's garment (881–3: *Detrahere cultus uxor hostiles iubet,/induere potius coniugis fidae manu/ textos amictus*), and the putting on of the treacherous attire that Clytemnestra has woven for him and in whose folds Agamemnon will finally be entangled (887–9: *mortifera vinctum perfidae tradit neci/induta vestis: exitum manibus negant/caputque laxi et invii claudunt sinus*).

As the narration of Cassandra progresses towards the climactic moment of the killing, her words increasingly gain in focus: she describes the first blow given to Agamemnon by the trembling hand of Aegisthus (890–1: *haurit trementi semivir dextra latus,/nec penitus egit: vulnere in medio stupet*) and his freezing in the middle of the striking; she then lingers on depicting Agamemnon's attempts to free himself from the bindings of the treacherous garment which, instead, tighten the folds more; in describing this, Cassandra resorts to an extended simile which compares the king to a boar caught in a net.[86] Then Cassandra focuses on Clytemnestra striking the fatal blow and hitting Agamemnon in different parts of the body;[87] also in this case, Cassandra employs an extended simile to describe Clytemnestra's actions comparing her with a *sacerdos* attending a sacrifice.[88] The death of the king is stylistically framed with the use of gladiatorial language *habet, peractum est* (901).[89]

Such a detailed description together with the ambiguous handling of spatial and temporal coordinates prompts the question as to its intended function. The above-mentioned features could well have been employed to perform onstage something which is, in fact, just taking place in Cassandra's mind; if this is the case, the scene of Cassandra's vision of the killing of Agamemnon seems suitable to be enacted as a 'silent performance' narrated by Cassandra's words. Such a peculiar handling may then reflect the influence of the aesthetics of pantomimic performances, in which the dancer performed silently the story told in the libretto as sung by the chorus or a soloist.[90]

The scene of Cassandra's vision could be defined, by using a modern terminology that increasingly scholars find appropriate for Seneca's tragedy, as a case of metatheatre.[91] Boyle has underlined the pervasively metatheatrical nature of Seneca's plays and how this aspect of Seneca's tragedies was influential on the Renaissance playwrights.[92]

Medea (670–751): Nurse on Medea

The fourth act of the *Medea* is given over to two monologues, one of the nurse (670–751) and the other of Medea. Both speeches involve the description of the preparation of the poison in which Medea will dip the lethal garment for Creusa; basically, the two speeches duplicate each other. Additionally, this large expansion into a secondary event, which becomes the major focus of the act, causes a minimum progression of the main plot. In relation to dramatic technique, the speech of the nurse describing Medea's preparation of the poison presents the frequently found ambiguity in relation to the place and the time at which it takes place. We infer from the nurse's words (675–6: *ut attonito gradu/evasit et penetrale funestum attigit*) that the action of Medea's incantation scene takes place inside the innermost part of her house (*penetrale*); as the description of the nurse goes on, it seems that Medea is onstage since the nurse repeatedly uses demonstrative pronouns (686: *hic*; 694: *huc*; 720: *illas*; 721: *has, illa*; 723: *has*; 724: *illas, has*; 728: *haec*; 729: *illius*; 730: *huius*), which seem to point out that Medea is gathering herbs onstage and under the eyes of the nurse. Furthermore, since the nurse uses the past tense at the beginning of her speech, it seems that she is remembering what she saw Medea doing inside the house and is now reporting it to the audience; but soon the nurse switches from the past tense (676: *evasit, attigit*; 677: *effudit*; 705: *evocavit*) to the present tense (678: *promit, explicat*) thus giving the impression of actions taking place at the moment she is speaking.[93] The impression of the nurse's speech being contemporaneous to Medea's actions seems to be confirmed by the presence of the demonstrative pronouns. In addition, the description is so lengthy and detailed that it does not seem plausible that the nurse can just remember by heart all the steps in the preparation of the poison as well as Medea's own words reported in direct speech.[94] A possible solution for the scene may be to imagine that the nurse sees what Medea is doing inside the house and reports it to the audience, but this would not solve the difficulty of the presence of the many demonstrative pronouns. The whole scene seems simply to be extremely fluid in place and time.[95] The scene makes sense if the nurse describes Medea's actions as taking place just in the background of the stage and this background is meant to be understood as inside the house. Thus, Medea's actions are then actually performed onstage and narrated by the nurse.

The incantation scene consists of different phases and actions in the preparation of the poison which the nurse describes at length: first Medea gathers the magical tools she has in stock (677–9) and then those that must be summoned from a distance (680–4): she pours out her magical resources and brings forth everything she has long feared herself (677–8: *totas opes effudit, et quidquid diu/ etiam ipsa timuit promit*); she deploys all her evils (678–9: *omnem explicat/turbam malorum*); she makes prayer at the sinister shrine with her left hand (680–1: *et triste laeva comprecans sacrum manu/pestes vocat*);[96] she summons a scaly throng (685: *squamifera turba*) which then approaches (*adest*). The fact that Medea prays with her left hand is worth noticing (there are several instances in the tragedies in which Seneca uses the word *manus*, or more specifically the word *dextra*, but this is the only occurrence of a reference to the left hand), since it is attested that in the ancient world it was customary to pray with both hands and, even more importantly, the use of the left hand was sinister.[97] The use of left hand is, instead, well attested in the preparation of magical sacrifices by magicians.[98] The gesture is thus fully appropriate to Medea since she is making a sinister prayer before attending to the preparation of a magical concoction. The nurse then describes the snakes called forth by Medea (686–90): she opens the description with the adverb *hic*, which points to the fact that the serpent is there; the snake hauls its body (686: *corpus immensum trahit*) and flicks out its three-forked tongue (687: *trifidamque linguam exertat*); as soon as it hears Medea's spell, it is mesmerised and twines its swollen body into folds upon folds and forces it into coils (689–90: *tumidumque nodis corpus aggestis plicat/cogitque in orbes*).

This section is then expanded by Medea's direct speech summoning mythological snakes and a constellation (690–704): Draco (the Northern constellation compared to a river, 694–5) whose coils are felt by the Greater and Lesser Bear (695–6); Ophiulcus (698–9); Python (700); the Hydra of Lerna (701–2); the Colchian dragon (703–4).

In the subsequent section, the nurse describes Medea gathering herbs for her concoction (706: *congerit*; 719: *attrectat manu*). This section is again expanded by a detailed list of plants, which specifies the place from where they come from (707–27) or the manner of collection (728–30);[99] the section of the list involving the description of the manner of collection of the plants is characterized by a recurrent use of demonstrative pronouns (720: *illas*; 721: *has, illa*; 723: *has*; 724: *illas, has*; 728: *haec*; 729: *illius*; 730: *huius*), as if the nurse were pointing out herbs that are in front of her eyes; as soon as the herbs are gathered, Medea crumbles them (731: *Mortifera carpit gramina*), bleeds the venom from the snakes (731–2: *ac serpentium/saniem exprimit*), and mixes everything with the entrails of different birds (732–4: *miscetque et obscenas aves/maestique cor bubonis et raucae strigis/exsecta vivae viscera*); she then separates the concoction in two parts (734–5: *haec scelerum artifex/discreta ponit*, the sense of the line is obscure), and finally she sings her magical formulae (737: *addit venenis verba*).

As far as we know, Medea's incantation scene is unique in extant classical tragedy.[100] Seneca must have strongly felt the spectacular appeal that such a scene could provide with its expansion into the supernatural and horrific; similarly, the description of the necromancy and extispicy in the *Oedipus*, which has no counterpart in its model, Sophocles' *Oedipus*, allowed analogous sensational effects. As discussed in Chapter 1, the representation of wonders and horrors was highly favoured in pantomimic performances.

Phoenissae (427–42): Messenger on Jocasta

The third act of the *Phoenissae* features an opening monologue of Jocasta (363–86) followed by an intervention of a messenger (387–402) who compels the queen to stop lamenting and act quickly to prevent the impending fight of her two sons (387–9: *Regina, dum tu flebiles questus cies/terisque tempus, saeva nudatis adest/acies in armis*). The messenger then describes in detail the battlefield and the armies ready to attack by actually pointing them out to Jocasta (394: *vide*). So the scene must be envisaged as taking place on the battlements of the royal palace, from where the messenger and Jocasta are able to see the offstage actions.[101] A few lines later, after Antigone's intervention, which includes an appeal to her mother and an additional description of the battle, the messenger (427–42) describes Jocasta leaving for the battlefield (426) and her subsequent offstage action there (from 427 onwards):

> Vadit furenti similis aut etiam furit.
> sagitta qualis Parthica velox **manu**
> excussa fertur, qualis insano ratis
> premente vento rapitur aut qualis cadit   430
> delapsa caelo stella, cum stringens polum
> rectam citatis ignibus rumpit viam,
> attonita cursu fugit et binas statim
> diduxit acies. victa materna prece
> haesere bella, iamque in alternam necem   435
> illinc et hinc miscere cupientes **manus**
> librata **dextra** tela suspensa tenent.
> paci favetur, omnium ferrum latet
> cessatque tectum-vibrat in fratrum **manu**.
> laniata canas mater ostendit comas,   440
> rogat abnuentes, irrigat fletu genas.
> negare matri, qui diu dubitat, potest.

Such a handling of a scene has no antecedent in classical drama and it is also unique within the Senecan *corpus*, since it describes simultaneous onstage and offstage actions that require a change of setting;[102] in fact, the setting described as offstage becomes the actual setting of the scene that follows. As Tarrant has observed 'the physical limitations of the ancient theater seem completely left behind'.[103]

Seneca opens the description of Jocasta with a long simile, comparing the queen rushing into the middle of the two armies to an arrow (428–9: *sagitta qualis Parthica velox manu/excussa fertur*), to a ship whirled by the wind (429–30: *qualis insano ratis/premente vento rapitur*), and then to a shooting star falling from the sky (430–1: *qualis cadit/delapsa caelo stella*).[104] Seneca then turns to describe the effect produced by Jocasta's prayer on the armies (434–9) and then back to Jocasta again: she displays and tears her hair (440: *laniata canas mater ostendit comas*), she begs as they shake their heads (441), and she cries (441: *irrigat fletu genas*).[105]

The fluid handling of space in the battlefield scene of the *Phoenissae* is an extreme case in Senecan tragedies. However, Seneca never seems to be much concerned with a realistic handling of time and space.

As a general tendency, offstage running commentaries show features that are to be found even in narrative set-pieces, a category which will be analysed in the last chapter. Both in the handling of offstage running commentaries and in narrative set-pieces, Seneca seems to stick to the tragic tradition of messenger's speeches reporting offstage actions; but, at the same time, he seems to change and adapt the convention to his own dramaturgical goals. Basically, Seneca just maintained the typical and well-recognizable building frame of this conventional messenger scene in its more general and distinctive features. For instance, the tendency to begin the descriptions in the past tense and then to shift it to the present as well as the ambiguity between exterior and interior seems to point out that Seneca was well aware of the traditional features of the convention of messenger's speeches, but he reshaped it by setting the narration in the present and moving onstage what was usually suggested as happening or had happened offstage (the case of Oedipus' self-blinding illustrates this point well). Even more importantly, all the events dealt with are extremely spectacular and constitute climactic moments of the plot, which are narrated with a plethora of visual details.

As an overall tendency, this may be explained as a feature borrowed from pantomimic performances, which, as discussed in the first chapter, tended to invade the onstage space with the intense and violent actions which, in tragedy, were relegated to offstage space.[106]

Monologues of Self-analysis

Introduction

In Seneca's tragedies, monologues are numerous. As has been discussed in Chapter 2, the preponderantly monologic nature of Seneca's tragedy is a feature possibly prompted by pantomime, which, as the evidence suggests, was a performance of a predominantly soloistic nature and favoured the dramatization of emotional dilemmas. Grysar has suggested that pantomimic libretti contained a high proportion of monologues.[1] Thus the influence of the aesthetics of pantomime on Seneca's tragedies can be seen working at the level of structure, since the plays are built along an alternation of monologues, and in one category of monologues in particular, i.e. monologues of self-analysis in which a character gives an extended and detailed self-description of the divided feelings he is experiencing.[2] Monologues of self-analysis are to be found already in Euripides, but, as Gill has argued, there is a substantial difference between the handling of this type of monologue in Euripides and Seneca; in Euripides monologues retain the character of a dialogue (i.e. they are addressed to others), while in Seneca monologues have a 'soliloquizing' and 'self-related (even solipsistic) character'.[3] Gill has further argued that 'the obsessively interior character of the Senecan monologue constitutes a deliberate realization of a certain kind of figure in a distinctive dramatic style, and not a failed attempt to create a real character who interacts with other such characters'.[4]

I would suggest that monologues of self-analysis recall closely, share common stylistic features of, and have the same function as running commentaries. The most important element that connects them with running commentaries is the fact that they seem uttered by an external narrator (running commentaries are actually pronounced by other characters). In addition, this type of monologue (as well as running commentaries) has no real dramatic function but to portray, often redundantly, emotional dilemmas (as in the case of the *Phaedra*) in which the pathetic element is over-emphasized. As observed by Tarrant, a striking feature of Seneca's monologues involving self-description is that they feature a 'combination of emotional chaos and detached intellectual analysis'.[5] The fact that a character in a frantic state describes his/her inner turmoil in a detailed and analytic manner produces the impression that the character becomes virtually an external narrator of his/her own psychic state. On the same line of thought, Gill claims that in monologues of self-analysis 'the immediate effect is of a narrator's voice over, analysing the psychological conflict of the figure involved'.[6] The impression of a narrator's voice is strengthened by the use of a peculiar stylistic device, namely a shift from first-person to narrative self-description in third-person form; the impression of an external narrator's voice is further enhanced by the use of epic similes and of a large number of personified abstractions.[7] As to similes, their use is usually circumscribed in dramatic speech; for example, Euripides employs very carefully just brief similes.[8] Seneca's characters, on the contrary, employ extended and artificial similes;[9] in addition to this, similes are not only used by a character describing the attitudes of another one, but, most awkwardly, also in the case of a character describing himself/herself. A good example of extended similes used by a character to describe another one is in the *Agamemnon* (892–6) where Cassandra employs it to describe Agamemnon: *at ille, ut altis hispidus silvis aper/cum casse vinctus temptat egressus tamen/artatque motu vincla et in cassum furit,/cupit fluentes undique et caecos sinus/dissicere et hostem quaerit implicitus suum*. As discussed above, Seneca heavily strains psychological realism by putting similes in the mouth of a character who uses them to describe himself/herself; for instance, in the *Trojan Women* (672–7), Andromache uses an extended simile to describe herself:

> qualis Argolicas ferox
> turmas Amazon stravit, aut qualis deo
> percussa Maenas entheo silvas gradu
> armata thyrso terret atque expers sui   675
> vulnus dedit nec sensit, in medios ruam
> tumuloque cineris socia defenso cadam.

In the *Thyestes*, Atreus employs an extended simile in his self-description (497–505):

> sic, cum feras vestigat et longo sagax
> loro tenetur Umber ac presso vias
> scrutatur ore, dum procul lento suem
> odore sentit, paret et tacito locum   500

rostro pererrat; praeda cum propior fuit,
cervice tota pugnat et gemitu vocat
dominum morantem seque retinenti eripit.
cum sperat ira sanguinem, nescit tegi
tamen tegatur.   505

As to the use of abstracts (such as *dolor, furor, pudor, amor, timor, ira*), they are usually described as personified and tend to become external and active forces outside the character; stylistically, such an impression is provided by the fact that the abstracts are actually subjects of active verbs. An example of this feature is to be found in the *Thyestes*, in a passage in which Thyestes is describing his feeling (942–4): *quid me revocas/festumque vetas celebrare diem,/quid flere iubes,/nulla surgens dolor ex causa?* A similar case features in the *Agamemnon* (288–90 Clytemnestra): *Surgit residuus pristinae mentis pudor;/quid obstrepis?quid voce blandiloqua mala/consilia dictas?*; in the *Phaedra* (99 Phaedra): *Sed maior alius incubat maestae dolor*; in the *Trojan Women* (642 Andromache): *Quid agimus?animum distrahit geminus timor*; and in the *Medea* (916–17 Medea): *Quo te igitur, ira, mittis, aut quae perfido/intendis hosti tela?*.[10] Furthermore, the fact that the characters describe the symptomatic reactions that the feelings provoke in their bodies sharpens the impression that they are external spectators of what is happening; for example, in the *Hercules furens* (1298–9 Amphitryon): *Ecce quam miserum metu/cor palpitat pectusque sollicitum ferit*; or in the *Trojan Women* (623–4 Andromache): *Reliquit animus membra, quatiuntur, labant,/torpetque vinctus frigido sanguis gelu*; or in the *Medea* (926–8 Medea): *Cor pepulit horror, membra torpescunt gelu/pectusque tremuit.* All these features have as a result that the protagonist 'has become the narrator of her experiences instead of a speaking character', since the voices of speaking character and narrator tend to merge.[11]

Unlike running commentaries, the fact that the monologues are uttered by the character himself/herself may be accounted as a variation between speaking voices, which might have been rendered with different intonations from the part of the singer of the tragic libretto. For example, in the case of the *Phaedra*, we have a running commentary spoken by the nurse (360–86) followed by a monologue of Phaedra (387–403). Even in the *Medea* we have a similar handling; a running commentary spoken by the nurse (670–739) and a following monologue by Medea (740–848). Interestingly, the nurse describes Medea's preparation of the poison and then Medea describes it again. Basically, the two speeches describe and expand on the same theme: Medea's witchcraft. The theme itself is very suitable for pantomime; first of all because it is spectacular and offers potential for virtuoso display. Dramatically, the length of the scene and the tangential relevance of the events for the advancement of the plot points suggestively in this direction. Here the change of voices may have been made clearer by the fact that Medea's utterance happens in lyric metre, while that of the nurse is in the dialogic one. The different metrical pattern is quite suggestive; since lyric delivery is often associated with a state of mental turmoil (as, for example, in Euripides, *Alc* 244–72 and *Hipp* 208–39; Aeschylus *Ag* 1085 ff.), the metrical shift may have the purpose of underlining the mood of Medea's utterance. This interpretation better explains the function of the recurring use of monologues often dismissively labelled as mere rhetorical expansion.

As previously discussed, this type of monologue primarily deals with a dramatization of emotions in the same way that running commentaries do. However, unlike running commentaries, which usually describe the effect of a single emotion experienced by the characters, monologues tend to deal with a dramatization of conflicting emotions: for example, in the *Phaedra* the conflict between Phaedra's illicit passion for her stepson and her *pudor*; in the *Agamemnon*, the conflict between Clytemnestra's passion for her new lover, jealousy of her unfaithful husband and bridal *pudor* (Clytemnestra's conflict is the one which involves several different feelings and not just the more frequent emotional dichotomy); in the *Thyestes*, the conflict portrayed is between fear and joy; in the *Trojan Women*, the conflict at play is between bridal and maternal love.

It is easy to understand that monologues are the most suitable means to portray such conflicts, which are more plausibly narrated by the same characters that experience them. Running commentaries are best suited to describe the effect of a single emotion, which expresses itself in its outward physical manifestation and can thus be described also by an external narrator. Nonetheless, the two dramatic devices perform the same function, especially because monologues tend to be delivered as if by the voice of an external narrator.

Stylistically, the monologues present features similar to those of running commentaries, such as the tendency to externalize the emotions by using several abstracts as subjects of active verbs, to refer constantly to bodily parts, and to make large use of extended epic similes. In relation to similes, the limited variety of comparisons that occurred in the running commentaries is further reduced in the monologues; basically one comparison is employed and adapted with slight variations on the same theme, namely that between a character and a ship swept by the force of a stormy sea: **Phae** (181–4) *sic, cum gravatam navita adversa ratem/propellit unda, cedit in vanum labor/et victa prono puppis aufertur vado./ quid ratio possit?*; **Ag** (138–40) *Fluctibus variis agor,/ut, cum hinc profundum*

ventus, hinc aestus rapit,/incerta dubitat unda cui cedat malo; **Med** (939–43)
anceps aestus incertam rapit;/ut saeva rapidi bella cum venti gerunt,/utrimque
fluctus maria discordes agunt/dubiumque fervet pelagus, haud aliter meum/cor
fluctuatur; **Thy** (438–9) *sic concitatam remige et velo ratem/aestus resistens remigi*
et velo refert.

The simile is well suited to portray in a dynamic way the pulling in different
directions of the emotional conflicts undergone by the characters. As in the
running commentaries, the linguistic register is stereotyped and repetitious and
the syntax adopts a staccato mode produced by rare use of connectives,
preference for paratactic and asyndetic constructions, and limited use of
subordinate clauses. The overall impression produced by these devices is that of
a *sermo praeruptus*, which matches the mental turmoil suffered by the characters.

The passages are the following and it is worth analysing them in detail:

- *Phaedra* (99–144; 177–94): Phaedra's self-analysis
- *Agamemnon* (131–44): Clytemnestra's self-analysis
- *Medea* (926–8; 937–44; 951–3): Medea's self-analysis
- *Thyestes* (434–9; 496–505; 920–69): Thyestes' self-analysis
- *Trojan Women* (642–62): Andromache's self-analysis

Phaedra (99–144; 177–94): Phaedra's Self-analysis

The first act of the *Phaedra* contains two passages in which Phaedra gives a
lengthy narrative self-analysis of her emotional feelings (99–114; 177–94):

(Lines 99–113):
Sed maior alius incubat maestae dolor.
non me quies nocturna, non altus sopor   100
solvere curis. alitur et crescit malum
et ardet intus, qualis Aetnaeo vapor
exundat antro. Palladis telae vacant
et inter ipsas pensa labuntur manus;
non colere donis templa votivis libet,   105
non inter aras, Atthidum mixtam choris,
iactare tacitis conscias sacris faces,
nec adire castis precibus aut ritu pio
adiudicatae praesidem terrae deam:
iuvat excitatas consequi cursu feras   110

et rigida molli gaesa iaculari manu.
Quo tendis, anime? quid furens saltus amas?
fatale miserae matris agnosco malum;

(Lines 177–85):
　　　　　　... Quae memoras scio
vera esse, nutrix; sed furor cogit sequi
peiora. vadit animus in praeceps sciens
remeatque frustra sana consilia appetens.　　　　　　　　　　　180
sic, cum gravatam navita adversa ratem
propellit unda, cedit in vanum labor
et victa prono puppis aufertur vado.
quid ratio possit? vicit ac regnat furor,
potensque tota mente dominatur deus.　　　　　　　　　　　　185

The first passage (85–128) falls in the category of entrance monologues; Phaedra's emotional speech begins *in medias res* and does not provide any information about the facts which caused it.[12] It does not address anyone in particular, so that the speech is delivered in a void. We learn by her words that she is afflicted by a fierce and tormenting love. She does not even mention the name of her beloved in all the passage. We implicitly infer that he must be Hippolytus because she affirms that she forgot about all her female duties and lists what her preferred pursuits are now (110–11: *iuvat excitatas consequi cursu feras/et rigida molli gaesa iaculari manu*), namely her desire to hunt.[13] Both passages belong to the category of 'passion-restraint' act, which is a recurring dramatic situation adopted by Seneca.[14] Usually, a subordinate character (the nurse or the *satelles*) is in charge to mitigate and restrain the destructive and foolish emotions and desires of a major character.

The passages are heavily modelled on and reminiscent of Virgil (*Aen.* 4) and Ovid (*Heroides* 4). Seneca actually blended Virgilian and Ovidian motifs and poetic colouring.[15] The first passage is much indebted to Virgil's description of Dido.[16]

Both passages feature two similes; the one in the first passage is short, while that in the second is extended. The first simile (102–3: *qualis Aetnaeo vapor/exundat antro*) compares the fire of love to that of Etna; the fire as imagery of love had a long literary tradition and is adopted repeatedly in the passages; the simile is borrowed from two Ovidian ones and reworked (*Her.* 15, 12: *me calor Aetnaeo non minor igne tenet*; and *Met.* 13, 867–9: *uror enim, laesusque exaestuat acrius ignis,/cumque suis videor translatam viribus Aetnen/pectore ferre meo*). Seneca's simile does not contain any reference to Phaedra experiencing a personal emotion; on the contrary, it is the *malum* itself that overflows as the fire of Etna. The extended simile (181–3) in the second passage is closely modelled on Virgil (*Geor.* 1, 201–3): *non aliter quam qui adverso vix flumine lembum/remigiis subigit, si bracchia forte remisit,/atque illum in praeceps prono rapit alveus amni.* As Fantham has pointed out, Seneca adhered closely in syntax and word sequence to the Virgilian model. There is also an echoing of words as *adverso ... flumine* corresponds with *adversa ... unda* and *prono ... amni* with *prono ... vado.* Nonetheless, the linguistic register chosen by Seneca avoids elevated or rare words (such as the Virgilian *lembum* where Seneca uses the more common *ratem*) and prefers simple and plain ones, as, for example, *navita, ratem, puppis, vado.*[17] There is also an echo of Ovid (*Am.* 2, 4, 8: *auferor ut rapida concita puppis aqua*); interestingly, Seneca substitutes the first person singular verb (*auferor*) with the third person (*aufert* whose subject is in Seneca *puppis*), so that the comparison set out by the simile remains impersonal. Several abstracts feature in the two passages. In the first one we find, *dolor* (*dolor ... incubat*) and *malum* (*non me quies nocturna, non altus sopor/solvere curis; malum ... alitur, crescit, ardet*).[18] In the second passage, *furor* is the active force that takes hold of Phaedra (*furor ... cogit sequi/peiora; vadit animus in praeceps; vicit ac regnat furor,/potensque tota mente dominatur deus*).[19] The abstracts are always subjects of active verbs, apart from one instance in which the passive *alitur* is used, but with a reflexive meaning.

Agamemnon (131–44): Clytemnestra's Self-analysis

Clytemnestra's self-analysis takes place in the second act of the *Agamemnon*, which features a confrontation between Clytemnestra and the nurse who attempts to restrain the queen (a passion-restraint scene).

> Maiora cruciant quam ut moras possim pati.
> flammae medullas et cor exurunt meum;
> mixtus dolori subdidit stimulos timor;
> invidia pulsat pectus, hinc animum iugo
> premit cupido turpis et vinci vetat;
> et inter istas mentis obsessae faces
> fessus quidem et devictus et pessumdatus
> pudor rebellat. fluctibus variis agor,
> ut, cum hinc profundum ventus, hinc aestus rapit,

135

incerta dubitat unda cui cedat malo.   140
proinde omisi regimen e manibus meis:
quocumque me ira, quo dolor, quo spes feret,
hoc ire pergam; fluctibus dedimus ratem.
ubi animus errat, optimum est casum sequi.

According with Senecan practice, Clytemnestra adopts an epic simile to describe the contrasting feelings she is experiencing (139: *ut, cum hinc profundum ventus, hinc aestus rapit,/incerta dubitat unda cui cedat malo*).[20] The nautical metaphor, which is one of the most favoured by Seneca, is employed again at 141, *proinde omisi regimen e manibus meis*, and at 143, *fluctibus dedimus ratem*. Clytemnestra's self-analysis is particularly rich in abstracts, which contributes to give to the description what Tarrant has defined as a 'combination of emotional chaos and detached intellectual analysis':[21] *timor* (*subdidit*), 133; *invidia* (*pulsat*), 134; *cupido* (*premit*), 135; *pudor* (*rebellat*), 138 with three adjectives: *fessus, devictus, pessumdatus; ira, dolor, spes* (*feret*), 142; *animus* (*errat*), 144.

Medea (926–8; 937–44; 951–3): Medea's Self-analysis

(Lines 926–8):
Cor pepulit horror, membra torpescunt gelu
pectusque tremuit. ira discessit loco
materque tota coniuge expulsa redit.

(Lines 937–44):
quid, anime, titubas? ora quid lacrimae rigant
variamque nunc huc ira, nunc illuc amor
diducit? anceps aestus incertam rapit;
ut saeva rapidi bella cum venti gerunt,   940
utrimque fluctus maria discordes agunt
dubiumque fervet pelagus, haud aliter meum
cor fluctuatur: ira pietatem fugat
iramque pietas. cede pietati, dolor.

(Lines 951–3):
       ... rursus increscit dolor
et fervet odium, repetit invitam manum
antiqua Erinys. ira, qua ducis, sequor.

In the final act of the *Medea*, the protagonist delivers an extremely long monologue (893–977), which has its culmination in the killing of one of her sons (970–1); the monologue dramatizes the conflict between Medea's maternal feelings and her desire to take revenge on Jason's betrayal and emphasizes the 'quick swerving of her thoughts into opposite directions'.[22]

At the end of her speech, the hatred for Jason prevails and Medea accomplishes her revenge. Strangely, the climax of the scene is not made clear by the words (at lines 970–1: *victima manes tuos/placamus ista* she here refers to the shadow of her brother Absyrtus); only at line 974, do the words explicitly provide a clue that Medea has perpetrated the *scelus*, since she claims that the killing has begun (*caede incohata*).[23] As to dramatic technique, the fact that Medea kills the sons onstage has raised a huge debate among scholars; according to the practice in Greek theatre and to the precepts of Aristotle and Horace, death ought not to be shown onstage. If we think that Seneca may have been influenced by pantomimic performances, which emphasized and gave central place to such displays, the difficulty may be easily resolved. A dancer may have mimed such a scene in a more allusive way than an actor onstage; the allusiveness of the art of the dancer would have added even more pathos to the scene.[24]

Stylistically, the monologue is characterized by shifts between the first-, second-, and third-person form: the speech is addressed to herself, to her children, or to her soul and emotions (895: *anime*; 914: *dolor*; 916: *ira*; 930: *furor*; 937: *anime*; 938: *ira, amor*; 944: *dolor*). As usual, the emotions are portrayed as external forces possessing Medea, as for example, at lines 916–17: *Quo te igitur, ira, mittis, aut quae perfido/intendis hosti tela?*; or 927–8: *ira discessit loco/ materque tota coniuge expulsa redit*; or 943–4: *ira pietatem fugat/iramque pietas*.

Epic phrasing is recurrently employed, as, for example, at lines 926–7: *Cor pepulit horror, membra torpescunt gelu/pectusque tremuit*, including an extended epic simile (939–43): *anceps aestus incertam rapit;/ut saeva rapidi bella cum venti gerunt,/utrimque fluctus maria discordes agunt/dubiumque fervet pelagus, haud aliter meum/cor fluctuatur*.[25]

Thyestes (434–9; 496–505; 920–69): Thyestes' Self-analysis

The third act of the *Thyestes* features a dialogue between Thyestes and his son Tantalus who spurs his father to rejoice over the reconciliation offered by his brother Atreus; Thyestes replies to his son describing the inexplicable fear that he is not able to overcome (434–9):

> Causam timoris ipse quam ignoro exigis.
> nihil timendum video, sed timeo tamen.   435
> placet ire, pigris membra sed genibus labant,
> alioque quam quo nitor abductus feror.
> sic concitatam remige et velo ratem
> aestus resistens remigi et velo refert.

Thyestes' self-analysis of his fear employs the common nautical simile (see *Agamemnon, Medea*, and *Phaedra*); the simile, which does not aim at any kind of linguistic variety (see the close repetition of *remige/remigi* and *velo/velo* at lines 438–9), simply expands on the preceding line *alioque quam quo nitor abductus feror* (437); the simile thus recasts the image of the movement of two opposite forces moving Thyestes in different directions.

  Later on in the act, Atreus provides a self-description comparing himself to a hunting dog chasing after a prey:

> (Lines 496–505):
> vix tempero animo, vix dolor frenos capit.
> sic, cum feras vestigat et longo sagax
> loro tenetur Umber ac presso vias
> scrutatur **ore**, dum procul lento suem
> odore sentit, paret et tacito locum   500
> **rostro** pererrat; praeda cum propior fuit,
> **cervice** tota pugnat et gemitu vocat
> dominum morantem seque retinenti eripit.
> cum sperat ira sanguinem, nescit tegi
> tamen tegatur.   505

This simile featuring in Atreus' self-analysis is the most extended one in the Senecan *corpus* and heavily strains psychological realism. The simile echoes Virgil (*Aen.* 12, 749–57 describing Aeneas fighting with Turnus) and Ovid (*Met.* 1, 533–8 Apollo chasing after Daphne); nonetheless, while Virgil and Ovid describe the entire process involved in the hunting (the seeing of the prey, the chase, and the capture), Seneca concentrates on a detailed and climactic description of the dog carefully and silently tracking the beast (497: *vestigat*; 498–9: *presso vias/scrutatur ore*; 500–1: *paret et tacito locum/rostro pererrat*), then sensing it closer (501: *praeda cum propior fuit*), and becoming more and more impatient (502: *cervice tota pugnat*) up to the point to breaking from restraint (503: *seque retinenti eripit*). Thus, the simile conveys a crescendo in the movements of the dog. Interestingly, Seneca provides concreteness to the description of the dog by enumerating the bodily parts of it (499: *ore*, 501: *rostro*, 502: *cervice*) which is paralleled by the use of a descriptive and vivid linguistic register (497: *vestigat*; 499: *scrutatur*; 500: *sentit, paret*; 501: *pererrat*; 502: *pugnat*; 503: *eripit*).

Thyestes' lyric monody (920–69):[26]

(Fitch)	(Zwierlein)
Pectora longis hebetata malis,	Pectora longis hebetata malis,
iam sollicitas ponite curas.	iam sollicitas ponite curas.
fugiat maeror fugiatque pavor,	fugiat maeror fugiatque pauor,
fugiat trepidi comes exilii	fugiat trepidi comes exilii
tristis egestas	tristis egestas
rebusque gravis pudor afflictis.	rebusque grauis pudor afflictis:
magis unde cadas quam quo refert.	magis unde cadas quam quo refert.
magnum, ex alto culmine lapsum	Magnum, ex alto culmine lapsum
stabilem in plano figere gressum;	stabilem in plano figere gressum;
magnum, ingenti strage malorum	magnum, ingenti strage malorum
pressum fracti pondera regni	pressum fracti pondera regni
non inflexa cervice pati,	non inflexa ceruice pati,
nec degenerem victumque malis	nec degenerem uictumque malis
rectum impositas ferre ruinas.	rectum impositas ferre ruinas.
sed iam saevi nubila fati	Sed iam saeui nubila fati
pelle ac miseri temporis omnes	pelle ac miseri temporis omnes
dimitte notas;	dimitte notas;
redeant vultus ad laeta boni,	redeant uultus ad laeta boni,
veterem ex animo mitte Thyesten.	ueterem ex animo mitte Thyesten.
Proprium hoc miseros sequitur vitium,	Proprium hoc miseros sequitur uitium,
numquam rebus credere laetis;	numquam rebus credere laetis:
redeat felix fortuna licet,	redeat felix fortuna licet,
tamen afflictos gaudere piget.	tamen afflictos gaudere piget.
quid me revocas	Quid me reuocas festumque uetas
festumque vetas celebrare diem,	celebrare diem, quid flere iubes,
quid flere iubes,	nulla surgens dolor ex causa?
nulla surgens dolor ex causa?	quis me prohibet flore decenti
quis me prohibet	uincire comam, prohibet, prohibet?
flore decenti vincire comam,	Vernae capiti fluxere rosae,
prohibet, prohibet?	pingui madidus crinis amomo

vernae capiti fluxere rosae,
pingui madidus crinis amomo
inter subitos stetit horrores,
imber vultu nolente cadit,
venit in medias voces gemitus.
maeror lacrimas amat assuetas,
flendi miseris dira cupido est.
libet infaustos mittere questus,
libet et Tyrio
saturas ostro rumpere vestes,
ululare libet.
Mittit luctus signa futuri
mens ante sui praesaga mali:
instat nautis fera tempestas,
cum sine vento tranquilla tument.
_ Quos tibi luctus quosve tumultus
fingis, demens?
credula praesta pectora fratri:
iam, quidquid id est,
vel sine causa vel sero times.
_ Nolo infelix,

sed vagus intra terror oberrat,
subitos fundunt oculi fletus,
nec causa subest.
dolor an metus est?
an habet lacrimas magna voluptas?

inter subitos stetit horrores,
imber uultu nolente cadit,
uenit in medias uoces gemitus.
Maeror lacrimas amat assuetas,
flendi miseris dira cupido est.
libet infaustos mittere questus,
libet et Tyrio saturas ostro
rumpere uestes, ululare libet.
Mittit luctus signa futuri
mens ante sui praesaga mali:
instat nautis fera tempestas,
cum sine uento tranquilla tument.
Quos tibi luctus quosue tumultus
fingis, demens?
credula praesta pectora fratri:
iam, quidquid id est, uel sine causa
uel sero times.
Nolo infelix, sed uagus intra
terror oberrat, subitos fundunt
oculi fletus, nec causa subest.
dolor an metus est? an habet
lacrimas
magna uoluptas?

The first scene of the fifth act of the *Thyestes* features a monologue by Atreus (885–919) and most probably a monologue (in lyric metre, 920–69) by Thyestes; in fact, the manuscript tradition is not in agreement in the assignment of lines 920–69. In the E tradition the lines occur as an antiphonal song between Thyestes and the chorus (920–37 chorus; 938–42 Thyestes; 942–4 chorus; 945–60 Thyestes; 961–4 chorus; 965–9 Thyestes); in the A tradition all the lines are assigned to Thyestes. Zwierlein and Fitch follow the A tradition and print the lines as an uninterrupted *canticum* by Thyestes.[27] Bishop, on the contrary, defends the reading of the E tradition on the basis of marked shifts between third-person and second-person speech. That the lines are to be assigned to Thyestes seems to be confirmed by Atreus' words at lines 918–19 (*ecce, iam cantus ciet/festasque voces, nec satis menti imperat*) and by a parallel passage in the *Medea* where the nurse announces Medea's entrance onstage with similar words (738–9: *Sonuit ecce vesano gradu/canitque. mundus vocibus primis tremit*); even in Medea's case the speech delivered by the protagonist is a lyric monody. It is worth noting that both Atreus and the nurse remark with the use of the verb *cieo* and *cano* respectively that Medea and Thyestes are actually singing (namely delivering their lines in lyric metre); thus the lyric metre is used to convey the impression of an altered frame of mind: in fact Medea is about to use her magic power and Thyestes is heavily drunk.

In relation to the emotional climate provided by the lyric metre, Fitch's arrangement of the colometry of the anapaestic lines, which features a larger number of monometers than Zwierlein (namely 12 to 5), better underlines the heightened emotional part of the speech; in fact, the monometers come to coincide with Thyestes' self-apostrophe or direct address.[28] Furthermore, Fitch observes that 'the broken rhythm created by the monometers in 942–6 matches the impassioned outburst of the lines, in contrast to the more controlled utterance which precedes and follows'.[29]

Thyestes' entrance onstage is announced by Atreus at lines 901–2 (*Turba famularis, fores/templi relaxa, festa patefiat domus*) who then gives a description of Thyestes inside the palace at 908–11 (*Aperta multa tecta conlucent face./ resupinus ipse purpurae atque auro incubat,/vino gravatum fulciens laeva caput./ eructat*).[30]

Thyestes' monologue is better seen as a soliloquy since it does not address or come as a reply to Atreus or any other character onstage. Tarrant has described Thyestes' monologue as a 'harrowing portrayal of psychological disintegration, unique in ancient literature'.[31] For what concerns the shifts from the third to the second person (self-address), this device is a recurring and constant technique of Seneca's dramatic writing (see the monologues described above) and thus the monologue can be accounted as a further example of it.

The first 17 lines (920–37) are delivered in the third-person form and the speech is constituted by two self-exhortations (920–5; 933–7) and a more generalizing section (925–33); in the first self-exhortation, Thyestes addresses his *pectora* (920) to release negative emotions, namely *maeror, pavor* (922: grief, fear), *egestas* (924: misery), *pudor* (925: shame), which are presented all the way through as active agents.[32] In the second, the same idea of releasing past misery and sorrow is stated further; here Thyestes does not address his emotions, but rather describes the symptoms associated with the negative emotions that must be abandoned (935–6: *pelle ac miseri temporis omnes/dimitte notas*) and those that must be subsumed for the new and positive situation (937–8: *redeant vultus ad laeta boni,/veterem ex animo mitte Thyesten*).

The central part (926–33) deals with a more general description of how to withstand negative events in a dignified way; this section is remarkable from a stylistic and metrical point of view:

> magis unde cadas quam quo refert.
> magnum, ex alto culmine lapsum
> stabilem in plano figere gressum;
> magnum, ingenti strage malorum
> pressum fracti pondera regni   930
> non inflexa cervice pati,
> nec degenerem victumque malis
> rectum impositas ferre ruinas.

Stylistically, the passage features a large use of alliteration (especially of the sound *m*); metrically, the passage employs a frequent use of spondees which 'convey not only physical but also emotional heaviness, and are therefore particularly appropriate for sorrow';[33] in addition to this, the sense of heaviness conveyed by the metre could match the sense of fatigue produced by the long struggle against misfortunes. The sense of heaviness is then expressly made clear by the text itself at lines 929–30 (*magnum, ingenti strage malorum/pressum fracti pondera regni*) and at line 933 (*rectum impositas ferre ruinas*); thus, misfortunes metaphorically become a weight that physically pulls down and forces human beings to bend; in front of such misfortunes, Thyestes has managed to keep standing straight (931: *non inflexa cervice pati*; 933: *rectum*) and yet stable (927–28: *magnum ex alto culmine lapsum/stabilem in plano figere gressum*). The struggle is visually depicted by the play of two opposite forces producing on the one side a pulling down movement and on the other a standing up one.

The generalizing and gnomic tone of this section is resumed again at lines 938–41; afterwards a sudden shift of tone comes about and Thyestes' speech (942–6) becomes personal and heavily emotional (see especially the emphatic series of interrogative sentences and the repetition of the verb *prohibet* thrice): Thyestes addresses his *dolor* (pain) complaining that it forbids him to rejoice over the change of situation; the *dolor* is experienced here as an external force that compels him to weep (*quid flere iubes?*); similarly, in the following self-description, which is cast in the third-person form, the symptoms through which Thyestes' *dolor* expresses itself are treated as external entities; it is notable that in this long descriptive section there is careful avoidance of any kind of personal pronoun that could refer to Thyestes as experiencing the emotion; even the *maeror* (sorrow), the *cupido flendi* (desire to weep), and the *mens* (mind) seem not to belong to the character and have a life on their own: 952, *maeror lacrimas amat assuetas*; 953, *flendi miseris dira cupido est*; 958, *mittit luctus signa futuri/ mens ante sui praesaga mali*.

The bodily effects produced by the emotion contain a familiar repertoire of symptoms: the hair bristles in fear (948–9: *pingui madidus crinis amomo/inter subitos stetit horrores*), tears fall from the unwilling eyes (950: *imber vultu nolente cadit*), a groan comes amidst the words (951: *venit in medias voces gemitus*); the pain longs to lament (954: *libet infaustos mittere questus*), to tear the garments (955–6: *libet et Tyrio/saturas ostro rumpere vestes*), and to howl (957: *ululare libet*; note the emphatic position of the verb at the beginning of the line and the repetition of the verb *libet* thrice in four lines). The section is rounded off by a nautical simile, which compares Thyestes' inexplicable foreboding of future misfortunes to the sailors on a calm sea threatened by an unpredictable storm (959–60).[34]

At lines 965–9, after an interruption containing self-exhortation (961–4), Thyestes provides another list of symptoms of his distress; the use of the first-person (965: *nolo*), with which the section opens, is followed again by a sudden shift from first-person to third-person form and this final section repeats the content and matches in tone the preceding more extended passage;[35] again, psychological and physical symptoms are described as external entities (966: *sed vagus intra terror oberrat*; 967: *subitos fundunt oculi fletus*).

Trojan Women (642–62): Andromache's Self-analysis

Quid agimus? animum distrahit geminus timor:
hinc natus, illinc coniugis cari cinis.
pars utra vincet? testor immites deos,
deosque veros coniugis manes mei: 645
non aliud, Hector, in meo nato mihi
placere quam te. vivat, ut possit tuos
referre vultus. -prorutus tumulo cinis
mergetur? ossa fluctibus spargi sinam
disiecta vastis? potius hic mortem oppetat.-   650
poteris nefandae deditum mater neci
videre, poteris celsa per fastigia

missum rotari? potero, perpetiar, feram,
dum non meus post fata victoris manu
iactetur Hector.-hic suam poenam potest   655
sentire, at illum fata iam in tuto locant.
quid fluctuaris?statue, quem poenae extrahas.
ingrata, dubitas? Hector est illinc tuus-
erras, utrimque est Hector: hic sensus potens,
forsan futurus ultor extincti patris-   660
utrique parci non potest: quidnam facis?
serva e duobus, anime, quem Danai timent.

Andromache's monologue features in the third act of the *Trojan Women* and deals with the attempt to conceal Astyanax from the Greeks (namely in the person of Ulysses). The monologue is delivered as a long aside (20 lines); in fact, her thoughts are not meant to be heard by Ulysses. Such an extended aside does not feature as a dramatic device in Greek tragedy, but they are well attested in New Comedy.[36] However, Seneca's asides present a length that is unparalleled even in New Comedy. Usually, asides are employed when a character is planning deception in relation to another one, as, for example in the *Medea* (549–50: *Sic natos amat?/bene est, tenetur, vulneri patuit locus*), where Medea's words are clearly not meant to be heard by Jason; a similar occurrence is to be found in the *Trojan Women* during the confrontation between Ulysses and Andromache; as soon as the cunning hero detects Andromache's fear, which reveals her lie about Astyanax, he delivers a brief aside (625–6: *Intremuit: hac, hac parte quaerenda est mihi./matrem timor detexit: iterabo metum*). However, Andromache's lengthy aside monologue in the *Trojan Women* is not unparalleled, since a similar one occurs in the *Thyestes* (491–507); Atreus actually delivers an extended monologue aside in which he first catches sight of Thyestes and his sons and then pours out his feelings of happiness since he has almost accomplished his revenge.[37]

Andromache's monologue deals with an emotional dilemma on the course of action she should choose, i.e. the choice between saving Hector's tomb (Ulysses has threatened to destroy it if she does not reveal where Astyanax is hidden) or the life of his little son. Andromache's perplexity appears to be totally incongruous, since the destruction of Hector's tomb will also cause the death of the boy who is hidden there.[38] Despite the incongruity, Andromache's speech is highly emotional and pathetic; it is different from those of Phaedra, Medea, and Clytemnestra in which the heroines analyse mainly their feelings and the symptoms produced by them. Here, Andromache's self-analysis is more concerned with portraying a conflicting choice between her maternal instinct and her bridal devotion to her husband (or better, his tomb!). Stylistically, the passage gives the impression of two voices speaking in Andromache; in fact, she addresses herself either in the first and in the second person (649: *sinam*; 651: *poteris*; 652: *poteris*; 653: *potero, perpetiar, feram* in asyndeton; 657: *fluctuaris, statue, extrahas*; 658: *dubitas*; 659: *erras*; 661: *facis*; 662: *serva* where she addresses her *animus*).

The passage includes several demonstrative pronouns relating to Astyanax and Hector (643: *hinc, illinc*; 650: *hic*; 655: *hic*; 656: *illum*; 658: *illinc*; 659: *hic*); the first two occurrences of the demonstrative pronouns seem to provide and set out a concrete space for the metaphorical interior feeling that on one side there is her son and on the other the ashes of her husband (643–4: *hinc natus, illinc coniugis cari cinis./pars utra vincet?*). Later on in her speech, she again asks herself whether it is preferable to see the profanation of Hector's ashes (649–50: *ossa fluctibus spargi sinam/disiecta vastis?*) or the death of her son (652–3: *poteris celsa per fastigia/missum rotari?*); in this case, she vividly portrays the two concrete outcomes her choice would produce. Remarkably, both of them are quite awkward. In the case of Hector's ashes, she fears that the Greeks will throw them into the sea. In the case of Astyanax, Andromache foreshadows that Astyanax will be thrown from the walls of Troy and it is not clear how she can know the exact type of death the small boy will endure. As to the last point, it seems that Andromache is aware of her own mythological story and uses it to add pathos to her speech with no concern for dramatic illusion. From the above analysis of Andromache's monologue, it emerges that Seneca purposely created an emotional dilemma for his self-conciously mythical heroine, no matter how awkward and implausible, and conceived it in a way that offered plenty of pathetic possibilities amenable to be depicted in strikingly visual effects.

Pantomime and Descriptive Narrative Set-pieces of Seneca's Tragedies

Introduction: General Features of Narrative Set-pieces

Lengthy narratives occur in almost every tragedy of the Senecan *corpus* with the exceptions of *Medea* and *Phoenissae*. They are developed as independent set-pieces which have little or no importance for the advancement of the plot. I list them as follows:

- Theseus' description of the descent to the Underworld of Hercules in the *Hercules furens* (act III: 662–827);
- the messenger's description of the sea monster in the *Phaedra* (act V: 1000–114);
- the messenger's description of Atreus' murder and dismemberment of Thyestes' sons in the *Thyestes* (act IV: 641–782);
- the messenger's description of Polyxena's and Astyanax's deaths in the *Trojan Women* (act V: 1056–179);
- Creon's description of the necromancy in the *Oedipus* (act III: 509–708);
- Eurybates' description of the sea storm in the *Agamemnon* (act III: 421–578).

Formal Frame

These narratives take the form of speeches in which a character brings information of some preceding action occurring offstage to the characters onstage. The speeches are either delivered by 'true' messengers or by characters who perform the same dramatic function. As Larson states, it is legitimate to classify them as messenger speeches since they display some of the conventional formal features of messenger speeches of Greek tragedy, and especially Euripidean tragedy.[2] Senecan messenger speeches, however, differ from their Greek counterparts in many respects. First, while the Greek messenger speech is employed to narrate events that are strictly connected and needed for the advancement of the plot, or that are not conventionally shown onstage (such as death and violence), Seneca's messenger speeches expand and elaborate on episodes and themes that, albeit belonging to the myth in question, are needed neither to advance the plot nor to overcome difficulties conventionally connected with the representation of bloodshed onstage. Furthermore, while the Greek messenger delivers a speech implicitly expressing his emotions, thoughts, and perspective on the events, the Senecan messenger 'excludes himself completely from the story he tells'.[3] The Senecan messenger represents thus more an epic narrator or a 'medium' (to use Larson's term) than a dramatic character. Since Seneca knew his Greek models, from which he could draw well-established and more obviously economical dramatic conventions, we have to interpret his different use of the messenger as a dramatic device intended for a highly specific purpose other than a means for rhetorical display or to replace stage performance. Their occurrence in almost every tragedy makes them a regularly recurring tool whose adoption should be interpreted and not simplistically dismissed as ornamental.

According to Garelli, 'the tendency to develop these scenes well beyond the dramatic necessities is a clear evidence of a choice which is fully conscious and literary, a choice of theatrical writing'.[4] She points out three aspects of the set-pieces that show Seneca's different aesthetic perspective on the material. First, the extreme length of the set-pieces indicates that their role is intended to be pivotal; in the structure of the play, in fact, they actually acquire the status of an episode in itself, which often occupies a whole act.[5] According to Garelli, these pieces are not conceived as elements of the drama, but as *equivalents* of it.[6] Furthermore, the narratives dramatize epic poetry, and the characters are depicted by Seneca in the most theatrical attitude offered by the epic text.[7] Finally, Seneca tends to simplify the dramatic structure of the set-pieces and develop and elaborate, instead, the narrative element in it. Thus, the structural frame is reduced to a minimum and the development of the action is not linear; on the contrary, the narrative seems to proceed by leaps. This is due to the fact that Seneca tends to elaborate secondary elements at the expense of the coherence of the whole.

Garelli exemplifies this tendency to simplify the action and to elaborate secondary elements by comparing the description of the storm in Aeschylus' (636–80) and Seneca's *Agamemnon* (421–578): in Aeschylus the description of the storm is brief and the return of the Greek fleet, which the messenger comes to announce, remains the most important fact in relation to the further development of the plot; in Seneca the narration of the storm is so long and its details so prominent that the return of Agamemnon and the Greek fleet is neglected. The Senecan narratives thus show clearly that he neglected structural unity, temporal and spatial continuity, as well as verisimilitude in favour of an accumulation and expansion of baroque descriptions.

This point of view is shared by Larson as well, who describes the Senecan messenger speech as dealing 'with a limited scope of time and action – with one event – and describes it in elaborate detail'.[8] This tendency becomes even more evident when the Senecan messenger speech and the Greek one are compared; in fact the latter 'is generally more concerned to present a chain of events in chronological perspective, that is, to compose a narrative', while the Senecan messenger speech 'concentrates rather on accumulating details to make a picture of one stage in this chain of events'.[9]

As to the themes, the narratives usually deal with literary *topoi* typical of the epic tradition where descriptions of events of such a kind are employed to arouse emotional effects; the secondary episodes treated in Seneca's narratives tend either to deal, generally speaking, with a sort of performance of wonders (such as for example, the description of the descent to the Underworld, the necromancy, the appearance of shades, descriptions of storms and shipwrecks, sacrifices and invocation to the souls of the dead), or with a dramatization of death and murder, especially of children (such as the description of the killing of Thyestes' sons or of Polyxena and Astyanax in the *Trojan Women*). Seneca's fondness for the treatment of supernatural and horrific events seems designed to create theatrical and spectacular effects reminiscent of pantomime.

Seneca's narrative set-pieces tend to feature the same structure; in particular, narrative set-pieces are constituted by the following three elements:

1) introductory *ecphrasis*;
2) description of characters, human-like figures, mythical animals/monsters;
3) reactions of the natural elements to the character's deeds (in the case of the *Trojan Women* the reactions of the natural elements are substituted by the reactions of a crowd gathered to assist in Astyanax's and Polyxena's deaths).

Ecphrasis: Imaginary Landscape

Seneca's set-pieces invariably open with an *ecphrasis topou*; the position of the lengthy *ecphrasis* at the beginning of the speech 'gives it the status of an entertaining opening to a story' and provides a background for the figures or characters.[10]

This background is described in a detailed and often graphic way, but, at the same time, the mode of depiction does not aim at being accurate or realistic (for example, it does not provide spatial or temporal coordinates); it pictures a scenario that is more imagined than real and thus quite fluid. The details also aim more at creating the general atmosphere of the location rather than defining a spatial framework. Seneca's *ecphraseis* seem a deliberate attempt to create an 'imaginary frame', within which his characters move. It is, of course, obvious that such a landscape (an imaginary and often phantasmagorical atmosphere) may not be portrayed as materially evident by means of theatrical business; but such a background or 'verbal scenery', which sidesteps the 'realistic' constraints imposed by theatrical conditions, would have been extremely suitable for pantomimic performances;[11] in fact, the very nature of these performances allowed (if not required) an expansion of the scenic space, indeed an imaginary one. The mime or pantomime that was performed could move in a fluid imaginary setting, more evocative than concrete, and created by the words of the libretti. Moreover, the verbal scenery portrayed in the libretti could have been translated from verbal into bodily images by means of allusive gestures and movements by the skilful dancer.

As seen in Chapter 1, Libanius (*Orations* 64, 116) attests that the dancer was able to convey pastoral landscapes.[12] The picture evoked by Libanius is a complex one since natural elements, animals, and human beings feature in it and a similar complexity is typical of Seneca's narrative set-pieces.

Mimetic Present

Besides spatial coordinates, time becomes rather vague as well. In fact, narrative set-pieces are usually couched in the present tense, which 'establishes the place in permanency'.[13] The past tense is seldom employed and never to describe a proper past action. For example, in the case of the narrative set-pieces in the *Hercules furens* (658–829), the narration consistently adopts the present, while the past tense features only scantily.[14] The past tense is used mainly in the perfect and is either employed to describe an instantaneous action or to convey temporal relationships between two actions swiftly taking place in close succession. The instantaneous perfect, which describes a sudden and thus frozen action, may be used to convey a static pose.[15]

As a consequence, even though the messenger is reporting actions that happened in the past, the use of the present makes the narration seem to describe an event simultaneously taking place as the narration proceeds, rather than a past event.[16]

The adoption of the present tense on Seneca's part seems to be a device chosen to provide immediacy and to reinforce the impression of vividness of the messenger's account. This immediacy is further reinforced by the extensive use of demonstrative adjectives and pronouns to point to different directions, or objects, or group of people. For example, the narrative set-piece of the *Hercules furens* is punctuated by deictic pronouns, adjectives, and adverbs.[17] The combined use of the present tense and of demonstrative determiners enhances the impression that the messenger or the character in charge of the speech is describing an action or a place or a character in front of his eyes.

Now, since the events, places, and characters that are the subjects of the narratives are away from the scene of the action and since the messenger is reporting actions that took place in the past, no matter how recent, the fact that Seneca's narrative set-pieces strive for immediacy sharply contrasts with these very premises.

Seneca seems to have adopted a well-established device of the tragic genre and reshaped it. Thus the tendency to present the events as if taking place at the moment and to describe characters as if acting conterminously with the narration may be the sign of the influence of pantomime, in which the temporal dimension was somehow irrelevant and the actions enacted by the dancer were taking place in a timeless present.

Running Commentaries: Characters, Animated Natural Elements, and Personified Abstractions

In narrative set-pieces several different figures make their appearance: there are proper characters, human-like figures (such as personifications of abstractions like Grief, Dolour, Disease, Death), but also monsters (such as the sea monster in the *Phaedra*), or mythological animals (such as Cerberus in the *Hercules furens*). Usually, the attitudes or physical appearances or actions of all these figures populating the narrative are described in detail. For example, in the *Trojan Women*'s narrative set-piece, Astyanax and Polyxena are described; in that of *Phaedra*, there is a minute description of Hippolytus and the sea monster. In that of the *Hercules furens*, a plethora of different figures appears: the personified abstractions (*Fames, Pudor, Senectus*), Dis, Charon, and Cerberus. Similar to the *Hercules furens*, in the *Oedipus* first Tiresias, then the personified abstractions such as *Luctus* (Grief) and *Morbus* (Disease), and lastly Laius' ghost are described; in the *Thyestes*, Atreus and Thyestes, while in the *Agamemnon*, Ajax and Nauplius.

When characters are described, the descriptions differ in no way from those found in 'running commentaries' and can be interpreted accordingly; for instance, the description of Tiresias in the *Oedipus* presents all the typical features outlined in the case of 'running commentaries':[18]

(Lines 548–55):
Huc ut sacerdos intulit senior gradum,
haud est moratus: praestitit noctem locus.
tum effossa tellus, et super rapti rogis   550
iaciuntur ignes. ipse funesto integit
vates amictu corpus et frondem quatit;
squalente cultu maestus ingreditur senex,
lugubris imos palla perfundit pedes,
mortifera canam taxus astringit comam.   555

(Lines 559–68):
Vocat inde manes teque qui manes regis
et obsidentem claustra letalis lacus,   560
carmenque magicum volvit et rabido minax
decantat ore quidquid aut placat leves
aut cogit umbras; sanguinem libat focis
solidasque pecudes urit et multo specum
saturat cruore; libat et niveum insuper   565
lactis liquorem, fundit et Bacchum manu
laeva, canitque rursus ac terram intuens
graviore manes voce et attonita citat.

Tiresias' entrance is shaped as that of a character entering onstage and closely resembles the conventional entrances of characters found in the acts (lines 548–9: *Huc ut sacerdos intulit senior gradum,/haud est moratus;*[19] the instance in the *Oedipus* is not an isolated case, since the entrance of Atreus (*Thy* 682–3: *Quo postquam furens/intravit Atreus liberos fratris trahens*) and that of Hippolytus (*Phae* 1000–1: *ut profugus urbem liquit infesto gradu*) are devised in the same way; such a handling, which is common in the acts, is awkward in the case of a messenger's narration in which the entrance of a character does not need to be announced nor his movements minutely described, since the messenger usually reports past events or events occurring offstage. It can be accounted thus as an additional device adopted to provide immediacy to the narrative.

As discussed above, Seneca tends to populate his narratives with personified abstracts portrayed as human-like figures. The personification of abstracts is a common feature in poetry, but while in the poetic representation the personifications are posing like instant images, Seneca's personifications are performing actions. For instance, if in Virgil *Senectus* (Old Age) is simply described as sad (*tristis*), in Seneca it is described as supporting its steps with a stick (*iners Senectus adiuvat baculo gradum*);[20] in this way, the personified abstracts acquire an even more pronounced human-like nature becoming similar to proper characters as described in 'running commentaries'.

In the case of the sea monster featuring in the narrative set-piece of the *Phaedra* (1000–114), Seneca provides such a long and detailed description of its bodily parts that it acquires a human-like, although phantasmagorical, appearance: the monster has body (*corporis*), neck (*colla*; *cervix*), forehead (*fronte*), ears (*aures*), eyes (*orbibus*; *oculi*), muscles (*toros*); nostrils (*nares*), chest (*pectus*), flanks (*latus*). A similar description of Cerberus is found in the narrative set-piece of the *Hercules furens* (662–827).

Now, all these figures (either human, vegetal, animal, or simply imaginary), which accumulate in Seneca's narrative, contribute to the impression of a human-like polymorphism expressed by a realm of figures continuously changing shapes and transforming from one to the other. Thus, this protean nature of Seneca's narratives seems to parallel that of the pantomime dancer who, as the mythical Proteus, was mostly praised for his ability to metamorphose into, imitate, and embody everything he wished to.[21]

Another recurrent element of narrative set-pieces is the description of transient aspects of environmental change, which usually take place in the form of the reactions of natural elements to the character's deeds. As Larson has shown, descriptions dealing with transient aspects of environmental disturbances are almost totally absent in Greek tragedy.[22] Such disturbances usually take place in correspondence to the characters' misdeeds or misfortunes, thus the landscape usually tends to mirror or respond to the characters' states of mind; as Herington has argued, the description of external landscape serves as the 'amplifying medium which conveys the state of the subject's soul'.[23] Because of this, natural phenomena are presented as being animated and possessing a sentient nature and thus even these descriptions portray a landscape that is emotional more than naturalistic.[24] The landscape and natural elements are often portrayed as if animated or as sentient beings through the use of a metaphorical language; the most explicit example of this tendency is found at *Oedipus* (574–7).[25] More generally, grove, trees, and earth tremble and shake in fear and fire burns unwillingly.[26] The prominent role given to inanimate objects and their reactions together with the tendency to present them as personified seems a tool intended to translate as much as possible into a language suitable for being performed in actions; this tendency may stand also as a sign of the influence of pantomime in Seneca's tragedies (no matter here whether Seneca consciously and purposely chose these stylistic devices to write a script suitable for pantomime, or adopted the language of pantomime for other reasons).[27]

From a stylistic point of view, the narratives combines two different qualities; in fact, some descriptions have an almost scientific nature because of the precision of the details provided, while some others have an imaginary, baroque, and totally unrealistic one. I would suggest that these opposite and contrasting qualities have a specific function connected with the different purposes they were meant to achieve. These qualities find a correspondence in pantomime where a dancer would embody quite literally a character's action, while suggesting an imaginary landscape, monsters, and phantasmagorical animals by means of more symbolic gestures.

Scholars tend to relate the distinctive aesthetic techniques of the Senecan set pieces to his integration of epic forms into the tragic genre and dismiss them as bombastic, excessive, and redundant. Alternatively, they could be interpreted as a sign of Seneca's creative engagement with the aesthetics of pantomime.

Analysis of the Narrative Set-pieces

Hercules Furens (662–827): The Descent to the Underworld

Theseus' description of the Underworld is the lengthiest one of the numerous set-pieces in Seneca's tragedies. Shelton states that 'in its function as a rhetorical showpiece, the scene gives Seneca an opportunity to exhibit his skills at descriptions.'[28] Fitch's interpretation is that 'undeniably such scenes have a considerable degree of independence from the body of the play, and offer an opportunity for display of rhetorical-poetic technique and in particular for δείνωσις, that is, treatment of the gruesome and horrific.'[29] Henry and Walker rightly claim that 'the long central scene of the play, by its position, length, and impressive power is clearly intended to be pivotal' and further add that 'a scene whose verse is of such compelling and astonishing power cannot be dismissed as merely an interruption of the dramatic development.'[30] In addition to this, since the narrative develops for almost 200 lines and thus forms a whole act, it seems hard to believe that Seneca built it up just to display his rhetorical skills and ability in engaging with a literary topic that had a blatantly famous antecedent in Virgil's narration of Aeneas' descent to the Underworld in the sixth book of the *Aeneid*. I submit that the conspicuous prominence of the set-piece begins to make more sense if we suppose that Seneca, no matter whether he envisaged his tragedies to be performed or to be recited, wrote the piece in dialogue with pantomime and the formal and stylistic features of the genre. From a formal point of view, three features may be ascribed to the influence of pantomime: the fact that the set-piece has a self-contained character; the role of Theseus as a speaking voice rather than a character involved in the action, and the bipartite arrangement of the narrative. From the point of view of stylistic composition, two features may be ascribed to the influence of pantomime: the recurring use of *ecphraseis topou* and description of the physical appearance of the mythical and hellish figures (the personified abstractions, Dis 721–7; Charon 764–7; the sinners in the increased number of seven, and Cerberus 783–97; and also the lengthy description of the fight between Hercules and Cerberus). The *ecphraseis topou* create the background where the characters move which is, however, not static, but a realm swarming with polymorphic shapes in constant movement. Theseus' speech is basically a monologue interrupted by brief questions asked by Amphitryon, which Seneca introduced mainly to avoid the necessity of providing linking transitions between the different sections of the narrative. Despite Amphitryon's brief interventions, Theseus' speech is basically a soliloquy.

Impersonality of the Narrator and Dramatic Inconsistency of the Character

Theseus' narration of the Underworld is totally impersonal and there is almost no hint (apart from the very last part of his speech; 821: *intulimus orbi*) of his own personal feeling or experience of the Underworld; even in replying to Amphitryon's questions, Theseus never reveals his point of view or his direct participation. On the contrary, all his replies begin with a new *ecphrasis topou*, which does not reflect or is meant to delimit the initial position of the characters (namely Theseus or Hercules) in the space. As rightly pointed out by Larson, the position of the lengthy *ecphrasis* at the beginning of the speech 'gives it the status of an entertaining opening to a story' and 'the present tense in which it is couched establishes the place in permanency and makes a background for the figures'.[31]

As Henry and Walker have aptly remarked, 'the character of Theseus remains resolutely undeveloped';[32] in fact, Theseus performs the function of an impersonal narrator or of a speaking voice rather than a character directly engaged in the action. His figure has basically no dramatic reality or consistency and he is just a mouthpiece for a story.

In the economy of the play, the figure of Theseus seems purposely and almost uniquely introduced to narrate Hercules' labour in the Underworld. In fact, Theseus' first appearance occurs in the third act where he and Hercules arrive at Thebes directly from the Underworld. As soon as Hercules is informed by Amphitryon about Lycus' threat towards them, he quickly decides to face Lycus and compels Theseus to remain with his family while he is away. At this point, Amphitryon asks Theseus to narrate Hercules' exploit in the Underworld. After the narration is concluded, Theseus leaves the stage and appears again only in the last act of the play to offer to Hercules purification and a home in Athens. Despite the importance of his role in relation to Hercules' future after the killing of his family, Theseus' final intervention is concentrated in three lines and a half (1341–6).[33] In Euripides' *Heracles*, Theseus appears much later in the play, but Seneca needs to have him onstage earlier because Theseus is the only character who can be in charge of the description of the Underworld.

Lack of Concern for Dramatic Illusion

From the point of view of dramatic illusion, Theseus' speech is highly implausible. This is because Theseus' long narration of Hercules' quest for Cerberus takes place at a moment in which the life of Hercules and his family is in danger because of Lycus' menace. In fact, Amphitryon asks Theseus to narrate Hercules' deed in the Underworld while Hercules is fighting with Lycus. Now, in such a moment of crisis, such a request, especially from Amphitryon's part, seems awkward at the very least; Theseus' reply is no less awkward since his speech starts off with an *ecphrasis topou* of the Underworld that lasts approximately for 100 lines (662–96; 698–706; 709–27; 731–47; 750–9) and will be followed by the proper narration of Hercules' deed (at line 762). This apparent lack of concern for dramatic illusion, which is an overall characteristic of this piece in many respects, is due to the fact that the scene is a combination of elements typical of a tragic messenger-like *rhesis* and an epic *ecphrastic* set-piece told by an external narrator. This mixed character of the piece, which seems to cross the boundaries of tragedy and epic, may be evidence of pantomime's free appropriation and fusion of both tragic and epic elements in pursuit of its own goal.[34] Furthermore, pantomimic libretti may have been composed by assembling elements typical of different literary genres in the well-established literary tradition. Tragedy and epic were possibly the main poetic resources from which the librettist could draw this new type of mythological verse, although they were by no means the only ones.

Structure: Juxtaposition of Two Tableaux

The narrative is sharply divided into two parts, the first one being concerned with a description of the geography of the Underworld (662–759) and the second one with the last of Hercules' labours: the conquest of Cerberus (760–827). This sharp division arises mainly from the fact that Hercules makes his appearance only very late in the narrative, right after Theseus has introduced Cerberus. Because of this, Theseus' description of the Underworld is not arranged in order to narrate, for example, how Hercules made his way into the Underworld or what he encountered and experienced there. Hercules' last labour (the capture of Cerberus), which was accomplished in the Underworld, allowed Seneca to deal with the theme of the Underworld at large. This being the case, the impression we get from the bipartite arrangement of the narrative is that Seneca aimed at treating somehow separately the Underworld at large and the labour. The two parts, although thematically unified, are, in fact, not structurally integrated; they rather consist of two separate tableaux, each of which develops independently from the other and elaborates its own theme.

The extant sources on pantomime attest that pantomimic performances featured themes such as those connected with the realm of Hades, as, for example, the descent to the Underworld of Theseus and Peirithous (Lucian, 60).[35] With regard to Hercules' labours, we know from Lucian (41) and Libanius (70) that the hero's exploits were very popular in pantomime. I suggest that the two sections of the narrative stand as two tableaux and, although they are different in tone and content, they share common stylistic features which suggest the influence of the aesthetics of pantomime.

Ecphrasis of the Underworld: Imaginary Background and Animated Landscape

The first tableau consists basically of a long *ecphrasis topou* of the Underworld (662–96) in which numerous mythical figures move and whose physical appearance is described at length. From a stylistic point of view, as pointed out by Henry and Walker, 'the description of Hell is written in verse which is precise and effective; so that so far from being composed in the abstract, often generalizing way which Roman poets conventionally use for such scenes, the detail is particular and selective'.[36] In fact, even though the depiction of the hellish landscape exhibits all the sinister elements topically associated with it such as deep woods, rocks, and darkness, the imaginary landscape tends to be presented as if animated and not in abstract terms; thus the opening (lines 662–7):

> Spartana tellus nobile attollit iugum,
> densis ubi aequor Taenarus silvis premit.
> hic ora solvit Ditis invisi domus
> hiatque rupes **alta** et **immenso** specu   665
> **ingens** vorago faucibus **vastis** patet
> latumque pandit omnibus populis iter.

Seneca combines here two Virgilian passages (*Aen.* 6, 237: *spelunca alta fuit vastoque immanis hiatu*; 7, 569–70: *ruptoque ingens Acheronte vorago/pestiferas aperit fauces*). The Senecan picture is vivid and atmospheric but impressionistic rather than precise, and the heavy presence of pleonasm (*alta, immenso, ingens, vastis*; *ora solvit, hiat, patet, pandit*) conveys the image of a rapaciously threatening *locus*, which resembles the embodiment of the devouring rapaciousness of death itself.

The description of the path to the Underworld (675–9) is handled in a similar way; Seneca here aims at portraying the actual agents or forces that make the way back from the Underworld irretrievably impossible: *nec ire labor est: ipsa deducit via./**ut saepe puppes aestus invitas rapit**,/sic pronus aer urget atque avidum chaos,/**gradumque retro flectere** haud umquam sinunt/umbrae tenaces*. The passage is modelled on Virgil (*Aen.* 6, 126–9): *facilis descensus Averno:/ . . . sed **revocare gradum** superasque evadere ad auras,/hoc opus, hic labor est*. In Virgil the Sybil states that the way down to the Underworld is easy to cover, while the difficult toil for Aeneas is to retrace his steps; but while the Sybil's statement is purposely addressed to the difficulties Aeneas could face in leaving the Underworld, Theseus' one is more generalizing and does not refer to the actual difficulties Hercules and he himself could face in returning from the Underworld. Seneca reworks the Virgilian model by adding and emphasizing the concrete agents which make the way down easy (the void and the breeze) and those which make the way backwards difficult (the clutching shadows). Thus we get the image of two forces, one which pulls down and the other which clutches firmly. The presence of an irresistible force is then already presented in the almost formulaic simile of the current that sweeps ships off course. Reactions to concrete agents would be much easier to dance mimetically in an attempt to create a supernatural atmosphere than abstract statements of the kind Virgil's Sybil makes.

Another detail added by Seneca in the hellish landscape serves to animate the landscape, namely the presence of 'ill-boding birds at large in the Underworld' (a vulture, an owl, and a screech-owl).[37]

Yet another good example is the description of the sterility of the Underworld (698–705), which is conveyed through negative clauses that evoke vividly the fertility missing from the Underworld; the construction allows the narrator to describe actions that are normally associated with fertility such as the sprouting forth of the fields and the fluctuation of the cornfield;[38] the natural elements of the landscape presented as active agents and abstractions (as, for example, in the case of *vastitas*) tend to be personified; the natural elements have a human-like nature since anthropomorphic adjectives are employed to describe them (*prata . . . laeta facie; pigro . . . mundo*):

Non prata viridi laeta facie germinant,	
nec adulta leni fluctuat Zephyro seges;	
non ulla ramos silva pomiferos habet;	700
sterilis profundi **vastitas** squalet soli	
et foeda tellus torpet aeterno situ . . .	
immotus aer haeret et pigro sedet	
nox atra mundo;	705

Running Commentary

As previously discussed, Seneca includes numerous descriptions of physical appearance, namely Dis (721–5), the great sinners (750–9), and Charon (764–7); the descriptions, to a greater or lesser extent, are modelled on Virgil's corresponding ones and a comparison between the two reveals how Seneca reworked his models for his own purposes.

Here is the description of Charon and of the personified abstractions in Seneca and Virgil respectively:

Seneca (764–7)	Virgil (*Aen.* 6, 298–301)
hunc servat amnem cultu et aspectu horridus	portitor has horrendus aquas et flumina servat
pavidosque manes squalidus gestat senex	terribili squalore Charon, cui plurima mento
impexa pendet barba, deformem sinum	canities inculta iacet, stant lumina flamma,
nodus coercet, concavae lucent genae;	sordidus ex umeris nodo dependet amictus.

The first remark to make is that, as Fitch has rightly pointed out, 'the tendency of Seneca's reworking is toward a simple, direct, less elevated (and less evocative) style'.[39] Secondly, Seneca tends to present pictures in clipped segments rather than as a continuous sequence, so that each line presents a single image; since the image is self-contained in one line, it can be more easily conveyed by means of gestures.

With regard to the personified abstractions, Seneca has as many as eleven, whereas Virgil lists seven of them (*Aen.* 6, 274–7). The number of adjectives applied by Seneca to them in comparison to Virgil where they have just a single one or none is also higher. Furthermore, Seneca's description tends to be more concrete and to be conveyed by a portrayal of the characteristic activity of the personified abstractions (which can be quite simple or more elaborate), while in Virgil the description is conveyed by emphasizing the more abstract qualities connected with them.

According to Fitch, 'Seneca adds more *color* by describing a characteristic activity of three of his figures, *Fames*, *Pudor*, and *Senectus*'.[40] In fact Hunger (*Fames*) 'lies with wasted jaws' (691: *Famesque maesta tabido rictu iacet*), Shame (*Pudor*) 'covers its guilty face' (692: *Pudorque serus conscios vultus tegit*), and Old Age (*Senectus*) 'supports its steps with a stick' (696: *iners Senectus adiuvat baculo gradum*). Similarly, the other personified abstractions are accompanied by graphic adjectives which describe the negative and concrete effects associated with them: Sleep (*Sopor*) is 'sluggish' (*segnis*), Resentment (*Dolor*) is 'gnashing' (*frendens*), Disease (*Morbus*) is 'trembling' (*tremens*); Virgil, instead, uses adjectives that describe the negative and more abstract qualities associated with them: thus Diseases (*Morbi*) are pale (*pallentes*), Old Age (*Senectus*) is sad (*tristis*), Hunger (*Fames*) is temptress to sin (*malesuada*), Want (*Egestas*) is loathsome (*turpis*). All these 'action' details are highly suggestive of an imagination producing verse with gestural and choreographical accompaniment in mind.

When it comes to the second tableau, the capture of Cerberus, we find that the Senecan tragedy provides the fullest extant treatment of this episode. It opens with a brief *ecphrasis topou*, which 'has no functional purpose but helps to create a grim, oppressive atmosphere'.[41] As analysed above, in the first part of the narrative the description of the landscape played a major role; quite differently, instead, the atmospheric landscape in the second part is just briefly sketched and the description of Cerberus and of the fight between Hercules and the watchdog of the Underworld is prominent. Even the tone of Theseus' speech, which was solemn in the description of the Underworld and becomes rhetoric-comical as soon as Hercules makes its appearance at line 770, is consistently different.[42] Shelton and Fitch state that the whole aim of the scene is to provide a negative characterization of Hercules; thus its 'comical' character purposely aims at providing a negative portrayal of Hercules by presenting him as a heroic-comic character whose achievements against monsters are not morally valuable and by emphasizing his attitude of always resorting to violence and brutal force. A different interpretation is however possible, since its character is markedly mimic, concentrated as it is on fully describing at length and with graphic and pictorial details each stage of Hercules' and Cerberus' fight. The stages of the encounter almost stand as vivid pictures in motion that follow one after the other.

The first picture presents Cerberus' physical appearance and him sensing the approaching of Hercules (783–93):

> hic saevus umbras territat Stygius canis,
> qui trina vasto capita concutiens sono
> regnum tuetur. sordidum tabo caput   785
> lambunt colubrae, viperis horrent iubae
> longusque torta sibilat cauda draco.
> par ira formae: sensit ut motus pedum,
> attollit hirtas angue vibrato comas
> missumque captat aure subrecta sonum,   790
> sentire et umbras solitus. ut propior stetit
> Iove natus antro, sedit incertus canis
> et uterque timuit.

The second one (793–827) presents the fight between Hercules and Cerberus and the hero's victory over the monstrous creature (797–802):

>   solvit a laeva feros
> tunc ipse rictus et Cleonaeum caput
> opponit ac se tegmine ingenti tegit,
> victrice magnum dextera robur gerens   800
> huc nunc et illuc verbere assiduo rotat,
> ingeminat ictus.

Cerberus immediately resigns himself and lowers its head (802–3): *domitus infregit minas/et cuncta lassus capita summisit canis.*

The third one presents the detailed description of Cerberus' transformation after its capture (808–12): *oblitus sui/custos opaci pervigil regni canis/componit aures timidus et patiens trahi,/erumque fassus, ore summisso obsequens,/utrumque cauda pulsat anguifera latus.* In fact, once captured, Cerberus undergoes a quite comical transformation from the fearful watchdog of the Underworld (793–802) into a submissive pet that drops its ears and wags its tail.

The last picture presents Hercules dragging Cerberus away from the Underworld (813–27). As soon as Cerberus sees the light of the day, it becomes so scared and frightened that it pulls Hercules violently backward (just a few lines previously Hercules' strength overwhelmed the dog very easily) and the dog can be dragged further only with the additional help of Theseus. Finally, Cerberus must yield and finds shelter from the light of the day under Hercules' shadow. In relation to the final part of Cerberus' capture, Shelton rightly observed that 'at the end of the scene we are left with the puzzling picture of a frightened dog and two men dragging it towards the light it fears.'[43]

Phaedra (989–1122): The Sea Monster

The fourth act of the *Phaedra* deals with the messenger's narration of Hippolytus' death. The *rhesis* is a patchwork of different models freely adapted by Seneca, namely Euripides' treatment of the same episode in the *Hippolytus* (1173–248), Ovid (*Met.* 15, 497–529), and Virgil (*Aen.* 2, the description of Laocoon's death). However, the closest parallel to the Senecan *rhesis* is to be found in Petronius (*Sat.* 89) which features a similar reworking of epic material (Eumolpus delivers a messenger-like *rhesis* in *senarii* about the Virgilian episode of Laocoon). The *rhesis* is preceded by an introductory dialogue between Theseus and the *nuntius* (991–9) and closed by a dialogue between the two characters (1114–22); the speech of the messenger (1000–114) runs uninterrupted for 114 lines.[44] In the Euripidean model the messenger's *rhesis* runs for 76 lines, thus Seneca almost doubled the length of his primary model. The conspicuous length of the passage in Seneca results from a specific interest in 'developing narrative into description'.[45] In relation to this tendency, it is worth noticing that Seneca includes five similes (1011–14; 1029–30; 1048–9; 1072–5; 1090–2), whereas Euripides has just two brief ones (1201 and 1221). As Coffey and Mayer have observed 'these similes increase the bulk of the speech but not its impact';[46] for example, the comparison of Hippolytus' death to that of Phaethon is not particularly fitting and it provides a redundant image to the description (1090–2: *talis per auras non suum agnoscens onus/Solique falso creditum indignans diem/Phaethonta currus devium excussit polo*).[47]

Impersonality of the Narrator

Furthermore, when compared with the Euripidean messenger speech, the Senecan *nuntius* reports the fact in the utmost impersonal way. There are just two hints to the messenger's reaction to what he is reporting: the first one at line

1025 (*haec dum stupentes quaerimus*), but the hint remains vague since it is made in the first person plural and it is not really clear to whom this 'we' refers; the second one at line 1034 (*os quassat tremor*).[48] He resembles more an external narrator than a character involved in the action. In Euripides, on the contrary, the *nuntius* repeatedly alludes to his actual presence and emotional participation in the event (1173; 1187; 1195–7; 1198; 1204; 1206; 1208; 1216; 1240). The Euripidean messenger not only provides the reason why he assisted in the event (he is one of Hippolytus' servants since he calls him master thrice: 1187, 1196, 1219), but also concrete spatial coordinates of the place where it took place (namely the shore: 1173, 1179, 1199; 1209 where Hippolytus and his servants happened to be combing and scraping the horses; there Hippolytus came to know about Theseus' decree of exile). In Seneca all these details are missing; the messenger's speech begins with a description of Hippolytus in flight from his fatherland (1000–5 the reason for him to flee is not, as in Euripides, caused by Theseus' decree since he did not come to know about it); the messenger does not provide any explanation for his presence there and does not mention that Hippolytus is accompanied by his servants or companions.

Mimetic Present

Besides, the Senecan messenger's speech is delivered in the present tense (in the Euripidean model, the messenger relates the facts in the past tense); when the perfect is employed, it describes an instantaneous action (1007: *tonuit*; 1008: *crevitque*; 1022: *latuere*; 1031: *inhorruit*; 1032: *solvit, invexit*; 1050: *tremuere*; 1069: *rapuere*; 1088: *sensere*; 1101: *haesere*; usually in the first foot of the iambic metre for emphasis);[49] moreover, the perfect is also employed to provide the temporal escalation in a series of action, as, for example: at lines 1000–3: *Ut profugus urbem* **liquit** *infesto gradu/celerem citatis passibus cursum explicans,/ celso sonipedes ocius* **subigit** *iugo/et ora frenis domita substrictis* **ligat**.[50] The use of the present tense has the function to provide immediacy to the messenger's account by enhancing its vividness; such an impression is further reinforced by the handling of the narration, which does not seem to describe a past event, but one simultaneously taking place as the narration proceeds.

Running Commentary

A remarkable structural feature of the speech is that it involves a large number of changes of subjects, namely the shift between Hippolytus and the monster. The alternations can be summarized as follows:

1) Description of Hippolytus (1000–6);
2) Description of a sudden turbulence of the sea and the appearance of the sea monster (1007–49);
3) Description of the reaction of animals, men, and Hippolytus to the monster (1050–6);
4) Description of the monster chasing after Hippolytus introduced by a brief *ecphrasis topou* (1057–63);
5) Description of Hippolytus' and the horses' reactions to the monster (1064–75);
6) Description of the second attack of the monster (1077–81);
7) Description of the horses' flinging Hippolytus from the chariot (1082–104);
8) Description of the *famuli* gathering Hippolytus' dismembered body (1105–14).

Each of the eight stages described above features a running commentary. In more detail, the first running commentary describes Hippolytus hastening to yoke his horses to flee from the city (1000–6):

> Ut profugus urbem liquit infesto gradu   1000
> celerem citatis passibus cursum explicans,
> celso sonipedes ocius subigit iugo
> et ora frenis domita substrictis ligat.
> tum multa secum effatus et patrium solum
> abominatus saepe genitorem ciet,   1005
> acerque habenis lora permissis quatit.

In the second one, the running commentary describes at length the sea monster (1035–48).[51] In the third one, the running commentary deals with a description of Hippolytus trying to hold his horses (1055: *Hippolytus artis continet frenis equos*). The fourth describes the monster preparing to attack Hippolytus (1060–3).[52] The fifth deals again with Hippolytus trying to maintain the control of his horses crazed with fear (1072–7); Seneca uses a long epic simile, which compares Hippolytus' efforts to those of a helmsman holding a ship steady in the sea (1072–5):

> at ille, qualis turbido rector mari
> ratem retentat, ne det obliquum latus,
> et arte fluctum fallit, haud aliter citos
> currus gubernat ...   1075

The sixth describes a second attack of the monster (1077–81):

> sequitur assiduus comes,
> nunc aequa carpens spatia, nunc contra obvius
> oberrat, omni parte terrorem movens.
> non licuit ultra fugere: nam toto obvius   1080
> incurrit ore corniger ponti horridus.

The seventh describes the horses flinging down Hippolytus and Hippolytus' entangling in the reins of his chariot (1082–114). Suggestively, the description of Hippolytus' entanglement features a 'rapid alternation from excited movements to sudden halt ... then back to energetic movement';[53] for example, the quick movement described at line 1097 (*celeres ... pervolvunt rotae*) comes to a stop at line 1100 (*domino currus affixo stetit*); the fast speed is resumed at line 1101–2 (*et pariter moram/dominumque rumpunt*); at lines 1085–7 (*Praeceps in ora fusus implicuit cadens/laqueo tenaci corpus, et quanto magis/pugnat, sequaces hoc magis nodos ligat*), Seneca plays again with the contrast between movement (*praeceps, cadens, pugnat*) and stasis (*implicuit ... laqueo tenaci, nodos ligat*).

The final stage depicts the slaves gathering Hippolytus' dismembered body (1105–14): 1105–8: *Errant per agros funebris famuli manus, ... /maestaeque domini membra vestigant canes*; 1113–14: *passim ad supremos ille colligitur rogos/ et funeri confertur.*

In comparison with his models, it is evident that Seneca aims at emphasizing the supernatural and phantasmagorical elements of the event, so that the human scale, which is carefully looked after in Euripides, is here completely left behind. Thus the human boundaries are consciously and purposely overtaken and, as Segal has brilliantly argued, Seneca's description 'shifts from a more or less realistic human setting to a fantastic realm of changing shapes' aimed at producing 'an interiorized atmosphere of nightmarish terror'.[54] For instance, while Euripides does not describe the sea monster at all, Seneca devotes 14 lines (1035–49) to a detailed and colourful description of it:[55]

> quis habitus ille **corporis** vasti fuit!   1035
> caerulea taurus **colla** sublimis gerens
> erexit altam **fronte** viridanti iubam.
> stant hispidae **aures**, **orbibus** varius color,
> et quem feri dominator habuisset gregis
> et quem sub undis natus: hinc flammam vomunt   1040
> **oculi**, hinc relucent caerula insignes nota.

opima **cervix** arduos tollit **toros**
naresque hiulcis haustibus patulae fremunt.
musco tenaci **pectus** ac palear viret,
longum rubenti spargitur fuco **latus**;   1045
tum pone **tergus** ultima in monstrum coit
facies et ingens belua immensam trahit
squamosa partem. talis extremo mari
pistrix citatas sorbet aut frangit rates.[56]

Interestingly, even though the monster described is an imaginary beast, Seneca makes a detailed reference to the bodily parts of it: (1035: *corporis*; 1036: *colla*; 1037: *fronte*; 1038: *aures*; 1041: *oculi*; 1042: *cervix*; *toros*; 1043: *nares*; 1044: *pectus*; 1045: *latus*; 1046: *tergus*); in comparison with the Ovidian model, 'Seneca stresses the separately masses of the flesh, the massive heavy neck and the bulging hard muscles'.[57] Furthermore, lines 1036–7 (*caerulea taurus colla sublimis gerens/ erexit altam fronte viridanti iubam*) and 1046–8 (*tum pone tergus ultima in monstrum coit/facies et ingens belua immensam trahit/squamosa partem*) recall closely Virgil (*Aen. 2, 206–8: pectora quorum inter fluctus arrecta iubaeque/ sanguineae superant undas, pars cetera pontum/pone legit sinuatque immensa volumine terga*); from the comparison, it emerges that Seneca 'stresses metamorphosis and fusion of shape' (especially lines 1046–47: *ultima in monstrum coit/facies*).[58] Seneca adapts another Virgilian passage (*Georgics 3, 232–4: et temptat sese atque irasci in cornua discit/arboris obnixus trunco, ventosque lacessit/ictibus, et sparsa ad pugnam proludit harena*) at lines 1059–63:

hic se illa moles acuit atque iras parat.
ut cepit animos seque praetemptans satis   1060
prolusit irae, praepeti cursu evolat,
summam citato vix gradu tangens humum,
et torva currus ante trepidantes stetit.

The monster is called *illa moles* (1059), an indefinite mass, which awkwardly becomes animated with anger (1059: *iras parat*; 1060: *cepit animos*; 1061: *prolusit irae*). Moreover, the juxtaposition of *moles* (1059) and *animos* (1060) produces a 'baroque fluidity between animate and inanimate, reality and fantasy, movement and stasis'.[59] In addition, Seneca tends to 'blur the division between realistic and fantastic details'.[60]

A good example of this feature is the intentional portrayal of the sea and the monster as virtually one (1031–4):

inhorruit concussus undarum globus
solvitque sese et litori invexit malum
maius timore; pontus in terras ruit
suumque monstrum sequitur.[61]

In the passage, the monster and the wave are blended at 1032 (*solvitque sese*) and at 1034 (*suumque monstrum sequitur*). The use of the verb *inhorruit* provides 'a sinister quasi-personification on the mass of water' (*inhorruit concussus undarum globus* 1031).[62]

Lack of Advancement of the Plot

In terms of the advancement of the plot, the actions involved in the eight stages tend to repeatedly expand and recast the same issues, mostly the disturbance of the sea caused by the monster and Hippolytus' fight to control his horses terrified by the monstrous creature. As Segal has observed, while the Euripidean and Ovidian narrations of the same event proceed in a 'linear and distinctly articulated progression', the Senecan one moves in 'a succession of stages', which are repeated over and over again producing a series of 'individual climaxes'.[63] For example, the sea turbulence in the Senecan narrative occurs at 1007 (*cum subito vastum tonuit ex alto mare/crevitque in astra*), is repeated at 1015 (*consurgit ingens pontus in vastum aggerem*), and again at 1025–6 (*totum en mare immugit*) producing three climaxes; the fight of Hippolytus with his horses and the fact that the hero does not fear the monster is stated at 1054–6 (*solus immunis metus/Hippolytus artis continet frenis equos/pavidosque notae vocis hortatu ciet*), at 1064–77, and at 1082–4 (*Tum vero pavida sonipedes mente exciti/imperia solvunt seque luctantur iugo/eripere rectique in pedes iactant onus*), where Hippolytus is finally entangled in the reins.

From the analysis proposed above, it emerges that Seneca tries to create the impression of 'an unstable shifting between the real and the imaginary'. This shifting is produced by a constant contrast between two opposite features: on the one hand, the striving for vividness and immediacy (especially in the use of the present tense, of detailed descriptions, which provide an almost concrete physical and bodily reality to imaginary creatures and natural elements as well as the tendency to personify inanimate elements); on the other, the striving for emphasizing and piling up as many supernatural and phantasmagorical elements as possible. This tension (which Segal defines as the eminently peculiar feature of baroque style), in my opinion, finds a plausible explanation if we think that the aesthetics of pantomime may have been in Seneca's mind when composing the passage. In fact immediacy and vividness would have been needed in pantomime since the dancer was enacting the story of the libretto as the singer was singing it; but, at the same time, pantomimic performances would have allowed room for fantastic depictions of events and creatures since the gestural art of the dancer could allude freely to imaginary elements as he was not constrained by the protocols of more conventional theatrical performances.

Thyestes (623–788): Thyestes' Banquet

The fourth act of the *Thyestes* features a long messenger *rhesis* (147 lines) which narrates to the chorus Atreus' killing and dismemberment of Thyestes' sons; the messenger's report is basically a monologue, since the chorus, besides the usual introductory dialogue with the messenger (623–40), is in charge of just seven brief interventions (690; 715; 719; 730–1; 743; 745–6; 747–8). The dialogue deals primarily with the chorus trying to overcome the conventional unwillingness on the messenger's part to reveal the terrible events that he has witnessed (line 633: chorus: *Effare, et istud pande, quodcumque est, malum*; lines 634–6: messenger: *Si steterit animus, si metu corpus rigens/remittet artus. haeret in vultu trucis/imago facti*).

Despite his reluctance in relating the dreadful news, the messenger is then persuaded to speak and opens his speech with an extremely long and accurate *ecphrasis topou* (641–82);[64] the messenger's repeated unwillingness to speak as well as his worried attitude oddly turns into a speech starting with a detailed landscape digression. In relation to this, it is worth remembering that messengers in Greek tragedies tend to provide just limited spatial coordinates, which have the function of either defining the setting of the narration or their position in it. In relation to dramatic illusion, it is similarly awkward that the messenger is able to see Atreus' actions, since Atreus is performing them in the innermost part of the royal palace (652: *penetrale regni*), inaccessible to a messenger;[65] more importantly, even if present at the cruel killings, he did not make any attempt at restraining Atreus.[66]

Impersonality of the Narrator

Here as in all the other instances of the Senecan messenger *rheseis*, the messenger has the role of an external narrator detached from the actions he is describing. In fact, he makes no hints at his position in the action and to the reason why he happened to witness Atreus' inhuman and bestial slaughters. More importantly, even though at the very beginning of his speech the messenger shows fear, horror, and disgust for what he saw, as his speech moves forward all the signs of his initial frightened attitude have disappeared and he has just become a mouthpiece of the story so much so that he can reply with irony and black humour to the worried questions of the chorus (718: *avo dicatur: Tantalus prima hostia est*).[67]

The speech can be divided into five main sections:

1) *Ecphrasis* (641–82);
2) Description of the killings (682–729);
3) Atreus' *extispicium* (748–8);
4) Thyestes' feast (779–83);
5) The reversal of the course of the sun (784–8).

Ecphrasis: Imaginary Background and Animated Landscape

As mentioned above, the messenger's speech opens with a long *ecphrasis topou* describing the palace of Pelops and its innermost part where Atreus is going to perform his dreadful and sacrilegious misdeed. The description of the royal house and of the *nemus* (grove) enclosed in its interior emphasizes the darkness and hostility of the place, elements which provide an overall threatening and sinister atmosphere to the scene. The description tends to be hyperbolic, as, for example, in depicting the house of the Pelopidai as rising up high as a mountain (643: *aequale monti crescit*) and shares common elements with the description of the house of Dis in the *Hercules furens* (662–7) and of the sacred grove where Laius' ghost is raised from the Underworld (530–47) in the *Oedipus*.[68] For instance, the threatening nature of the royal palace in the *Thyestes* (643–5: *atque urbem premit/ et contumacem regibus populum suis/habet sub ictu*) closely resembles the similar oppressive environment surrounding the house of Dis in the *Hercules furens* (662–3: *Spartana tellus nobile attollit iugum,/densis ubi aequor Taenarus silvis premit*), where the sense of oppressiveness is conveyed by the verb *premere* used in both contexts. The description of the grove (650–8) inside the palace has also parallels in the *Oedipus* and in the *Hercules furens*, as, for example, in the presence of a set of ill-omened trees (*taxus, cupressus*, and *ilex*) above which a high oak towers; in the *Oedipus*, a more varied number of trees makes its appearance, but we find again a massive tree (542: *ingens arbor*) oppressing (543: *urget*) the smaller ones. Similarly, in the *Hercules furens* (689–90) a yew tree (*taxo*) hangs menacingly over the lower ones (690: *imminente*). Another common element is the presence of sluggish waters, a stagnant spring ending up in a black swamp in the *Thyestes* (665–6: *fons stat sub umbra tristis et nigra piger/haeret palude*), again a spring surrounded by a muddy swamp in the *Oedipus* (547: *limosa pigrum circumit fontem palus*), and the sluggish river of the Underworld which grows torpid with languid waters in the *Hercules furens* (763: *stupente ubi unda segne torpescit fretum*). Furthermore, the grove is characterized by the absence of light (678: *nox propria luco est*) as in the *Oedipus* (549: *praestitit noctem locus*) and in the *Hercules furens* (704–5: *et pigro sedet/nox atra mundo*). Finally, Seneca tends to personify the inanimate trees and plants of the grove; in relation to this, Seneca's choice of verbs in the description of it is remarkable: *nutat, eminens* (655), and *despectat* (656) strongly convey the impression that the grove is actually animated.[69] Similarly, the description of the fearful reactions of nature caused by Atreus' plans of revenge (696–702) tends to present inanimate objects as animated: the grove trembles in fear (696: *Lucus tremescit*), the palace sways and seems to waver (696–8: *tota succusso solo/nutavit aula, dubia quo pondus daret/ac fluctuanti similis*; it is interesting that Seneca uses here again the verb *nutare* as in 655), and ivory weeps in the temples (702: *flevit in templis ebur*).[70]

Sight and Sound Effects

The description of the grove is also characterized by a repeated interplay between sight (678 the appearance of a crowd of shades) and sound effects (668: *gemere*; 669: *catenis excussis, sonat*; 670: *ululant*; 675: *latratu*; 676: *remugit*; 681: *immugit*), which is introduced by the awkward statement that 'anything fearful to *hear* can be *seen* there' (670–1: *quidquid audire est metus/illic videtur*); Tarrant has remarked that the line stresses 'the progression upward in terror, from sound to sight', but the progression is not a linear one, going from sight to sound; on the contrary, the two different senses of perception are treated as a single one;[71] more precisely, the effects of sound tend to become effects of sight. In relation to this, it is worth noticing that some effects of sounds can be easily transformed into gestures; for instance, a mute cry could mime the verbs *gemere, ululant, latratu, remugit, immugit*. That Seneca aimed at stressing the effects of sound here is confirmed by the way he reworked a Virgilian line describing Tartarus (*Aen.* 6, 557–8: *hinc exaudiri gemitus, et saeva sonare/verbera, tum stridor ferri tractaeque catenae*): Seneca transforms the Virgilian *tractaeque catenae* into *catenis . . . excussis* as if the ghosts were actually shaking their chains.

Running Commentary

In the next section of the narrative, the messenger describes at length Atreus' slaughtering of Thyestes' sons. Atreus is described entering in a frenzy (682–3: *Quo postquam furens/intravit Atreus liberos fratris trahens*) and dragging Thyestes' sons.[72] As observed by Tarrant, Atreus 'plays all the parts in his sacrificial drama';[73] Atreus acts as if he were a *sacerdos* making a sacrificial rite: all the elements of the sacrifice are present: the altars, the incense, wine, the knife, and the *mola salsa*, a mixture of wheat and salt, which was used to sprinkle the victims; he also utters the formula required by the rite (691–2: *ipse funesta prece/letale carmen ore violento canit*).[74] Even more importantly, Atreus is the only character described in action, while the other characters involved, Thyestes' sons, are just passive victims who strangely do not even attempt the smallest resistance when he drags them, binds their hands behind their back, and wraps their heads with a purple band (683: *liberos fratris trahens*; 685–6: *post terga iuvenum nobiles revocat manus/et maesta vitta capita purpurea ligat*); then, he handles, arranges, and readies them for the knife (693–4: *ipse devotos neci/contrectat et componit et ferro apparat*). Even though the killings of the three young men are described as a slaughter, it is remarkable that just in one case, more specifically that of Tantalus, the narrator hints at the way in which the young boy faced death (720–1: *Stetit sui securus et non est preces/perire frustra passus*); the brief remark is followed by the crude description of the way Atreus kills Tantalus; thus, the narrative focuses primarily on giving a detailed account of the most gruesome aspects of the killing, indulging in the description of severed body parts, spray of gore, and the like (e.g. lines 727–9 in relation to Plisthenes' death: *colla percussa amputat;/cervice caesa truncus in pronum ruit,/querulum cucurrit murmure incerto caput*). To a certain extent, Thyestes' sons are already presented as simple pieces of flesh, thus foreshadowing the end their corpses will undergo. It is worth singling out the language chosen by Seneca to depict quite pictorially Tantalus' bravery in facing death by means of his bodily attitude: his steadiness is conveyed by the use of the verb *stetit*, which is remarkably common in such descriptions; for example, just a few lines before and after, the verb is used twice for Atreus (693: *stat ipse ad aras*; 704: *immotus Atreus constat*) and for the corpse of Tantalus (723–4: *educto stetit/ferro cadaver*). The verb produces a freezing of the action in which the character assumes a sort of statuary pose.[75] Usually, a new and sudden acceleration of the action follows the picture-like preceding moment; in the specific case examined here, the description of Tantalus' inner strength, translated into the image of physical immobility, is followed by the description of a quickly resuming of the action on the part of Atreus, who all of a sudden buries his sword in Tantalus' throat (721–3: *ast illi ferus/in vulnere ensem abscondit, et penitus premens/iugulo manum commisit*). Tarrant has singled out the 'grotesque juxtaposition of Atreus' hand and Tantalus' throat', where the insistence on the single parts of the body of the two characters is remarkable;[76] the same insistence characterizes also the descriptions of Plisthenes and of the third unnamed child of Thyestes: 727–8 *colla, cervice, truncus, caput*; 740–1 *corpus, pectore, tergo*. After the sword has been pulled out from Tantalus' body, the corpse hesitates on where to follow resulting in a 'depiction of a macabre mime of hesitation' (723–5: *educto stetit/ferro cadaver, cumque dubitasset diu/hac parte an illa caderet, in patruum cadit*).[77]

As previously mentioned, the scene is completely dominated by Atreus whose actions are the main centre of focus; to describe him Seneca also employs two extended similes, which very closely recall the type of similes also found in running commentaries used to describe the characters in violent action. In the first simile (707–14) Atreus is compared to a tiger, in the second one (732–40) to a lion.

> ieiuna silvis qualis in Gangeticis
> inter iuvencos tigris erravit duos,
> utriusque praedae cupida, quo primum ferat
> incerta **morsus**; flectit hoc **rictus** suos,   710
> illo reflectit et famem dubiam tenet:
> sic dirus Atreus **capita** devota impiae
> speculatur irae. quem prius mactet sibi,
> dubitat, secunda deinde quem caede immolet.

> Silva iubatus qualis Armenia leo
> in caede multa victor armento incubat;
> cruore **rictus** madidus et pulsa fame
> non ponit iras: hinc et hinc tauros premens   735
> vitulis minatur, **dente** iam lasso piger:
> non aliter Atreus saevit atque ira tumet.
> ferrumque gemina caede perfusum tenens,
> oblitus in quem fureret, infesta manu
> exegit ultra corpus.   740

As pointed out in relation to the similes in running commentaries, the comparison with an animal is common and used over and over again (*Med* 863: *tigris*; *HO* 241–2: *Armenia . . . tigris*; *Oed* 919: *Libycus . . . leo*; *Ag* 892: *hispidus . . . aper*; *Tro* 795: *iuvencus*; 1093–4: *ingentis ferae . . . fetus*). The emphasis in the two similes on dynamic elements such as anger, more specifically the outcome produced by anger and the uncertainty on which course of action to choose, can be considered standard motifs. The first simile is modelled on Ovid (*Met.* 5, 164–7: *tigris ut auditis diversa valle duorum/exstimulata fame mugitibus armentorum/nescit, utro potius ruat, et ruere ardet utroque, sic dubius Perseus, dextra laevane feratur*). Here as elsewhere, Seneca's reworking effects a simplification in the choice of the range of the linguistic register and in the image conveyed. It is remarkable how the language is repetitious and unvaried (710: *flectit*, 711: *reflectit*; 710: *morsus* and *rictus* in the same line and *rictus* again in the second simile 734). Furthermore, Seneca appropriates the Ovidian idea of the tiger wavering between two preys, but this uncertainty is conveyed by the image of the jaws and teeth of the wild beast not knowing where to bite first, while in Ovid the animal is uncertain as to which prey to direct its assault. The emphasis on jaws and teeth is also present in the second Senecan simile (734: *rictus*; 736: *dente*). There is also a difference in length between the Ovidian and the Senecan simile; the former is two lines long, while the latter is expanded by a 'loosely appended set of phrases elaborating the general description of the scene' (lines 710–11); the same is also true for the second simile at lines 734–6.[78] This tendency of elaborating and redundantly expanding on the same theme as well as the repetitious character of the linguistic register is also true for the simile of the lion.

In the third section of the narrative, Atreus performs an *extispicium* (748–78): he looks into destiny through the entrails of Thyestes' sons, he dismembers their limbs, and then cooks them. The single steps of the gruesome operation are described in detail: the organs torn from the living chests tremble (755: *erepta vivis exta pectoribus tremunt*); the veins pulse and the heart throbs in terror (756: *spirantque venae corque adhuc pavidum salit*); he handles the entrails and takes note of the still hot veins on the viscera (757–8: *at ille fibras tractat . . . /et adhuc calentes viscerum venas notat*). Then he cuts the body limb by limb (760–1: *ipse divisum secat/in membra corpus*); he chops away from the trunk the broad shoulder and the sinews of the arms (761–2: *amputat trunco tenus/umeros patentes et lacertorum moras*); he lays bare the joints and bones (763: *denudat artus durus atque ossa amputat*); he keeps just the faces and the hands given in trust (764: *tantum ora servat et datas fidei manus*).

The dismemberment is followed by the cooking: some bits of flesh are roasted on spits, while some others are boiled (765–7). Seneca ends this section of the narrative with the description of the reaction of the natural elements such as fire, flames, and smoke to Atreus' misdeed. Once again, the natural elements are animated as if personified; for instance, the fire leaps and refuses to burn (768: *transiluit ignis*; 770: *invitus ardet*); the flames tremble (768: *trepidantes focos*); the bodies and the flames groan (771–2: *nec facile dicam corpora an flammae magis/ gemuere*); the smoke does not go straight or rise into the air, but it smothers the household gods in a dense cloud (773–5: *et ipse fumus, tristis ac nebula gravis,/ non rectus exit seque in excelsum levat:/ipsos penates nube deformi obsidet*).

At this point in the narrative, all of a sudden the messenger abandons Atreus and moves to Thyestes; in fact the last lines of the act describe Thyestes' banquet (778–84), thus anticipating what is 'the starting-point in both time and setting for the next act'.[79] For what concerns dramatic illusion, the narrative requires that the messenger moves from the innermost part of the royal palace where Atreus performed the killings to the dining room where Thyestes' feast takes place in order to describe Thyestes in such a close focus (778–84):

> . . . lancinat natos pater
> artusque mandit ore funesto suos.
> nitet fluente madidus unguento comam   780
> gravisque vino est; saepe praeclusae cibum
> tenuere fauces. in malis unum hoc tuis
> bonum est, Thyesta, quod mala ignoras tua.
> sed et hoc peribit . . .

The description of Thyestes will continue then in the following act (908–19):

> (Lines 908–11):
> Aperta multa tecta conlucent face.
> resupinus ipse purpurae atque auro incubat,
> vino gravatum fulciens laeva caput.   910
> eructat.
> (Lines 913–19):
> satur est; capaci ducit argento merum-
> ne parce potu: restat etiamnunc cruor
> tot hostiarum; veteris hunc Bacchi color   915
> abscondet. hoc, hoc mensa claudatur scypho.
> mixtum suorum sanguinem genitor bibat:
> meum bibisset. ecce, iam cantus ciet
> festasque voces, nec satis menti imperat.

It is worth noting that the description of Thyestes in both passages echoes the Virgilian description of the Cyclops (*Aen.* 3, 626–7; 630–2):

> vidi atro cum membra fluentia tabo
> **manderet** et tepidi tremerent sub dentibus artus.
> nam simul expletus dapibus vinoque sepultus
> cervicem inflexam posuit, iacuitque per antrum
> immensus, saniem **eructans**.

In relation to Virgil, Lobe has suggested that the description of the Cyclops eating Ulysses' fellows was inspired by one of the stock characters of the Atellane, Dossenus;[80] Dossenus was a glutton and was alternatively named *manducus*.[81]

Thus, Manducus, the Virgilian Cyclops, and the Senecan Thyestes share features in common; they all eat as animals would. The verb *mandere*, in fact, describes the way animals eat and it strongly suggests an unnatural behaviour when used of men. In addition to this, the word suggests the noise made by the eater's teeth while biting the food. This characteristic belongs to Atreus as well; in fact, in the two similes discussed above, the vengeful king is compared to a hungry animal tusking his preys with his jaws (710–11: *flectit hoc rictus suos,/illo reflectit*) and the 'repeated ct sound may suggest the gnashing of teeth'.[82]

As discussed in Chapter 1, the story of Atreus and Thyestes was a very popular subject in pantomimic performances.[83] It is possible to suggest that in the story of Atreus and Thyestes, the theme of dismemberment (*sparagmos*)and cannibalism was what pantomime was most interested in. More generally, both themes were very popular and ancient authors repeatedly make reference to them.[84] Suggestively, the body itself of the dancer is said to be sinewless and fragmented by the ancient writers. Libanius (103), in describing the training of the dancer, claims that the training master actually dismembers the body of his pupil in order for him to achieve the suppleness and ability to move in isolation the single parts of the body. It is thus possible to suggest that the body of the dancer was 'equipped' to portray such a phenomenon.

In Seneca's tragedies too the theme of dismemberment recurs several times: in the case of the death of Hippolytus, Seneca describes in detail the dismemberment of Hippolytus' body which is emphasized to the point that the severed pieces of it are scattered in different and far-reaching directions.[85] Similarly, in the description of the death of Astyanax (1110–17), the messenger provides a detailed account of Astyanax's dismembered body after he has been hurled from the tower of Troy.

As underlined by Most, the theme of dismemberment in Neronian poetry is a pervasive one; he has suggested that one of the reasons for its presence in authors such as Seneca and Lucan may derive from the cruel spectacles of the circus where criminals, playing the roles of mythical characters such as Orpheus or Attis, were torn to pieces by animals.[86] I would add that the theme may also derive from pantomime, where, as we have seen, it was widely popular.

Trojan Women (1056–179): The Death of Astyanax and Polyxena

The fifth act of the *Trojan Women* features a long narrative recounting the deaths of Astyanax and Polyxena. In the whole *corpus* of Senecan tragedies this is the only play that presents a messenger's speech in the last act (usually final acts are devoted to a confrontation between the two major characters of the play). In some sense, the fact that the play ends with a description of Astyanax's and Polyxena's deaths is an unambiguous sign that they can be considered the two major characters, albeit silent, of Seneca's *Trojan Women*. Hecuba and Andromache play also a major role in the play and in this last act their presence justifies the messenger's narration.

The most striking feature of the narrative resides in the original and untraditional union of two events, namely Astyanax's and Polyxena's deaths, which were previously never combined together as a single episode. In Euripides' *Hecuba* (523–79), which was the major inspiring model for Seneca's narrative, the messenger *rhesis* narrates Polyxena's death; Astyanax's burial (and not death) was instead treated in Euripides' *Trojan Women* (1117–24).[87] The combination of the two events is thus most probably Seneca's own invention, which seems mainly motivated by the spectacular opportunities offered by the double dramatization of death.

The comparison between Seneca's narrative and Euripides' one in the *Hecuba* is worthy of scrutiny with the aim of outlining similarities and differences, since it can enable us to better evaluate Seneca's own purposes as compared to the Greek tragedian. The most substantial difference between the two narratives is primarily structural. In fact, the scene set up by Seneca is reduced to the minimum compared to the articulate and complex structure of the Euripidean one made up of blocks of narration developing a linear action. In Seneca, spatial and temporal coordinates are overlooked or unevenly treated; characters make sudden appearances and disappearances; lines and lines are devoted to describe a place but never to provide concrete spatial coordinates relative to the positions of the characters in the scene. For example, Seneca devotes several lines to the description of the place surrounding Achilles' tomb, but where is the crowd exactly positioned? Then, when Helen enters and leads the procession and Polyxena, where do they come from and where do they stop?[88] The handling of Pyrrhus' presence is similar; was he waiting for Polyxena by the tomb or was he in the procession as well?[89] In Euripides, the messenger says that he is standing by Achilles' tomb where also the Greek army and Polyxena are.

From a general point of view, this tendency to overlook a congruent structural development of the scene in the acts parallels the same tendency of structural looseness in the construction of the play as a whole, which has been discussed in Chapter 2.

The final act of the *Trojan Women* shows clearly that Seneca neglected structural unity, temporal and spatial continuity, as well as verisimilitude in favour of an accumulation and expansion of baroque descriptions juxtaposed one to the other.

Monologic and Impersonal Nature of the Speech

The narrative opens with a brief dialogue between the messenger, Andromache, and Hecuba (1056–68) and closes with Hecuba's lamentation over Troy's destiny (1165–77). The narration runs almost uninterrupted apart from two interventions of Andromache (1104–10; 1117).[90]

The messenger in charge of the narration, as in the other Senecan messenger's *rheseis*, fulfils the function of an external narrator who has somehow witnessed the facts he reports, but without taking a direct part in them. He does not give any information about his physical position in the event or his emotional reaction to it; only at the very beginning of the speech the messenger traditionally expresses his horror for the facts (1056: *O dura fata, saeva miseranda horrida!*; 1058–9: *quid prius referens gemam, tuosne potius, an tuos luctus, anus?*), but after this no other hints are made.[91]

Mimetic Present

The narrative is couched in the present tense (e.g. 1077: *cingitur; coit*; 1082: *gerit*; 1089: *incedit*; 1091: *pergit*; 1123: *cingit*; 1129: *odit; spectat*; 1131: *vident*; 1143: *stupet*; 1147: *antecedit*) which provides immediacy and vividness to the account (qualities which are further enhanced through the use of demonstrative adjectives or pronouns: 1071: *turre in hac*; 1075: *haec nota quondam turris*; 1078: *his*; 1080: *his*; 1082: *hunc; illum; hunc*; 1126: *hi*; 1127: *hi*; 1144: *hos*; 1145: *hos*).

The perfect is used to convey an instantaneous action (1158: *cecidit*; 1160: *flevit*; 1162–4: *non stetit fusus cruor/humove summa fluxit: obduxit statim/ saevusque totum sanguinem tumulus bibit*) or with *ut* in order to convey temporal relationships between two actions; the *ut* plus perfect construction is used to indicate that an action closely precedes the main one; thus it also conveys the sense of a rapid succession of two actions (1091–3: *ut summa stetit/pro turre, vultus huc et huc acres tulit/intrepidus animo*; 1118–21: *Praeceps ut altis cecidit e muris puer,/flevitque Achivum turba quod fecit nefas,/idem ille populus aliud ad facinus redît/tumulumque Achillis*; 1148–51: *Ut primum ardui/sublime montis tetigit, atque alte edito/iuvenis paterni vertice in busti stetit,/audax virago non tulit retro gradum*; lines 1155–8: *ut dextra ferrum penitus exactum abdidit,/subitus recepta morte prorupit cruor/per vulnus ingens*).

Structure

The narrative can be divided into ten sections, the first five devoted to Astyanax and the last five to Polyxena:

1) Opening *ecphrasis* describing the tower of Troy (1168–74);
2) Description of the crowd gathering around the tower to witness Astyanax's death (1075–87);
3) Description of Astyanax's death (1088–103);
4) Description of Astyanax's dismembered body after the fall from the tower (1110–17);
5) Description of the reactions of the crowd of Trojans and Greeks to Astyanax's death (1118–21);
6) *Ecphrasis* describing Achilles' tomb (1121–5);
7) Description of the crowd gathering around Achilles' tomb to witness Polyxena's death (1125–31);
8) Description of Polyxena's death (1132–59);
9) Description of the reactions of the crowd of Trojans and Greeks to Polyxena's death (1160–1);
10) Description of Polyxena's blood swallowed by Achilles' tomb (1162–4).

As is apparent from the above schematization, the sections of the narrative show that the narration is characterized by a re-iterated structure, which performs the function of presenting the deaths of Astyanax and Polyxena in a similar way.[92] In addition to this, it emerges that the main protagonists of the narrative are not just the two young Trojans condemned to death, but also the crowd watching the event. The physical location of the crowd in the space as well as its attitude and reaction to the sorrowful deaths play a major role in the narrative. The overall impression produced by the narrative is thus that Astyanax's and Polyxena's deaths are a sort of theatrical attraction in which the crowd is eager to participate, similar to an audience taking part in a show.

The fact that the deaths of the two young Trojans are treated as spectacle is confirmed by the fact that the crowd/audience sits in a location closely recalling an amphitheatre in Astyanax's case (lines 1076–7: *(turris) ... undique adfusa ducum/plebisque turba cingitur*) and a theatre in Polyxena's one (1123–5: *adversa cingit campus, et clivo levi/erecta medium vallis includens locum/crescit theatri more*). In addition to this, the impression that the crowd is an audience is enhanced by the use of the word *spectator* (1087) and of the verb *spectare* (1129 *spectat*), which are technical terms used for describing an audience looking at theatrical performances of different kinds.[93]

To shift from the two different locations of Astyanax's death and Polyxena's, Seneca also needs to introduce a sudden change of setting, since the messenger and the crowd need to move from the tower where Astyanax is killed to Achilles' tomb by the shore where Polyxena is sacrificed (1118–21: *Praeceps ut altis cecidit e muris puer,/flevitque Achivum turba quod fecit nefas,/idem ille populus aliud ad facinus redit/tumulumque Achillis*). With reference to dramatic illusion, the change of setting can still be acceptable since a freer handling of either space or time are traditionally accepted in messenger speeches. Nonetheless, the movement of the crowd from one place to the other gives the impression that the crowd is taking part in a sort of publicly organized event. In the case of Polyxena, it was established by tradition that her ritual killing was performed in front of the Greek army (although no mention was made of any Trojan participation in it); this public dimension was thus motivated by the fact that her death was meant to be a sacrifice in honour of Achilles. On the contrary, the decision to kill Astyanax was prompted more as a precautionary measure in order to avoid a future war and not as a ritual sacrifice. Seneca seems here to be manipulating his sources in order to construct a narrative which, by combining Astyanax's and Polyxena's deaths (1065: *duplex nefas*) in a single act, allows him plenty of spectacular as well as pathetic possibilities.

Ecphrasis

Conventionally, the proper narration begins with an *ecphrasis topou* (1068–74) which sets the scene for Astyanax's death; that is the tower of Troy enclosed within the city walls from which the young boy was hurled according to the literary tradition (e.g. Euripides' *Trojan Women* 1119–22; 1133–5); the messenger describes first the tower as it was before the war and as it is at the present moment after the conclusion of the conflict. The tower was the place where Priam used to direct the war from (1068–71: *Est una magna turris e Troia super,/assueta Priamo, cuius e fastigio/summisque pinnis arbiter belli sedens/regebat acies*) and was also the place where grandfather and son used to meet and watch Hector's victories over the Greeks (1071–4: *turre in hac blando sinu/fovens nepotem, cum metu versos gravi/Danaos fugaret Hector et ferro et face,/paterna puero bella monstrabat senex*).[94]

The *ecphrasis* is followed by the description of the gathering of a crowd to watch Astyanax's death-fall (1075–87). The messenger provides a detailed account of the different locations chosen by the crowd to watch the event: some prefer a distant but clear view provided by a hill (1078–9: *his collis procul/aciem patenti liberam praebet loco*); others choose a high cliff and stand on tip toe to get a better sight (1080–1: *his alta rupes, cuius in cacumine/erecta summos turba libravit pedes*); another group climbs up different trees so that the wood trembles under their weight (1082–3: *hunc pinus, illum laurus, hunc fagus gerit/et tota populo silva suspenso tremit*); someone chooses the edge of a sheer scarp (1084: *extrema montis ille praerupti petit*), someone else puts his weight on a half-burnt roof or a rock jutting from the collapsing wall (1085–6: *semusta at ille tecta vel saxum imminens/muri cadentis pressit*), and one most cruel spectator even sits on Hector's tomb (lines 1086–7: *atque aliquis (nefas)/tumulo ferus spectator Hectoreo sedet*).

The question arises as to what Seneca wanted to achieve with such a description, whose expected tragic impact is greatly diminished by the inclusion of tangentially relevant details, such as the position of the crowd and its movements, which continously keep shifting the focus from the main central action. In addition, the description does not have a pronounced ornamental nature, since the landscape portrayed does not produce an impression either of beauty or of fearful desolation. Secondly, the description does not aim at being functional (i.e. it does not provide verisimilar and economical spatial coordinates of the crowd in the space; on the contrary, the mob is scattered in locations quite distant from one another and some of them are quite unlikely since people even sit in trees). The description portrays rather a scene suitable to be mimetically enacted; such an impression is supported by the presence of two contrastive qualities, which are height and weight; lines 1078–81 are concerned with height (*collis*; *alta*; *cacumine*; *erecta*; *summos*; *libravit*); lines 1082–7 are concerned with weight (*gerit*; *suspenso*; *imminens*; *pressit*; *sedet*).

Running Commentary

The subsequent section of the narrative (1088–103) concentrates on Astyanax's death and opens with the description of Ulysses' and Astyanax's entrance, who are both characterized by their respective manner of walking: grand in the case of Ulysses (1088–9: *sublimi gradu/incedit Ithacus parvulum dextra trahens*), not lagging in that of Astyanax (1090: *nec gradu segni puer/ad alta pergit moenia*). The following description of Astyanax is similar in content and style to those found in 'running commentaries':

(Lines 1091–8):

... ut summa stetit
pro turre, vultus huc et huc acres tulit
intrepidus animo. qualis ingentis ferae
parvus tenerque fetus et nondum potens
saevire dente iam tamen tollit minas   1095
morsusque inanes temptat atque animis tumet:
sic ille dextra prensus hostili puer
ferox superbit ...

The description is conventional in several respects: the use of the verb *stetit* as soon as a character makes his/her entrance is a standard element; the gazing around is also a recurring feature (e.g. *Tro* 458: *oculosque nunc huc pavida, nunc illuc ferens*). Conventional is also the extended simile that compares Astyanax to the cub of a wild animal; already in the third act of the same play, Astyanax was compared to a young calf attacked by a lion whose mother tries to defend in vain (794–8: *fremitu leonis qualis audito tener/timidum iuvencus applicat matri latus,/ at ille saevus matre summota leo/praedam minorem morsibus vastis premens/ frangit vehitque*).

In addition, Seneca tends to accumulate synonyms to convey the idea of Astyanax's bravery in facing death (1090–8: *nec gradu segni, acres, intrepidus, animis tumet, ferox, superbit*);[95] the boy's courage is stressed again a few lines later by the remark that he, who is wept for, is the only one who does not cry (1099–100: *non flet e turba omnium/qui fletur*);[96] his heroic attitude has moved even Ulysses (1098–9: *moverat vulgum ac duces/ipsumque Ulixem*). This accumulation of pathetic elements reaches its climax with Astyanax's voluntary leap to death (1100–3: *ac, dum verba fatidici et preces concipit Ulixes vatis et saevos ciet/ad sacra superos, sponte desiluit sua/in media Priami regna*).

The next section of the narrative describes at length Astyanax's dismembered body after the fall from the tower (1110–17):

           Quos enim praeceps locus   1110
reliquit artus? ossa disiecta et gravi
elisa casu; signa clari corporis,
et ora et illas nobiles patris notas,
confudit imam pondus ad terram datum;
soluta cervix silicis impulsu, caput   1115
ruptum cerebro penitus expresso: iacet
deforme corpus.

Seneca's report echoes Euripides' parallel passage in the *Trojan Women* where Hecuba hints at the pitiful state of the boy's body after the fall (lines 1173–4; 1176–7). Nonetheless, the precision and length of the physical detail provided by the Roman writer is not found in his Greek antecedents. The description parallels those of Hippolytus and of Thyestes' sons, whose dismembered bodies are graphically portrayed.[97] It is indeed remarkable that the passage opens with an awkward rhetorical question about what kind of body the steep place has left (1110–11: *Quos enim praeceps locus/reliquit artus?*). As a reply to this odd question, the messenger gives an explicit and almost scientific account of the dismembered body, which in Euripides is only hinted at in Hecuba's words. In this way, the explicit account of the dismemberment, purposely framed as it is, seems to stand for itself and to have its own role in the passage.

Ecphrasis

The account of the dismembered body of the Trojan young boy closes the section on Astyanax. The transition between the two sections of the narrative is abrupt and the connection is awkward (1118–21: *Praeceps ut altis cecidit e muris puer,/flevitque Achivum turba quod fecit nefas,/idem ille populus aliud ad facinus redît/tumulumque Achillis*). The transition provides the new setting of the scene: Achilles' tomb, to which is devoted the second *ecphrasis topou* of the narrative (1121–5):

> . . . cuius extremum latus
> Rhoetea leni verberant fluctu vada;
> adversa cingit campus, et clivo levi
> erecta medium vallis includens locum
> crescit theatri more . . .   1125

The following section describes the gathering of the crowd, which parallels the same description in Astyanax's narrative:

> (Lines 1125–31):
>   . . . concursus frequens   1125
> implevit omne litus. hi classis moras
> hac morte solvi rentur, hi stirpem hostium
> gaudent recidi; magna pars vulgi levis
> odit scelus spectatque. nec Troes minus
> suum frequentant funus et pavidi metu   1130
> partem ruentis ultimam Troiae vident

Unlike the parallel section on the gathering for Astyanax's death, where the locations chosen by the crowd are portrayed, the description here addresses the different reactions provoked in the crowd of Greeks and Trojans by Polyxena's death;[98] some rejoice (lines 1127–8: *hi stirpem hostium/gaudent recidi*); others are horrified by the crime but eager to watch (lines 1128–9: *magna pars vulgi levis/odit scelus spectatque*); the Trojans are frightened and full of sorrow since they are assisting the final act of Troy's destruction (lines 1129–31: *nec Troes minus/suum frequentant funus et pavidi metu/partem ruentis ultimam Troiae vident*). Similar to the Astyanax section, demonstrative pronouns (1126: *hi*; 1127: *hi*) as well as other distinguishing nouns (*magna pars*; *Troes*) are employed, but this time to differentiate the groups in the crowd reacting in different ways. Indeed the reactions of the crowd play a major role across all the sections relative to Polyxena. As she enters, both Greeks and Trojans are held paralysed by terror (1136–7: *terror attonitos tenet/utrosque populos*). At her sight the people are astonished for different reasons (1143: *stupet omne vulgus*); some are moved by her beauty (1144: *hos movet formae decus*); some by her tender age (1145: *hos mollis aetas*); some others by the inconstant alternation of human life (1145: *hos vagae rerum vices*); but all of them are deeply touched by the braveness of her spirit in facing death head-on (1146: *movet animus omnes fortis et leto obvius*; 1153: *tam fortis animus omnium mentes ferit*) and they admire as well as feel pity for her (1148: *mirantur ac miserantur*). The climax in the description of the reactions is reached after Polyxena has received the fatal blow, when the entire crowd literally weeps (1160: *uterque flevit coetus*); the emotional peak is built up through the increase of sound effects produced by the Greeks and Trojans: in fact, the Trojans just utter timid laments (1160–1: *et timidum Phryges/misere gemitum*), while the Greeks lament loudly (1161: *clarius victor gemit*).

The description of the crowd's reactions in both passages dealing with Astyanax and Polyxena closely parallels the reactions of the natural elements caused by the perpetuation of evil actions found in the other narrative set-pieces and can be thus interpreted accordingly.

Running Commentary

The next section of the narrative deals with Polyxena's sacrifice (lines 1132–59); Helen is the character in charge to lead the Trojan girl to Achilles' tomb where she will be sacrificed (1132–4):

> cum subito thalami more praecedunt faces
> et pronuba illi Tyndaris, maestum caput
> demissa.

Helen is characterized as the bride woman (*pronuba*) who leads the wedding procession; this would imply that the deception of the marriage has not yet been uncovered. Nonetheless, this is not the case, since not only Polyxena but even the crowd already know what her destiny is about to be. This kind of incongruence is not isolated in the Senecan *corpus*; on the contrary, Seneca often overlooks details of this kind. In this specific case, I think Seneca's neglect for an obvious contradiction may be explained by the fact that presenting Polyxena in bridal dress while led by Helen to her execution was visually a spectacular *coup de théâtre* to exploit.

The description of Polyxena is divided in two parts; the first one describes her physical appearance characterized by her shining beauty (1137–42), while the second one involves a long account of the heroic way in which she faces death (1147–59).

(Lines 1137–42):
           ... Ipsa deiectos gerit
vultus pudore, sed tamen fulgent genae
magisque solito splendet extremus decor,
ut esse Phoebi dulcius lumen solet   1140
iamiam cadentis, astra cum repetunt vices
premiturque dubius nocte vicina dies.

The description insists on Polyxena's modesty, which is conveyed by the lowering of her gaze (1137–8: *ipsa deiectos gerit/vultus pudore*) and her attitude is contrasted to that of Helen who lowers her eyes too (1133–4: *maestum caput/demissa*) but out of shame instead of modesty.[99] The description conventionally resorts to an extended simile to convey Polyxena's glimmering beauty, which is compared to heavenly bodies; the comparison has a long tradition especially in the elegiac genre from where Seneca most probably appropriated it.[100]

(Lines 1148–59):
           ... Ut primum ardui
sublime montis tetigit, atque alte edito
iuvenis paterni vertice in busti stetit,   1150
audax virago non tulit retro gradum;
conversa ad ictum stat truci vultu ferox.
tam fortis animus omnium mentes ferit,
novumque monstrum est Pyrrhus ad caedem piger.
ut dextra ferrum penitus exactum abdidit,   1155
subitus recepta morte prorupit cruor

per vulnus ingens. nec tamen moriens adhuc
deponit animos: cecidit, ut Achilli gravem
factura terram, prona et irato impetu.

In contrast to the death-narrative of Astyanax, Seneca could rely on Euripides'
and Ovid's treatment of Polyxena's death to shape his own account; even
though the narration bears similarities with its models, nonetheless, differences
are by far more conspicuous. One of the main substantial divergences is
Polyxena's silence, which some scholars have argued Seneca took from Sophocles'
Polyxena.[101] However, Polyxena's silence ensures that the image of her moral
attitude in facing death is conveyed through her physical attitude: she does not
step back in front of her executioner and she faces the blow frowning in defiance
(1151–2: *audax virago non tulit retro gradum;/conversa ad ictum stat truci vultu
ferox*). The description of the fatal blow also deserves a close reading. Seneca
describes almost scientifically and in a sort of slow motion the starting and the
finishing movement of the striking hand (*dextra*) plunging the sword in
Polyxena's body;[102] the gesture's path is from the outside to the inside beginning
with the unsheathing of the sword (*exactum*) and ending with the plunging of it
deeply into the body (*penitus*). The juxtaposition of *penitus* and *exactum*
emphasizes the two relevant moments (1155–7: *ut dextra ferrum penitus exactum
abdidit,/subitus recepta morte prorupit cruor/per vulnus ingens*).

The description in Euripides, instead, employs a metaphor and carefully
avoids providing too precise details (566–8); similarly, Ovid briefly hints at the
blow and portrays it through a poetic and elusive image (*Met.* 13, 476: *praebita
coniecto rupit praecordia ferro*). In the description of Polyxena's fall after she has
been struck, Seneca insists anew on her fierce resistance and hatred towards her
enemies. The verb *cecidit*, usually used to describe the fall of trees after they have
been cut or uprooted, gives the impression of a weighty and massive fall and also
suggests the noise produced by its impact on the ground.[103] The heavy and
violent fall matches the angry force (*irato impetu*) Polyxena imposes upon
Achilles' tomb. In Euripides and Ovid, by contrast, Polyxena falls composedly
down to the earth taking care to cover her body and guarding the honour of her
modesty (Euripides 568–70; Ovid 479–80).

The narration ends with the tragic and violent image of Achilles' tomb greedily
drinking Polyxena's blood (1162–4: *non stetit fusus cruor/humove summa fluxit:
obduxit statim/saevusque totum sanguinem tumulus bibit*); the close position of
the verb *fluxit* and *obduxit* in the line is remarkable especially in relation to the
sound produced by the repetition of the same ending (*-xit*) which seems to
match the noise produced by the mound swallowing the blood.

Oedipus (509–708): The Necromancy of Laius' Ghost

The third act of the *Oedipus* features a long narrative dealing with the account of the necromancy of Laius' ghost.[104] Creon delivers the narrative, since Oedipus charged him with the report of Tiresias' raising of Laius' ghost whom the seer thought could reveal the reasons why Thebes was afflicted by a devastating and long-lasting plague. The narrative does not have parallels in any extant tragic antecedents and may have been Seneca's own invention; in Sophocles' *Oedipus* there are no elements that may be remotely flagged as precedents for Seneca's motif. However, the tendency to linger in the treatment of events of a supernatural and wondrous nature is at any rate a peculiar mark of Seneca's tragedies. We have already mentioned the incantation scene in the *Medea*, the descent to the Underworld in the *Hercules furens*, the several apparitions of ghosts and shadowy figures. As has been discussed in Chapter 1, pantomime seems to have been particularly fond of such supernatural themes.[105]

Impersonality of the Narrator

The role of Creon is here equivalent to that of a messenger, who is usually in charge of relating offstage actions. The account is as impersonal as an account can be and just three hints are made by Creon to his personal reactions to the events he is describing (595: *nos liquit animus*; 583–6: *ipse pallentes deos/vidi inter umbras, ipse torpentes lacus/noctemque veram: gelidus in venis stetit/haesitque sanguis*; 623: *fari horreo*). No spatial coordinates are provided for Creon's position within the narrative, or for that of Manto who is also present, as we infer from the only remark made in the narrative about her (595–6: *ipsa quae ritus senis/artesque norat stupuit*). Creon does not describe how Tiresias, Manto, and he himself reached the grove, since his speech begins in the most impersonal way possible with the traditional epic formula *est locus*. Because of this, Creon does not even seem to have taken part in the rite; in the case of Tiresias, instead, his initial position is provided (548: *huc ut sacerdos intulit senior gradum*); but, since no mention of him has been made in the narrative so far (530–47), his appearance comes not only unexpectedly but is also shaped as that of a character entering onstage; afterwards, Tiresias' exit is also uncued since he simply disappears with no further notice after he has performed the rite and Laius' ghost has been raised.

As to the location of the rite, Creon sets the scene in two different places: firstly under the huge tree in the grove of the Dircean valley (530–1: *est procul ab urbe lucus ilicibus niger/Dircaea circa vallis inriguae loca*; 542–7: *medio stat ingens arbor atque umbra gravi/silvas minores urget et magno ambitu/diffusa ramos una defendit nemus./tristis sub illa, lucis et Phoebi inscius,/restagnat umor frigore aeterno rigens;/limosa pigrum circumit fontem palus)*; then, inside a cave (556–7: *nigro bidentes vellere atque atrae boves/antro trahuntur;* 564–5: *multo specum/saturat cruore)*. The fluidity of the location contrasts with the presence of the deictic adverb (*huc*), which points to a precise spot. In summary, the spatial coordinates of the narrative are neither consistently nor accurately provided and are not aimed at giving a clear and fixed setting for the scene. Seneca seems thus interested just in sketching an atmospheric location in which there are a traditional threatening grove and a conventional dark cave.

Mimetic Present

As to temporal coordinates, the narrative is couched in the present tense and the perfect tense is used either to convey the temporal coordinates to the actions performed or to describe instantaneous actions.[106] Temporal coordinates thus mirror the function of spatial ones in terms of fluidity and vagueness since they convey an invariably present and depthless time. The present in permanency gives the impression that the action unfolds along a timelessly flat surface and the vague spatial coordinates the impression of characters moving in a fluidly atmospheric vacuum.

The narrative is opened and closed by two dialogues between Oedipus and Creon (511–29; 659–708), while in the central part (530–658) the account of Creon runs uninterrupted. The narrative is divided into five main sections:

1) *Ecphrasis topou* (529–47);
2) Description of Tiresias performing the rite to raise Laius' ghost (549–69);
3) Reactions of the natural elements (569–81);
4) Opening of the earth and appearance of the creatures of the Underworld (582–619);
5) Appearance of Laius' ghost (619–58).

Ecphrasis

The narrative opens with the standard *ecphrasis topou*. The description portrays the Theban grove where Tiresias performs his magical rite (530–47) and is heavily indebted to the Virgilian description of the Underworld, thus sharing several features in common with the *ecphraseis* in the *Hercules furens* and *Thyestes*. Like the *ecphraseis* of the *locus horridus* in the *Hercules furens* and *Thyestes*, the one in the *Oedipus* is conventional in many respects: the grove is characterized by darkness and absence of light, which does not filter because of the density of the trees (530: *Est procul ab urbe lucus ilicibus niger*; 545: *lucis et Phoebi inscius*; 549: *praestitit noctem locus*);[107] the traditional set of ill-omened trees associated with death such as holm oaks (530: *ilicibus*) and cypresses (532: *cupressus*) is present as well as sluggish waters (546–7: *restagnat umor frigore aeterno rigens; limosa pigrum circumit fontem palus*).[108]

Here as in the parallel *ecphraseis topou*, the landscape tends to be presented as if animated; the use of dynamic active verbs capture the activities of the several kinds of trees that feature in the narrative: a cypress, lifting its head above the lofty wood, holds the grove in its evergreen embrace (532: *cupressus altis exerens silvis caput/ virente semper alligat trunco nemus*);[109] an ancient oak spreads its gnarled branches crumbling in decay (534–5: *curvosque tendit quercus et putres situ/annosa ramos*); a pine-tree, facing the sun, lifts its knotless bole to front the winds (540–1: *et Phoebo obvia/enode Zephyris pinus opponens latus*); a huge tree overwhelms and defends the smaller ones (542–4: *medio stat ingens arbor atque umbra gravi/silvas minores urget et magno ambitu/diffusa ramos una defendit nemus*).

Running Commentary

The landscape digression is followed by the description of Tiresias attending the rite of raising the spirit of Laius from the Underworld. The second part of the narrative deals with a description of the ritual performed by Tiresias (559–68) and is modelled on the Virgilian parallel sacrificial scene (*Aen.* 6, 243 ff.). Töchterle has remarked that the structure of this section does not have a clear and logical sequence, but is built up through a repetitious doubling of recurrent elements.[110] For example, Tiresias' entrance (548; 554) and his attire (550–4) are described twice; the sacrifice of the animals is performed first at 558 and again at 564; the libation of blood occurs two times (563; 564); Tiresias twice sings the magical formula (561–2; 567–8); the splitting of the earth occurs first at 570–1 and again at 582–3.

(Lines 548–55):
Huc ut sacerdos intulit senior gradum,
haud est moratus: praestitit noctem locus.
tum effossa tellus, et super rapti rogis   550
iaciuntur ignes. ipse funesto integit
vates amictu corpus et frondem quatit;
squalente cultu maestus ingreditur senex,
lugubris imos palla perfundit pedes,
mortifera canam taxus astringit comam.   555

In this first part of the description, the narrative focuses on redundantly portraying the physical appearance of the old seer: as he enters the grove, he covers his body with a funeral vestment (551–2: *ipse funesto integit/vates amictu corpus*); he then advances in a squalid garb of mourning (554: *squalente cultu maestus ingreditur senex*) and wears a mantle (*palla*), which sweeps over his feet (553: *lugubris imos palla perfundit pedes*);[111] his white hair is bound with a wreath of death-dealing yew.

> (Lines 559–68):
> Vocat inde manes teque qui manes regis
> et obsidentem claustra letalis lacus,   560
> carmenque magicum volvit et rabido minax
> decantat ore quidquid aut placat leves
> aut cogit umbras; sanguinem libat focis
> solidasque pecudes urit et multo specum
> saturat cruore; libat et niveum insuper   565
> lactis liquorem, fundit et Bacchum manu
> laeva, canitque rursus ac terram intuens
> graviore manes voce et attonita citat.

The second part of the description properly deals with the sacrificial rite. The actions performed by Tiresias recall closely those of Medea in the incantation scene (*Med* 670–843) and of Atreus' killings of Thyestes' sons, which configures itself as a sacrificial rite (*Thy* 623–788); for instance, both Tiresias and Medea wave branches (*Oed* 552: *et frondem quatit*; *Med* 804–5: *tibi iactatur/tristis Stygia ramus ab unda*), perform the rite with their left hand (*Oed* 566–7: *fundit et Bacchum manu/laeva*; *Med* 680: *et triste laeva comprecans sacrum manu*), prepare the fire on which to burn the sacrificial victims (*Oed* 550: *et super rapti rogis/ iaciuntur ignes*; *Med* 799–800: *tibi de medio rapta sepulcro/ fax nocturnos sustulit ignes*), and make libation of blood (*Oed* 563: *sanguinem libat focis*; *Med* 811: *sacrum laticem percussa dedi*). Tiresias, Medea, and Atreus sing the ritual formulae (*Oed* 561: *carmenque magicum volvit et rabido minax/decantat ore*; 567–8: *canitque rursus ac terram intuens/graviore manes voce et attonita citat*; *Med* 738–9: *Sonuit ecce vesano gradu/canitque*; *Thy* 691–2: *Ipse est sacerdos, ipse funesta prece/letale carmen ore violento canit*). As in the case of Seneca's *ecphraseis*, repetitiousness and unvaried handling are present in sacrificial scenes, which, no matter what type of rite is described, all recast the same set of stereotyped elements.

The following section (569–81) deals with a detailed description of the reactions of the natural elements to Tiresias' rite:

(Lines 569–71):
latravit Hecates turba; ter valles cavae
sonuere maestum, tota succusso solo
pulsata tellus . . .

(Lines 574–81):
subsedit omnis silva et erexit comas,
duxere rimas robora et totum nemus   575
concussit horror; terra se retro dedit
gemuitque penitus, sive temptari abditum
Acheron profundum mente non aequa tulit,
sive ipsa tellus, ut daret functis viam,
compage rupta sonuit, aut ira furens   580
triceps catenas Cerberus movit graves.

The description of the reactions of the natural elements is extremely extended, especially when we compare it with its Virgilian model (*Aen.* 6, 255–8: *ecce autem primi sub lumina solis et ortus/sub pedibus mugire solum et iuga coepta moveri/silvarum, visaeque canes ululare per umbram/adventante dea*); despite its singular extension, the description is conventional in the set of phenomena portrayed, in the animated nature of the reactions of inanimate objects, and in the linguistic register adopted to describe them. As to phenomena described, the reactions of the natural elements are traditionally characterized by the production of trembling, laments, bays, mournful noises (569–80: *latravit*; *sonuere*; *concussit*; *gemuitque penitus*; *sonuit*) and tend to metamorphose themselves into sound effects, of which the shaking of the chains is one of the most peculiar, though not unparalleled (580–1: *aut ira furens/triceps catenas Cerberus movit graves*).[112] Here as in the *ecphraseis*, the impression that the reactions of the natural elements are those of animate beings is produced by the use of active verbs, which have as subjects inanimate objects: thrice the deep valley gave out a mournful noise (569–70: *ter valles cavae/sonuere maestum*); the wood shrank down and bristled its foliage/hair (574: *subsedit omnis silva et erexit comas*); the trunks split open, (575: *duxere rimas robora*); horror shook the whole wood (575–6: *et totum nemus/concussit horror*); the earth also shrank back and gave a groan from her depths (576–7: *terra se retro dedit/gemuitque penitus*).

As to the linguistic register, the language adopted is almost formulaic; compare for example the barking of Hecate's dogs in *Oed* (569–70: *latravit Hecates turba; ter valles cavae/sonuere maestum*) with *Med* (840–1: *ter latratus audax Hecate/dedit*) and *Med* (765: *sonuere fluctus*); *Oed* (570–1: *tota succusso solo/pulsata tellus*) with *Thy* (696–7: *tota succusso solo/nutavit aula*); *Oed* (574: *subsedit omnis silva et erexit comas*) with *Tro* (173: *movere silvae capita*); *Oed* (575–6: *totum nemus/concussit horror*) with *Med* (926: *Cor pepulit horror*), *Tro* (168: *artus horridus quassat tremor*), and *Phae* (1034: *Os quassat tremor*); *Oed* (576–7: *terra . . . /gemuitque penitus*) with *Phae* (350: *tum silva gemit murmure saevo*) and *Ag* (468: *tractuque longo litus ac petrae gemunt*); *Oed* (579–80: *sive ipsa tellus, ut daret functis viam,/compage rupta sonuit*) with *Tro* (173–4: *excelsum nemus/fragore vasto tonuit*), *Tro* (171–2: *cum subito caeco terra mugitu fremens/concussa totos traxit ex imo sinus*), and *Phae* (1007: *cum subito vastum tonuit ex alto mare*).

The following section (582–619) describes the splitting of the earth and the appearance of the hellish creatures. As discussed above, the opening of the earth first happens at 579–80 and again at 582–3 (*Subito dehiscit terra et immenso sinu/ laxata patuit*);[113] the presence of the adverb *subito* ('suddenly', even though contrasting with the fact that the earth has already opened) and the emphasis on the width of the cavity (*immenso sinu*) are recurrent features that provide pathos to the description. The hellish creatures appear in two groups; in the first one, mythical figures such as the whole snaky brood (586–8: *saeva prosiluit cohors/et stetit in armis omne vipereum genus*), the armed men sown from Dircean teeth (588: *fratrum catervae dente Dircaeo satae*), the Erinys (590: *tum torva Erinys sonuit*), and personified abstractions such as Rage, Horror, Grief, Disease, Old Age, Fear, and Plague (590–5) make their parade.[114]

Here as in the *Hercules furens*, the proper activity of some of the personified abstractions is described: Grief tears away its hair (592: *Luctus avellens comam*);[115] Disease barely supports its weary head (593: *aegreque lassum sustinens Morbus caput*), Plague is hungry for the Ogygian people (589: *avidumque populi Pestis Ogygii malum*).

The second group of creatures is summoned by Tiresias' further utterance (597: *convocat*, 607: *vatis eduxit sonus*) which brings forth the bloodless multitude of cruel Dis;[116] the parade features Zethus, Amphion, Niobe, Agave, and Pentheus. Here as in the case of the personified abstractions, the individual activity of the mythical figures is described: Zethus restrains with his right hand a fierce bull by the horns (609–11: *primus emergit solo,/dextra ferocem cornibus taurum premens,/Zethus*); Amphion holds with his left hand the lyre (611–12:

manuque sustinet laeva chelyn/qui saxa dulci traxit Amphion sono);[117] Niobe carries her head high in arrogance and counts her ghosts (613–15: *interque natos Tantalis tandem suos/tuto superba fert caput fastu grave/et numerat umbras);*[118] Agave is frenzied (615–17: *peior hac genetrix adest/furibunda Agave, tota quam sequitur manus/partita regem*); Pentheus fiercely continues his threats (617–18: *sequitur et Bacchas lacer/Pentheus tenetque saevus etiamnunc minas*).

The last section of the narrative deals with the emerging of Laius' shade (619–58); the section first provides a description of Laius' physical appearance (619–21; 622–3) and a report of his words delivered in direct speech:

(Lines 624–6):
stetit per artus sanguine effuso horridus,
paedore foedo squalidam obtentus comam,
et ore rabido fatur . . .

The description of Laius is conventional; the verb *stetit* is widely employed in these kinds of descriptions;[119] from a stylistic point of view, I would suggest that the instantaneous perfect *stetit* may perform the function of depicting a static and tableau-like pose, which strongly contributes to the fear and surprise, in this specific case, to Laius' ghostly appearance. The hair or the hairstyle is also a constant feature; the expression employed to describe it is almost the same (*Tro* 450: *squalida obtectus coma*) as the one used of Hector in the *Trojan Women*;[120] similarly, the phrase employed to convey the way the character speaks (*ore rabido*) recurs;[121] because the first meaning of the word *os* is mouth/face, but the word can be used as a metonym for voice, there is an ambiguity whether Seneca is describing (here as well as in the other instances of the word) the expression of the face or the tone of voice of the character.

Laius' appearance shares several features in common with the appearance of Achilles' ghost in the *Trojan Women* (164–202), even though the shade of Achilles is not raised from the dead by an appropriately organized ritual, but just happens to appear of its own accord to demand Polyxena's sacrifice. Since the Achilles' scene has the shape of an abridged version of the conventional Senecan messenger's scene, the two narratives seem to be equivalent also from a formal point of view. Even in the case of Achilles' ghost, its appearance is preceded by a series of similar supernatural events that closely recalls those in the *Oedipus*.[122] Furthermore, both the shades of Laius and that of Achilles deliver their accusations and requests, which are reported in direct speech.[123] The recurrence of ghostly travesties in Seneca's tragedies and the stereotyped handling of their appearances enhance the impression that these supernatural figures played a prominent role and had a specific function in the tragedies.[124] The horrific though spectacular presence of such supernatural figures may have been again a sign of the influence of pantomime, which heavily relied on such means to impress its audience.

Agamemnon (421–578): The Sea Storm

The third act of Seneca's *Agamemnon* is devoted to the messenger's long description of the storm that wrecked the Greek fleet. In the tragic tradition the first treatment of this episode is found in Aeschylus' *Agamemnon*, but Seneca's treatment of the storm seems to owe very little to its Greek predecessor.[125] For instance, the extremely broad length of the Senecan messenger's narration of the storm (157 lines: 421–578) appears as the most conspicuous difference when compared with the length of Aeschylus' treatment of the same topic in his *Agamemnon* (56 lines: 636–80).

In the context of Latin literature, descriptions of storms held a long and well-established tradition.[126] In tragedy, Pacuvius' storm in the *Teucer* was most celebrated. In epic, Virgil's and Ovid's storms (*Aen.* 1, 81–156; 3, 192–208; *Met.* 11, 474–572) are the closest models from which Seneca drew the material for his account. The mythological arrangement given to it by Seneca, which combines three distinct episodes, namely the sea storm that destroys the Greek fleet on its way home, the death of Ajax Oileus, and Nauplius' treachery, is peculiar. As possible sources for Seneca's storm, Tarrant names Lycophron's *Alexandra* and a five-act mechanical puppet-show on Nauplius as referred to by Hero of Alexandria.[127] Both Lycophron and Hero of Alexandria present the three episodes but in a slightly different order than Seneca, i.e. storm, Nauplius, and death of Ajax. In pantomime, Lucian's catalogue of pantomimic themes (46) attests that the episode of the storm shipwrecking the Greek fleet was performed in this medium. In Lucian's list, the same three distinct episodes are connected as in Seneca's passage, but again in a different order: the wrath of Nauplius and the death of Ajax between the rocks. That these episodes take place during the sea storm in which the Greek fleet was destroyed can be inferred from the context of the Lucianic passage. Besides, that shipwreck featured as a theme of pantomimic performances also finds support in Seneca's *De Ira* (2, 2, 5): *Quae non sunt irae, non magis quam tristitia est, quae ad conspectum **mimici naufragii** contrahit frontem.*[128]

Impersonality of the Narrator

The narrative set-piece of the *Agamemnon* is conventionally constituted by an introductory dialogue between Clytemnestra and the messenger (394–420) and closed by a monologue of Clytemnestra (579–88) in which the queen does not even utter a single comment on the event narrated at length by Eurybates, but debates with herself about what her course of action should be in relation to the return of her husband Agamemnon. The proper narrative of the storm thus runs completely uninterrupted. Because of this, the messenger's speech in the *Agamemnon* is characterized by an even greater degree of impersonality than the other *rheseis* within the *corpus* and, aside from the initial and conventional reluctance to relate unfortunate events (416–18: *Acerba fatu poscis, infaustum iubes/miscere laeto nuntium, refugit loqui/mens aegra tantis atque inhorrescit malis*), no personal hints are made by Eurybates; he basically tells the event as if he did not take part in it, since he uses the first person plural only on one occasion (557: *Nos alia maior naufragos pestis vocat*) and the third one all the way through.[129]

Mimetic Present

The narrative is couched in the present and the perfect is employed just to provide the temporal sequence of consequent actions.[130] The high number of active verbs describing actions that occur in the passage is also remarkable.[131]

Non-linear Progression of the Narration

The narrative of the storm progresses through a succession of stages rather than in a linear manner. Tarrant has divided the narrative into seven major sections:[132]

1) Departure from Troy with favourable winds (421–8);
2) Appearance of dolphins (449–55);
3) Nightfall (456–66);
4) Storm (466–527);
5) Punishment of Ajax (528–56);
6) Treachery of Nauplius (557–76a);
7) Dawn and subsiding of the storm (576b–8).

Each section of the narrative is somehow juxtaposed to the preceding and following ones and develops in detail a single event. Thus, the forward movement of the narration is quite slowed down by the expansion of the single units. If the overall movement of the narration is static, the single units depict a series of vignettes that include a large amount of action portrayed in a moving picture.

The first section of the narration describes the departure from Troy and the activities of the soldiers preparing for the seafaring are mimetically portrayed: they unbuckle their weary sides from the swords (423: *iamque ense fessum miles exonerat latus*), abandon their shields on the ship's decks (424: *neglecta summas scuta per puppes iacent*), and the oars are fitted to their military hands (425: *ad militares remus aptatur manus*). Then, as soon as the sign of departure has been given (428: *et clara laetum remigem monuit tuba*), the oarsmen prepare to leave: the whole army hastens in bending the oars and pulling them together (437–8: *properat iuventus omnis adductos simul/lentare remos*), helps the winds with its hand (438: *adiuvat ventos manu*), and moves the strong arms with rhythmical effort (439: *et valida nisu bracchia alterno movet*). After the ships are set in motion and the favourable wind makes the sailing easy, the oarsmen can abandon the oars and look at the landscape or recall the most memorable events of the war (442–8). The description of the activities of the army is interwoven with the description of the favourability of the winds and of the effects produced by the ships on the sea; as in the case of the *ecphraseis*, the watery elements tend to be personified; for instance, the calm wave trembles for the gentle breath of Zephyr (432–3: *unda vix actu levi/tranquilla Zephyri mollis afflatu tremit*); it is possible that Seneca was inspired by a passage in Ovid (*Heroides* 11, 75: *ut mare fit tremulum/tenui cum stringitur aura*) and Virgil (*Aen.* 7, 9: *splendet tremulo sub lumine pontus*), though in Seneca's description the grammatical construction (in which the wave is the subject of the active verb *tremit*) underscores the animated nature of the wave; furthermore, the phrase recalls very closely the description of the bristling of Cassandra's hair (*Ag* 712: *mollis horrescit coma*). The grammatical construction of line 440 (*sulcata vibrant aequora et latera increpant*), with the presence of active verbs and the absence of the agents producing the glistening and the hissing, gives the impression that both the waters and the sides of the ships are agents voluntarily acting; in Ovid there are similar descriptions of the noise produced by the water hitting the sides of ship (*Met.* 11, 507: *saepe dat ingentem fluctu latus icta fragorem*; *Tr.* 1, 4, 24: *increpuit . . . unda latus*), but the grammatical constructions always specify the agents producing the noise.[133] In addition to this, the use of *vibrare* for the glistening of the water is rare. Usually, Seneca uses the verb to indicate the brandishing of a weapon.[134] The meaning 'shimmer' is attested by Cicero and Lucan;[135] Claudian employs it for the shimmering of silk tunics in a breeze.[136] Thus, the glistening of the waters may have been mimed through an appropriate movement of the silk tunic, which we know was the versatile costume worn by the pantomime dancer. Similarly, line 442 (*aura plenos fortior tendit sinus*) may be mimed through the use of the tunica or of the mantel. In this respect, the high occurrence of the word *sinus* in Seneca's tragedies is remarkable (in the storm narrative the word is employed here and at 483 *quatiens sinus*).

The second section of the narrative deals with a description of the traditional appearance of dolphins. Seneca's description echoes the Ovidian metamorphosis of the Tyrrhenian sailors.[137] In the *Oedipus* (449–67), the metamorphosis of pirates into dolphins employs again the same material. This specific passage is also noteworthy for the amount of mimetic movements it contains: the dolphin weaves, jumps, leaps with arching back, and dashes about in circles (449: *ludit*, 450: *pando transilit dorso*; 451: *exultat*; 452: *agitat gyros*; 454: *lascivit*; 455: *ambit*; *lustrat*). The linguistic register used deserves closer scrutiny, since it is recurrently employed, especially in narrative set-pieces to describe a set of movements; the verb *ludit* is used also at *Hf* 684–5 (*incerta vagus/Maeander unda ludit*) to describe a serpentine movement; the verb *transilit* at *Thy* 767–8 (*impositas dapes/transiluit ignis*) to describe the leaps of the fire; the verb *exultat* at *Ag* 773–4 (*exultat et ponit gradus/pater decoros Dardanus*) to describe Dardanus' dance; the verb *ambit* at *Tro* 16 (*regiam flammae ambiunt*), *Oed* 325 (*ambitque densus regium fumus caput*), and *Oed* 543–4 (*magno ambitu/diffusa ramos una defendit nemus*) to describe a circular movement.

The section dealing with the effects of the storm on the ships is striking for the motion picture it provides (497–506):

> Ipsa se classis premit
> et prora prorae nocuit et lateri latus.
> illam dehiscens pontus in praeceps rapit
> hauritque et alto redditam revomit mari;   500
> haec onere sidit, illa convulsum latus
> summittit undis, fluctus hanc decimus tegit;
> haec lacera et omni decore populato levis
> fluitat, nec illi vela nec tonsae manent
> nec rectus altas malus antemnas ferens,   505
> sed trunca toto puppis Ionio natat.

The description of the effects of the storm on the ships is already in Virgil (*Aen.* 1, 104–17) and Ovid (11, 501–15), and Seneca is clearly indebted to their treatments. Unlike his predecessors, Seneca adopts a predominantly paratactic and simple style of diction in which to couch its description, whose hyperbolic nature is again reminiscent of Virgil and Ovid; still the Senecan description remains easy to visualize and to convey through gestures. In Ovid, instead, the hyperbolic content is somehow matched by the highly complex and hypotactic syntax in which the description is couched.[138]

Thus whereas Virgil's and Ovid's descriptions are grandiose in content and style, the Senecan one is rather prosaic and schematic. The presentation of the ships as sentient beings is crafted in a way that verges on the trivial more than on the sublime.[139] Galinsky has remarked that Ovid's storm stands as a 'virtuoso play on the literary conventions and precedents';[140] unlike Ovid, Seneca's combination of hyperbolic imagery with a rather simple and paratactic style does not seem then to be meant as an improvement on his predecessors; the combination of Virgilian and Ovidian elements seems rather to be interpreted as a means to adapt a conventional literary *topos* to the requirements of the new aesthetics of pantomime.

Personified Natural Phenomena

According to Senecan practice, the natural phenomena that accompany the storm are portrayed in a personified way (466–90): first a murmur falls from the high hills and the shore and the rocks moan (466–8: *tum murmur grave,/maiora minitans, collibus summis cadit/tractuque longo litus ac petrae gemunt*); the wave, roused by the approaching winds, swells (469: *agitata ventis unda venturis tumet*).[141] The action of the winds on the sea is mimetically described as a struggle between Zephyrus against Eurus and Notus against Boreas (474–6: *incumbunt, rapiunt, mittunt tela*).

Even though the fight of the wind is a traditional theme, Seneca portrays the struggle of the winds as one between personified entities. In Virgil, the struggle of the wind features as well, but he maintains the simile-form (*Aen.* 1, 82–3: *ac venti, velut agmine facto,/quo data porta, ruunt et terras turbine perflant*):

(Lines 474–84):

                    undique incumbunt simul
rapiuntque pelagus infimo eversum solo   475
adversus Euro Zephyrus et Boreae Notus.
sua quisque mittunt tela et infesti fretum
emoliuntur, turbo convolvit mare:
Strymonius altas Aquilo contorquet nives
Libycusque harenas Auster ac Syrtes agit   480
[nec manet in Austro; fit gravis nimbis Notus]
imbre auget undas; Eurus orientem movet
Nabataea quatiens regna et Eoos sinus;
quid rabidus ora Corus Oceano exerens?

In addition to this, Seneca expands the description of the struggle of the winds by depicting the single activity of each wind, whereas Virgil provides a briefer and summary account of the effects of the winds on the sea.[142]

From a stylistic point of view, the description is remarkable for the use of a repetitive linguistic register.[143] In this respect, as Pratt has remarked, it is noteworthy that the language employed to describe the actual storm in the *Agamemnon* parallels that used as a metaphor to portray the figurative emotional storm experienced by the characters in such a way that they become basically indistinguishable.[144]

For instance, lines 488–9 (*vento resistit aestus, et ventus retro/aestum revolvit. non capit sese mare*) are worth comparing with the description of Clytemnestra (*Ag* 138–40):

> ... fluctibus variis agor,
> ut, cum hinc profundum ventus, hinc aestus rapit,
> incerta dubitat unda cui cedat malo.

The description of the ships swept away by the current at lines 499–502:

> illam dehiscens pontus in praeceps rapit
> hauritque et alto redditam revomit mari;   500
> haec onere sidit, illa convulsum latus
> summittit undis, fluctus hanc decimus tegit;

can be compared with the description of Medea's inner fluctuations (939–43):

> ... anceps aestus incertam rapit;
> ut saeva rapidi bella cum venti gerunt,   940
> utrimque fluctus maria discordes agunt
> dubiumque fervet pelagus, haud aliter meum
> cor fluctuatur ...[145]

Similarly, the boiling of the sea (*Ag* 560: *aestuat scopulis fretum*) can be compared with the boiling of the character's passions (e.g. *Med* 390: *haeret minatur **aestuat** queritur gemit*) and the burning of the wave (*Ag* 561: *fervetque semper fluctus*) with the boiling of the character's feelings (*Phoe* 352: *fervet immensum dolor*; *Med* 942: *dubiumque fervet pelagus, haud aliter meum/cor fluctuatur*; 952: *fervet odium*; *Hf* 946–7: *Leo/iraque totus fervet*; *Phae* 362: *torretur aestu tacito ... furor*; 641: *pectus insanum vapor/amorque torret*). The whirling of the winds heaves the sea (478: *turbo convolvit mare*) as the whirling of the emotions heaves the hearts of the characters (*Thy* 260–1: *tumultus pectora attonitus quatit/penitusque volvit*; *Thy* 1041: *volvuntur intus viscera*).

If we go back now to Seneca's reference to the 'mimicum naufragium', it is possible to suggest that the adjective 'mimic' does not refer strictly to the type of performance, but rather means 'mimetically enacted'. This mimetic representation of a shipwreck together with the fact that it produces saddening effects on the audience seems to point to a pantomimic more than a mimic performance. Whether Seneca is then referring to an actual shipwreck or to a metaphoric shipwreck of the soul, such as the one undergone by his tragic characters, it is not possible to establish. However, the actual and the figurative shipwreck would not have entailed a sharply different enactment because, according to Nonnus, pantomime often consisted in a symbolic rendition of the myth or plot enacted.[146] For instance, such a symbolic representation can be inferred from Nonnus' account of the performance of the pantomimic dancer Silenus who mimed the flowing water of a river (*Dionysiaca* 19, 288–95) and from Lucian's (19) claim that the dancer can even imitate 'the liquidity of water' (ὕδατος ὑγρότητα).[147]

Conclusion

Viewed as dramatic texts, Seneca's tragedies are controversial. This is largely due to the fact that some formal characteristics of his tragic *corpus* diverge from the theatrical conventions of tragedy as exemplified in the classical Greek plays of the fifth century BC. Taking into account that the theatrical landscape in the Imperial age was extremely varied, I have argued that some of the controversial features of Seneca's tragedies are to be ascribed to the influence of one of them in particular, i.e. pantomime, which was an extremely popular genre of performance in his time. Since Seneca must have been well aware of this popularity, he may have included pantomimic elements to make his tragedies more appealing to his audience. The popularity of pantomime would have encouraged poets and writers either to write texts suitable for this genre or to experiment with the generic enrichment of more traditional literary genres through the aesthetics of this type of performance. We know, for instance, that authors such as Silo, Statius, and Lucan composed pantomimic libretti.[1] Still several centuries later, the Archbishop Isidore of Seville (560–636) attests the practice of poets of composing *fabulae* suitable to be enacted through the movement of the body.[2] As to generic enrichment, the cross-fertilization of tragedy through the aesthetics of pantomime ought not to surprise given the contiguity of these two theatrical genres. Seneca's adoption of compositional devices typical of pantomime is in keeping with the attested process of dialogue between sub-literary and literary genres in Latin culture at large, which I survey in Chapter 1.

The idea that pantomime played a part in the performance of the problematic scripts that have come down to us as 'Seneca's tragedies' can help to solve many of the problems associated with envisaging their performance as stage plays, such as unexplained references, un-cued exits and entrances, and extended descriptions.

In this work, I therefore explored the possibility that it is to the influence of pantomime that we may ascribe the singular medley of dramatic and narrative (or epic) features in Seneca's tragedies. With pantomime's aesthetics in mind, the highly descriptive character of Seneca's tragedies can be accounted for as a strategy of writing that enables us to achieve a novel and perhaps better understanding of his tragic *corpus*; alternatively, it is possible that the language of pantomime, which was so widespread, familiar and thus influential, may have affected Seneca's writing, no matter what destination for his tragedies he envisaged.

The influence of the aesthetics of pantomime can also explain four distinctive features of Seneca's plays, all of which have been found particularly troublesome by scholars assessing them as dramatic texts and evaluating their aesthetic value; these controversial features of Seneca's dramaturgy are the loose dramatic structure, the presence of 'running commentaries', monologues of self-analysis, and lengthy narrative set-pieces.

Even more importantly, pantomime can reconcile a dichotomy existing in Seneca's tragedies between the constant engagement in the portrayal of the emotions of the characters and the nature of such emotions, which are, surprisingly, far from being personal (i.e. based on individual experience); in fact, the emotions are rather objective, they stand as 'performed emotions'. Seneca's tragedies thus present an apparent incongruity between the emphasis on emotional responses and lack of a psychological dimension of the characters.[3] Despite this, Seneca's characters do not have a real psychological dimension, they 'do not express a human intelligibility . . . they are all of one piece; there is not that something within';[4] they lack a psychological interiority, even though they speak such a vocabulary.

This dichotomy can be explained if we think that pantomime consisted primarily in the display of the emotional life of the characters enacted, which relied on a set of stylized conventions to do so. In this medium, the different emotions were to a high extent portrayed in a stylized form; this semiotic system was needed both to express and to make intelligible the different emotions to the audience.

Moreover, the performative quality of the emotions of Seneca's characters is accompanied by a novel linguistic register adopted to shape them in a plastic way; these two features can be traced back to the influence of the aesthetics of pantomime, especially if we think about pantomime's engagement with the representation of emotions and the fact that its medium of expression was the plastic language of the body.

It is then precisely this engagement with the emotions that made the aesthetics of pantomime an attractive and apt means of expression for Seneca.

It is important to clarify at this point that I am not suggesting that the influence of pantomime on Seneca's conception of mythical narrative, which seems virtually inevitable given the cultural environment in which the plays came into being, necessarily bears the implication that Seneca intended his tragedies to be performed as pantomime or with pantomimic sequences. In fact, it is unnecessary to assume that he wrote them in a way that excluded the possibility of any of the forms of performance, whether rhetorical or theatrical, with or without elements of mimetic dance, that were popular in the mid-first century AD. My point is rather that Seneca wrote them 'with pantomime in mind', and that both the formal structure of the tragedies and the details of the verse they contain reveal characteristics which he took over from the pantomimic genre. They certainly reflect a familiar cultural language that had been well established by Seneca's day through the traditions of tragic pantomime.

Notes

Introduction

1. Zwierlein (1966) is still the most systematic and detailed study of this issue.
2. Against representation onstage see: Schlegel (1809–11: 27): 'Die Tragödien Senecas sind über alle Beschreibung schwülstig und frostig, ohne Natur in Charakter und Handlung, durch die widersinnigsten Unschicklichkeiten empörend, und so von aller theatralischen Einsicht entblößt, daß ich glaube, sie waren nie dazu bestimmt, aus den Schulen der Rhetoren auf die Bühne hervorzutreten'; Leo (1878–79: 147–59); Zwierlein (1966). For staging see: Herrmann (1924: 195): 'toutes les tragédies de Sénèque, sans exception, étaient destinées par lui à la présentation sur un théâtre public ou privé de ces œuvres, avec acteurs, chœurs et musique'; Herington (1966: 422–71); Walker (1969: 183–7); Hadas (1939: 220); Kelly (1979: 96); Dihle (1983: 162–71); Sutton (1986). Littlewood (2004: 3) although not addressing the issue of representation in particular, implicitly endorses this possibility when he claims that 'if Ovid's non-dramatic poetry could be danced and applauded in the theatre (*Tristia* 5, 7, 25–8), it seems perverse to argue that Senecan tragedy is a literary not a theatrical art form.'
3. Concerning the question of evidence, it is worth remembering that a line from Seneca's *Agamemnon* (*Idai cernu nemura* 730) appears on a Pompeian graffito and has been interpreted as a proof of a stage-production of the tragedy by Gigante (1979: 150–1). By contrast, Tarrant (1976: 307) states that this line cannot be accounted as a proof of a stage-production, but simply as a proof of the knowledge of the tragedy. In my opinion, even though Tarrant's statement is methodologically correct, the appearance of this very line, which is spoken by Cassandra in the moment of her spectacular clairvoyant vision, on a wall of the city of Pompeii, whose theatrical life and love of pantomime is well attested, seems strongly suggestive of some kind of performance of the *Agamemnon*.
4. Tarrant (1976: 7–8).
5. Tarrant (1978: 213–61); Kelly (1979: 21–44).
6. Tarrant (1978: 217) defines the term post-classical as a 'conveniently brief designation for ancient drama after the end of the fifth century'.
7. Herrmann (1924: 220–32). Unfortunately, his work was not taken into serious account mostly because Herrmann's edition of the tragedies was not very accurate and his point of view was opposed to the established judgement formulated by Leo

(1878–79) in his fundamental and (from a text-critical and philological point of view) reliable, edition of the tragedies.

8. See also: *Troades* (705–35); *Phaedra* (1201–12); *Oedipus* (223–32); *Agamemnon* (759–74); *Thyestes* (920–69).

9. Hall (2002: 27) argues that 'there is evidence for almost every conceivable combination of performers of tragedy under the Roman empire'.

10. In contrast with this view, Seneca's disregard for pantomime and theatrical performances has been argued on the basis of the following passage (*Naturales Quaestiones*, 7, 32, 2–3): *Itaque tot familiae philosophorum sine successore deficiunt. Academici et veteres et minores nullum antistitem reliquerunt. [. . .] At quanta cura laboratur, ne cuius pantomimi nomen intercidat! Stat per successores Pyladis et Bathylli domus; harum artium multi discipuli sunt multique doctores.* I would interpret these words not so much as proof of his dislike of pantomime in itself, but rather as criticism of certain excesses. The quoted passage also provides evidence of the popularity of pantomime in Seneca's age as well as the link between pantomime and the representation of emotions.

11. See Lucian, *De Saltatione* (31).

12. Wagenvoort (1920: 112): 'Es versteht sich, daß der Pantomimus, als er sich einmal eingebürgert hatte, starken Einfluß übte auf die Tragödie. Denn, wollte die letztere ihre Popularität nicht völlig einbüßen, so mußte sie mit dem Pantomimus wetteifern, zuerst in der Jagd nach Pathos'.

13. Boyle (1987: 86–7).

14. Harrison (2007: 16).

15. *Epistle* (8, 8): *quam multi poetae dicunt quae philosophis aut dicta sunt aut dicenda! Non attingam tragicos nec togatas nostras (habent enim hae quoque aliquid severitatis et sunt inter comoedias ac tragoedias mediae): quantum disertissimorum versuum inter mimos iacet! Quam multa Publilii non excalceatis sed coturnatis dicenda sunt!*; *De Tranquillitate animi* (11, 8): *Publilius, tragicis comicisque vehementior ingeniis quotiens mimicas ineptias et verba ad summam caveam spectantia reliquit, inter multa alia cothurno, non tantum sipario fortiora et hoc ait: Cuivis potest accidere quod cuiquam potest.*

16. Leo (1878–79: 148): 'Novum autem genus tragoedia rhetorica inventa est, cuius indoles breviter sic describi potest ut ἦθος in ea nullum, πάθος omnia esse dicatur'; and 158: 'Istae vero non sunt tragoediae sed declamationes ad tragoediae amussim compositae et in actus deductae; in quibus si quid venuste vel acute dictum, floride et figurate descriptum, copiose narratum esset, plaudebant auditores, arti satisfactum erat'.

17. Leo (1878–79: 148): 'Periculum in mimo factum erat qui cum natura arti rhetoricae affinis esset quantum ab illa receperit et in illam valuerit Senecae patris lectores sciunt'.

18. Tacitus, *Annales* (14, 52): *obiciebant etiam eloquentiae laudem uni sibi adsciscere et carmina crebrius factitare, postquam Neroni amor eorum venisset.* Tacitus' account has not been unanimously accepted by scholars as evidence that the *carmina* mentioned by the historian are to be identified with the tragedies.

19. Suetonius, *Nero* (54): *sub exitu quidem vitae palam voverat, si sibi incolumis status permansisset, proditurum se partae victoriae ludis etiam hydraulam et choraulam et utricularium ac novissimo die histrionem saltaturumque Vergili Turnum.*

20. Sandy (1974: 341–2).

21. Zimmermann (1990: 161–7); Erasmo (2004: 134).

Chapter 1

1. Wiseman (2008b: 146–53) argues that a considerable overlap between mime and pantomime existed and warns against setting mutually exclusive categories for genres as heterogeneous as mime and pantomime. Wiseman offers as example of this a notice reported by a scholiast on Lucan about a mimetic enacting of the story of Thyestes and Atreus. The scholiast uses the term 'mime', but, since the subject in question is tragic, we should admit either the existence of tragic themes in mime or that the scholiast is actually referring to pantomime.

2. Fantham (1988–89: 153–63).

3. For a discussion of the problems of the origins see Rotolo (1957: 18–48); Bier (1917: 48–54), relying on Aelius Aristides (in Libanius 64, 80), claimed that pantomime has its origins in Egypt in connection with the sacred rites of the goddess Isis in which it had a cultic function. Despite the fact that Bier's theory has been dismissed by scholars, his idea of a cultic origin of the genre deserves consideration.

4. Jory (1981: 147).

5. Lawler (1943: 60–71) has argued that Ionian dances were most probably forerunners of pantomime; in the Roman world, Ionian dancers were equated with *cinaedi*, as is attested by Plautus (*Stich.* 769–70: *qui Ionicus aut cinaedicust, qui hoc tale facere/possiet*); Scipio Aemilianus disparagingly attests that *cinaedi* run dancing schools in Rome (fr. 30 Malcovati: *eunt, inquam, in ludum saltatorium inter cinaedos virgines puerique ingenui*); see also Horace, *Odes* (3, 6, 21–4): *motus doceri gaudet Ionicos/matura virgo et fingitur artibus/iam nunc et incestos amores/de tenero meditatur ungui;* and Lucian, *De mercede conductis* (27) who says that *cinaedi* were part of the household as trainers of Ionic songs and dances.

6. Athenaeus, *Deipnosophistae* (1, 20d–e) defines pantomime as the 'Italian dance' (Ἰταλικὴν ὄρχησιν) thus attesting the perceived Italian ancestry of the genre in the Greek world; for the connections between pantomime and the *ludus talarius* see

Jory (1995: 139–52) and Garelli (2000: 101–2) who argues against Jory's suggestion; see Garton (1972: 232) for the connections between pantomime and mime.

7. See Garelli (2001: 234–5).

8. For a detailed discussion of mime and its development at Rome see Nicoll (1931: 80–131); Duckworth (1952: 13–15); Giancotti (1967) focuses on the literary mime of Laberius and Publilius Syrus.

9. Gellius, *Noctes Atticae* (I, XI, I2) speaks of a *planipes saltans*; a fragment (Ribbeck, 188) of a comedy by a certain Atta (first century BC) has *exultat planipes*.

10. *ILS* 5201 = *CIL* 6.10118 = *CLE* 411 = Courtney (1995: 121). Slater (2002: 319–20) objects to Courtney's translation of *mimi saltantes* as pantomimes since the performers in question danced as well as acted, while the dancers did not speak. Festus (438, 22, L) reports that a mime of secondary parts had also the role of dancing to the music of the flute: 'Volumnius who danced to the flute, was an actor of secundarum, who is introduced in nearly all mimes as a parasite'.

11. See Jory (1981: 147–61) for a detailed discussion of the origins and development of pantomime.

12. Athenaeus, *Deipnosophistae* (I, 20 D).

13. Suetonius, *De Poetis*, frag. 3 (Rostagni p. 65): *Pylades Cilex pantomimus, cum veteres ipsi canerent atque saltarent, primus Romae chorum et fistulam sibi praecinere fecit.*

14. Macrobius, *Saturnalia* (II, 7, 18): *hic quia ferebatur mutasse rudis illius saltationis ritum, quae apud maiores viguit, et venustam induxisse novitatem, interrogatus ab Augusto quae saltationi contulisset, respondit:* Αὐλῶν συρίγγων τ᾽ ἐνοπὴν, ὁμαδόν τ᾽ ἀνθρώπων (the line quoted by Pylades is from Homer's *Iliad* 10, 13).

15. Macrobius, *Saturnalia* (II, 7, 12): *Sed quia semel ingressus sum scaenam loquendo, nec Pylades histrio nobis omittendus est, qui clarus in opere suo fuit temporibus Augusti.*

16. Lucian, *De Saltatione* (34): ἀλλὰ τό γε ἐν τῷ παρόντι μοι κεφάλαιον τοῦ λόγου τοῦτό ἐστιν, τὴν νῦν ὄρχησιν καθεστῶσαν ἐπαινέσαι καὶ δεῖξαι ὅσα ἐν αὐτῇ τερπνὰ καὶ χρήσιμα περιλαβοῦσα ἔχει, οὐ πάλαι ἀρξαμένη ἐς τοσοῦτο κάλλος ἐπιδιδόναι, ἀλλὰ κατὰ τὸν Σεβαστὸν μάλιστα; Zosimus, *Historia Nova* (I, 6): αὐτὴ σαφῶς ἔδειξε τῶν ἐκβεβηκότων ἡ πεῖρα καὶ τὰ εὐθὺς συμπεσόντα κατὰ τὴν Ὀκταβιανοῦ βασιλείαν· ἥ τε γὰρ παντόμιμος ὄρχησις ἐν ἐκείνοις εἰσήχθη τοῖς χρόνοις, οὔπω πρότερον οὖσα, Πυλάδου καὶ Βαθύλλου πρώτων αὐτὴν μετελθόντων, καὶ προσέτι γε ἕτερα πολλῶν αἴτια γεγονότα μέχρι τοῦδε κακῶν.

17. Jerome, *Annotations to Eusebius' Chronicon*, Ol. 180, 3: *Anno XXII Pylades Cilex pantomimus cum veteres ipsi canerent atque saltarent, primus Romae chorum et fistulam sibi praecinere fecit.*

18. Jory (1981: 147 and 157) and Hall (2002: 25–6) have convincingly argued that Livy's famous account of the development of Roman drama can be better

understood as an 'aetiological narrative' illustrating the invention of pantomime. Since Livy's account has been shown to have Varro's *Antiquitates divinae* as its source, which was published around 47 BC, we can be sure that 'a solo mimetic dance form' was in existence well before 22 BC. Wiseman (2008b: 146–7) has claimed that a passage in Cicero's *Pro Rabirio Postumo* (35) could possibly attest that pantomime had already been introduced in Rome in 54 BC, the year of composition of Cicero's speech: *audiebamus Alexandream, nunc cognoscimus. illinc omnes praestigiae, illinc, inquam, omnes fallaciae, omnia denique ab eis mimorum argumenta nata sunt.* Wiseman (2008b: 147) further observes that 'the combination of mime, novelty, and Alexandria' would point to the introduction of a new style of performance, since Cicero can hardly refer to mime as something new.

19. See Weinreich (1941: 96–100).
20. See Wiseman (2008a: 213–14).
21. Macrobius reports that Pylades performed during a dinner offered by Augustus in the imperial palace, *Saturnalia* (II, 7, 16–18): *cum in Herculem furentem prodisset et nonnullis incessum histrioni convenientem non servare videretur, deposita persona ridentes increpuit: μωροί, μαινόμενον ὀρχοῦμαι. hac fabula et sagittas iecit in populum. eandem personam cum iussu Augusti in triclinio ageret, et intendit arcum et spicula immisit. nec indignatus est Caesar eodem se loco Pyladi quo populum Romanum fuisse.*
22. Cassius Dio, *Historia Romana* (54, 17, 5); Macrobius, *Saturnalia* (11, 7).
23. Beacham (1999: 146).
24. Garelli (2004: 362–7). The perceived 'universal' nature of the pantomimic language is attested by a passage in Lucian (64) in which this type of performance is shown to enable cross-cultural communication.
25. Tacitus, *Annales* (1, 54, 77): *Ludos Augustales tunc primum coeptos turbavit discordia ex certamine histrionum. Indulserat ei ludicro Augustus, dum Maecenati obtemperat effuso in amorem Bathylli.* Lucian (32): ἐῶ λέγειν ὅτι πόλις ἐν Ἰταλίᾳ, τοῦ Χαλκιδικοῦ γένους ἡ ἀρίστη, καὶ τοῦτο ὥσπερ τι κόσμημα τῷ παρ' αὐτοῖς ἀγῶνι προστέθεικεν; see Geer (1935: 208–11) for the Greek games held at Sebasta. See Slater (1995, 1996) for a discussion of pantomime's introduction into the regular Greek agonistic festivals, which did not take place until the early 170s AD.
26. For a description of the frieze of the propylon of the Sebasteion at Aphrodisias see Chaisemartin (1987: 135–54) and Chaisemartin (2006: 33–82). Other pantomimic masks have been found at Aspendos: see Moretti (1993: 212–13); at Jerash in Trans-Jordan: see Iliffe (1945: 4–5 and plate V); pantomimic masks are possibly represented on ash-chests found in Ostia: the material is published by Bianchi and Bonanno Aravantinos (1991: 1–32).
27. Jory (2002: 244).
28. Tacitus, *Annales* (1, 77).

29. Suetonius, *Tiberius* (37, 2); Tacitus, *Annales* (1, 77); Dio, *Historia Romana* (59, 2, 5).

30. Suetonius, *Caligula* (11, 54 and 55).

31. Seneca, *Apocolocyntosis* (13, 15).

32. Suetonius (*Nero*, 6, 3) disparagingly claims that Nero had as tutors a dancer and a barber: *apud amitam Lepidam nutritus est sub duobus paedagogis saltatore atque tonsore.* Nero's most favoured roles were, according to Suetonius (*Nero*, 21, 3), 'Canacen parturientem, Oresten matricidam, Oedipodem excaecatum, Herculem insanum'; Dio (*Historia Romana*, 61, 20, 2) reports that Nero sang an 'Attis or Bacchants' and similarly, Persius (*Sat.*, 1, 105) says that he sang the same roles (*in udo est Maenas et Attis*). The preferred singing roles played by Nero are interestingly some of the most popular in pantomimic performances. For instance, 'Canace in labour' matches the Lucianic claim that 'Ledo's labour' was a subject of danced performances; similarly, Attis and the Bacchic thiasos, the maddened Hercules, and Oedipus' self-blinding were very popular subjects in pantomimic performances. It is thus possible to suggest that the arias sung by Nero may well have been those that accompanied the pantomimic dancer enacting through his movements the stories told by the libretto.

33. Suetonius, *Nero* (54): *Et sunt qui tradant Paridem histrionem occisum ab eo quasi gravem adversarium.* Servius (ad *Aen.* V, 370) reports that Nero's poem entitled *Troica* had Paris as its hero: *sane hic Paris secundum Troica Neronis fortissimus fuit, adeo ut in Troiae agonali certamine superaret omnes, ipsum etiam Hectorem.* It seems then no coincidence that Nero's favourite dancer took the stage name Paris, which is attested to have been adopted by several pantomimic dancers thereafter, see Bonaria (1959: 226–7); the dancer Paris in question here most probably adopted such stage name because his fame was attached to his outstanding impersonation of the Phrygian hero. For a discussion of Nero's poetic compositions, see Bardon (1936: 337–49) and Charlesworth (1950: 69–76).

34. Garelli (2004b: 353–68) has claimed that Nero did not actually ever perform as a dancer and that his interest in pantomime was just politically motivated following, in this respect, Augustus' instrumentalization of public entertainments to enhance personal popularity and celebration of Imperial ideology.

35. For a portrait of the dancer Pylades see Lawler (1946: 241–7) and Jory (2004: 147–56).

36. Athenaeus, *Deipnosophistae* (I, 20–1); ancient writers report that Pylades excelled in the roles of Dionysus (*Anth. Pal.* 209) and the maddened Hercules (*Anth. Pal.* 9. 248; Macrobius, *Sat.* II, 7, 16); Bathyllus in those of Echo, Pan, Eros and Satyr (*CIL* 9, 344; Persius *Sat.* 5, 122–23: *cum sis cetera fossor,/tris tantum ad numeros Satyrum moveare Bathylli*).

37. For Pylades see Cassius Dio (54, 17, 4); for Bathyllus see Tacitus, *Ann.* (1, 54, 2); schol. Ad Pers. (5, 123): *Bathylli: pantomimus fuit libertus Maecenatis.*

38. See Bonaria (1959: 224–42).

39. Seneca, *Naturales Quaestiones* (7, 32, 3): *At quanta cura laboratur, ne cuius pantomimi nomen intercidat! Stat per successores Pyladis et Bathylli domus; harum artium multi discipuli sunt multique doctores. Privatum urbe tota sonat pulpitum.*

40. Suetonius, *Augustus* (45, 4): *Nam histrionum licentiam adeo compescuit, ut Stephanionem togatarium, cui in puerilem habitum circumtonsam matronam ministrasse compererat, per trina theatra virgis caesum relegaverit, Hylan pantomimum querente praetore in atrio domus suae nemine excluso flagellis verberarit et Pyladen urbe atque Italia summoverit, quod spectatorem, a quo exsibilabatur, demonstrasset digito conspicuumque fecisset.*

41. Macrobius, *Saturnalia* (II, 7, 13–16): *populus deinde inter utriusque suffragia divisus est, et cum canticum quoddam saltaret Hylas cuius clausula erat* τὸν μέγαν Ἀγαμέμνονα, *sublimem ingentemque Hylas velut metiebatur. non tulit Pylades et exclamavit e cavea:* σὺ μακρὸν οὐ μέγαν ποιεῖς. *tunc eum populus coegit idem saltare canticum cumque ad locum venisset quem reprehenderat, expressit cogitantem, nihil magis ratus magno duci convenire quam pro omnibus cogitare. saltabat Hylas Oedipodem, et Pylades hac voce securitatem saltantis castigavit:* σὺ βλέπεις.

42. Cassiodorus, *Variae* (4, 51, 9).

43. The protean nature of the pantomimic dancer is a feature emphasised by ancient writers; Lucian (19) states that the myth about the Egyptian Proteus, who could mould himself in any shape he wanted to, meant that he was nothing else than a dancer; actually, transformations were a major topic of the pantomimic repertoire as attested by Lucian (57) who generally states that the dancer should know all the mythical plots involving transformation such as Cadmus' metamorphosis into a snake (Lucian 41) or human beings changed into stones (Lucian 39 the Deucalion myth; the petrified Niobe) or Callisto's transformations into a bear (48).

44. Nonnus, *Dionysiaca* (19, 288–95) describes the pantomimic performance of the dancer Silenus who imitates the flowing of a river. See also Velleius Paterculus, *Historia Romana* (2, 83, 2) who describes the performance of Munatius Plancus who danced the sea-god Glaucus at a banquet: *cum caeruleatus et nudus caputque redimitus arundine et caudam trahens, genibus innixus Glaucum saltasset in convivio, refrigeratus ab Antonio ob manifestarum rapinarum indicia, transfugit ad Caesarem.*

45. Lucian (19): ὡς καὶ ὕδατος ὑγρότητα μιμεῖσθαι καὶ πυρὸς ὀξύτητα ἐν τῇ τῆς κινήσεως σφοδρότητι καὶ λέοντος ἀγριότητα καὶ παρδάλεως θυμὸν καὶ δένδρου δόνημα, καὶ ὅλως ὅ τι καὶ θελήσειεν.

46. Lucian (60): καὶ τὴν ἐν Ἅιδου ἅπασαν τραγῳδίαν καὶ τὰς κολάσεις καὶ τὰς ἐφ' ἑκάστῃ αἰτίας καὶ τὴν Πειρίθου καὶ Θησέως ἄχρι τοῦ Ἅιδου ἑταιρείαν.

47. Augustine, *De Magistro* (3, 5).

48. Isidore of Seville, *Etymologiae* (18, 49).

49. Quintilian, *Institutio Oratoria* (6, 3, 65). Weinreich (1948: 144 n. 1) has interpreted the performance of the two pantomimes (*saltator* and *interpellator*) as a 'Zeichendisput'. See Slater (1990: 215–20).

50. This is the interpretation of Harmon (1936: 271); Jory (1998: 220–1) thinks, instead, that the actor impersonating Odysseus 'was in fact the rival pantomime dancer who had just left the stage after playing his Odyssean role'.

51. Additional evidence is provided by the large cast involved in the pantomimic performance of the Judgment of Paris described by Apuleius (*Met.* 10, 30–4).

52. See Jory (2001: 1–20; 2002: 238–53). The decorative frieze of the Propylon of the Sebasteion at Aphrodisias displays a series of fifteen masks representing Dionysus, his thiasos, and Heracles, which can be designated as pantomimic with certainty since they present the closed mouth typical of this theatrical genre.

53. Cicero, *De Orat.* (2, 193).

54. Apuleius, *Met.* (10, 32): *nunc mite coniventibus, nunc acre comminantibus gestire pupulis, et nonnunquam **saltare solis oculis***; Augustine, *De doctrina christiana* (2, 4, 5). Nonnus, *Dionysiaca* (5, 104–07): καὶ παλάμας ἐλέλιζε Πολύμνια, μαῖα χορείης,/ μιμηλὴν δ᾽ ἐχάραξεν ἀναυδέος εἰκόνα φωνῆς,/φθεγγομένη παλάμῃσι σοφὸν τύπον ἔμφρονι σιγῇ,/ὄμματα δινεύουσα; (19, 201–2): ὀφθαλμοὺς δ᾽ ἐλέλιζεν ἀλήμονας, εἰκόνα μύθων/νεύματι τεχνήεντι νοήμονα ῥυθμὸν ὑφαίνων.

55. Fronto, *On Orations* (4): *Ut histriones, quom palliolatim saltant, caudam cycni, capillum Veneris, Furiae flagellum eodem pallio demonstrant: ita isti unam eandemque sententiam multimodis faciunt.*

56. Webb (2008: 53–4).

57. *Anthologia Latina* n. 100 = Weinreich n. 20 (Epigramm und Pantomimus).

58. Webb (2008: 50).

59. Seneca the Elder, *Controv.* (3 *praef.* 10): *Nomio, cum velocitas pedum non concedatur tantum, sed obiciatur, lentiores manus sunt.*

60. Augustine, *Sermones* (311, VII, 7).

61. Habinek (2002: 52–3) and Habinek (2005: 176).

62. Lada-Richards (2004: 31 and 44 n. 59).

63. Lada-Richards (2004: 31 and 44 n. 59).

64. Beacham (1999: 144).

65. For a list of pantomimic themes see Wüst (1949) complemented by Kokolakis (1959).

66. See the section in this chapter entitled 'The Pantomimic Show'.

67. See also Lucian (11) and (38) where he explicitly affirms that the power of the two Loves is a very suitable theme for pantomimic performances. See Brunelle (2000–2001: 123–40) for a discussion of the Ovidian passage.

68. Ovid's poem is echoed in one of the *Carmina Priapea* (19): *Hic quando Telethusa circulatrix,/quae clunem, tunica tegente nulla,/extis latius altiusque motat,/crisabit*

tibi fluctuante lumbo/haec sic non modo te, Priape, posset,/privignum quoque sed movere Phaedrae; and in Martial (14, 203): *(puella Gaditana) tam tremulum crisat, tam blandum prurit, ut ipsum masturbatorem fecerit Hippolytum.* See Fear (1991: 75–9) about the fame of Gaditane dancing girls.

69. See also Varro fr. 513 from the *Synephebus: crede mihi, plures dominos servi comederunt quam canes. quod si Actaeon occupasset et ipse prius suos canes comedisset, non nugas saltatoribus in theatro fieret.*

70. Lada-Richards (2007: 35).

71. See Note 21 of this chapter.

72. Hall (2008: 258–82) has recently proposed that the Barcelona *Alcestis* (a Latin hexameter poem perhaps composed in the fourth century AD) might be a pantomimic libretto. See Marcovich (1988) for an edition with commentary of the *Alcestis Barcinonensis*.

73. Suetonius, *Nero* (54, 1): *Sub exitu quidem vitae palam voverat, si sibi incolumis status permansisset, proditurum se partae victoriae ludis etiam hydraulam et choraulam et utricularium ac novissimo die histrionem saltaturumque Vergili Turnum*; Lucian (46), the wandering of Aeneas and the love of Dido; Macrobius, *Saturnalia* (V, 17, 5): *quod ita elegantius auctore digessit, ut **fabula lascivientis Didonis**, quam falsam novit universitas, per tot tamen saecula speciem veritatis obtineat et ita pro vero per ora omnium volitet, ut pictores fictoresque et qui figmentis liciorum contextas imitantur effigies, hac materia vel maxime in effigiandis simulacris tamquam unico argumento decoris utantur, **nec minus histrionum perpetuis et gestibus et cantibus celebretur**;* Augustine, *Sermones* (241.5 = PL 38, 1135–6).

74. Seneca the Elder, *Suasoriae* (2, 19) about Silo: *qui pantomimis fabulas scripsit*; Juvenal, *Satire* (7, 86–7) about Statius: *sed cum fregit subsellia versu/esurit, intactam Paridi nisi vendit Agaven*; about Lucan, see *Vita Lucani de commentario Vacca sublata:* 'extant eius salticae fabulae XIV'.

75. Lada-Richards (2007: 13) claims that pantomime was a 'hybrid mode of performance, . . . a spectacle of excess, a lavish multi-media extravaganza'.

76. The *ecphrasis topou* that opens the description of the pantomimic performance of the Judgment of Paris in Apuleius' *Metamorphoses* (10, 30–4) seems to have the function of setting the scene in which the action takes place.

77. The term 'pictorial dramaturgy' is from Lada-Richards (2004: 18) and Lada-Richards (2007: 47–8 and 55).

78. Pantomime employed such frozen and statuesque-like positions as well; see Lada-Richards (2004, 2007).

79. See Beacham (1999: 143–4) and Lada-Richards (2004: 31).

80. Claudian, *In Eutropium* (2, 402–5): *fit plausus et ingens/concilii clamor, qualis resonantibus olim/exoritur caveis, quotiens crinitus ephebus/aut rigidam Nioben aut flentem Troada fingit.*

81. For the topic see: Fantham (1982b, 2002); Graf (1992); Aldrete (1999); Hall (2004).

82. See also Cicero, *Brutus* (278): *Ubi dolor? ubi ardor animi, qui etiam ex infantium ingeniis elicere voces et querelas solet? Nulla perturbatio animi nulla corporis, frons non percussa non femur, pedis, quod minimum est, nulla supplosio.*

83. Plutarch, *Cicero* (5); Macrobius, *Saturnalia* (III, 14).

84. Macrobius, *Saturnalia* (III, 14, 12): *quae res ad hanc artis suae fiduciam Roscium abstraxit ut librum conscriberet quo eloquentiam cum histrionia compararet.*

85. The passages are echoed in Quintilian (*Inst. orat.* 6, 3, 29): *Oratori minime convenit distortus vultus gestusque, quae in mimis rideri solent.*

86. Aulus Gellius, *Noctes Atticae* (1, 5, 2): *Ad eundem modum Q. Hortensius omnibus ferme oratoribus aetatis suae, nisi M. Tullio, clarior, quod multa munditia et circumspecte compositeque indutus et amictus esset manusque eius inter agendum forent argutae admodum et gestuosae, maledictis compellationibusque probris iactatus est multaque in eum, quasi in histrionem, in ipsis causis atque iudiciis dicta sunt. Sed cum L. Torquatus, subagresti homo ingenio et infestivo, gravius acerbiusque apud consilium iudicum, cum de causa Sullae quaereretur, non iam histrionem eum esse diceret, sed gesticulariam Dionysiamque eum notissimae saltatriculae nomine appellaret, tum voce molli atque demissa Hortensius 'Dionysia', inquit, 'Dionysia malo equidem esse quam quod tu, Torquate, ἄμουσος, ἀναφρόδιτος, ἀπροσδιόνυσος'.*

87. Cicero, *Brutus* (225): *Quos Sex. Titius consecutus, homo loquax sane et satis acutus, sed tam solutus et mollis in gestu ut saltatio quaedam nasceretur cui saltationi Titius nomen esset.*

88. See also Quintilian, *Institutio Oratoria* (1, 11, 12).

89. Quintilian, *Institutio Oratoria* (1, 11, 3): *Ne gestus quidem omnis ac motus a comoedis petendus est. Quamquam enim utrumque eorum ad quendam modum praestare debet orator, plurimum tamen aberit a scaenico, nec vultu nec manu, nec excursionibus nimius.*

90. See Beacham (1991: 126) for the process of cross-fertilization between oratory and theatrical rhetoric.

91. Quintilian, *Institutio Oratoria* (11, 3, 184): *Sed iam recepta est actio paulo agitatior et exigitur et quibusdam partibus convenit, ita tamen temperanda ne, dum actoris captamus elegantiam, perdamus viri boni et gravis auctoritatem.* See Aldrete (1999: 67–73).

92. Pratt (1983: 145).

93. Quintilian, *Institutio Oratoria* (11, 3, 89): *Abesse enim plurimum a saltatore debet orator, ut sit gestus ad sensus magis quam ad verba accommodatus.* The prescription was already stated at (1, 11, 19): *Neque enim gestum oratoris componi ad similitudinem saltationis volo, sed subesse aliquid ex hac exercitatione puerili;* similarly at (11, 3, 181): in closing the section devoted to *actio*, Quintilian states

again the principle of moderation that needs to be applied to gesturing in order for the apprentice orator not to be confused with the comic actor (*non enim comoedum esse, sed oratorem volo*).

94. Similar precepts appear in Cicero's *De orat.* (3, 220): *Omnes autem hos motus subsequi debet gestus, non hic verba exprimens scænicus, sed universam rem et sententiam non demonstratione, sed significatione declarans, laterum inflexione hac forti ac virili, non ab scæna et histrionibus, sed ab armis aut etiam a palaestra; manus autem minus arguta, digitis subsequens verba non exprimens, brachium procerius proiectum . . . supplosio pedis in contentionibus aut incipiendis aut finiendis; Orator* (18, 59): *idemque motu sic utetur, nihil ut supersit: in gestu status erectus et celsus; rarus incessus nec ita longus; excursio moderata eaque rara; nulla mollitia cervicum, nullae argutiae digitorum, non ad numerum articulus cadens.*

95. Tacitus, *Dial.* (26, 2–3): *Neque enim oratorius iste, immo hercle ne virilis quidem cultus est, quo plerique temporum nostrorum actores ita utuntur ut lascivia verborum et levitate sententiarum et licentia compositionis histrionales modos exprimant. Quodque vix auditu fas esse debeat, laudis et gloriae et ingenii loco plerique iactant cantari saltarique commentarios suos; unde oritur illa foeda et praepostera, sed tamen frequens exclamatio, ut oratores nostri tenere dicere, histriones diserte saltare dicantur.* A passage in Pliny (*Epistulae*, IX, 34) indicates the extent to which the figure of orators and actors progressively tended to merge; Pliny is here concerned whether he should have one of his freedmen read the speech for him, since he considers himself a bad reader. He also ponders whether he should accompany the reading with gestures, as some orators do. At the end, he resolves to read himself, since he thinks that his gesticulation is not better than his reading: *Ipse nescio, quid illo legente interim faciam, sedeam defixus et mutus et similis otioso an, ut quidam, quae pronuntiabit, murmure oculis manu prosequar. Sed puto me non minus male saltare quam legere.* The passage is possibly ironic, but it attests that such practice existed.

96. See Lucian, *Rhetorum praeceptor* (15): ἀλλὰ καὶ βοὴν ὅτι μεγίστην καὶ μέλος ἀναίσχυντον καὶ βάδισμα οἷον τὸ ἐμόν. Lucian advises the novice orator to employ the postures and the rhythmic cadences of a mime in order to achieve popularity; see also Tacitus, *Dial.* (26, 2).

97. See Lada-Richards (2007: 116–20).

98. Kroll (1924: 202–24).

99. Harrison (2007: 1).

100. Pasquali (1994: 275–82).

101. See Conte (1986; 1994: 120–3) for the discussion of the inadequacy of the Krollian notion of 'Kreuzung der Gattungen' and Barchiesi (2001: 142–63).

102. Harrison (2007: 1).

103. Aulus Gellius calls the mimographer Cn. Matius *homo impense doctus* (*Noctes Atticae* 10, 24, 10) and *vir eruditus* (15, 25, 1). Seneca (apud Augustine, *De Civitate Dei*, 6, 10 = fr. 36 Haase) calls a chief mimic actor learned (*doctus archimimus, senex iam decrepitus, quotidie in Capitolio mimum agebat*).

104. Fantham (1988–89: 153–63).

105. Andreassi (1997: 17–20).

106. See Santelia (1991) for a full discussion of the Charition-mime.

107. Wiemken (1972: 139); Steinmetz (1982: 367); the Adulteress-mime has its model in the Fifth mime of Herodas.

108. Finkelpearl (1998: 149–83); the Euripidean, Virgilian, and Ovidian echoes are already present in Seneca's description.

109. Quintilian (11, 3, 88–9): *alii sunt qui res imitatione significant, ut si aegrum temptantis venas medici similitudine aut citharoedum formatis ad modum percutientis nervos manibus ostendas, quod est genus quam longissime in actione fugiendum. Abesse enim plurimum a saltatore debet orator, ut sit gestus ad sensus magis quam ad verba accommodatus, quod etiam histrionibus paulo gravioribus facere moris fuit.*

110. The title of an Atellan farce by Pomponius was the Doctor (*Medicus*).

111. Epyllion: Quinn (1970: 283); Fedeli (1978: 157–69); Traina (1998: 191, 196); hymn commissioned to Catullus by an aedile for the Megalesia: Wiseman (1985: 205 ff.); combination of hymn and epyllion: Elder (1947: 34); tragedy: Guillemin (1949: 153 [in three acts]); Thomson (1997: 374); pantomime: Newman (1990: 348). See also Fantuzzi and Hunter (2004: 477–85).

112. Morisi (1999: 31): 'la sua apparente irriducibilità sui molteplici piani dell'intreccio, dell'atmosfera, dell'intonazione, della lingua, del registro stilistico, del ritmo, ad una forma tipizzata e tributaria di una gamma coerente di norme e convenzioni, complicano terribilmente la possibilità di ascriverlo ad alcuno dei generi conosciuti'.

113. Hephaestion, *Enchiridion* (12, 3).

114. The gloss is attributed to Georgius Choeroboscus (a sixth-century Byzantine scholar).

115. Wilamowitz-Möllendorff (1879: 194–201). For a detailed counter-argument to Wilamowitz-Möllendorff, see Mulroy (1976: 61–72) who has impugned the integrity of Hephaestion's text and consequently Wilamowitz-Möllendorff's suggestion.

116. Ross (1969: 33) strongly claimed that 'Catullus' twist to the usual story is original'. Courtney's proposal (Courtney, 1985: 88–91) has also had some credit among scholars; he suggested that Catullus 63 drew its models from the *Garland* of Meleager; he thus names as inspiring models the epigrams of Alcaeus of Messene (*AP* 6, 218), Simonides (*AP* 6, 217), Antipater of Sidon (*AP* 6, 219), and Dioscorides (*AP* 6, 220) which all narrate the story of the encounter of a Gallus

with a lion that is frightened off by the sound of the tympanon; Shipton (1987: 444–9), although in agreement with Courtney's reconstruction, points out that only two of the four epigrams (those by Alcaeus and Dioscorides) can be said to come from the *Garland*.

117. Thomson (1997: 374) has singled out the lack of 'details of the cult, with allusions to the underlying myths' in Catullus 63 as an argument against the influence of Alexandrian poems on Cybele-worship on it.

118. Morisi (1999: 32–3): 'il soggetto, tuttavia, è eminentemente drammatico nella misura in cui gli eventi appaiono estratti dal decorso temporale intrinseco alla narrazione e attualizzati, vissuti come presenti dalla prospettiva individuale del protagonista, i cui atti e sentimenti tendono a tradursi in enfatici gesti di scena'.

119. Guillemin's interpretation has been followed by several scholars, for instance by Thomson (1997: 374) who claims that poem 63 'is clearly in essence a tragedy'.

120. Thomson (1997: 371–2) divides the poem as follows: Day one: outset of religious frenzy, resulting in enslavement to the goddess by self-mutilation; day two: remorse and desire to flee followed by re-enslavement.

121. The poem alternates narratives (1–11; 27–49; 74–7; 84–90) and monologues (12–26; 50–73; 78–83); emotions: in the poem a great emphasis is given to *furor* which actually leads Attis' actions (compare here the parallel emphasis on emotions in Seneca's running commentaries); diction: use of repetitions, of the first person, of the interjection 'ah' (especially attested in tragedy and comedy), and of the self-apostrophe 'anime', which is widely employed by Seneca *tragicus*.

122. Newman (1990: 343–66).

123. See Lada-Richards (2007: 20).

124. For a discussion of Dioscorides' epigram as evidence of the existence of a primeval form of the fully-fledged pantomime in the middle of the third century BC in Greece see the section entitled 'Origins and Development of Pantomime' in this chapter. The *Galli* were the eunuch priests of Cybele. Tertullian (*Apol.* XV, 5): *vidimus aliquando castratum Attin, illum deum ex Pessinunte*; Arnobius (*Adv. Nat.* VII, 33): *tranquillior, lenior Mater Magna efficitur, si Attidis conspexerit priscam refricari ab histrionibus fabulam?*

125. See Wooton (1999: 314–55); *oscilla* are 'small scale marble sculptures in relief'.

126. Madness was a popular theme in pantomime: see Lucian (41) madness of Hercules and Athamas; Lucian (46) Ajax.

127. The word *furor* and its cognates are repeatedly employed: *furenti rabie* (4); *rabidus furor* (38); *rabie* (44); *furibunda* (31, 54); *rabie* (57); *furor* (78); *furoris* (79).

128. *citata* (8); *tremebunda* (11); *Gallae* (12, 34); *notha mulier* (27); *furibunda, vaga* (31); *comitata* (32); *lassulae* (35); *excitam* (42); *ipsa* (45); *allocuta* (49); *furibunda* (54); *mulier* (63); *ministra, famula* (68); *maenas* (69); *teneramque* (88); *illa* (89); *famula* (90).

129. Lada-Richards (2003: 24).

130. Elder (1947: 34); Ross (1969: 150).

131. The cult of the goddess was brought to Rome in 204 BC and her temple on the Palatine was dedicated in 191 BC.

132. The galliambic metre is very rarely employed in Latin poetry. It was used by Varro in one of his Menippean satires entitled *Eumenides* to describe the ritual of Cybele's acolytes.

133. Kirby (1989: 72–3). The performative nature of the poem was already suggested by Wiseman (1985) who claimed that the poem was officially commissioned from Catullus by an aedile for the Megalensia; to Wiseman's theory Kirby objects that it would need to be established 'how much narrative such choric hymns contained'.

134. The sotadean verse was raised to literary recognition by Sotades of Maronea who employed this metrical pattern in the composition of his satires (often obscene in content) for which he was credited with the foundation of cinaedography. See Strabon (14, 1, 41); Athenaeus (XIV, 62e) says that such compositions were recited by a cinaedologus.

135. Ennius (Var. 25–9 Vahlen), Varro (fr. 2, 3), Plautus (*Amph.* 168 ff.), Martial (*Ep.* 3, 29), and Petronius (*Satyricon* 23, 3; 132, 8) composed poems in sotadeans.

136. Martial, *Ep.* (2, 86, 1–5): *Quod nec carmine glorior supino/nec retro lego Sotaden cinaedum/nusquam Graecula quod recantat echo/nec dictat mihi luculentus Attis/ mollem debilitate galliambon.* See Merkelbach (1973: 92): 'Der Rhythmus ist völlig identisch mit dem Sotadeum, nur ist das Versende um eine Stelle verschoben'.

137. Demetrios, *De eloc* (189) associates the sotadean verse directly with *galli*.

138. Martial (9, 2, 13): *i nunc et miseros, Cybele, praecide cinaedos*; see Carcopino (1942: 76–92).

139. See also Plautus, *Miles Gloriosus* (667): *tum ad saltandum non cinaedus malacus aeque est/atque ego*; *Poenulus* (1317–20): **Anta**. *Quin adhibuisti, dum istaec loquere, tympanum?/nam te cinaedum esse arbitror magis quam virum./**Ag**. Scin quam cinaedus sum?ite istinc, servi, foras,/ecferte fustis*; Macrobius, *Saturnalia* (14).

140. See also Lucian's *De mercede conductis* (27): a *cinaedus* talented in singing Ionic songs is said to be the ballet-master in a wealthy household. That *cinaedi* were often part of the household is attested by other ancient writers, for example, Juvenal (6, 01–03): *In quacumque domo vivit luditque professus/obscenum et tremula promittens omnia dextra,/invenies omnis turpes similesque cinaedis.*

141. See Juvenal (6, 63–6): *chironomon Ledam molli saltante Bathyllo/Tuccia vesicae non imperat, Apula gannit,/attendit Thymele: Thymele tunc rustica discit*; the remark that Bathyllus' impersonation of Leda had something to teach even to the mime actress Thymele is telling. Lada-Richards (2007: 69): '(the pantomime) excels in a language of movement that becomes by turn both male and female'.

142. Lada-Richards (2007: 69). See Novatian, *On the Spectacles* (6, 6): *vir ultra mulierem mollitiem dissolutus*.

143. Athenaeus, *Deiph.* (I, 20–1). See the section entitled 'Founders of the Genre' in this chapter.

144. Geffcken (1973).

145. Cicero, *Pro Caelio* (1).

146. See paragraphs 35; 38; 49.

147. See Geffcken (1973: 34 n. 1) for the occurrences of the word *meretrix* and *meretricius*.

148. Wiseman (1985: 48); see Cicero, *In Verrem* (III, 36, 83): . . . *Tertiae mimae condonavit. Utrum impudentius ab sociis abstulit an turpius meretrici dedit an improbius populo Romano ademit an audacius tabulas publicas commutavit?*; Horace, *Satires* (I, 2, 58–9): *verum est cum mimis, est cum meretricibus, unde/fama malum gravius quam res trahit*.

149. The question whether the lines quoted by Petronius are genuinely Publilian or a Petronian original reworking does not bear any consequence on the presence of the theme *matrona/meretrix* in Publilius' mime. See Giancotti (1967: 231–74) for an in-depth discussion of the issue of authenticity of Publilius' lines in Petronius. See also Wiseman (1985: 48).

150. Cicero, *Pro Caelio* (68): the slaves were then manumitted by Clodia because of their act of loyalty towards their mistress.

151. Wiseman (1985: 29).

152. Compare Cicero, *Pro Rabirio Postumo* (35) for evidence that deceptions and intrigues were the bread and butter of mimes: *Audiebamus Alexandream, nunc cognoscimus. Illinc omnes **praestigiae**, illinc, inquam, omnes **fallaciae**, omnia denique ab eis mimorum argumenta nata sunt*.

153. *Pro Caelio* (18), the lines are from Ennius' Medea: *Nam nunquam era errans/hanc molestiam nobis exhiberet/Medea animo aegra, amore saevo saucia. Sic enim, iudices, reperietis, quod, cum ad id loci venero, ostendam, hanc Palatinam Medeam migrationemque hanc adulescenti causam sive malorum omnium sive potius sermonum fuisse*. Geffcken (1973: 15–17) has underlined the pronounced parodist flavour of the analogy Medea–Clodia provided by the epithet Palatinam, and by the fact that Cicero compares Caelius' moving to the Palatine, next to Clodia's own house, to the unfortunate sea trip of Jason and his encounter with Medea; the comparison of a mythical situation with a prosaic one involves, in fact, a degradation of the model meant to provoke amusement and it is a typical device used in comedy. See Austin (1960: 148–50) for the discussion of Clodia's identification with Catullus' Lesbia which relies on Apuleius (*Apologia* 10): *C. Catul[l]um, quod Lesbiam pro Clodia nominarit*.

154. Compare this with the description of Sempronia in Sallust, *Bellum Catilinae* (25, 2): *Sed in eis erat Sempronia, quae multa saepe virilis audaciae facinora commiserat*.

> *Haec mulier genere atque forma, praeterea viro atque liberis satis fortunata fuit;*
> *litteris Graecis et Latinis docta, psallere et saltare elegantius, quam necesse est probae,*
> *multa alia, quae instrumenta luxuriae sunt;* with Macrobius, *Saturnalia* (III, 14, 5):
> *quid enim ait Sallustius: 'psallere saltare elegantius quam necesse est probae'? adeo et*
> *ipse Semproniam reprehendit non quod saltare, sed quod optime scierit.*

155.   *ILS* 5213.

156.   Macrobius, *Saturnalia* (II, 6, 6): *cum iratus esse P. Clodius D. Laberio diceretur*
         quod ei mimum petenti non dedisset, 'quid amplius', inquit, 'mihi facturus es, nisi ut
         Dyrrhachium eam et redeam?', ludens ad Ciceronis exilium.

157.   Wiseman (1985: 38).

158.   Ovid, *Tristia* (2, 515): *scribere si fas est imitantes turpia mimos;* Valerius Maximus
         (2, 6, 7): *Eadem civitas severitatis custos acerrima est, nullum aditum in scaenam*
         mimis dando, quorum argumenta maiore ex parte stuprorum continent actus . . .;
         Seneca the Elder, *Controversiae* (2, 4, 5): *vere mimicae nuptiae, [in] quibus ante in*
         cubiculum rivalis venit quam maritus; Juvenal (6, 41–4); Tertullian, *Apologeticus*
         (15, 1) refers to 'moechum Anubin' as one of the characters typical of the mime of
         his days; Minucius Felix, *Octavius* (37, 12): *In scenicis etiam non minor furor et*
         turpitudo prolixior; nunc enim mimus vel exponit adulteria vel monstrat, nunc
         enervis histrio amorem dum fingit, infligit.

159.   The fifth mime of Herodas and the Oxyrhynchus Jealous Lady mime (Page 1941:
         77) both deal with a jealous mistress in love with a slave, but, as Reynolds has
         remarked (1946: 77–8), both of them tend to be more 'a psychological study of
         the adulteress than an attempt at bringing out the dramatic possibilities inherent
         in the situation' as in the later adultery-mime.

160.   Reynolds (1946: 84) has suggested that 'a trial scene was of common occurrence
         in the Imperial mimes'.

161.   See Juvenal (1, 36) and Martial, *Ep.* (1, 4, 5–6): *qua Thymelen spectas derisoremque*
         Latinum,/illa fronte precor carmina nostra legas; (2, 72, 3–4): *os tibi percisum*
         quanto non ipse Latinus/vilia Panniculi percutit ora sono; (3, 86, 3–4): *sed si*
         Panniculum spectas et, casta, Latinum,/non sunt haec mimis improbiora . . .; (5, 61,
         11–12): *o quam dignus eras alapis, Mariane, Latini:/te successurum credo ego*
         Panniculo; (9, 28): *Dulce decus scaenae, ludorum fama, Latinus/ille ego sum,*
         plausus deliciaeque tuae,/qui spectatorem potui fecisse Catonem,/solvere qui Curios
         Fabriciosque graves./sed nihil a nostro sumpsit mea vita theatro/et sola tantum
         scaenicus arte feror;/nec poteram gratus domino sine moribus esse:/interius mentes
         inspicit ille deus./vos me laurigeri parasitum dicite Phoebi,/Roma sui famulum
         dum sciat esse Iovis; (13, 2, 3): *et possis ipsum tu deridere Latinum.*

162.   McKeown (1979: 74); already Yardley (1972: 135) pointed out that the situation
         described is not a biographical one and Hubbard (1974: 151) suggested the
         influence of mime on this elegy.

163. Juvenal (6, 275–9): *tu credis amorem,/tu tibi tunc, uruca, places fletumque labellis/ exorbes, quae scripta et quot lecture tabellas/si tibi zelotypae retegantur scrinia moechae!/sed iacet in servi complexibus aut equitis*; Petronius (45) *Videbis populi rixam inter zelotypos et amasiunculos*; (69) *Tu autem, Scintilla, noli zelotypa esse.* Fantham (1986: 45–57) has argued that jealousy (*ZHΛΟΤΥΠΙΑ*) was a stock theme already in Greek mimes (Herodas' fifth mime about the jealous mistress); the term *zelotypus* entered into Latin where it also had clear mimic overtones.

164. Yardley (1974: 431).

165. Scholars have assumed that Lycinna was Propertius' first love on the basis of line 5–6 *illa rudis animos per noctes conscia primas/imbuit, heu nullis capta Lycinna datis.* Thus, they usually tend to interpret the situation described in 3, 15 as an autobiographical one. Yardley, on the contrary, thinks the poem describes a fictional one since the scenario depicted by Propertius seems borrowed from a mime (with Lesky 1951: 173) or from Comedy (with Day 1938: 85–101). See Wyke (1987: 47–61) in relation to the fictional character of Propertius'women.

166. McKeown (1979: 73–4).

167. McKeown (1979: 74).

168. See also Jacob of Serugh (*Hom.* 5, F22vb, text in Moss 1935: 112) where the Syriac homilist affirms that the danced story of Zeus' adulteries 'is famous among the spectacles'.

169. The story of the love of Ares and Aphrodite appears already in Homer (*Odyssey,* VIII, 266–320).

170. See Wiseman (2008a: 210–30).

171. Cunningham (1949: 100): 'I wish to suggest that the *Heroides* were originally written as lyric-dramatic monologues to be presented on the stage with music and dancing'.

172. Ovid, *Ars Amatoria* (3, 346): *ignotum hoc aliis ille novavit opus.* Cunningham (1949: 100) remarks that the poetical epistle was not new in itself, since already Lucilius, Horace, and Propertius employed this form; however, the novelty of Ovid's *Heroides* resides in the 'adoption of situations and characters from mythology and legend.'

173. Sargent (1996) offered an analysis of *Heroides* 7 and 10 (the letter of Ariadne to Theseus and that of Dido to Aeneas) trying to highlight the hallmarks of their composition as pantomimic libretti.

174. Owen (1924: 271).

175. Galinsky (1975: 68) remarked how strikingly pantomimic are the qualities of the Narcissus episode. In addition to this, 'the scope of the pantomimic artist's undertaking', which Lucian said to range from chaos to the story of Cleopatra, is very similar to Ovid's scope in the *Metamorphoses* (1, 3–4: *primaque ab origine mundi/ad mea . . . tempora*). Compare Lucian, *De Saltatione* (37): ἀπὸ γὰρ χάους

εὐθὺς καὶ τῆς πρώτης τοῦ κόσμου γενέσεως ἀρξάμενον χρὴ αὐτὸν ἅπαντα εἰδέναι ἄχρι τῶν κατὰ τὴν Κλεοπάτραν τὴν Αἰγυπτίαν.

176. Ingleheart (2008: 198–217).

177. Horsfall (1979: 319–32).

178. Varro, *Antiquitates rerum divinarum* fr. 3 (Cardauns): *Ex eo enim poterimus ... scire, quem cuiusque causa deum invocare atque advocare debeamus, ne faciamus, ut mimi solent, et optemus a Libero aquam, a Lymphis vinum.*

179. Tertullian, *Ad. Nat.* (1, 10, 45); *Apol.* (15, 2): *Sed et histrionum litterae omnem foeditatem eorum designant. Luget Sol filium de caelo iactatum laetantibus vobis, et Cybele pastorum suspirat fastidiosum non erubescentibus vobis, et sustinetis Iovis elogia cantari, et Iunonem, Venerem, Minervam a pastore iudicari*; Minucius Felix, *Oct.* (23, 2): *Cybelae Dindyma pudet dicere, quae adulterum suum infeliciter placitum, quoniam et ipsa deformis et vetula, ut multorum deorum mater, ad stuprum inlicere non poterat, exsecuit, ut deum scilicet faceret eunuchum. Propter hanc fabulam Galli eam et semiviri sui corporis supplicio colunt.* See Hepding (1903: 116).

180. Fantham (1983: 185–216); already McKeown (1979: 76) and Littlewood (1980: 301–21) had signalled the influence of sub-literary dramatic genres on the four episodes in the *Fasti*. See also Barchiesi (1997: 238–46) and Wiseman (2002: 275–99).

181. Barchiesi (1997: 241) agrees with Fantham: 'There is no traditionally accepted explanation to justify these stories of Priapus and Faunus as the causes of Roman rituals and festivals'. See Littlewood (1980: 316–17) who, on the contrary, thinks that the inclusion of material drawn from low forms of comic drama fits pertinently and congruously in the *Fasti*, since 'the earliest dramatic productions in the ancient world had their first origins in rustic and religious festivals.'; mimes, for example, were associated with the festival of the Floralia since the second century BC.

182. It is remarkable that the description of the exchange of garments features several times in Seneca's tragedies: *Hf* (465–71); *Phae* (317–24); *HO* (371–7); such a theme was highly suitable to be exploited in mimic or pantomimic performances where parodist travesty was one of the most common ingredients.

183. For a detailed analysis of the story see Fantham (1983: 192–201).

184. Fantham (1983: 200).

185. Bömer (1954: II, 179); Giancotti (1967: 61–5).

186. See Ingleheart (2008: 200) who provides the following instances: Ovid, *Rem.* (755): *illic assidue ficti saltantur amantes*; Horace, *Sat.* (I, 5, 63): *pastorem saltaret uti Cyclopa rogabat*; Juvenal (6, 63): *chironomon Ledam molli saltante*; and Velleius Paterculus (2, 83, 2): *Plancus ... Glaucum saltasset.*

187. See McKeown (1979: 75–6 and 81 n. 23).

188. Giancotti (1967: 63–5). For a discussion of the popularity of the theme of the jealous mistress in mimes, see the end of the section entitled 'The Adultery-mime in the Elegiac Poets' in this chapter. See McKeown (1979: 76) on window entrances and exits as a typical feature of amatory mimes. He quotes Ovid, *Ars Amatoria* (3, 605–8): *Cum melius foribus possis, admitte fenestra,/inque tuo vultu signa timentis habe./callida prosiliat dicatque ancilla 'perimus'!/tu iuvenem trepidum quolibet abde loco.*

189. Fantham (1983) has remarked the oddity that the tale of Priapus' sexual disappointment is told twice with the only change being that of the victim undergoing Priapus' attempts at raping; thus the two passages are basically doublets.

190. Cicero, *Pro Caelio* (65): *mimi ergo est iam exitus, non fabulae; in quo cum clausula non invenitur, fugit aliquis e manibus, deinde scabilla concrepant, aulaeum tollitur.*

191. Barchiesi (1997: 240): *causa pudenda quidem est . . . iocis non alienus* (Priapus 1, 392 ff.); *traditur antiqui fabula plena ioci* (Faunus 2, 304); *nunc mihi cur cantent superest obscena puellæ/dicere . . . inde ioci veteres obscenaque dicta canuntur* (Anna and Mars 3, 675 ff.); *non habet ingratos fabula nostra iocos* (Silenus 3, 738); *scaena ioci morem liberioris habet . . . Mater, ades, florum, ludis celebranda iocosis* (apparitions of Flora 5, 183); *est multi fabula parva ioci* (Priapus and Vesta 6, 320); *et canere ad veteres verba iocosa modos* (flute players 6, 692).

192. Fantham (1983: 190).

193. Barchiesi (1997: 246).

194. For a different dating of the satire, see Toynbee (1942: 83–93) who thinks that the *Apocolocyntosis* was written for the *Neronia* of 60 AD. In Toynbee's argument there is one compelling point; she remarks that in the satire Apollo is presented as *citharoedus* and Nero is said to be his double (4, 1), an equation which did not begin before 59/60 AD.

195. Eden (1984: 8).

196. Weinreich (1923: 19).

197. Fantham (1988–89: 160).

198. Kehoe (1984: 89–106).

199. Purcell (1999: 182–3).

200. A funerary inscription (*CIL* VI 4886) attests the existence of an imitator of the emperor Tiberius (*Caesaris lusor*); it has been suggested that this imitator was the mime who impersonated the emperor at his funeral; Suetonius gives evidence that an *archimimus* impersonated Vespasian at his funeral (*Vesp.* 19): *Sed et in funere Favor archimimus personam eius ferens imitansque, ut est mos, facta ac dicta vivi . . .* See Sumi (2002: 559–85) for a discussion of 'funerary mimes' who impersonated the emperors at their funeral and mimed their life.

201. Richter (1913: 149–56).

202. Paschal (1939: 10).

203. Purcell (1999: 182).

204. Generally speaking, scholars think that the reference here is to Claudius' addiction to banquets and dicing.

205. Suetonius, *Claudius* (2, 2; 3, 2; 15, 4; 38, 3): *Ac ne stultitiam quidem suam reticuit simulatamque a se ex industria sub Gaio, quod aliter evasurus perventurusque ad susceptam stationem non fuerit, quibusdam oratiunculis testatus est; nec tamen persuasit, cum intra breve tempus liber editus sit, cui index erat μωρῶν ἐπανάστασις, argumentum autem stultitiam neminem fingere.*

206. The pun lies on *mŏrari* (to linger) and *mōrari* (to be a fool).

207. The title *Apocolocyntosis* is only attested by Cassius Dio (60, 35, 2 ff.) who attributes a satire thus entitled to Seneca. The medieval title of the satire in the manuscript tradition is *Ludus de morte Divi Claudii*.

208. Pace Eden (1984: 3): 'It must be stressed here that there is no evidence that κολοκύντη and *cucurbita* necessarily conveyed an implication of stupidity'. In Italian, expressions such as 'zucca vuota', 'zucca dura', or 'non avere sale in zucca' are proverbially used for singling out someone's stupidity.

209. Petronius *Satyricon* (39, 12): in the passage Trimalchio explains the kind of people born under each sign of the Zodiac; he says that under the Aquarius (the Water Carrier) innkeepers and numbskulls are born (*in aquario [sc. nascuntur] copones et cucurbitae*); as the innkeepers dilute wine with water, so the numbskulls have a diluted brain, which means that they are stupid. In Italian, the dialectal expressions 'vino annacquato' and 'avere il cervello annacquato' have the same meaning; Apuleius, *Met.* (1, 15, 2): *nos cucurbitae caput non habemus ut pro te moriamur* (*cucurbitae* is genitive of definition).

210. Coffey (1976: 168).

211. See Eden (1984: 109). This type of mime is not otherwise known apart from the mention of it found in the Senecan passage (*famam/fama mimum*) and in Cicero (*Ad Att.* I, 16, 13), which has *fabam mimum* instead of *famam/fama mimum* as in Seneca: *sed heus tu, videsne consulatum illum nostrum, quem Curio antea ἀποθέωσιν vocabat, si hic factus erit, fabam mimum futurum?*; see Allen (1959: 1–8) for a discussion of the Ciceronian passage; Watt (1955: 496–500) has proposed to emend *famam/fama* in *Phasma*, which is the attested title of a mime by Catullus.

212. Eden (1984: 109) with Watt (1955: 251 ff.); in relation to a mimic antecedents of Seneca's *Apocolocyntosis*, Laberius' *Cancer*, which seem to have consisted in a parody of the Pythagorean doctrine of transmigration of souls, may stand as such. See Bonaria (1965: 42–3) and Giancotti (1967: 55–6). A passage in the *De ira* (II, 11, 3) attests that Seneca was familiar with Laberius' mimes.

213. See Reynolds (1946: 84): Philo (*Legatio ad Gaium* 358 ff.); Petronius (106–7); the mime *Laureolous* may have very plausibly presented a trial scene; Apuleius (*Met.*

10, 2–12); Origen (*Ep. ad Afric. de Hist. Sus.* II = Migne, P.G. XI 73 ff.); Ammianus Marcellinus (30, 4, 21); Choricius of Gaza (*Apologia mimorum*, 30).

214. *ILS* 5225 [= *CIL* VI 4886]. See Purcell (1999: 181–93).

215. Abbot (1911: 257–70): 'the romance of Petronius … may be related to the epic, to the serious heroic romance, to the bourgeois story or adventure developed out of the rhetorical exercise, to the prologue of comedy, to the verse-mélange of comedy or the mime, or to the prose-poetical Menippean satire'; Conte (1996: 130) argues convincingly that the most salient feature of Petronius' *Satyricon* is its creativity, which cannot be fixed in a category of genre, since the very first aim of the work is the accumulation of different languages, the grafting of a genre onto another one, the inexhaustible contamination of diverse literary forms. Zeitlin (1971: 631–84) has remarked that the generic anarchy of the *Satyricon* is, paradoxically, the cipher of its artistic integrity.

216. Marius Mercator, *Lib. Subnot. in verba Juliani* (4.1 = Migne, P.L. 48, 126–7). See Sullivan (1968: 112–13).

217. Collignon (1892: 273–83); Preston (1915: 260–9); Sandy (1974: 329): 'Petronian studies … agree almost unanimously that Roman theatre, especially mimes, and its tastes, techniques, and concerns have left many recognizable traces throughout the *Satyricon*'.

218. See Walsh (1970: 24–31).

219. Sandy (1974: 324–43).

220. Augustine, *De Civitate Dei* (6, 75).

221. Sandy (1974: 339–40). For the presence of the theme of the *cena* in Roman satire and its legacy on Petronius' *Cena Trimalchionis* see Shero (1923: 126–43).

222. See Panayotakis (1995: 31–51).

223. Rostovtzeff (1937: 87–91) interprets a scene on a bowl now in the Louvre where slaves sexually arouse a donkey as 'a well-known scene of a famous mime'; Sandy (1974: 340) argues that the 'attempts made by the *cinaedus* to arouse Ascyltos and Encolpius are strikingly similar' to that of the bowl of the Louvre.

224. See also Seneca the Elder, *Contr.* (2, 4, 5): *vere mimicae nuptiae [in] quibus ante in cubiculum rivalis venit quam maritus*; pseudo-Quintilian, Dec. (ed. C. Ritter, 139, 21–2): *ecquid semoto illo nuptiarum mimo atque inani tantummodo nomine virum esse cogitatis et dignum, qui abdicetur, quod hominem non occiderit?*; Bonaria (1965: 117–18).

225. For an analysis of the *Cena Trimalchionis* see Sandy (1974: 330–9); Rosati (1983: 213–27); Panayotakis (1995: 52–109).

226. For a discussion about the authenticity of the lines of Publilius quoted by Trimalchio see: Skutch (1959: 1923–4); Giancotti (1967: 238–74); Sandy (1976: 286–7).

227. For the role of music in the *Cena* see Panayotakis (1995: 60 n. 19) who quotes the work of: Sandy (1974: 331); Bonaria (1982: 136–8); Rosati (1983: 217); Horsfall (1989: 197–8).

228. Sandy (1974: 342).
229. Sandy (1974: 337–8).
230. See Giancotti (1967: 119–28).
231. The word is employed by Plautus: *Curc.* (2, 3, 44); *Ps.* (1, 2, 33); *Capt.* (3, 4).
232. See Collignon (1892: 276–9); Panayotakis (1995: 136–57).
233. The P. Berol. 13927 (= Manteuffel, 1930, no. 17; Wiemke 192 ff.) contains a list of stage properties for mimes, which includes ship's tackle.
234. Aulus Gellius, *Noctes Atticae* (16, 7, 10): (Laberius) *in Anna Peranna 'gubernium' pro 'gubernatore' dicit.*
235. Giancotti (1967: 63–5).
236. Panayotakis (1995: 153). For the Laureolus-mime see Suetonius (*Gaius*, 57) who reports that such a mime was performed on the day of Caligula's death (41 AD): *et cum in Laureolo mimo, in quo actor proripiens se ruina sanguinem vomit, plures secundarum certatim experimentum artis darent, cruore scaena abundavit.*
237. See Wiemken (1972: 139 ff.); Steinmetz (1982: 367 ff.).
238. For evidence of the popularity of the theme see: Cicero (*Phil.* II, 27, 65): *in eius igitur viri copias cum se subito ingurgitasset, exsultabat gaudio persona de mimo, 'modo egens, repente dives'. Sed, ut est apud poetam nescio quem, 'Male parta male dilabuntur';* Seneca, *Epistulae* (114, 6): *hunc esse qui [in] tribunali, in rostris, in omni publico coetu sic apparuerit ut pallio velaretur caput exclusis utrimque auribus, non aliter quam in mimo fugitivi divitis* solent. *Heres petitor* is the title of an Atellan farce by Pomponius.
239. Fedeli (1988: 12) argues that the old man functions as the 'Prologue' of the ensuing mime that Eumolpus and his friends will stage at Croton. He thus performs the function of providing the information needed for the following actions to ensue.
240. See Panayotakis (1995: 157–60).
241. Panayotakis (1994: 327).
242. See Steinmetz (1982: 352–5) and Fick (1990: 225).
243. See Hall (2002: 29) who rightly claims that 'there was no single correct way to stage a pantomime'.
244. However, an expression such as *vultu honesta* could refer to the mask rather than to the face of the dancer, and it could have been the way the libretto hinted at the actual mask of the dancer in a somehow implicit way.
245. See Zimmerman (2000: 366–92); e.g. *ad instar incluti montis illius; instructus fabrica; consitus; de manibus fabri; in modum Paridis, Phrygii pastoris; pecuarium simulabat magisterium; cognatione simili; indicabant; qui Paris videbatur; in deae Iunonis speciem similis; scaenici pueri;* for the fictional nature of pantomimic performances see Ovid, *Remedia Amoris* (751–66): *illic assidue ficti saltantur amantes.*
246. See Lucian (72); the Judgement of Paris is attested as a very popular one in pantomimic performances (Lucian, 45); Augustine, *De Civitate Dei* (18, 10): *illud*

quod de tribus deabus, Iunone scilicet et Minerva et Venere, quae pro malo aureo adipiscendo apud iudicem Paridem de pulchritudinis excellentia certasse narrantur et . . . inter theatricos plausus cantantur atque saltantur; Tertullian, *Apol.* (15, 2); see also Steinmetz (1982: 350 and n. 148).

247. See Lada-Richards (2007: 39–40).
248. See Zimmerman (2000: 366–9).
249. Zimmerman (2000: 371–2) remarks that the adverb *saltatorie* is attested only here, while the adjective *saltatorius* is attested only twice: Scip. min. orat. 20 and Cicero, *in Pisonem* (X, 22): *cum collegae tui domus cantu et cymbalis personaret, cumque ipse nudus in convivio saltaret; in quo cum suum illum **saltatorium** versaret orbem, ne tum quidem fortunae rotam pertimescebat.*
250. The nods of the head seem to play a relevant role in the dance vocabulary of pantomime (*honestis nutibus; nutu significans; adnutante capite*); compare Quintilian (11, 3, 182) which attests the use of nodding by actors at large: *Hic enim dubitationis moras, vocis flexus, varias manus, diversos **nutus** actor adhibebit. Aliud oratio sapit nec vult nimium esse condita: actione enim constat, non imitatione.*
251. See also the dance of Fotis which shows a similar wave-like quality, *Met.* (2, 7, 30, 20): *illud cibarium vasculum floridis palmulis rotabat in circulum et in orbis flexibus crebra succutiens et simul membra sua leniter illubricans, lumbis sensim vibrantibus, spinam mobilem quatiens placide decenter **undabat**.* Compare the overall charming quality of Venus' solo with Ovid, *Amores* (2, 4, 29–30): *illa placet gestu numerosaque bracchia ducit/et tenerum molli torquet ab arte latus* and Juvenal, *Satires* (6, 63): *chironomom Ledam molli saltante Bathyllo.*
252. For a discussion of the emphasis on the beautiful quality of the performance see Zimmerman (1993: 143–61).
253. See Webb (2005: 3–11).
254. Windisch (1924: 316).
255. Welborn (1999: 137).
256. Betz (1972: 82–3).
257. Betz (1972: 162); on the theatrical life at Corinth see Engels (1990: 47–8). Mason (1971: 160) argues that Apuleius chose Corinth for the 'reputation of the city, which he employed as a symbol of the secular world and contrasted with the life of the devotee of Isis presented in the final book'.

Chapter 2

1. This is due to the lack of transitions and connections between the acts themselves or between single scenes within the acts.
2. Regenbogen (1927–28: 430).

3. The tragedies are listed according to the order of the E manuscript tradition (*Hercules, Troades, Phoenissae, Medea, Phaedra, Oedipus, Agamemnon, Thyestes, Hercules*). The A manuscript tradition gives them in a different order and, in some cases, with different titles (*Hercules furens, Thyestes, Thebais, Hippolytus, Oedipus, Troas, Medea, Agamemnon, Octavia, Hercules Oetaeus*). Most editors adopt the order of E, but distinguish the two Hercules plays following A (*furens* and *Oetaeus*).

4. The fifth act of the *Oedipus* has a peculiar structure even by Senecan standards. It is constituted by two scenes separated by a choral intervention (980–96); in no other Senecan play does a choral interlude feature between the scenes of a single act. The first scene deals with the messenger's narration of Oedipus' self-blinding; the second scene, separated from the first by the chorus, presents the confrontation between the blind Oedipus and Jocasta which will lead to Jocasta's suicide (*coram populo*). The chorus leader, who is actively involved in this final unfolding of the dramatic action, fulfils the role of an external commentator more than that of a character; in fact, he is in charge of the description of the entrance of a frenzied Jocasta (1004–9) and of her final suicidal blow (1040–1).

5. The *Thyestes* is the only play that presents a dialogic prologue.

6. *Tro* (168–202 and 203–370); *Med* (380–430 and 431–578; 879–90 and 891–977; 978–1027); *Thy* (404–9 and 491–545); *Ag* (108–225 and 226–309).

7. See Regenbogen (1927–28: 461).

8. Owen (1969: 295).

9. Fitch (1987a: 116). Tarrant (1985: 85) has claimed that the Senecan prologue is 'less an introduction than a microcosm of the play'.

10. In the prologue of the *Oedipus* in particular, the *dénouement* is exceptionally foreshadowed; in fact, Oedipus is already aware that he is the cause of the plague that is devastating Thebes (36: *fecimus caelum nocens*). In the prologue of the *Thyestes* (54–62), the *dénouement* is similarly foreshadowed.

11. See Fitch (1987a: 116–17): see Virgil, *Aen.* (1.37 ff., 7.293 ff.); Ovid, *Met.* (2.508 ff., 3.259 ff., 4.420 ff.).

12. Bragington (1933: 13). The different length of Juno's soliloquy (124 lines) and the speeches of Iris and Lissa (52 lines) points in this direction too.

13. See especially Pratt (1939).

14. Tarrant (1978: 230): 'Indirect evidence confirms the impression that postclassical drama sacrificed structural coherence to the emotional or rhetorical effect of a single scene. Aristotle records the damaging effects of the actor's supremacy on fourth-century tragedy: the highly developed rhetorical and pathetic skills of the performers encouraged writers of tragedy to emphasize histrionically effective solo writing at the expense of a coherent whole. These pressures could only have grown stronger in the Hellenistic period, when evidence for the performance of selections from classical tragedy is most abundant. Seneca's neglect of classical norms of

coherence may thus be the natural outcome of a long evolution in dramatic history'.

15. Erasmo (2004: 134).

16. On the same line of thought, Motto and Clark (1972: 70) describe Seneca's tragedies as presenting neither an 'interlocking chain of events nor inevitable unfolding of action', but 'pictures in clipped segments, each picture being but a miniature portrayal of a single phase'.

17. Tarrant (1976: 3–6).

18. Tarrant (1976: 333–5).

19. See Tarrant (1978: 229–30): 'The *Phoenissae* displays Seneca's emancipation from classical tragic form at its most extreme'. The play lacks the choruses, it does not feature the common five-act division to which the other plays basically conform, and it requires two changes of setting. Because of the absence of choral odes and the uneven length of the four acts in which the play can be divided, the play has been considered incomplete by some scholars, while others, such as Tarrant, have maintained that the play is indeed complete and have interpreted its structural unconventional peculiarities as a sign that the play is 'an essay in a distinct sub-genre of tragedy' an example of which is Ezekiel's *Exagoge*.

20. Frank (1995: 27). In this respect, the case of the *Phoenissae* is not isolated since the *Trojan Women* also features a similar combination of events which, in the antecedents, belong to different plays.

21. Expansion is particularly conspicuous in the narrative set-pieces of the *Medea* (the incantation scene), *Oedipus* (the necromancy), *Hercules furens* (the descent to the Underworld), *Agamemnon* (the storm), *Phaedra* (the sea-monster), *Trojan women* (the double death of Astyanax and Polyxena), and *Thyestes* (the banquet), which are analysed in Chapter 4.

22. The scene requires a change of setting; in fact, the previous acts take place in front of the royal palace, but in this one Medea is said by the nurse to have moved inside her house, where she attends to the preparation of the poison.

23. A similar concentration characterizes the last act of the play since several events crowd the finale. First, a messenger announces the death of Creon and Creusa; then Medea appears onstage and, after having been long torn between her motherly feelings and her desire of revenge on Jason, kills her first child; then Jason arrives with soldiers and the protagonist has to escape on the roof of the palace where, in front of Jason, she finally kills the second child and throws the corpses of the children to their desperate father.

24. Tarrant (1976: 5) has remarked that the action of the finale is extremely fragmented.

25. Awkwardly, the encounter between Clytemnestra and Agamemnon occupies two lines and no dialogue features between the two of them; in fact, Clytemnestra remains mute in the entire scene.

26. The second act deals with the unclear response given by the Delphic oracle in relation to the cause of the plague afflicting Thebes and with the divinatory sacrifice (extispicy) ordered by Tiresias in order to disclose the truth. The third deals with the description of the necromancy of Laius' ghost narrated by Creon to a distraught Oedipus.

27. Act II is 196 lines long and Act III is 199.

28. The first act features a love-sick Phaedra revealing, in an emotionally charged monologue, her love for Hippolytus (85–128). In the second, it is the nurse who presents the distraught state of mind of the queen. Such doubling of the same material is common in Seneca's tragedies; for instance, the second act of the *Medea* consists basically of a recasting of Medea in the grip of *furor* already provided in the prologue; she is here accompanied by the nurse who tries to persuade her to opt for a milder and safer course of action.

29. The second act runs for 375 lines, while the average length of the other acts amounts to around 130 lines.

30. This shift between first and third person narration is a Senecan hallmark; the technique is employed widely either in scenes such as this in which two characters are in charge of the narration or also in scenes in which a single character adopts at times a first person narration and at others a third one in the same speech. In this second case, this technique produces a displacing effect, since the voice of a single character is capable of an extremely subjective and emotional account of his/her state as well as a detached and objective anamnesis of the same. Tarrant (1976: 199) says that the 'combination of emotional chaos and detached intellectual analysis' is distinctively Senecan.

31. See Coffey and Mayer (1990: 89).

32. This act features a dramatic technique, largely used by Seneca, which scholars have called 'passion-restraint' scene; it features in the *Med* (116 ff.), *Phae* (85 ff.), *Thy* (176 ff.), *Hf* (1186 ff.), and *Oed* (81 ff.). Usually, a minor character tries to restrain the protagonist; this dramatic technique allows Seneca to present the emotional state of the characters through the reactions they have to the attempts at restraint made by the minor ones.

33. Tarrant (1976: 193).

34. Zeitlin (1971: 653–4) has borrowed the term 'dance-pattern' from Miller (1967: 13–20).

35. Zwierlein (1966: 38–45) provides a list of 'vague and inconsistent information about the scenography'.

36. Fantham (1982a: 38).

37. This change of setting has long troubled scholars who have tried to make the play conform to the 'in-front-of-the-palace-setting'; Kragelund (2008: 181–94) claims that in the *Phaedra* Seneca adopts a 'symbolic scenography', which is not bound to a single setting.

38. Marshall (2000: 27–51) offers a discussion of 'the fluid sense of space on Seneca's stage'.
39. Larson (1994: 19).
40. Larson (1994: 56).
41. Seneca's predilection for monologic prologues as well as for monologues in general over dialogues is due to the fact that they constitute a fitting dramatic device well suited to better convey emotional paroxysm.
42. This pattern is common in Senecan tragedy; characters rarely engage in proper dialogues, but they utter monologues in turn. The result is that characters are juxtaposed one to the other and thus they do not give the impression of interacting, but rather of speaking in isolation.
43. Hippolytus' speech has been judged as a 'declamation' on a common theme by Coffey and Mayer (1990: 134–5).
44. See Tarrant (1985: 180).
45. Tarrant (1978: 231).
46. Tarrant (1978: 237).
47. Eliot (1951: 68) has remarked that Senecan characters actually 'recite in turn'.
48. *Sententiae* were moral maxims usually short and epigrammatic; they were widely employed by the rhetoricians. Seneca makes a large use of them both in his prose writings and in the tragedies. A large number of the *sententiae* employed by Seneca are by the mimographer Publilius Syrus, who became widely popular among the rhetoricians from the Augustan age onwards, as is attested by a passage in Seneca the Elder (*Controversiae* VII, 3, 8); see Giancotti (1967: 282–4); the affinity between Publilius and Seneca is attested not only by the large use of Publilian *sententiae* found in Seneca's writings at large and by Seneca's words of praise for Publilius, but also, quite suggestively, by the title '*Proverbia Senecae*' given to the collection of Publilius' *sententiae* in the medieval codices which transmit it. See Giancotti (1967: 335–6) who suggests that the compiler of the Publilian collection may have been Seneca himself or someone closely related to him. That the collection of Publilian *sententiae* formed in Seneca's age and not before seems attested by a passage in Seneca in which, referring to the learned *sententiae* of Publilius, he uses the expression *quantum disertissimorum versuum inter mimos iacet*; Giancotti (1967: 298) claims that such an expression implies that Seneca is not referring to isolated *sententiae* detached from their context, but to *sententiae* as they were found in the mimes as a whole.
49. See Canter (1925: 88–93) for a list of the occurrences.
50. The passage in Quintilian together with another in Lucian (83) and in Plutarch (*Quaestiones Conviviales* 711e) attest that pantomime not always consisted of a solo performance (pace Jory, 1998), but that the dancer could be accompanied by an assistant playing secondary roles (as in the episode referred to by Lucian in

which the dancer playing Ajax was flanked by one playing Odysseus). See Rotolo (1957: 16) and Hall (2002: 29) who rightly states that it is difficult to maintain that there was a 'single correct way to stage pantomime'.

51. Weinreich (1948: 144 n. 1); see Slater (1990: 217–18). See the section in Chapter 1 entitled 'The Pantomimic Cast' and Isidore of Seville, *Etymologiae* (18, 49).

52. In relation to this issue, a passage in Choricius of Gaza (*Apologia mimorum*, 110), in which he provides a list of all the things that mimes can imitate, is particularly relevant; among them, Choricius includes the imitation of an angry character who is being quieted by another one: *Τίς δε οὐκ ἂν ἀπείποι καταλέγειν ἐπιχειρῶν, ὅσα μιμοῦνται; δεσπότην, οἰκέτας, καπήλους, ἀλλαντοπώλας, ὀψοποιούς, ἑστιάτορα, δαιτυμόνας, συμβόλαια γράφοντας, παιδάριον ψελλιζόμενον, νεανίσκον ἐρῶντα, θυμούμενον ἕτερον, ἄλλον τῷ θυμουμένῳ πραΰνοντα τὴν ὀργήν.* Choricius is referring to mimes, but it is possible that he is using the term 'mime' as a general one which could in fact include pantomime as well; for instance, the same ambiguity of terminology is to be found in Isidore of Seville (*Etymologiae* 18, 49): *Mimi sunt dicti Graeca appellatione quod rerum humanarum sint imitatores; nam habebant suum auctorem, qui antequam mimum agerent, fabulam pronuntiare[n]t. Nam fabulae ita componebantur a poetis ut aptissimae essent motui corporis.* It is clear that the last sentence of the passage refers to pantomime.

53. For example *Ag* (57–107); *Phae* (274–375).

54. Tarrant (1972: 196; 1976: 324).

55. See Hall (2002: 29). She quotes Apuleius' description of the marriage of Cupid and Psyche (*Met.* 6). The danced performance with which the marriage is celebrated is most likely a pantomimic one in which 'Venus dances, the Muses sing choral odes, Apollo sings to the cithara, while Satyrus and Paniscus speak to the pipe'. Thus, pantomime could 'accommodate both solo singing and accompanied recitation'.

56. *Ag* (57–107); *Hf* (524); *Phae* (972ff.; 1141 ff.); *Oed* (987 ff.); *Thy* (546 ff.).

57. *Astronomica* (5, 483): *omnis fortunae vultum per membra reducet*; suggestively, Cicero (*In Pis.*, X, 22) equates the circle of dances (*saltatorium orbem*) to the wheel of Fortune (*fortunae rotam*) possibly attesting to the way in which the theme was rendered in a danced performance.

58. See Zeitlin (1971: 656–8). See e.g. Cicero *Phil.* (2, 65): *in eius igitur viri copias cum se subito ingurgitasset, exsultabat gaudio persona de mimo, modo egens, repente dives. Sed, ut est apud poetam nescio quem 'male parta male dilabuntur'*; Seneca, *De Brevitate vitae* (12, 8): *I nunc et mimos multa mentiri ad exprobrandam luxuriam puta. plura me hercules praetereunt quam fingunt et tanta incredibilium vitiorum copia ingenioso in hoc unum saeculo processit, ut iam mimorum arguere possimus neglegentiam*; in Petronius' *Satyricon*, the characters obsessively fear a reversal of fortune.

59. See Giancotti (1967: 387–95): the theme of Fortune's mutability is all pervasive in the Publilian sentences: *Fortuna cum blanditur, captatum venit; Fortunam citius*

reperias quam retineas; Fortuna unde aliquid fregit, quassat omnia; Fortuna nimium quem fovet, stultum facit; Fortuna obesse nulli contenta est semel; Fortuna vitrea est: tum cum splendet frangitur; Facit gratum Fortuna, quem nemo videt; Fortuna plus homini quam consilium valet; Homo semper aliud, Fortuna aliud cogitat; Homo ne sit sine dolore, Fortunam invenit; Levis est Fortuna: cito reposcit, quod dedit; Legem nocens veretur, Fortunam innocens; Minimum eripit Fortuna, cui minimum dedit; Nec vita hominibus nec fortuna perpes est; Plures tegit Fortuna, quam tutos facit; stultum facit Fortuna, quem vult perdere.

60. Tarrant (1978: 227–8) and Henry and Walker (1985: 28) consider this ode as a lyric interlude barely connected with the action; for an opposite interpretation of this chorus see Davis (1993: 202–7) and Stevens (1999: 281–307). The juxtaposition of scenes whose atmosphere is strikingly in contrast is indeed a technique much favoured by Seneca. A case similar to that of the *Oedipus* is to be found in the *Medea*; in fact, Medea's first soliloquy is a speech full of rage and hatred, while the following chorus is a joyous wedding song. Interestingly, the contrast is not given just by the opposite mood of the two scenes, but it is also conveyed, so to say, in a pictorial way which one could call baroque or expressionistic; in fact, whereas in Medea's monologue the prominent colour is black and darkness, in the chorus it is the bright quality of the white colour that is insisted upon. Such a visual device may have been inspired by pantomimic performances, which must have relied on contrasting colours in costumes and scenery to create the atmosphere of the scene or to typify the characters.

61. As Töchterle (1994: 372) has remarked, the syntactical construction, *decet* plus infinitive, provides dynamism and immediacy to the description.

62. Compare this with *Phaedra* (370–2: *iubet/. . . solvi comas/rursusque fingi* and 401–2: *nodo comas/coegit emisitque*).

63. Lucian (19).

64. Boyle (1994: 144–5).

65. Boyle (1994: 144–5).

66. Fantham (1982a: 226).

67. Claudian, *In Eutropium* (2, 402–5): *Hic dictis iterum sedit; fit plausus et ingens/ concilii clamor, qualis resonantibus olim/exoritur caveis, quotiens crinitus ephebus/ aut rigidam Niobem aut flentem Troada fingit.*

68. I follow Fitch's arrangement of the colometry (Fitch 2002–2004), which is still debated by scholars. The A tradition writes a series of anapaestic dimeters irregularly closed by monometers, while the *Etruscus* writes each of Hecuba's utterances as anapaestic dimeters. See Fantham (1982a: 110–13) and Fitch (1987b) for a fuller discussion of the colometry of anapaests.

69. Boyle (1994: 147). See also Boyle (2006: 217) for the similar case at *Medea* (1021–2: *coniugem agnoscis tuam?/sic fugere soleo*). Medea's final words to Jason have always

troubled scholars because of their enigmatic meaning. Boyle's interpretation that 'the metatheatrical sense is that this is how Medea leaves her play' seems to make the meaning clear.

70. See Lateiner (1996: 225–53) for a study of non-verbal behaviours in Ovid.

Chapter 3

1. Bain (1977: 61).
2. Larson (1994: 135).
3. Zwierlein (1966).
4. Larson (1994: 53) [italics are mine].
5. Larson (1994: 53 and 135).
6. See the section entitled 'The Pantomimic Libretto' in Chapter 1.
7. See the section entitled 'The Pantomimic Libretto' in Chapter 1.
8. Suetonius, *Nero* (54, 1): *Sub exitu quidem vitae palam voverat, si sibi incolumis status permansisset, proditurum se partae victoriae ludis etiam hydraulam et choraulam et utricularium ac novissimo die histrionem saltaturumque Vergili Turnum*; Lucian (46) the wandering of Aeneas and the love of Dido; Macrobius, *Saturnalia* (V, 17, 5): *quod ita elegantius auctore digessit, ut **fabula lascivientis Didonis**, quam falsam novit universitas, per tot tamen saecula speciem veritatis obtineat et ita pro vero per ora omnium volitet, ut pictores fictoresque et qui figmentis liciorum contextas imitantur effigies, hac materia vel maxime in effigiandis simulacris tamquam unico argumento decoris utantur, **nec minus histrionum perpetuis et gestibus et cantibus celebretur**;* Augustine, *Sermones* (241.5 = PL 38, 1135–6).
9. I adopt here Larson's definition (Larson, 1994: 31).
10. Larson (1994: 28).
11. Zwierlein (1966: 56–63); 58: 'Der Zuschauer müßte den Eindruck bekommen, er werde Zeuge einer Pantomime, die ihm -lästig genug- auch noch pedantisch von dritter Seite beschrieben wird, als sei er blind'.
12. Zimmermann (1990: 161–7).
13. Lucian, *De Saltatione* (67); epigram in the *Latin Anthology* (100).
14. We know that Seneca was extremely interested in the effects of passions and that he explored them in his philosophical works, especially in the *De Ira*.
15. (714–15) *incerta nutant lumina et versi retro/ torquentur oculi, rursus immoti rigent*.
16. See Lada-Richards (2004: 31 and 44 n. 59); she rightly claims that a 'very significant amount of stylisation in the bodily enactment of particular motifs or types or stories' must have featured; as evidence of this, she refers to a passage in Lucian (80), in which he says that a dancer, depicting the tecnophagy of Cronus, went off

in presenting that of Thyestes; the mistake that occurred was probably due to the fact that 'tecnophagy was conveyed by a set choreographic pattern, making it quite easy for a pantomime to confuse the stories of Cronus and Thyestes'.

17. Canter (1925: 14) and Bonner (1949: 162) think that the characterization in Seneca's tragedies was directly inspired by the rhetorical practice of impersonation (*ethopoeia*).

18. Schlegel (1809–11): '[Seneca's] characters are neither ideal nor real beings, but misshapen gigantic puppets, who are set in motion at one time by the string of an unnatural heroism, and at another by that of a passion equally unnatural . . .' (as translated into English in Schlegel, 1846: 211); Eliot (1951: 68); Jung (1963: 180) states that 'archetypes speak the language of high rhetoric, even of bombast'.

19. See also *Thy* (252–4 and 273–5).

20. Lada-Richards (2007: 115).

21. The passage seems to expand on Ovid's *Medea: feror huc illuc ut plena deo.*

22. The passage dealing with Medea's *furor* recalls closely Seneca's description of this destructive emotion in the *De Ira* (1, 1, 3–4): *nam ut furentium certa indicia sunt audax et minax vultus, tristis frons, torva facies, citatus gradus, inquietae manus, color versus, crebra et vehementius acta suspiria, ita irascentium eadem signa sunt: flagrant ac micant oculi, multus ore toto rubor exaestuante ab imis praecordiis sanguine, labra quatiuntur, dentes comprimuntur, horrent ac surriguntur capilli, spiritus coactus ac stridens, articulorum se ipsos torquentium sonus, gemitus mugitusque et parum explanatis vocibus sermo praeruptus et complosae saepius manus et pulsata humus pedibus et totum concitum corpus magnasque irae minas agens, foeda visu et horrenda facies depravantium se atque intumescentium.*

23. A similar asyndetic construction is to be found in an epigram of the *Anthologia Latina* (n. 100 = Weinreich n. 20 *Epigramm und Pantomimus*) in praise of the art of a pantomimic dancer: *pugnat, ludit, amat, bacchatur, vertitur, adstat.*

24. Apuleius, *Apologia* (78, 3ff.): *Tune effeminatissime, tua manu cuidam viro mortem minitari[s]?At qua tandem manu? Philomelae an Medeae an Clytemnestrae? Quas tamen cum saltas-tanta mo[l]litia animi, tanta formido ferri est-, sine cludine saltas.* See also for Medea, Sidonius Apollinaris, *Carmina* (23, 272–3): *sive Aeetias et suus Iason/inducuntur*; Lucian (40, 52–3).

25. The term 'psychoplastic' is Regenbogen's (1927–28: 207).

26. Compare Ovid, *Met.* (8, 465–6) about Althaea: *saepe metu sceleris pallebant ora futuri,/saepe suum fervens oculis dabat ira ruborem.*

27. The simile is borrowed from Ovid, *Met.* (13, 547–9): *utque furit catulo lactente orbata leaena/signaque nacta pedum sequitur, quem non videt, hostem*; *Met.* (6, 636–7): *nec mora, traxit Ityn, veluti Gangetica cervae/lactentem fetum per silvas tigris opacas.*

28. Costa (1973: 148); Zwierlein (1986: 464).

29. Häuptli (2002: 316–17).
30. Leo (1878–79: 136).
31. Häuptli (2002: 313–17).
32. See Dodds (1960: 72).
33. Terenzianus Maurus, *De Metris* (lines 2899–900): *Sonat hoc subinde metro Cybeleium nemus,/nomenque galliambis memoratur hinc datum,/tremulos quod esse Gallis habiles putant modos;/adeo ut frequenter illum prope ab ultimo pedem,/ mage quo sonus vibretur, studeant dare tribrachym./Anapaestus esse primus, spondeus aut solet,/duo post erunt iambi, tribrachysve subicitur,/linquitque comma primum catalecticam brevem./Pariambus et trochaei duo comma posterum/ tribrachysve continebunt, superatque semipes./Servasse quae Catullum probat ipse tibi Liber:/'super alta vectus Attis celeri rate maria'.*
34. See Cèbe (1977: vol. 4); Wiseman (1985: 269–72). Fragment 139 is a galliambic: *Phrygius per ossa cornus liquida canit anima*; fragment 140 contains 3 galliambics: *tibi typana non inanis sonitus Matri'deum/tonimus [chorus] tibi nos; tibi nunc semiviri/teretem comam volantem iactant, [domine] tibi/galli.*
35. See Dodds (1960: 72–4; 118; 142); and West (1982: 22).
36. Hephaestion, 12.3 (Westphal 39). In Rome, the cult of Cybele was instituted in 204 BC and a temple in her honour was dedicated on the Palatine in 191. Annual celebrations were held during the Megalensia (4–9 April) and included stage performances, chariot racing, and beast hunts.
37. See Kirby (1989) for a detailed metrical analysis of the galliambics in Catullus 63.
38. Morisi (1999: 33).
39. Newman (1990: 343–66).
40. See the section entitled 'Pantomime in Catullus' Attis (Poem 63)' in Chapter 1.
41. See the section entitled 'Pantomime in Catullus' Attis (Poem 63)' in Chapter 1.
42. Compare the alternation of complexion in the *Medea* (858–61).
43. The description of an emotion buried within the character and striving to come out is used by Seneca over and over again: compare e.g. *Phaedra* (362–3): *torretur aestu tacito et inclusus quoque,/quamvis tegatur, proditur vultu furor.*
44. The symptom described was typical of an ecstatic and paranormal mental state: see Euripides' *Bacchae* (1122–3) and *Medea* (1173–4).
45. The lines expand Virgil's *maiorque videri* (*Aen.* 6, 49).
46. For example, in the *Medea* where the nurse and the chorus use it to describe Medea (382–3 and 849–50); in the *Trojan Women* where Andromache uses the simile to describe herself (373–6); in the *Hercules Oetaeus* where the nurse uses it to describe Deianira (243–5).
47. The principle in relation to Senecan tragedy was first stated by Marx (1932) and later resumed by Bishop (1968).
48. Fitch (1987a: 350).

49. Fitch (1987a: 46).
50. Lucian (42) attests that the theme of madness was generally extremely popular in pantomime. Macrobius' passage is interesting in relation to the Senecan mad-scene, for which it may provide a source; Macrobius describes a performance of the famous dancer Pylades dancing the role of Hercules *furens* thus: *cum in Herculem furentem prodisset et non nullis incessum histrioni convenientem non servare videretur, deposita persona ridentes increpuit:* μωροί, μαινόμενον ὀρχοῦμαι. *hac fabula et sagittas iecit in populum. eandem personam cum iussu Augusti in triclinio ageret, et intendit arcum et spicula immisit. nec indignatus est Caesar eodem se loco Pyladi quo populum Romanum fuisse.*
51. MacKay (1975: 151).
52. Fantham (1982a: 306).
53. Calder (1984: 225).
54. Fantham (1982a: 309).
55. Zwierlein (1986: 78).
56. Richter (1899: 32–47) postulated that 'in the majority of Seneca's anapaests, metrical units coincide with units of sense, syntax and style'; Fitch's colometry has been judged too radical by some scholars such as Wilson (1990: 189–94) and Boyle (1994: 237). Since the corruption of the manuscript tradition is well established in regard to the colometry of anapaests and is then quite unreliable, I think that his arrangement is the only one that restores the poetic colour of the lines.
57. Fitch (1987b: 75).
58. I include this monometer as one implying movement, because of the simile between the young Priam and the young Astyanax present here. Due to the association between the two, Astyanax could well perform the role of young Priam, which requires the same kinds of movements acted out by Astyanax just a few lines above. In relation to this, the presence of the verb *flectere* is particularly indicative; the verb *flectere* (with the meaning of *flectere animus*) is used to describe Priam's successful attempt to move Hercules' *animus*. The verb has also the meaning of bending the limbs (*flectere membra*) which is the physical action performed by Astyanax to act as a suppliant. According to this, the use of *flectere* in the Priam's passage recalls the action performed by Astyanax and, in my opinion, allows the possibility to make Astyanax perform a bending movement as if in the role of Priam.
59. See Owen (1969: 136–7): he states that the fourth act 'demands some visual component, perhaps pantomime, in order to affect clearly its multiple levels for an audience'.
60. Fitch (2002: 165–6). Some scholars have claimed that the play has a double plot, one dealing with Astyanax, the other with Polyxena. The double plot is unified then in the last act where the deaths of both characters are acted out.

61. Boyle (1994: 207).

62. Those lines are attributed by both the *Etruscus* and the A tradition (EA) to Hecuba
     but some scholars felt that an emendation was needed because of the sudden
     change of Polyxena's attitude from joy to sorrow; in my opinion, the difficulty of
     the passage is the sudden change from the first to the third person in Hecuba's
     speech, if one has to think that she is describing herself and not Polyxena, which is
     what Fantham (1982a: 349–50) suggests. Richter (Peiper and Richter, 1867)
     claimed that the lines do not describe Polyxena but Hecuba and assigned them to
     Andromache; he had then to place lines 967–8 after 978 because Andromache
     cannot call Hecuba *nata*. Zwierlein (1966: 174–6) writes the text as transmitted by
     the manuscripts and states that the lines describe Polyxena and belong to Hecuba.
     Fantham assigns the lines to Hecuba but she states that they describe Hecuba
     herself; she also then has to transpose lines 967–7 after 978 where they, in her
     opinion, are needed as a response to 975–8. Fitch (2002: 297–8) accepts both
     Richter's transposition and the assignment of lines 965–6 to Andromache instead
     of Hecuba; they thus describe Hecuba's condition and not Polyxena's. Since EA
     agree on this point and the text as it is does not present particular difficulties, I
     think that Zwierlein's conservative reading, which does not alter the text as the
     emendations proposed by the other scholars, is to be preferred.

63. Fantham (1982a: 335).

64. There is a parallel instance at lines 826–8 where the chorus, at the end of its song,
     describes Phaedra: *quaerit crine lacerato fidem,/decus omne turbat capitis, umectat
     genas:/instruitur omni fraude feminea dolus.* The queen must be again inside the
     palace since later on Theseus (*Reserate clausos regii postes laris* 863) compels the
     slaves to open the door of the royal house in order to know from Phaedra's own
     words (it is the nurse who informs Theseus of Phaedra's distraught state) why she
     wants to die.

65. Fantham (1975: 6–7); Virgil (4, 66–9): *est mollis flamma medullas/interea et tacitum
     vivit sub pectore vulnus./uritur infelix Dido totaque vagatur/urbe furens.*

66. In relation to the *vox propria iactare*, it is worth quoting a passage in Tacitus in
     which he blames the orators of his time who praise themselves for the fact that
     their speeches can be sung and danced (*Dial.* 26, 3): *Quodque vix auditu fas esse
     debeat, laudis et gloriae et ingenii loco plerique iactant cantari saltarique
     commentarios suos*; Tacitus employs the verb *iactare*, here with the meaning of
     boasting, but, given the context, the verb is clearly and purposely chosen for the
     allusive pantomimic overtones.

67. Libanius (67): Φαίδραν ὀρχηστὴς ἐποίησεν ἐρῶσαν.

68. Compare the similar passage in the *Medea* where the nurse describing Medea
     rushing to her house employs a similar expression (674–5): *namque ut attonito
     gradu/evasit et penetrale funestum attigit.*

69. That the shift is awkward is confirmed by the fact that Fitch translates the messenger's speech in the past and Oedipus' direct speech in the present.

70. See Chapter 4 for a discussion of characters describing themselves in the third person. In the specific case of Oedipus, we have the extreme case of a messenger reporting a direct speech of a character describing himself in the third person. The voice of the narrator and that of Oedipus basically merge together.

71. Segal (1983: 152) has remarked that the language of corporeality used in Seneca's description of the self-blinding is totally absent in Sophocles' parallel one.

72. See Jakobi (1988: 133–5).

73. Lucian (41): story of Oedipus.

74. Suetonius, *Nero* (21): *Inter cetera cantavit Canacen parturientem, Oresten matricidam, Oedipodem excaecatum, Herculem insanum.* See Chapter 1, n. 32.

75. The *Hercules Oetaeus* is considered spurious by the large majority of scholars. Nonetheless, the play is much indebted in its phrasing and tone to the Senecan ones. The author of the *Hercules Oetaeus* had Seneca's tragedies as his models, thus I draw examples of running commentaries from it, since they do not differ from the Senecan ones.

76. *attonita fertur* is the reading of the E tradition, while *lymphata rapitur* is that of the A tradition.

77. Watson (1995: 121).

78. See the section entitled 'The Adultery-mime in the Elegiac Poets' in Chapter 1.

79. Libanius (67) also mentions the story of Deianira.

80. Here as in the *Phaedra* and *Oedipus*, Fitch (2002–2004) translated all the passage in the past, even where the Latin has the present tense. Again, Fitch must have felt the awkwardness of the shift and the temporal ambiguity of the passage.

81. See Note 22 of this chapter.

82. Tarrant (1976: 335–6): 'it seems quite probable that Cassandra is relating a clairvoyant vision of Agamemnon's death, not describing what she can see by looking into the palace . . . The only apparent obstacle to this interpretation is *spectemus* (875)'.

83. Boyle (2006: 208–18). In addition to this, it is worth noticing that the conventional term used for prophetic visions is *cerno*, as, for example, at *Ag* (730). See also: Virgil (*Aen.* 6, 86–7) and Valerius Flaccus (*Arg.* 1, 226).

84. Tarrant (1976: 336).

85. *P. Oxy* (2746): Coles (1968: 110–18; 1970: 9–11); see Tarrant (1978: 254).

86. Lines 892–96: *at ille, ut altis hispidus silvis aper/cum casse vinctus temptat egressus tamen/artatque motu vincla et in cassum furit,/cupit fluentes undique et caecos sinus/dissicere et hostem quaerit implicitus suum.*

87. Line 897: *armat bipenni Tyndaris dextram furens . . . 900 sic huc et illuc impiam librat manum.*

88. Lines 898–99: *qualisque ad aras colla taurorum popa/designat oculis antequam ferro petat*.
89. Tarrant (1976: 343).
90. Lucian (43) attests that Agamemnon's slaughter was a theme of pantomimic performances; Macrobius (*Saturnalia* II, 7, 12) reports that the dancer Hylas played the role of the Greek king and his impersonation was much criticized by his former tutor, Pylades, the founder of the pantomimic genre.
91. Curley (1986: 187–217); Boyle (1997: 193–207; 2006: 208–18); Littlewood (2004); Erasmo (2004: 122–39).
92. Boyle (1997: 193–207); Ewbank (2005: 45–6) has suggested that the dumb show contained in *The True Tragedy of Herod and Antipater* (1622) by Gervase Markham and William Sampson could have been inspired by the above passage in the *Agamemnon*. According to Ewbank, the play 'makes use of a telescoped Agamemnon'. Similar to many passages in Seneca's tragedies in which the Furies are invoked in order to produce a maddening effects, Antipater 'calls on Furies to come and possess him': the calling of the Furies produces then a 'dumb show' representing, in a way quite suggestively reminiscent of the Cassandra's scene in Seneca, Clytemnestra's and Aegisthus' killing of Agamemnon: 'Musique: and enter Egystus and Clitemnestra dancing a Curranto, which is broken off by the sound of Trumpets: then, enter Agamemnon, and divers Noblemen in Triumph: Egisthus whispers with Clitemnestra, and delivers her a sleevless shirt; then slip aside: Clitemnestra imbraces Agamemnon, he dismisses his Traine; she offers him the shirt, he offers to put it on, and being intangled, Egisthus and she kils him; then departs, leaving at Antipaters feete two Scrowles of paper'.
93. In relation to this passage, Hine (2000: 177) suggests that the present 'may be the vivid present describing past events . . . but it might be a genuine present tense, as the nurse describes what she sees happening while she speaks'.
94. The overall implausibility of the scene is further enhanced by the fact that a nurse delivers such an extremely learned speech, punctuated as it is by geographical, mythological, and astronomical catalogues.
95. Compare this with narrative set-pieces where past events are almost always reported in the present tense; compare also running commentaries for the handling of ambiguous interior actions. I would suggest that the nurse's speech stays in between narrative set-pieces and running commentaries and presents a blending of the characteristics of the two. In fact, similar to messengers' speeches, it reports facts that are supposed to take place offstage; similar to running commentaries it portrays the detailed actions of a character.
96. The manuscript tradition is not in agreement on the reading of line 680: the E tradition has *comprecans*, while the A tradition has *complicans*. Both readings have been much discussed by scholars, since they both seem to be unsatisfactory.

Zwierlein (1976: 205–6) prints Büchler's conjecture *comparans* and translates 'Sie bereitet das magische Opfer *laeua manu* zu'. Fitch (2004: 93–4) prints E's reading and translates 'Making prayers at the sinister shrine with her left hand'. Fitch translates *sacrum* as shrine; for *sacrum* in this sense he quotes a passage in the *Phaedra* (424): *ipsum intuor sollemne venerantem sacrum.*

97. See Zwierlein (1976: 205–6) where he collects evidence of the fact that the use of the left hand was felt as sinister. See Quintilian, *Inst.* (11, 3, 114): *Manus sinistra numquam sola gestum recte facit: dextrae se frequenter accommodat, sive in digitos argumenta digerimus sive aversis in sinistrum palmis abominamur sive obicimus adversis sive in latus utramque distendimus sive satisfacientes aut supplicantes (diversi autem sunt hi gestus) summittimus sive adorantes attollimus sive aliqua demonstratione aut invocatione protendimus.*

98. See Zwierlein (1976: 205–7).

99. Compare Ovid, *Met.* (7, 220–33) where he provides a list of mountains and rivers from which Medea collected herbs and plants to prepare the concoction to rejuvenate Jason's father. Ovid confines his list to geographical places in Greece, while Seneca's catalogue is far more wide ranging including Sicily (Eryx 707), Caucasus (709), Arabia (710), Media (711), and Germany (712–13).

100. Costa (1973: 129) quotes a Virgilian cento of the Medea story which has a messenger describing Medea preparing the magic (in Baeherens *PLM* IV, 232, 321 ff.).

101. Tarrant (1978: 252–3) quotes as parallel for such an account of offstage action a passage in the *Rudens* of Plautus (160 ff.).

102. See Frank (1995: 2 and 39–40): the setting changes from the area around Cithaeron to the walls of Thebes (362) and from the walls of Thebes to the battlefield (443); the last change of scene is particularly troublesome since it happens as the action unfolds, thus Jocasta is supposed to move from the walls of Thebes to the battlefield in the view of the *satelles* and Antigone.

103. Tarrant (1978: 252).

104. The simile of the shooting star or meteor is found also in the *Phaedra* to describe Hippolytus' flight (738–40): *ocior cursum rapiente flamma,/stella cum ventis agitata longos/porrigit ignes.*

105. Frank (1995) remarks that Seneca is 'the only classical author who uses *inrigo* of *umores corporis* outside a medical context'; see also *Oed* (346): *irrigat plagas cruor; Tro* (965): *inrigat fletus genas; Phae* (381–2): *genae/rore irrigantur.*

106. See Lada-Richards (2007: 35) for a discussion of this feature in pantomime. Lucian (43) attests that the theme of the 'Seven against Thebes' featured in pantomimic performances.

Chapter 4

1. Grysar (1834: 56); Sargent (1996: 89–90); Hall (2008: 277).
2. Tarrant (1976: 199–200) has remarked that Seneca borrows a technique deriving in part from Ovid and in part from Virgil; the dramatization of emotional dilemmas is Ovidian (Ovid's heroines often describe themselves as caught between conflicting forces, especially in the *Heroides* and in the *Metamorphoses*); as Tarrant has observed, the feelings presented in Ovid's descriptions are often more schematic and involve less complex feelings than Seneca's ones. The lengthier narration of more complex emotional situations is Virgilian, as, for example, in the description of Turnus (*Aen.* 12, 665–71) or of Lavinia's blush (*Aen.* 12, 64–70).
3. Gill (1987: 26).
4. Gill (1987: 37).
5. Tarrant (1976: 199).
6. Gill (1987: 33).
7. For example, see the shift at *Phae* lines 177 ff.
8. See Barlow (1971): similes in messenger speeches: *Hipp.* (1201 and 1221); in lyric and monody: *Hipp.* (564 and 828); *Med.* (1279); in dialogue: *Hipp.* (429); *Med.* (523).
9. Pratt (1963: 233–4) has remarked that in Greek drama images tend to be intrinsic; they are designed 'to be a natural expression of the thoughts and feelings associated with the dynamics of the action as a living phenomenon'; on the contrary, 'Seneca's whole dramaturgy is a system of commentary upon the action'.
10. See Henry and Walker (1985: 141–5).
11. Gill (1987: 33) gives as examples of this, one passage in Virgil (*Aen.* 4, 15–23) and two in Ovid (*Met.* 7, 18–21; 8, 506–11).
12. Coffey and Mayer (1990: 107) have aptly pointed out that 'Seneca takes the mythical basis of his story for granted.'
13. Compare Ovid (*Her.* 4, 41–44): *in nemus ire libet pressisque in retia cervis/hortari celeris per iuga summa canes,/aut tremulum excusso iaculum vibrare lacerto,/aut in graminea ponere corpus humo.*
14. *Med* (115–78; 382–430); *Ag* (108–225); *Thy* (176–335).
15. See Fantham (1975: 1–10).
16. Virgil, *Aen.* (4, 1–5): *At regina gravi iamdudum saucia cura/vulnus alit venis et caeco carpitur igni./Multa viri virtus animo multusque recursat/gentis honos; haerent infixi pectore vultus/verbaque, nec placidam membris dat cura quietem.*
17. Seneca is particularly fond of nautical similes compare: *Ag* (138–40); *Med* (939–43); *Thy* (438–9); the image of rowing against the normal flow of the water is also metaphorically used in *Epistle* (122, 19): *contra illam nitentibus non alia vita est quam contra aquam remigantibus.*

18. Compare with Virgil (*Aen.* 4, 2): *vulnus alit venis et caeco carpitur igni* where Dido is the subject experiencing the fire of love.

19. Compare with Ovid (*Met.* 7, 19–21): *aliudque cupido,/mens aliud suadet: video meliora proboque,/deteriora sequor.*

20. The simile is borrowed from Ovid (*Met.* 8, 470–72): *utque carina,/quam ventus ventoque rapit contrarius aestus,/vim geminam sentit paretque incerta duobus.*

21. Tarrant (1976: 199).

22. Costa (1973: 151–2).

23. See Braun (1982: 49): 'Da in den Tragödien Senecas aber die Handlung, auch die entscheidende Handlung, oftmals nicht unmittelbar in den Worten des Textes greifbar wird, kann der Autor diese Dramen nur für eine Aufführung auf der Bühne geschrieben haben. Erst wenn sie gespielt werden, begreift man, was geschieht'.

24. See also Phaedra's final monologue, which involves her committing suicide onstage.

25. The simile is borrowed from Ovid (*Met.* 8, 470–2); see above on Clytemnestra's self-description.

26. Fitch (2002–2004: 306–10) and Zwierlein (1986: 327–8) print a different colometry of the anapaestic lines.

27. Zwierlein (1986: 327–8); Fitch (2002–2004: 306–10). See Bishop (1988: 392–412) for a defence of the reading of the E tradition.

28. Compare the similar case of Andromache's lyric monody in the *Trojan Women* (705–35).

29. Fitch (1987b: 75).

30. Compare *Phaedra* (384–6) and *Hercules furens* (999–1053) for a similar handling of an interior scene.

31. Tarrant (1985: 221).

32. Bishop (1988: 394–6) claims that *pectora* is never used in self-address.

33. Fitch (1987b: 79).

34. For the recurrent use of nautical imagery see Note 17 of this chapter.

35. This is the only occurrence of a verb used in the first-person form.

36. See Bain (1977: 105–34); Tarrant (1978: 242–6); in Euripides there are four instances that can be accounted as *in fieri* development of the convention (*Hecuba* 726 ff., *Philoctetes* 572 ff., *Orestes* 669 ff., *Medea* 277–280). New Comedy, by contrast, offers many examples of the technique: Aristophanes, *Thesmophoriazusai* (603, 604, 609); *Plutus* (365 ff.); Plautus, *Cas.* (685 ff.); *Poen.* (647 ff., 653 ff.); Terentius, *Ad.* (548).

37. See Tarrant (1985: 161).

38. Owen (1969: 119) defines the monologue as a 'dramatic conundrum'; Fantham (1982a: 302); Pratt (1983: 110); pace Boyle (1994: 192).

Chapter 5

1. Larson (1994: 67) states that 'the consequence for the extension of the messenger-role to characters involved in the action of the tragedy, is that there are more opportunities for messenger-speeches'.
2. Larson (1994: 31).
3. Larson (1994: 65). See also Garelli (1998: 25) for a similar interpretation.
4. Garelli (1998a: 20–1).
5. See Henry and Walker (1965: 12) in relation to Theseus' description of the Underworld in the *Hercules furens*.
6. Garelli (1998: 26).
7. Garelli (1998: 27).
8. Larson (1994: 68).
9. Larson (1994: 34).
10. Larson (1994: 68).
11. The expression 'verbal scenery' is Lada-Richards' (2007).
12. See the section entitled 'The Pantomimic Libretto' in Chapter 1.
13. Larson (1994: 68).
14. I give here a list of the occurrences of the present and the past tense respectively in the narrative set-piece of the *Hercules furens* (the verb count does not include Amphitryon's interventions). A detailed analysis of the issue will be provided *ad locum* for each of the six narratives. **Present**: (662) *attollit*; (663) *premit*; (664) *solvit*; (665) *hiat*; (666) *patet*; (667) *pandit*; (668) *incipit*; (670) *cadit*; (671) *ludit*; *solet*; (673) *laxantur*; (674) *pergat*; (675) *est*; *deducit*; (676) *rapit*; (677) *urget*; (678) *sinunt*; (680) *labitur*; (681) *demit*; (682) *pateat*; (683) *involvit*; (684) *ludit*; *cedit*; (685) *instat*; *petat*; (686) *iacet*; (687) *gemit*; (688) *resonat*; (689) *horrent*; (690) *tenet*; (691) *iacet*; (692) *tegit*; (694) *sequitur*; (696) *adiuvat*; (698) *germinant*; (700) *habet*; (701) *squalet*; (702) *torpet*; (704) *haeret*; *sedet*; (706) *est*; (709) *est*; (710) *alligat*; (711) *manat*; (713) *iurant*; (714) *rapitur*; (715) *volvit*; (716) *cingitur*; (718) *tegitur*; (719) *pendent*; (720) *iacet*; (721) *digerit*; (723) *gerat*; (724) *est*; (726) *timet*; (727) *timetur*; (732) *sortitur*; (733) *aditur*; (734) *audit*; (735) *patitur*; (736) *repetit*; *premitur*; (739) *est*; (740) *servat*; (741) *regit*; (742) *parcit*; (743) *petit*; (745) *abstine*; (746) *regnas*; *taxantur*; (750) *rapitur*; (751) *sedet*; (753) *sectatur*; *alluit*; (755) *perit*; *destituunt*; (756) *praebet*; (757) *gerunt*; (757) *errant*; (758) *terret*; (762) *imminet*; (763) *torpescit*; (764) *servat*; (765) *gestat*; (766) *pendet*; (767) *coercet*; *lucent*; (768) *regit*; (770) *poscit*; (771) *exclamat*; (772) *pergis*; *siste*; (774) *domat*; (775) *scandit*; (781) *mergit*; (782) *apparet*; (783) *territat*; (785) *tuetur*; (786) *lambunt*; *horrent*; (787) *sibilat*; (789) *attollit*; (790) *captat*; (794) *terret*; *sibilat*; (797) *exterret*; (799) *opponit*; *tegit*; (801) *rotat*; (802) *ingeminat*; (805) *iubet*; (808) *vincit*; (810) *componit*; (812) *pulsat*; (813) *est*; (815) *resumit*; (816) *quassat*; (827) *abscondit*. **Past**: (735)

fecit; (737) *vidi*; (754) *dedit*; (770) *repetebat*; (776) *succubuit*; *sedit*; (777) *bibit*; (788) *sensit*; (791) *stetit*; (792) *sedit*; (793) *timuit*; (802) *infregit*; (803) *summisit*; (804) *cessit*; *extimuit*; (806) *dedit*; (814) *percussit*; (816) *abstulit*; (817) *vexit*; (818) *respexit*; (821) *intulimus*; *vidit*; (822) *conspexit*; (824) *compressit*; *expulit*; (825) *flexit*; *petit*.

15. As seen in Chapter 1, pantomime was characterized by the alternation of static poses and swift movements; I give some examples: *Thy* (720): *stetit sui securus*; *Thy* (723–4): *stetit . . . cadaver*; *Hf* (458): *mox fulminanti proximus patri stetit*; *Phae* (1063): *currus ante trepidantes stetit*; *Phae* (1100): *paulumque domino currus affixo stetit*; *Thy* (697): *nutavit aula*; *Phae* (1031): *inhorruit concussus undarum globus*; *Oed* (576–7): *terra . . . gemuitque penitus*.

16. Examples are provided later in this chapter.

17. (664) *hic*; (687) *hic*; *illic*; (711) *hinc*; (712) *hunc*; (714) *hic*; (718) *hic*; (719) *hoc*; (720) *haec*; *hanc*; (733) *illo*; (734) *illo*; *hoc*; (764) *hunc*; (769) *hic*; (783) *hic*; (801) *huc*; *illuc*.

18. See Chapter 3.

19. Compare e.g. *Med* (675–6): *namque ut attonito gradu/evasit et penetrale funestum attigit*.

20. A detailed analysis of the handling of personifications of abstracts in comparison to Virgil is provided in the chapter on the narrative set-piece in the *Hercules furens*. The tendency to endow personified abstractions with a human-like nature is to be found already in Ovid: Envy (*Invidia*): *Met.* (2, 760–96); Grief (*Luctus*), Terror (*Pavor*), Dread (*Terror*); Madness (*Insania*): *Met.* (4, 484–5); Hunger (*Fames*): *Met.* (8, 799–822); Sleep (*Somnus*): (11, 592–649); Rumor (*Fama*): *Met.* (12, 39–63). See Miller (1916: 516–34) for a discussion of this feature of Ovid's style.

21. Lucian (19): δοκεῖ γάρ μοι ὁ παλαιὸς μῦθος καὶ Πρωτέα τὸν Αἰγύπτιον οὐκ ἄλλο τι ἢ ὀρχηστήν τινα γενέσθαι λέγειν, μιμητικὸν ἄνθρωπον καὶ πρὸς πάντα σχηματίζεσθαι καὶ μεταβάλλεσθαι δυνάμενον.

22. Larson (1999: 34–36).

23. Herington (1966: 451); this feature, among others, has prompted a psychoanalytical (namely Lacanian) interpretation of the tragedies; such an approach has been first pioneered by Segal (1986), followed by Littlewood (2004), Fitch and McElduff (2002), and Schiesaro (2003).

24. Pratt (1963: 233) has claimed that Seneca's tendency to present inanimate objects as sentient beings was prompted by the desire to provide 'large graphic effect and vivid animation' to his tragedies and that this attitude was 'dramatic and poetic rather than philosophical'. See *Thy* (262–5; 990–5; 103–21); *Ag* (53–6); *Oed* (1–5; 37–51; 225–9; 569–85); *Hf* (692–702; 939–52); *Phae* (1007–54).

25. *subsedit omnis silva et erexit comas,/duxere rimas robora et totum nemus/concussit horror; terra se retro dedit/gemuitque penitus*.

26. *Thy* (696): *Lucus tremescit; Hf* (689–90): *horrent opaca fronde nigrantes comae/taxo imminente; Phae* (1050): *Tremuere terrae; Phae* (1031): *inhorruit concussus undarum globus; Thy* (768–70): *ignis . . . invitus ardet.*

27. In relation to this, it is worth quoting a passage in Lucian (19), which attests that the art of the dancer was able to imitate inanimate things such as 'the liquidity of water, the sharpness of fire in the liveliness of his movements, and the quivering of a tree' (ὡς καὶ ὕδατος ὑγρότητα μιμεῖσθαι καὶ πυρὸς ὀξύτητα ἐν τῇ τῆς κινήσεως σφοδρότητι καὶ λέοντος ἀγριότητα καὶ παρδάλεως θυμὸν καὶ δένδρου δόνημα, καὶ ὅλως ὅ τι καὶ θελήσειεν).

28. Shelton (1978: 50).

29. Fitch (1987a: 275).

30. Henry and Walker (1965: 12).

31. Larson (1994: 68).

32. Henry and Walker (1965: 19).

33. *Nostra te tellus manet./illic solutam caede Gradivus manum/restituit armis; illa te, Alcide, vocat,/facere innocentes terra quae superos solet.*

34. See the section entitled 'The Pantomimic Libretto' in Chapter 1.

35. Augustine, *Sermones*, 241.5 = PL 38, 1135–6 claims that his contemporaries used to know the Virgilian episode of Aeneas' descent to the Underworld more because of the theatre than because they actually read it.

36. Henry and Walker (1965: 12).

37. Fitch (1987a: 299).

38. Fitch (1987a: 302). Fitch notes that this is the first instance of an intransitive use of the verb *germinare*, which is generally 'used of the place rather than plants'.

39. Fitch (1987a: 320).

40. Fitch (1987a: 300).

41. Fitch (1987a: 319).

42. Henry and Walker (1965: 18).

43. Shelton (1978: 55).

44. In the *Agamemnon* and the *Oedipus* as well, the messenger's *rheseis* flow without interruption.

45. Larson (1994: 42).

46. Coffey and Mayer (1990: 176).

47. The simile is borrowed from Ovid (*Met.* 2, 161–2): *sed leve pondus erat nec quod cognoscere possent/Solis equi, solitaque iugum gravitate carebat.*

48. The text presents a difficulty here; the manuscripts have two different readings; E has *quaerimus*, while A has *querimur*. Scholars have objected to the A reading on the grounds that it is not possible to be amazed and lamenting at the same time. The E reading seems better in terms of meaning, but it presents a metrical difficulty that can be overcome by transposing *en* to achieve correct scansion. Zwierlein accepts Axelson's conjecture *sequimur*.

49. Coffey and Mayer (1990: 178); see Austin on Virgil (*Aen.* 1, 90: *intonuere poli*).

50. See also 1060–4; 1085–7.

51. See below for a more detailed analysis. Compare the description of the sea monster in the *Phaedra* with that of Cerberus (783–97) in the *Hercules furens*.

52. See below for a more detailed analysis.

53. Segal (1984: 323–4).

54. Segal (1984: 314, 316).

55. See Barlow (1971: 71–3) for a comparison between Euripides' sea monster in the *Hippolytus* and Seneca's.

56. For the closing position of the simile see *Phaedra* (382–3).

57. Segal (1984: 320). Compare: Ovid, *Met.* (15, 511–13): *corniger hinc taurus ruptis expellitur undis/pectoribusque tenus molles erectus in auras/naribus et patulo partem maris evomit ore.*

58. Segal (1984: 320).

59. Segal (1984: 321).

60. Segal (1984: 317).

61. Segal (1984: 319).

62. Compare with Ovid *Met.* (15, 508–11): *cum mare surrexit, cumulusque inmanis aquarum/in montis speciem curvari et crescere visus/et dare mugitus summoque cacumine findi./corniger hinc taurus ruptis expellitur undis.*

63. Segal (1984: 321–3).

64. See the *Hercules furens*, where Theseus' speech opens in the same way.

65. For the *penetrale* as a favoured setting for exceptional actions, compare *Med* (676) (*penetrale funestum*), which is the setting of the incantation scene.

66. In the *Hercules furens*, a similar passivity in front of an action that would require intervention on the part of the speaking character is shown by Amphitryon, who describes in detail Hercules' killings of his family without making any attempt at stopping his furious son.

67. See Tarrant (1985: 193–4).

68. The major model influencing the Senecan royal palace of Pelops is Virgil's description of the palace of Latinus in *Aen.* (7, 170–91). For further discussion of Virgilian borrowings in Seneca's piece, see Tarrant (1985: 183).

69. See also the discussion about this feature in relation to the *Hercules furens*.

70. The comparison proposed here is mainly meant to show how the descriptions of the *loci horridi* in Senecan tragedy tend to be stereotyped similarly to the repetitive and unvaried depictions of characters driven by extreme passions in the running commentaries.

71. Tarrant (1985: 187).

72. Compare here the seemliness of language used in the *Medea* (675–6) and the *Oedipus* (918–19) to announce, in this case, the exits of the protagonists.

73. Tarrant (1985: 190) at 691–5.

74. Compare here with *Medea* (739: *canitque. mundus vocibus primis tremit*).
75. See the section entitled 'Dance Vocabulary' in Chapter 1: features such as sudden halts and accelerations are mentioned as constitutive elements of pantomime by extant sources.
76. Tarrant (1985: 194 n. 722–3).
77. Tarrant (1985: 194 n. 723–4).
78. Tarrant (1985: 195).
79. Tarrant (1985: 202 n. 778).
80. Lobe (1999: 102–8). See Horace (*Serm.* 1, 5, 63: *pastorem saltaret uti Cyclopa rogabat*).
81. Lowe (1989: 169) who quotes a passage in Varro (*Ling.* 7, 95): *dictum mandier a mandendo, unde manducari, a quo et in Atellanis Dossenum vocant Manducum*.
82. Tarrant (1985: 193 n. 710).
83. Lucian, *De Saltatione* (43; 67); Thyestes' banquet in scholia ad Lucan (1, 543–4) (*Commenta Bernensia* edited by Usener, 1967: 35–6): *Atreus Thyestis fratris sui filios ob adulterium Aeropae uxoris suae ad aram mactavit simulato sacrificio. Vinum sanguine mixtum visceraque filiorum eius pro epulis Thyesti adposuisse dicitur. Quod nefas ne sol aspiceret, nubibus se abscondit hoc est eclipsin passus est, Mycenisque nox fuit. Sed hoc fabulosum esse inveni in libro Catulli †quis cribitur permimologiarum†*; Sidonius Apollinaris, *Carmina* (23, 277–80): *sive prandia quis refert Thyestae/seu vestros, Philomela torva, planctus,/discerptum aut puerum cibumque factum/iamiam coniugis innocentioris*.
84. Sparagmos: Lucian (39) Iacchus; (51) Orpheus; (53) Apsyrtus; Cannibalism: Lucian (80) Cronus and Thyestes.
85. See above for the analysis of the narrative.
86. Most (1992: 391–419).
87. Ovid (*Met.* 13, 449–82), who also dealt with the episode of Polyxena's death, does not include the account of Astyanax's one.
88. It is also remarkable that Helen's appearance is really shaped as that of a character entering onstage, which is an awkward feature since we are in a messenger *rhesis*.
89. A sign of the confusing and unclear handling of Pyrrhus' presence in the scene may be the interpolation at line 1147 *Pyrrhum antecedit* deleted by Zwierlein (1976).
90. Schiesaro (2003: 238) defines Andromache's interjection (1104–10) as a histrionic lament.
91. Compare e.g. Euripides' *Hecuba* (524) where the messenger gives his position in the events (he says that he stood by Polyxena and Pyrrhus) and actively participates in them since he is in charge of the speech to silence the Greek army (529–31).
92. Owen (1969: 121) has noted the 'structural and thematic parallelism of the Astyanax and Polyxena sequences'.

93. See Schiesaro (2003: 237–43) for a discussion of the layers of spectatorship present in the *Trojan Women*'s narrative.

94. Compare Ovid, *Met.* (13, 415–17): *mittitur Astyanax illis de turribus, unde/ pugnantem pro se proavitaque regna tuentem/saepe videre patrem monstratum a matre solebat.*

95. Fantham (1982a: 371).

96. Compare Ovid, *Met.* (13, 474–5): *at populus lacrimas, quas illa tenebat,/non tenet.*

97. See also *Hercules furens* (1006–7): *ast illi caput/sonuit, cerebro tecta disperso madent*; and (1025–6) *perfregit ossa, corpori trunco caput/abest nec usquam est.*

98. The reactions of the crowd are similarly subjected to a detailed description in the narrative set-pieces of the *Hercules Oetaeus* (1666–90) where the crowd bursts into tears at Hercules' death.

99. Fantham (1982a: 379) has pointed out that a passage in Seneca's letters (11, 7) describes how the lowering of the gaze was the device used by actors to convey modesty: *Artifices scaenici, qui imitantur adfectus, qui metum et trepidationem exprimunt, qui tristitiam repraesentant, hoc indicio imitantur verecundiam. Deiciunt enim vultum, verba summittunt, figunt in terram oculos et deprimunt: ruborem sibi exprimere non possunt; nec prohibetur hic nec adducitur.*

100. Compare the description of Creusa's beauty in the *Medea* (93–101) and that of Hippolytus in the *Phaedra* (743–52).

101. See Fantham (1982a: 376).

102. See also *Thy* (721–3): *ast illi ferus/in vulnere ensem abscondit, et penitus premens/ iugulo manum commisit*; and (738–41): *ferrumque . . ./infesta manu/exegit ultra corpus; ac pueri statim/pectore receptus ensis e tergo exstitit*; in relation to the second passage, Tarrant (1985: 196) has remarked that the awkward subordinate syntactical position of the child shifts 'the attention on the progress of the sword through the body'.

103. Compare e.g. *Thy* (1082–3): *montium/tergemina moles cecidit*; *Ag* (921): *cecidit decenni marte concussum Ilium.*

104. The necromancy scene has no counterpart in Sophocles' *Oedipus*.

105. The theme was also popular in mimes; the Roman Grammarian Aulus Gellius (16, 7, 17; 20, 6, 6) reports that Laberius, a distinguished writer of mimes, composed a *Necyomantia*.

106. For example line 548: *Huc ut sacerdos intulit senior gradum*; (551–2) *ipse funesto integit/vates amictu corpus et frondem quatit*; e.g. lines 569–70: *latravit Hecates turba; ter valles cavae/sonuere maestum.*

107. Compare Virgil (*Aen.* 6, 237–8): *spelunca alta fuit vastoque immanis hiatu,/ scrupea, tuta lacu nigro nemorumque tenebris.*

108. In addition to this, in Senecan descriptions of *loci horridi*, there is always a tree which dominates the grove: *Oed* (542–4): *medio stat ingens arbor atque umbra*

gravi/silvas minores urget et magno ambitu/diffusa ramos una defendit nemus;
Thy (655–7): *quam supra eminens/despectat alte quercus et vincit nemus; Hf*
(689–90): *horrent opaca fronde nigrantes comae/taxo imminente.* The image of the
dominating tree is derived from the Virgilian description of the tree of false
dreams (*Aen.* 6, 282–4): *In medio ramos annosaque bracchia pandit/ulmus*
opaca, ingens, quam sedem Somnia vulgo/vana tenere ferunt, foliisque sub omnibus
haerent.

109. The line echoes Virgil, *Egl.* (1, 24–5): *(Roma) . . . alias inter caput extulit urbes,/*
     quantum lenta solent inter viburna cupressi.
110. Töchterle (1994: 429).
111. Töchterle (1994: 442) has observed that the p-alliteration (*palla, perfundit, pedes*)
     at line 553 matches the sound of the impact of the fabric of the dress on the feet.
112. Compare *Thy* (669) (*catenis lucus excussis sonat*), where the shadows shake their
     chains; *Hf* (784–5) (*qui trina vasto capita concutiens sono/regnum tuetur*), where
     the noise is produced by the shaking of Cerberus' three heads; *Hf* (815–16) (*et*
     vastas furens/quassat catenas), where Cerberus shakes its chains.
113. Compare with *Hf* (665–6): *hiatque rupes alta et immenso specu/ingens vorago*
     faucibus vastis patet; and with *Tro* (178–80): *Tum scissa vallis aperit immensos*
     specus,/et hiatus Erebi pervium ad superos iter/tellure fracta praebet.
114. Compare the analogous troupe of personified abstractions in the *Hf* (689–96).
115. The gesture is extremely common in Seneca's tragedies.
116. The *exangue vulgus* is introduced through a comparison with leaves, flowers,
     swarms, waves, and birds (600–7). The simile is modelled on two Virgilian
     passages: *Aen.* (6, 309–12) and *Georg.* (4, 471–4).
117. The emphasis given to the hands in the description of Zethus and Amphion is
     remarkable.
118. Töchterle (1994: 467) has observed that the phrase *caput fastu grave* (614)
     actually describes a type; compare *Ag* (305) *pectus aerumnis grave; Phoe* (233)
     caput tenebris grave.
119. Compare *Tro* (443) *cum subito nostros Hector ante oculos stetit; Tro* (188)
     (Achilles) *cum superbo victor in curru stetit; Ag* (166) (Agamemnon) *cum stetit ad*
     aras ore sacrifico pater; Thy (720) (Tantalus) *stetit sui securus.*
120. Compare *Phae* (833) *staretque recta squalor incultus coma; Thy* (780) *nitet fluente*
     madidus unguento comam; (948) *pingui madidus crinis amomo; HO* (120) *crinis*
     patrio pulvere sordidus; (376) *hirtam Sabaea marcidus myrrha comam.*
121. Compare *Oed* (480) *ore deiecto;* (561–2) *rabido . . . ore; Ag* (166) *ore sacrifico; Thy*
     (2) *avido . . . ore;* (692) *ore violento;* (779) *ore funesto;* (988) *ore decepto; Tro* (34)
     ore lymphato; Hf (811) *ore summisso;* (902) *ore saxifico;* (947–8) *ingenti . . . ore;*
     (1059) *ore decoro; Phoe* (119–20) *semifero . . . ore;* (220) *ore pestifero; Med* (241)
     ore flagranti.

122. The earth groans and bellows at: *Tro* (171–4); *Oed* (569–70; 571); the earth splits open at: *Tro* (172); *Oed* (582–3); the trees are disturbed at: *Tro* (173–4); *Oed* (574–6); the ghost emerges at: *Tro* (179 ff.); *Oed* (586–8).

123. To Achilles' and Laius' shadowy appearances may be added that of Hector's ghost in the *Trojan Women* (443–56).

124. In Greek tragedy, only two ghosts make their appearance, namely Darius' ghost in Aeschylus' *Persians* (619–84) and Polydorus' one in Euripides' *Hecuba*.

125. See Tarrant (1976: 248) for a fuller discussion of the sources.

126. See Morford (1967: 20–36).

127. Tarrant (1976: 21).

128. Since Seneca's words imply a tragic and not a comic treatment of the topic, I assume that the term 'mimicus' is equivalent to and stands for 'pantomimicus'. It is possible that Seneca is using the word 'mimici' in a general and broad sense which would include pantomime, since mime and pantomime were sister arts, which shared many features in common and the boundaries between the two of them were not sharply marked.

129. In Aeschylus' *Agamemnon*, the herald uses the first person plural (e.g. lines 659; 660; 672; 673).

130. Perfect: (421) *cecidit*; (422) *divisa est*; (427) *fulsit*; (428) *monuit*; (443) *posuere, credita est*; (460) *relevabat*; (464) *fecit*; (465) *sparserat*; (498) *nocuit*; (507) *cessit*; (515) *meruit*; (534) *perstrinxit*; (536) *excussit*; (538) *tulit*; (542) *traxit*; (547) *fugavit*; (549) *pepulerunt*; (550) *vicimus*; (555) *tulit*. Compare Aeschylus' narration of the storm which is couched in the past.

131. In 157 lines, only twelve verbs in the passive occur: (422) *divisa est*; (425) *aptatur*; (456) *tegitur*; (470) *conditur*; (485) *revelli*; (487) *induci*; (471) *tollitur*; (491) *datur*; (515) *vocatur*; (535) *libratur*; 548) *tuli*; (573) *vehitur*.

132. Tarrant (1976: 249).

133. The verb *increpere* is used only twice in the tragic *corpus*: here and at *Tro* (302) *timide, cum increpuit metus*.

134. For example *Hf* (473–4) *nec manu molli levem/vibrare thyrsum*; *Oed* (441) *thyrsumque levem vibrante manu*; *Phoe* (439) *vibrat in fratrum manu*.

135. Cicero, *Acad.* (2, 105): *[mare] qua a sole collucet, albescit et vibrat*; Lucan, *Pharsalia* (5, 446): *[pontus] non horrore tremit, non solis imagine vibrat*.

136. Claudian, *In Rufinum* (2, 355–7): *hinc alii saevum cristato vertice nutant/et tremulos umeris gaudent vibrare colores,/quos operit formatque chalybs*.

137. *Met.* (3, 683–86): *undique dant saltus multaque adspergine rorant/emerguntque iterum redeuntque sub aequora rursus/inque chori ludunt speciem lascivaque iactant/corpora et acceptum patulis mare naribus efflant*. See Tarrant (1976: 259) for a full discussion of the Ovidian borrowings.

138. For an analysis of Virgil's and Ovid's storms see Otis (1966: 238–46); Solodow (1988: 119–25).

139. The description of the destruction of the ships is cast here and at lines 571–6. Line 504, *nec illi vela nec tonsae manent,* recalls the Virgilian *non comptae mansere comae* (*Aen.* 6, 48). In the second instance the ships are treated as sentient beings even more forcefully (575–6 *iam timent terram rates/et maria malunt*).

140. Galinsky (1975: 145).

141. Compare Virgil, *Georgics* (1, 356–9): *continuo ventis surgentibus aut freta ponti/ incipiunt agitata tumescere et aridus altis/montibus audiri fragor, aut resonantia longe/litora misceri et nemorum increbrescere murmur.* It is remarkable that the verb *tumere* and the adjective *tumidus* are either used in the tragedies to describe the swelling of the sea or the swelling of an emotion, usually *ira.*

142. Compare Virgil, *Aen.* (1, 82–6) and Ovid, *Met.* (11, 490–1): *omnique e parte feroces/bella gerunt venti fretaque indignantia miscent.*

143. The stereotyped nature of the language employed by Seneca can be well exemplified by e.g. line 484: *quid rabidus ora Corus Oceano exerens;* the same image is used at *Ag* (554) *Neptunus imis exerens undis caput* and *Oed* (532) *cupressus altis exerens silvis caput;* the adjective *rabidus* is both employed for inanimate beings as here and at *Thy* (360–2) (*non Eurus rapiens mare/aut saevo rabidus freto/ventosi tumor Hadriae*) and for animate ones as at *Thy* (254) (*Quid novi rabidus struis?*), at *Oed* (561–2) (*rabido minax/decantat ore*), and at *Oed* (626) (*et ore rabido fatur*).

144. See Pratt (1963: 225–6).

145. See also *Thy* (438–9): *Sic concitatam remige et velo ratem/aestus resistens remigi et velo refert;* (*Phae* 181–4): *Sic, cum gravatam navita adversa ratem/propellit unda, cedit in vanum labor/et victa prono puppis aufertur vado./quid ratio possit?;* *Hf* (676–9): *ut saepe puppes aestus invitas rapit,/sic pronus aer urget atque avidum chaos,/gradumque retro flectere haud umquam sinunt/umbrae tenaces.*

146. Nonnus, *Dionysiaca* (19, 226) says that the dancer used *symbola,* this meaning that the pantomimic performance was of a symbolic nature: πολυστρέπτοιο δὲ τέχνης σύμβολα τεχνήεντα κατέγραφε σιγαλέν χείρ.

147. See the section entitled 'The Pantomimic Show' in Chapter 1. See also Nonnus, *Dionysiaca* (1, 29–30): εἰ δὲ πέλοι μιμηλὸν ὕδωρ, Διόνυσον ἀείσω/κόλπον ἁλὸς δύνοντα κορυσσομένοιο Λυκούργου.

Conclusion

1. Elder Seneca, *Suasoriae* (2.19) about Silo: *qui pantomimis fabulas scripsit;* Juvenal, *Satire* (7, 86–7) about Statius: *sed cum fregit subsellia versu/esurit, intactam Paridi nisi vendit Agaven;* Lucan, see Lada-Richards (2003: 39: according to the so-called 'Vacca' life, XIV *salticae fabulae* are attributed to him.

2. Isidore of Seville (18, 49): *Nam fabulae ita componebantur a poetis ut aptissimae essent motui corporis.*

3. Segal (1983: 140) has remarked that 'emotional responses are magnified to a new level' and Seneca even created an apposite language capable to portray them in 'a new pictorial expressiveness', or, as Regenbogen (1927–8: 207) has called it, a 'psychoplastic portrait of emotional affect'.

4. Hook (2000: 55).

References

I. Editions of Seneca's Tragedies Consulted

Peiper, R. and G. Richter (1867), Leipzig (reprinted 1963).

Leo, F. (1878–79), Berlin.

Peiper, R. and G. Richter (1902), Leipzig (reprinted 1921, 1937).

Miller, F. J. (1917), London (reprinted 1927, 1938, 1953, 1960).

Moricca, U. (1917–23), Torino.

Herrmann, L. (1924), Paris.

Viansino, G. (1965), Torino.

Giardina, G. C. (1966), Bologna.

Zwierlein, O. (1986), Oxford.

Fitch, J. G. (2002–2004), Cambridge.

II. Works Cited in the Text

Abbot, F. F. (1911), 'The Origin of the Realistic Romance among the Romans', *CPh* 6, 257–70.

Aldrete, G. S. (1999), *Gestures and Acclamations in Ancient Rome*, Baltimore and London.

Allen, W. (1959), 'Stage Money (*fabam mimum*: Cic. Att. 1.16.13)', *TAPhA* 90, 1–8.

Andreassi, M. (1997), 'Osmosis and Contiguity between Low and High Literature', *GCN* 8, 1–21.

Austin, R. G. (ed.) (1960), *M. Tulli Ciceronis Pro M. Caelio oratio*, Oxford.

Bain, D. (1977), *Actors and Audience: a study of asides and related conventions in Greek drama*, Oxford.

Barchiesi, A. (1997), *The Poet and the Prince*, Berkeley.

Barchiesi, A. (2001), 'The Crossing', in S. J. Harrison (ed.) *Texts, Ideas, and the Classics*, 142–63, Oxford.

Bardon, H. (1936), 'Les poésies de Néron', *REL* 14, 337–49.

Barlow, S. A. (1971), *The Imagery of Euripides: a study in the dramatic use of pictorial language*, London.

Bauman, R. (1977), *Verbal Art as Performance*, Rowley.

Beacham, R. C. (1991), *The Roman Theatre and Its Audience*, London.

Beacham, R. C. (1999), *Spectacle Entertainments of Early Imperial Rome*, New Haven.

Betz, H. D. (1972), *Der Apostel Paulus und die sokratische Tradition: Eine exegetische Untersuchung zu seiner 'Apologie' 2 Korinther 10–13*, Tübingen.

Bianchi, L. and M. Bonanno Aravantinos (1991), 'Una tradizione di scultura microasiatica a Ostia', *Bollettino di Archeologia* 8, 1–32.

Bier, H. (1917), *De saltatione pantomimorum*, Bonn.

Bishop, J. D. (1968), 'The Meaning of the Choral Meters in Senecan Tragedy', *RhM* 111, 197–219.

Bishop, J. D. (1988), 'Seneca, *Thyestes* 920–969: an antiphony', *Latomus* 47, 392–412.

Bömer, F. P. (1954), *P. Ovidius Naso: Die Fasten*, Heidelberg.

Bonaria, M. (1959), 'Dinastie di pantomimi latini', *MAIA* 2, 224–42.

Bonaria, M. (1965), *Romani mimi*, Roma.

Bonaria, M. (1982), 'La musica conviviale dal mondo latino antico al medioevo', in F. Doglio (ed.), *Spettacoli conviviali dall'antichità classica alle corti italiane del '400*, 119–47, Viterbo.

Bonner, S. F. (1949), *Roman Declamation in the Late Republic and Early Empire*, Liverpool.

Boyle, A. J. (1987), 'Senecan Tragedy: twelve propositions', *Ramus* 16, 78–101.

Boyle, A. J. (ed.) (1994), *Seneca's Troades*, Leeds.

Boyle, A. J. (1997), *Tragic Seneca: an essay in the theatrical tradition*, London and New York.

Boyle, A. J. (2006), *Roman Tragedy*, London and New York.

Bragington, M. V. (1933), *The Supernatural in Seneca's Tragedies*, Menasha.

Braun, L. (1982), 'Sind Senecas Tragödien Buhnenstücke oder Rezitationsdramen?', *Res Publica Litterarum* 5, 43–52.

Brunelle, C. (2000–2001), 'Form vs. Function in Ovid's *Remedia Amoris*', *CJ* 96, 123–40.

Calder, W. M. III (1984), 'Seneca: *Thyestes* 101–6', *CPh* 79, 225–6.

Canter, H. V. (1925), *Rhetorical Elements in the Tragedies of Seneca*, Urbana.

Carcopino, J. (1942), *Aspects mystiques de la Rome païenne*, Paris.

Cèbe, J.-P. (ed.) (1977), *Varron, Satires ménippées*, Roma.

Chaisemartin, N. de (1987), 'Recherches sur la frise de l'Agora de Tibère', in J. de la Genière and K. Erim (eds), *Aphrodisias de Carie. Colloque du centre de recherches archéologiques de l'Université de Lille III* (13 November 1985), 135–54, Paris.

Chaisemartin, N. de (2006), 'La frise ionique à masques scéniques du propylon du Sébasteion d'Aphrodisias', *Revue Archéologique* 1, 33–82.

Charlesworth, M. P. (1950), 'Nero: some aspects', *JRS* 40, 69–76.

Coffey, M. (1976), *Roman Satire*, 165–77, London.

Coffey, M. and R. Mayer (1990), *Seneca: Phaedra*, Cambridge.

Coles, R. A. (1968), 'A new Fragment of Post-classical Tragedy from Oxyrhynchus', *BICS* 15, 110–18.

Coles, R. A. (1970), 'New Classical Text', *the Oxyrhynchus papyri* vol. XXXVI, 9–11.

Collignon, A. (1892), *Étude sur Pétrone. La critique littéraire, l'imitation et la parodie dans le Satiricon*, Paris.

Conte, G. B. (1986), *The Rhetoric of Imitation*, Ithaca and London.

Conte, G. B. (1994), *Genres and Readers*, Baltimore.

Conte, G. B. (1996), *The Hidden Author: an interpretation of Petronius' Satyricon*, London.

Costa, C. D. N. (1973), *Medea*, Oxford.

Courtney, E. (1985), 'Three Poems of Catullus: (2) How Catullus came to write the Attis', *BICS* 32, 88–91.

Courtney, E. (1995), *Musa Lapidaria: a Selection of Latin Verse Inscriptions*. Atlanta.

Cunningham, M. P. (1949), 'The Novelty of Ovid's *Heroides*', *CPh* 44, 100–6.

Curley, T. F. (1986), *The Nature of Senecan Drama*, Roma.

Davis, P. J. (1993), *Shifting Song: the chorus in Seneca's tragedy*, Hildesheim.

Day, A. A. (1938), *The Origins of Latin Love-Elegy*, 85–101, Oxford.

Dihle, A. (1983), 'Seneca und die Aufführungspraxis der römischen Tragödie', *Antike und Abendland* 29, 162–71.

Dodds, E. R. (ed.) (1960), *Bacchae*, Oxford.

Duckworth, G. E. (1952), *The Nature of Roman Comedy*, Princeton.

Eden, P. T. (ed.) (1984), *Seneca: Apocolocyntosis*, Cambridge.

Elder, J. P. (1947), 'The Art of Catullus' Attis', *AJPh* 68, 394–403.

Eliot, T. S. (1951), *Selected Essays*, London.

Engels, D. W. (1990), *Roman Corinth: an alternative model for the classical city*, Chicago.

Erasmo, M. (2004), *Roman Tragedy*, Austin.

Ewbank, I.-S. (2005), 'Striking Too Short at Greeks: the transmission of *Agamemnon* to the English Renaissance stage', in F. Macintosh, P. Michelakis, E. Hall, and O. Taplin (eds), *Agamemnon in Performance*, 37–53, Oxford.

Fantham, E. (1975), 'Virgil's Dido and Seneca's Tragic Heroines', *G&R* 22, 1–10.

Fantham, E. (ed.) (1982a), *Seneca's Troades*, Princeton.

Fantham, E. (1982b), 'Quintilian on Performance: traditional and personal elements in *institutio* 11.3', *Phoenix* 36, 243–63.

Fantham, E. (1983), 'Sexual Comedy in Ovid's *Fasti*: sources and motivation', *HSCP* 87, 185–216.

Fantham, E. (1986), 'ΖΗΛΟΤΥΠΙΑ: a brief excursion into sex, violence, and literary history', *Phoenix* 40, 45–57.

Fantham, E. (1988–89), 'Mime: the missing link in Roman literary history', *CW* 82, 153–63.

Fantham, E. (2002), 'Orator and/et Actor', in P. Easterling and E. Hall, *Greek and Roman Actors*, 362–76, Cambridge.

Fantuzzi, M. and R. Hunter (2004), *Tradition and Innovation in Hellenistic Poetry*, 477–85, Cambridge.

Fear, A. T. (1991), 'The Dancing Girls of Cadiz', *G&R* 38, 75–79.

Fedeli, P. (1978), 'Struttura e stile dei monologhi di Attis nel carme 63 di Catullo', *RFIC* 106, 39–52.

Fedeli, P. (1988), 'Encolpio-Polieno', *Materiali e Discussioni per l'Analisi dei Testi Classici* 20–21, 9–32.

Fick, N. (1990), 'Die Pantomime des Apuleius (*Met.* X, 30–34, 3)', in J. Blänsdorf (ed.), *Theater and Gesellschaft im Imperium Romanum*, 223–32, Tübingen.

Finkelpearl, E. D. (1998), *Metamorphosis of Language in Apuleius*, Ann Arbor.

Fitch, J. G. (ed.) (1987a), *Seneca's Hercules Furens*, Ithaca and London.

Fitch, J. G. (1987b), *Seneca's Anapaests*, Atlanta.

Fitch, J. G. (2002), 'Transpositions and Emendations in Seneca's Tragedies', *Phoenix* 56, 296–314.

Fitch, J. G. (2004), *Annaeana Tragica: notes on the text of Seneca's tragedies*, Leiden.

Fitch, J. and S. McElduff (2002), 'Construction of the Self in Senecan Drama', *Mnemosyne* 55, 18–40.

Frank, M. (ed.) (1995), *Seneca's Phoenissae*, Leiden.

Galinsky, G. K. (ed.) (1975), *Ovid's Metamorphoses*, Oxford.

Garelli, M.-H. (1998), 'Tradition littéraire et creation dramatique dans les tragedies de Sénèque: l'exemple des récits de messangers', *Latomus* 57, 15–32.

Garelli, M.-H. (2000), 'Le *ludus talarius* et les representations dramatiques à Rome', *RPh* 74, 87–102.

Garelli, M.-H. (2001), 'La pantomime entre danse et drame: le geste et l'écriture', *Cahiers du GITA* 14, 229–47.

Garelli, M.-H. (2004), 'Néron et la pantomime', in C. Hugoniot, F. Hurlet, and S. Milanezi (eds), *Le statut de l'acteur dans l' Antiquité greque et romaine*, 353–68, Tours.

Garton, C. (1972), *Personal Aspects of the Roman Theatre*, Toronto.

Geer, R. S. (1935), 'The Greek Games at Naples', *TAPhA* 66, 208–21.

Geffcken, K.A. (1973), *Comedy in the Pro Caelio*, Leiden.

Giancotti, F. (1967), *Mimo e gnome: studio su Decimo Laberio e Publilio Siro*, Firenze.

Gigante, M. (1979), *Civiltà delle forme letterarie nell'antica Pompei*, 150–2, Napoli.

Gill, C. (1987), 'Two Monologues of Self-Division: Euripides, *Medea* 1021–80 and Seneca, *Medea* 893–977', in M. Whitby, P. Hardie, and M. Whitby (eds), *Homo Viator*, 25–37, Bristol.

Graf, F. (1992) 'Gestures and Conventions: the gestures of Roman actors and orators', in J. Bremmer and H. Roodenburg (eds), *A Cultural History of Gestures from Antiquity to the Present Days*, 36–58, New York.

Grysar, C. J. (1834), 'Über die Pantomimen der Römer', *RhM* 2, 30–80.

Guillemin, A. (1949), 'Le poème 63 de Catulle', *REL* 27, 149–57.

Habinek, T. (2002), 'Ovid and Empire', in P. Hardie (ed.), *The Cambridge Companion to Ovid*, 46–61.

Habinek, T. (2005), *The World of Roman Song*, Baltimore and London.

Hadas, M. (1939), 'The Roman Stamp of Seneca's Tragedies', *AJPh* 60, 220–31.

Hall, E. (2002), 'The Singing Actors of Antiquity', in P. Easterling and E. Hall (eds), *Greek and Roman Actors: aspects of an ancient profession*, 3–38, Cambridge.

Hall, E. (2008), 'Is the *Barcelona Alcestis* a Latin Pantomime Libretto?', in E. Hall and R. Wyles (eds), *New Directions in Ancient Pantomime*, 258–82, Oxford.

Hall, J. (2004), 'Cicero and Quintilian on the Oratorical Use of Hand Gestures', *CQ* 54, 145–69.

Harmon, A. M. (ed.) (1936), *Lucian*, vol. III, Cambridge.

Harrison, S. J. (2007), *Generic Enrichment in Vergil and Horace*, Oxford.

Häuptli, B. (2002), 'Versteckte Galliamben bei Seneca: zu Metrik und Ethos von Seneca, Medea 848–878', *RhM* 145, 313–24.

Henry, D. and B. Walker (1965), 'The Futility of Action: a study of Seneca's *Hercules Furens*', *CPh* 60, 11–22.

Henry, D. and B. Walker (1985), *The Mask of Power: Seneca's tragedies and Imperial Rome*, Chicago.

Hepding, H. (1903), *Attis seine Mythen und sein Kult*, Berlin.

Herington, C. J. (1966), 'Senecan Tragedy', *Arion* 5, 422–71.

Herrmann, L. (1924), *Le Théatre de Sénèque*, Paris.

Hine, H. M. (ed.) (2000), *Medea*, Warminster.

Hook, B. S. (2000), 'Nothing within which passeth show', in G. W. M. Harrison, *Seneca in Performance*, 53–71, London.

Horsfall, N. (1979), 'Epic and Burlesque in Ovid, *Met*, VIII. 260 ff.', *CJ* 74, 319–32.

Horsfall, N. (1989), 'The Use of Literacy and the *Cena Trimalchionis*: II', *G&R* 36, 194–209.

Hubbard, M. (1974), *Propertius*, London.

Iliffe, J. H. (1945), 'Imperial Art in Trans-Jordan', *Quarterly of the Department of Antiquities in Palestine* 11, 1–26.

Ingleheart, J. (2008), '*Et mea sunt populo saltata poemata saepe* (*Tristia* 2. 519): Ovid and Pantomime', in E. Hall and R. Wyles (eds), *New Directions in Ancient Pantomime*, 198–217, Oxford.

Jakobi, R. (1988), *Der Einfluss Ovids auf der tragiker Seneca*, Berlin.

Jory, E. J. (1981), 'The Literary Evidence for the Beginnings of Imperial Pantomime', *BICS* 28, 147–61.

Jory, E. J. (1995), '*Ars Ludrica* and the *Ludus Talarius*', in A. Griffiths (ed.), *Stage Directions: essays in ancient drama in honour of E. W. Handley* (*BICS* Suppl. 66), 139–52, London.

Jory, E. J. (1998), 'The Pantomime Assistants', in T. W. Hillard, R. A. Kearsley, C. E. V. Nixon and A. M. Nobbs (eds), *Ancient History in a Modern University*, vol. 1, 217–21, Michigan and Cambridge.

Jory, E. J. (2001), 'Some Cases of Mistaken Identity? Pantomime masks and their context', *BICS* 45, 1–20.

Jory, E. J. (2002), 'The Masks on the Propylon of the Sebasteion at Aphrodisias', in P. Easterling and E. Edith (eds), *Greek and Roman Actors*, 238–53, Cambridge.

Jory, E. J. (2004), 'Pylades, Pantomime, and the Preservation of Tragedy', *Mediterranean Archaeology* 17, 147–56.

Jung, C. G. (1963), *Memories, Dreams, Reflections*, London.

Kehoe, P. H. (1984), 'The Adultery Mime Reconsidered', in D. F. Bright and E. S. Ramage (eds), *Classical Texts and their Traditions: Studies in Honor of C. R. Trahman*, 89–106, Chicago.

Kelly, H. A. (1979), 'Tragedy and the Performance of Tragedy in Late Roman Antiquity', *Traditio* 35, 21–44.

Kirby, J. C. (1989), 'The Galliambics of Catullus 63: that intoxicating meter', *Syllecta Classica* 1, 63–74.

Kokolakis, M. (1959), 'Pantomimus and the Treatise ΠΕΡΙΟΡΧΗΣΕΩΣ', *Platon* 11, 3–56.

Kragelund, P. (2008), 'Senecan Tragedy: back on stage?', in J. G. Fitch (ed.), *Seneca: Oxford Readings in Classical Studies*, 181–94, Oxford.

Kroll, W. (1924), *Studien zum Verständnis der Römischen Literatur*, 202–24.

Lada-Richards, I. (2003), ' "A Worthless Feminine Thing"? Lucian and the 'Optic Intoxication' of Pantomime Dancing', *Helios* 30, 21–75.

Lada-Richards, I. (2004), 'Μύθων Εἰκών: Pantomime Dancing and the Figurative Arts in Imperial and Late Antiquity', *Arion* 12.2, 17–46.

Lada-Richards, I. (2007), *Silent Eloquence: Lucian and Pantomime Dancing*, London.

Larson, V. T. (1994), *The Role of Descriptions in Senecan Tragedy*, Frankfurt am Main.

Lateiner, D. (1996), 'Nonverbal Behaviours in Ovid's Poetry, primarily *Metamorphoses* 14', *CJ* 91, 225–53.

Lawler, L. B. (1943), 'Ὄρχησις Ἰωνική', *TAPhA* 74, 60–71.

Lawler, L. B. (1946), 'Portrait of a Dancer', *CJ* 41, 241–7.

Leo, F. (ed.) (1878–79), *L. Annaei Senecae Tragoediae*, Berolini.

Lesky, A. (1951), *Aristaenetus: erotische Briefe*, Zürich.

Littlewood, C. A. (1980), 'Ovid and the Ides of March (*Fasti* 3.523–710): a further study in the artistry of the Fasti', in C. Deroux (ed.), *Studies in Latin Literature and Roman History* (Collection Latomus 168), 301–21, Bruxelles.

Littlewood, C. A. (2004), *Self-Representation and Illusion in Senecan Tragedy*, Oxford.

Lobe, M. (1999), *Die Gebärden in Vergils Aeneis. Zur Bedeutung und Funktion von Körpersprache in Römischen Epos*, Frankfurt.

Lowe, J. C. B. (1989), 'Plautus' Parasites and the Atellana', in G. Vogt-Spira (ed.), *Studien zur vorliterarischen Periode im frühen Rom*, 161–9, Tübingen.

MacKay, L. A. (1975), 'The Roman Tragic Spirit', *California Studies in Classical Antiquity* 8, 145–62.

Marcovich, M. (ed.) (1988), *Alcestis Barcinonensis: Text and Commentary* (Mnemosyne suppl. 103), Leiden and New York.

Marshall, C. W. (2000), 'Location!Location!Location! Choral absence and dramatic space in Seneca's *Troades*', in G. W. M. Harrison (ed.), *Seneca in Performance*, 27–51, London.

Marx, W. (1932), *Funktion und Form der Chorlieder in den Seneca-Tragödien*, Heidelberg.

Mason, H. J. (1971), 'Lucius at Corinth', *Phoenix* 98, 160–5.

McKeown, J. C. (1979), 'Augustan Elegy and Mime', *PCPhS* 25, 71–84.

Merkelbach, R. (1973), 'Fragment eines satirischen Romans: Aufforderung zur Berichte', *ZPE* 11, 81–100.

Miller, F. J. (1916), 'Some Features of Ovid's Style: I. Personification of Abstractions', *CJ* 11, 516–34.

Miller, S. (1967), *The Picaresque Novel*, 13–20, Cleveland.

Moretti, J.-C. (1993), 'Des masques et des théâtres en Grèce et en Asie Mineure', *REA* 95, 207–23.

Morford, M. P. (1967), *The Poet Lucan*, Oxford.

Morisi, L. (ed.) (1999), *Attis (carmen LXIII)* (L. Morisi trans.), Bologna.

Moss, C. (1935), 'Jacob of Serugh's Homilies', *Le Muséon* 48, 87–112.

Most, G. W. (1992), '*Disiecti Membra Poetae*: the Rhetoric of Dismemberment in Neronian Poetry', in R. Hexter and D. Selden (eds), *Innovations of Antiquity*, 391–419, New York.

Motto, A. L. and J. R. Clark (1972), 'Senecan Tragedy: patterns of irony and art', *CB* 48, 69–76.

Mulroy, D. (1976), 'Hephaestion and Catullus 63', *Phoenix* 30, 61–72.

Newman, J. K. (1990), *Roman Catullus and the Modification of the Alexandrian Sensibility*, Hildesheim.

Nicoll, A. (1931), *Masks, Mimes, and Miracles*, London.

Otis, B. (1966), *Ovid as an Epic Poet*, Cambridge.

Owen, S. G. (1924), *Ovid: Tristium Liber Secundus*, Oxford.

Owen, W. H. (1969), 'Time and Event in Seneca's *Troades*', *WS* 82, 118–37.

Page, D. L. (1941), *Greek Literary Papyri*, London.

Panayotakis, C. (1994), 'Quartilla's Histrionics in Petronius, *Satyrica* 16.1–26.6', *Mnemosyne* 47, 319–36.

Panayotakis, C. (1995), *Theatrum Arbitri: Theatrical Elements in the Satyrica of Petronius*, (Mnemosyne suppl. 146), Leiden & New York.

Paschal, D. M. (1939), 'The Vocabulary of Mental Aberration in Roman Comedy and Petronius', *Language* 15, 4–88.

Pasquali, G. (1994), *Pagine stravaganti di un filologo*, 275–82, Firenze. (Original work published in 1942.)

Pratt, N. T. (1939), *Dramatic Suspense in Seneca and in His Greek Predecessors*, Diss. Princeton.

Pratt, N. T. (1963), 'Major Systems of Figurative Language in Senecan Melodrama', *TAPhA* 94, 199–234.

Pratt, N. T. (1983), *Seneca's Drama*, Chapel Hill.

Preston, K. (1915), 'Some Sources of Comic Effect in Petronius', *CPh* 10, 260–9.

Purcell, N. (1999), 'Does Caesar Mime?', in B. Bergmann and C. Kondoleon (eds), *The Art of Ancient Spectacle*, 181–93, Washington.

Quinn, K. (1970), *Catullus: the Poems*, London.

Regenbogen, O. (1927–28), 'Schmerz und Tod in den Tragödien des Senecas', *Vorträge der Bibliothek Warburg* 7, 167–218. (Reprinted in *Kleine Schriften*, 1961, 411–64.)

Reynolds, R. W. (1946), 'The Adultery Mime', *CQ* 40, 77–84.

Richter, G. (1899), *Kritische Untersuchungen zu Senecas Tragödien*, Jena.

Richter, G. M. A. (1913), 'Grotesque and the Mime', *AJA* 17, 149–56.

Rosati, G. (1983), 'Trimalchione in scena', *MAIA* 35, 213–27.

Ross, R. C. (1969), 'Catullus 63 and the Galliambic Meter', *CJ* 64, 145–52.

Rostovtzeff, M. (1937), 'Two Homeric Bowls in the Louvre', *AJA* 41, 86–96.

Rotolo, V. (1957), *Il pantomimo: studi e testi*, Palermo.

Sandy, G. N. (1974), 'Scaenica Petroniana', *TAPhA* 104, 329–46.

Sandy, G. N. (1976), 'Publilius Syrus and *Satyricon* 55. 5–6', *RhM* 119, 286–7.

Santelia, S. (1991), *Chariton liberata (P.Oxy. 413)* and Bari.

Sargent, J. L. (1996), *The Novelty of Ovid's Heroides*, Diss. Bryn Mawr College.

Schiesaro, A. (2003), *The Passions in Play: Thyestes and the dynamics of Senecan drama*, Cambridge.

Schlegel, A. W. (1809–11), *Vorlesungen über dramatische Kunst and Literatur*, Heidelberg.

Schlegel, A. W. (1846), *A Course of Lectures on Dramatic Art and Literature* (English trans. John Black), London.

Segal, C. P. (1983), 'Boundary Violation and the Landscape of the Self in Senecan Tragedy', *Antike und Abendland* 29, 172–87. (Reprinted in Fitch, 2008, 136–56.)

Segal, C. P. (1984), 'Senecan Baroque: the death of Hippolytus in Seneca, Ovid and Euripides', *TAPhA* 114, 311–25.

Segal, C. P. (1986), *Language and Desire in Seneca's* Phaedra, Princeton.

Shelton, J.-A. (1978), *Seneca's* Hercules furens: *Time, Structure, and Style*, Göttingen.

Shero, L. R. (1923), 'The Cena in Roman Satire', *CPh* 18, 126–43.

Shipton, K. M. W. (1987), 'The Attis of Catullus', *CQ* 37, 444–9.

Skutch, O. (1959), 'Publilius Syrus', *RE* 23, 1923–4.

Slater, W. J. (1990), 'Orchestopala', *ZPE* 84, 215–20.

Slater, W. J. (1995), 'The Pantomime Tiberius Iulius Apolaustus', *GRBS* 36, 263–92.

Slater, W. J. (1996), 'Inschriften von Magnesia revisited', *GRBS* 37, 195–204.

Slater, W. J. (2002), 'Mime Problems: Cicero *ad Fam.* 7.1 and Martial 9.38', *Phoenix* 56, 315–29.

Solodow, J. B. (1988), *The World of Ovid's Metamorphoses*, Chapter Hill and London.

Steinmetz, P. (1982), *Untersuchungen zur römischen Literatur des zweiten Jahrhunderts nach Christi Geburt*, 295–373, Wiesbaden.

Stevens, J. A. (1999), 'Seneca and Horace: allegorical technique in Two Odes to Bacchus (Hor. *Carm.* 2.19 and Sen. *Oed.* 403–508)', *Phoenix* 53, 281–307.

Sullivan, J. P. (1968), *The Satyricon of Petronius*, London.

Sumi, G. S. (2002), 'Impersonating the Dead: mimes at roman funerals', *AJPh* 123, 559–85.

Sutton, D. F. (1986), *Seneca on the Stage*, Leiden.

Tarrant, R. J. (1972), Review of Seidensticker, *Phoenix* 26, 194–9.

Tarrant, R. J. (ed.) (1976), *Agamemnon/Seneca*, Cambridge.

Tarrant, R. J. (1978), 'Senecan Drama and Its Antecedents', *HSCP* 82, 213–63.

Tarrant, R. J. (ed.) (1985), *Seneca's Thyestes*, Atlanta.

Thomson, D. F. S. (ed.) (1997), *Catullus*, Toronto.

Töchterle, K. (ed.) (1994), *Lucius Annaeus Seneca: Oedipus*, Heidelberg.

Toynbee, J. M. (1942), 'Nero Artifex: the *Apocolocyntosis* reconsidered', *CQ* 36, 83–93.

Traina, A. (1998), 'L'ambiguo sesso. Il c. 63 di Catullo', in N. Criniti (ed.), *Commune Sermioni: società e cultura della Cisalpina dopo l'anno Mille*, 189–98, Brescia.

Wagenvoort, H. (1920), 'Pantomimus und Tragödie im augusteischen Zeitalter', *Neue Jahrbuch für klassische Philologie* 45, 101–13.

Walker, B. (1969), 'Review of Zwierlein 1966', *CPh* 64, 183–7.

Walsh, P. G. (1970), *The Roman Novel*, Cambridge.

Watson, P. A. (1995), *Ancient Stepmothers: myth, misogyny, and reality*, 92–134, Leiden and New York.

Watt, W. S. (1955), 'Fabam mimum', *Hermes* 83, 496–500.

Webb, R. (2005), 'The Protean Performer: mimesis and identity in late antique discussions of the theater', in L. Del Gudice and N. van Deusen (eds), *Performing Ecstasies: music, dance and ritual in the Mediterranean*, 3–11, Ottawa.

Webb, R. (2008), 'Inside the Mask: pantomime from the performers' perspective', in E. Hall and R. Wyles (eds), *New Directions in Ancient Pantomime*, 43–60, Oxford.

Weinreich, O. (1923), *Senecas Apocolocyntosis. Die Satire auf Tod/Himmel und Höllenfahrt des Kaisers Claudius*, Berlin.

Weinreich, O. (1941), 'Varro und die Geschichte des Pantomimus', *Hermes* 76, 96–100.

Weinreich, O. (1948), *Epigrammstudien I. Epigramm und Pantomimus nebst einem Kapitel über einige nicht-epigraphische Texte und Denkmäler zur Geschichte des Pantomimus*, SHAW 1944/48.1, Heidelberg.

Welborn, L. L. (1999), 'The Runaway Paul', *HTR* 92, 115–63.

West, M. L. (1982), *Greek Metre*, Oxford.

Wiemken, H. (1972), *Der griechische Mimus: Dokumente zur Geschichte des antiken Volkstheater*, Bremen.

Wilamowitz-Möllendorff, U. (1879), 'Die Galliamben des Kallimachos und Catullus', *Hermes* 14, 194–201.

Wilson, M. (1990), 'Review of Fitch (1987)', *Phoenix* 44, 189–94.

Windisch, H. (1924), *Der zweite Korintherbrief*, Göttingen.

Wiseman, T. P. (1985), *Catullus and His World*, Cambridge.

Wiseman, T. P. (2002), 'Ovid and the Stage', in G. Herbert-Brown (ed.), *Ovid's Fasti*, 275–99, Oxford.

Wiseman, T. P. (2008a), *Unwritten Rome*, Exeter.

Wiseman, T. P. (2008b), ' "Mime" and "Pantomime": Some Problematic Texts', in E. Hall and R. Wyles (eds), *New Directions in Ancient Pantomime*, 146–53, Oxford.

Wooton, G. E. (1999), 'A Mask of Attis, *Oscilla* as Evidence for a Theme of Pantomime', *Latomus* 58, 314–55.

Wüst, E. (1949), 'Pantomimus', *RE* 18.3, 833–69.

Wyke, M. (1987), 'Written Women: Propertius' *scripta puella*', *JRS* 77, 47–61.

Yardley, J. C. (1972), 'Comic Influences in Propertius', *Phoenix* 26, 134–9.

Yardley, J. C. (1974), 'Propertius' Lycinna', *TAPhA* 104, 429–34.

Zeitlin, F. I. (1971), 'Petronius as Paradox: Anarchy and Artistic Integrity', *TAPhA* 102, 631–84.

Zimmerman, M. (1993), 'Narrative Judgement and Reader Response in Apuleius' Metamorphoses 10, 29–34: the Pantomime of the Judgement of Paris', *GCN* 5, 143–61.

Zimmerman, M. (ed.) (2000), *Apuleius Madaurensis, Metamorphoses: Book X*, Groningen.

Zimmermann, B. (1990), 'Seneca und der Pantomimus', in G. Vogt-Spira (ed.), *Strukturen der Mündlichkeit in der römischen Literatur*, 161–7, Tübingen.

Zwierlein, O. (1966), *Die Rezitationsdramen Senecas*, Meisenheim am Glan.

Zwierlein, O. (1976), 'Versinterpolationen und Korruptelen in den Tragödien Senecas', *WJA* N.F. 2, 181–217.

Zwierlein, O. (1986), *Kritischer Kommentar zu den Tragödien Senecas* (Abh. Akad. Mainz, Geistes – u. Sozialwiss. Kl., Einzelveröffentlichung 6), Stuttgart.

III. Works Consulted But Not Cited in the Text

Ahl, F. (2008), *Two Faces of Oedipus: Sophocles'Oedipus Tyrannus and Seneca's Oedipus*, Ithaca and London.

Amoroso, F. (ed.) (2006), *Teatralità dei Cori Senecani*, Palermo.

Andreassi, M. (1999), 'P. Oxy. III 413 (*Moicheutria*), rr. 122–124 verso', *ZPE* 124, 17–21.

Andreassi, M. (2000), 'La Figura del Malakos nel Mimo della *Moicheutria*', *Hermes* 128, 320–326.

Andreassi, M. (2001a), 'Esopo sulla scena', *RhM* 144, 203–25.

Andreassi, M. (2001b), *Mimi greci in Egitto*, Bari.

Andreassi, M. (2002), 'Il mimo tra consumo e letteratura', *AncNarr* 2, 30–46.

Astbury, R. (1977), 'Petronius, P.Oxy. 3010, and Menippean Satire', *CPh* 72, 22–31.

Bagnani, G. (1919), 'The Subterranean Basilica at Porta Maggiore', *JRS* 9, 78–85.

Bagnani, G. (1954), *Arbiter of Elegance*, Toronto.

Barsby, J. A. (1996), 'Ovid's Amores and Roman comedy', in F. Cairns and M. Heath (eds), *Papers of the Leeds International Latin Seminar*, Vol. 9, 135–57, Leeds.

Bernini, F. (1915), 'Studi sul mimo', *Annali della R. Scuola Normale Superiore di Pisa* 21, 9–160.

Betts, J. H., J. T. Hooker and J. R. Green (eds) (1986), *Studies in Honour of T. B. L. Webster*, Bristol.

Bieber, M. (1953–54), 'Wurden die Tragödien des Senecas in Rom aufgeführt?', *Mitteilungen des Deutschen Archaelogischen Instituts* 60–61, 100–6.

Bishop, J. D. (1972), 'Seneca's *Troades*: Dissolution of a Way of Life', *RhM* 115, 329–37.

Blänsdorf, J. (1990), *Theater und Gesellschaft im Imperium Romanum*, Tübingen.

Boissier, G. (1861), 'De la signification des mots *saltare* et *cantare tragoediam*', *Revue Archéologique*, 333–43.

Boissier, G. (1899), 'A propos d'un théatre antique', *Revue des deux Mondes*, 303–32.

Bonaria, M. (1961), 'Marullo scrittore di mimi', *Dioniso* 35, 16–27.

Bonelli, G. (1978), 'Il carattere retorico delle tragedie di Seneca', *Latomus* 37, 395–418.

Bonfante, G. (1967), 'La lingua delle atellane e dei mimi', *MAIA* 19, 3–21.

Boyle, A. J. (ed.) (1987), *Seneca's Phaedra*, Liverpool.

Boyle, A. J. (1993), *Roman Epic*, London.

Boyle, A. J. (ed.) (2011), *Seneca Oedipus*, Oxford.

Braun, L. (1981), 'La forza del visibile nelle tragedie di Seneca', *Dioniso* 52, 109–24.

Braund, S. M. and C. Gill (eds) (1997), *The Passions in Roman Thought and Literature*, Cambridge.

Browning, R. (1952), 'The Riot of A.D. 387 in Antioch: the Role of the Theatrical Claques in the Later Empire', *JRS* 42, 13–20.

Cairns, F. (1972), *Generic Composition in Greek and Roman Poetry*, Edinburgh.

Castagna, L. (ed.) (1996), *Nove studi sui cori tragici di Seneca*, Milano.

Cervellera, M. A. (1973), 'La cronologia delle tragedie di Seneca in relazione al trimetro recitativo', *Rivista di Cultura Classica e Medioevale* 15, 19–34.

Cicu, L. (1991), 'Componere Mimum', *Sandalion* 14, 103–41.

Cicu, L. (1998), *Problemi e strutture del mimo a Roma*, Sassari.

Cignolo, C. (ed.) (2002), *Terentiani Mauri: de litteris, de syllabis, de metris* (trans. C. Cignolo), Hildesheim, Zürich and New York.

Coffey, M. (1961), 'Seneca, *Apocolocyntosis* 1922–1958', *Lustrum* 6, 239–71.

Coleman, K. M. (1993), 'Launching into History: aquatic displays in the early empire', *JRS* 83, 48–74.

Comotti, G. (1989), *Music in Greek and Roman Culture*, Baltimore and London.

Courtney, E. (1962), 'Parody and Literary Allusion in Menippean Satire', *Philologus* 106, 86–100.

Csapo, E. and W. J. Slater (1994), *The Context of Ancient Drama*, Ann Arbor.

Dale, A. M. (1969), *Collected Papers*, Cambridge.

Davis, P. J. (1989), 'The Chorus in Seneca's *Thyestes*', *CQ* 39, 421–35.

Del Giudice, L. and N. Van Deusen (eds) (2005), *Performing Ecstasies: Music, Dance, and Ritual in the Mediterranean*, Ottawa.

Depew, M. and D. Obbink (eds) (2000), *Matrices of Genre*, Cambridge.

Dickie, M. W. (2001), 'Mimes, Thaumaturgy, and the Theatre', *CQ* 51, 599–603.

Dickison, S. K. (1977), 'Claudius: *Saturnalicius princeps*', *Latomus* 36, 634–47.

D'Ippolito, G. (1962), 'Draconzio, Nonno e gli idromimi', *Atene e Roma* 7, 1–14.

Dunbabin, K. (2004), 'Problems in the iconography of Roman Mime', in C. Hugoniot, F. Hurlet, and S. Milanezi (eds), *Le statut de l'acteur dans l'Antiquité greque et romaine*, 161–81, Tours.

Duncan, A. (2006), *Performance and Identity in the Classical World*, Cambridge.

Dupont, F. (1985), *L'acteur-roi*, Paris.

Easterling, P. (ed.) (1997), *The Cambridge Companion to Greek Tragedy*, Cambridge.

Easterling, P. and E. Hall (eds) (2002), *Greek and Roman Actors: aspects of an ancient profession*, Cambridge.

Eitrem, S. (1941), 'La magie comme motif litteraire chez les grecs et les romains', *SO* 21, 39–83.

Eitrem, S., L. Amudsen and R. P. Winnington-Ingram (1955), 'Fragments of Unknown Greek Tragic Texts with Musical Notation', *SO* 31, 1–87.

Elam, K. (1980), *The Semiotics of Theatre and Drama*, London.

Elia, O. (1965), 'Rappresentazione di un pantomimo nella pittura pompeiana', in *Gli Archeologi Italiani in Onore di Amedeo Maiuri*, 169–79, Cava dei Tirreni.

Elsner, J. and J. Masters (1994), *Reflections of Nero*, London.

Emmanuel, M. (1917), *The Antique Greek Dance after Sculptured and Painted Figures*, London.

Evans, E. C. (1935), 'Roman Descriptions of Personal Appearance in History and Biography', *HSCP* 46, 43–84.

Evans, E. C. (1941), 'The Study of Physiognomy in the Second Century A.D.', *TAPhA* 72, 96–108.

Evans, E. C. (1948), 'Literary Portraiture in Ancient Epic: a study of the descriptions of physical appearance in classical epic', *HSCP* 58, 189–217.

Evans, E. C. (1950), 'A Stoic Aspect of Senecan Drama: portraiture', *TAPhA* 81, 196–184.

Fantham, E. (1981), 'Seneca's *Troades* and *Agamemnon*: continuity and sequence', *CJ* 77, 118–29.

Fantham, E. (1996), *Roman Literary Culture*, Baltimore and London.

Fiorencis, G. and G. F. Gianotti (1990), 'Fedra e Ippolito in provincia', *MD* 25, 71–114.

Fitch, J. G. (1979), '*Pectus o nimium ferum*: Act V of Seneca's *Hercules Furens*', *Hermes* 107, 240–248.

Fitch, J. G. (1981), 'Notes on Seneca's *Hercules Furens*', *TAPhA* 111, 65–70.

Fitch, J. G. (1981), 'Sense-Pauses and Relative Dating in Seneca, Sophocles and Shakespeare', *AJPh* 102, 289–307.

Fitch, J. G. (2000), 'Playing Seneca?', in G. W. M. Harrison (ed.), *Seneca in Performance*, 1–12, London.

Fitch, J. G. (ed.) (2008), *Oxford Readings in Classical Studies: Seneca*, Oxford.

Franklin, J. L. (1987), 'Pantomimists at Pompeii: Actius Anicetus and His Troupe', *AJPh* 108, 95–107.

Frassinetti, P. (1953), *Fabula atellana: saggio sul teatro popolare latino*, Pavia.

Frassinetti, P. (ed.) (1967), *Atellanae Fabulae*, Roma.

Friedländer, L. (1862–71), *Darstellungen aus der Sittengeschichte Roms in der Zeit von Augustus bis zum Ausgang der Antonine*, Leipzig.

Gaffney, G. E. (1995), '*Severitati Respondere*: character drawing in *Pro Caelio* and Catullus' *Carmina*', *CJ* 90, 423–31.

Garelli, M.-H. (1995), 'Le danseur dans la cité', *REL* 73, 29–43.

Garelli, M.-H. (1996), 'Médèe et les mères en deuil: échos, renvois, symmetries dans le théâtre de Sénèque', *Pallas* 45, 191–204.

Garelli, M.-H. (1998), 'Rome et le tragique: questions', *Pallas* 49, 9–19.

Garelli, M.-H. (1998), 'À propos du *Thyeste* d'Ennius: tragédie et histoire', *Pallas* 49, 159–71.

Garelli, M.-H. (2000), 'Ludions, homéristes ou pantomimes?', *REA* 102, 501–8.

Garelli, M.-H. (2004), 'La pantomime antique ou les mythes revisités: le répertoire de Lucien (Danse, 38–60)', *Dioniso* 3, 108–19.

Gentili, B. (1979), *Theatrical Performances in the Ancient World*, Amsterdam.

Gianotti, G. (1991), 'Sulle tracce della pantomima tragica: Alcesti tra i danzatori?', *Dioniso* 61, 121–49.

Gigante, M. (2001), 'Seneca tragico da Pompei all'Egitto', *SIFC* 19, 89–104.

Gill, C. (1973), 'The Sexual Episodes in the *Satyricon*', *CPh* 68, 172–85.

Giomini, R. (ed.) (1956), *L. Annaei Senecae Agamemnona*, Roma.

Goldhill, S. and R. Osborne (eds) (1999), *Performance Culture and Athenian Democracy*, Cambridge.

Goldman, H. (1943), 'Two Terracotta Figurines from Tarsus', *AJA* 47, 22–34.

Graham, L. (2002), 'Modern Visions of Greek Tragic Dancing', *Theatre Journal* 55, 467–80.

Green, E. (1995), 'The Catullan Ego: Fragmentation and the Erotic Self', *AJPh* 116, 77–93.

Green, W. M. (1933), 'The Status of Actors at Rome', *CPh* 28, 301–4.

Grimal, P. (ed.) (1965), *L. Annaei Senecae Phaedra*, Paris.

Grimal, P. (1983), 'Sénèque: le théatre latin entre la scène et le livre', *Vita Latina* 89, 2–13.

Guillemin, A. (1941), 'L'évolution d'un cliché poétique', *REL* 20, 101–12.

Hahlbrock, P. (1968), 'Beobachtungen zum jambischen Trimeter in den Tragödien des L. Annaeus Seneca', *WS* 81, 171–92.

Hall, E. (2005), 'Aeschylus' Clytemnestra versus her Senecan Tradition', in F. Macintosh, P. Michelakis, E. Hall, and O. Taplin (eds), *Agamemnon in Performance*, 53–75, Oxford.

Hall, E. and R. Wyles (eds) (2008), *New Directions in Ancient Pantomime*, Oxford.

Handley, E. W. (1969), 'Notes on the *Theophoroumene* of Menander', *BICS* 16, 88–101.

Hardie, W. R. (1920), *Res Metrica*, Oxford.

Harrison, G. W. M. (ed.) (2000), *Seneca in Performance*, London.

Harrison, S. J. (ed.) (2001), *Texts, Ideas, and the Classics*, Oxford.

Haslam, M. W. (1986), *the Oxyrhynchus Papiri 53*, 41–8, Oxford and London.

Henry, D. and B. Walker (1963), 'Seneca and the *Agamemnon*: some thoughts on tragic doom', *CPh* 58, 1–10.

Henry, D. and B. Walker (1966), 'Phantasmagoria and Idyll: an element of Seneca's *Phaedra*', *G&R* 13, 223–39.

Herrmann, L. (1985), 'Laureolus', *Latomus* 187, 225–34.

Hill, D. E. (2000), 'Seneca's Choruses', *Mnemosyne* 53, 561–87.

Hinds, S. (1998), *Allusion and Intertext*, Cambridge.

Horsfall, N. (2003), *The Culture of the Roman Plebs*, London.

Horsfall, N. (1989), 'The Use of Literacy and the *Cena Trimalchionis*: I', *G&R* 36, 74–89.

Hugoniot, C., F. Hurlet and S. Milanezi (eds) (2004), *Le statut de l'acteur dans l'Antiquité grecque et romaine*, Tours. Hutcheon, L. (2006), *A theory of adaptation*, New York.

Huys, M. (1993), 'P. Oxy. LIII 3705: A Line from Menander's *Periceiromene* with Musical Notation', *ZPE* 99, 30–32.

Jannot, J.-R. (1985), 'De l'agôn au geste ritual. L'exemple de la boxe étrusque', *Antiquité Classique* 54, 66–75.

Jocelyn, H. D. (ed.) (1967), *The Tragedies of Ennius*, Cambridge.

Johnson, W. A. (2000), 'Musical Evenings in the Early Empire: new evidence from a Greek papyrus with musical notation', *JHS* 120, 57–85.

Jones, C. P. (1986), *Culture and Society in Lucian*, Cambridge.

Jory, E. J. (1963), 'Algebraic Notation in Dramatic Texts', *BICS* 10, 65–78.

Jory, E. J. (1966), 'Dominus Gregis?', *CPh* 61, 102–4.

Jory, E. J. (1970), 'Associations of Actors in Rome', *Hermes* 98, 224–53.

Jory, E. J. (1984), 'The Early Pantomime Riots', in A. Moffat (ed.), *Maistor, Classical, Byzantine and Renaissance Studies for Robert Browning*, 57–66, Canberra.

Jory, E. J. (1986), 'Continuity and Change in the Roman Theatre', in J. H. Betts, J. T. Hooker and J. R. Green (eds), *Studies in Honour of T. B. L. Webster*, vol. 1, 143–52, Bristol.

Jory, E. J. (1988), 'Publilius Syrus and the Element of Competition in the Theatre of the Republic', in N. Horsfall (ed.), *Vir Bonus Discendi Peritus: studies in celebration of Otto Skutsch's eightieth birthday*, (*BICS* Suppl. 51), 73–81, London.

Jory, E. J. (1996), 'The Drama of the Dance: Prolegomena to an Iconography of Imperial Pantomime', in W. J. Slater (ed.), *Roman Theatre and Society*, 1–27, Ann Arbor.

Jory, E. J. (2008), 'The Pantomime Dancer and His Libretto', in E. Hall and R. Wyles (eds), *New Directions in Ancient Pantomime*, 157–68, Oxford.

Keulen, A. (ed.) (2001), *L. Annaeus Seneca Troades*, Leiden.

Knight, W. F. J. (1932), 'Magical Motifs in Seneca's *Troades*', *TAPhA* 63, 20–33.

Knoche, U. (1971), *Die römische Satire*, Göttingen.

Knox, P. (2004), 'Cynthia's Ghosts in Propertius 4.7', *Ordia Prima* 3, 153–69.

Kokolakis, M. (1960), 'Lucian and the Tragic Performances in His Time', *Platon* 12, 3–45.

Kraemer, C. J. (1931), 'A Greek Element in Egyptian Dancing', *AJA* 35, 125–38.

Lada-Richards, I. (2003), 'Mobile Statuary: Refractions of Pantomime Dancing from Callistratus to Emma Hamilton and Andrew Ducrow', *International Journal of the Classical Tradition* 10, 3–37.

Lada-Richards, I. (2005), 'In the Mirror of the Dance: a Lucianic metaphor in its performative and ethical contexts', *Mnemosyne* 58, 335–57.

Lada-Richards, I. (2008), 'Was Pantomime "good to think with" in the Ancient World?', in E. Hall and R. Wyles (eds), *New Directions in Ancient Pantomime*, 285–313, Oxford.

Larson, V. T. (1989), 'Seneca's Epic Theatre', in C. Deroux (ed.), *Studies in Latin Literature and Roman History* vol. V, 279–304, Bruxelles.

Lawall, J. (1982), 'Death and Perspective in Seneca's *Troades*', *CJ* 77, 244–52.

Lawler, L. B. (1939), 'The Dance of the Owl and Its Significance in the History of Greek Religion and Drama', *TAPhA* 70, 482–502.

Lawler, L. B. (1943), 'Proteus is a Dancer', *Classical Weekly* 36, 116–17.

Lawler, L. B. (1944), 'The Dance of the Ancient Mariners', *TAPhA* 75, 20–33.

Lawler, L. B. (1945), 'Diphl, Dipodia, Dipodismos in the Greek Dance', *TAPhA* 76, 59–73.

Lawler, L. B. (1946), 'The Geranos Dance: a new interpretation', *TAPhA* 77, 112–30.

Lawler, L. B. (1950), 'Ladles, Tubs, and the Greek Dance', *AJPh* 71, 70–2.

Lawler, L. B. (1954), 'Phora, Schema, Deixis in the Greek Dance', *TAPhA* 85, 148–58.

Lebek, W. D. (1985), 'Senecas *Agamemnon* in Pompeji (CIL IV 6698)', *ZPE* 59, 1–6.

Leigh, M. (2004), 'The *Pro Caelio* and Comedy', *CPh* 99, 300–35.

Leucci, T. (2005), 'Nartakî. Figurina eburnea indiana ritrovata a Pompei', *Dioniso* 4, 142–9.

Littlewood, C. A. (1981), 'Poetic Artistry and Dynastic Politics: Ovid at the Megalenses (*Fasti* 4. 179–372)', *CQ* 31, 381–95.

Luque Moreno, J. (1996), 'Séneca musicus', in M. Rodriguez-Pantoja (ed.), *Séneca, dos mil años después: actas del Congreso internacional conmemorativo del bimilenario de su nacimiento*, 77–115, Córdoba.

Macintosh, F., P. Michelakis, E. Hall and O. Taplin (eds) (2005), *Agamemnon in Performance*, Oxford.

Maguinness, W. S. (1956), 'Seneca and the Poets', *Hermathena* 88, 81–98.

Marcucci, S. (1999), *Modelli 'tragici' e modelli 'epici' nell'Agamemnon di L. A. Seneca*, Milano.

Markus, D. and G. Schwendner (1997), 'Seneca's *Medea* in Egypt (663–704)', *ZPE* 117, 73–80.

Markus, D. and G. Schwendner (2000), 'Seneca, *Medea* 680: an Addendum to ZPE 117 (1997) 73–80', *ZPE* 132, 149–50.

Marmorale, E. (ed.) (1967), *Petronius: Satyricon*, Firenze.

Marshall, C. W. (2006), *The Stagecraft and Performance of Roman Comedy*, Cambridge.

Marti, B. M. (1945), 'Seneca's Tragedies: a new interpretation', *TAPhA* 76, 216–45.

Marti, B. M. (1947), 'The Prototypes of Seneca's Tragedies', *CPh* 42, 1–16.

Mastronarde, D. J. (1970), 'Seneca's *Oedipus*: the Drama in the Word', *TAPhA* 101, 291–315.

May, R. (2006), *Apuleius and Drama: the ass on stage*, Oxford.

May, R. (2008), 'The Metamorphosis of Pantomime: Apuleius' *Judgement of Paris* (*Met.* 10.30–34), in E. Hall and R. Wyles (eds), *New Directions in Ancient Pantomime*, 338–62, Oxford.

Mazzoli, L. (1961), 'Umanità e poesia nelle *Troiane* di Seneca', *MAIA* 13, 51–67.

McDonald, M. and J. M. Walton (eds) (2007), *The Cambridge Companion to Greek and Roman Theatre*, Cambridge.

Merchant, F. I. (1905), 'Seneca the Philosopher and His Theory of Style', *AJPh* 26, 44–59.

Mitchell, S. (1990), 'Review: Festivals, Games, and Civic Life in Roman Asia Minor', *JRS* 80, 183–93.

Molloy, M. E. (1996), *Libanius and the Dancers*, Hildesheim and New York.

Momigliano, A. (1944), 'Literary Chronology of the Neronian Age', *CQ* 38, 96–100.

Montiglio, S. (1999), 'Paroles dansées en silence: l'action signifiante de la pantomime et le moi du danseur', *Phoenix* 53, 263–80.

Moor, T. J. (1998), 'Music and Structure in Roman Comedy', *AJPh* 119, 245–73.

Moorman, E. M. (1983), 'Rappresentazione teatrali su *scaenae frontes* di quarto stile a Pompei', *Bollettino dell'Associazione Internazionale Amici di Pompei* 1, 73–117.

Owen, W. H. (1968), 'Commonplace and Dramatic Symbol in Seneca's Tragedies', *TAPhA* 99, 291–313.

Owen, W. H. (1970), 'The Excerpta Thuanea and the Form of Seneca's *Troades* 67–164', *Hermes* 98, 361–8.

Panayotakis, C. (1994), 'A Sacred Ceremony in Honour of the Buttocks: Petronius, *Satyrica* 140.1–11', *CQ* 44, 458–67.

Panayotakis, C. (1997), 'Baptism and Crucifixion on the Mimic Stage', *Mnemosyne* 50, 302–19.

Parker, L. P. E. (1997), *The Songs of Aristophanes*, Oxford.

Pavese, C. (1966), 'Un frammento di mimo in un nuovo papiro fiorentino', *SIFC* 38, 62–9.

Pearl, O. M. and R. P. Winnington-Ingram (1965), 'A Michigan Papyrus with Musical Notation', *JEA* 51, 179–95.

Picone, G. (2004), 'La scena doppia: spazi drammaturgici nel teatro di Seneca', *Dioniso* 3, 134–43.

Pighi, G. B. (1932), 'Il canto di Attis', *Rivista Musicale Italiana* 39, 34–40.

Pighi, G. B. (1963), 'Seneca metrico', *Rivista di Filologia Classica* 91, 170–81.

Poe, J. P. (1969), 'An Analysis of Seneca's *Thyestes*', *TAPhA* 100, 355–76.

Pöhlmann, E. and M. L. West (2001), *Documents of Ancient Greek Music*, Oxford.

Potter, D. S. and D. J. Mattingly (eds) (2002), *Life, Death, and Entertainment in the Roman Empire*, Ann Arbor.

Putnam, M. C. (1992), 'Virgil's Tragic Future: Senecan drama and the *Aeneid*', in *La storia, la letteratura e l'arte a Roma*, Mantova.

Raina, G. P. (1997), 'Rossore e pallore sul volto dei personaggi tragici senecani', *Paideia* LII, 275–92.

Rawson, E. (1991), *Roman Culture and Society*, 468–87, Oxford.

Rawson, E. (1993), 'The Vulgarity of the Roman Mime', in H.D. Jocelyn and H. Hurt (eds), 'Tria Lustra: essays and notes to John Pinsent', *Liverpool Classical Paper* 3, 255–60, Liverpool.

Relihan, J. C. (1984), 'On the Origin of the Menippean Satire as the Name of a Literary Genre', *CPh* 79, 226–9.

Ries, F. W. D. (1977), 'Plato on the Dance', *Dance Scope* 11, 2, 53–60

Ries, F. W. D. (1977–78), 'Roman Pantomine: practice and politics', *Dance Scope* 12, 1, 35–47.

Robert, L. (1930), 'Pantomimen im griechischen Orient', *Hermes* 65, 106–22.

Robert, L. (1981), 'Amulettes grecques', *Journal des Savants*, 35–44.

Romano, D. (1991), '*Laserpiciarius mimus*: Petronio, *Sat.* 35,7', *Dioniso* 61, 289–94.

Rosati, G. (2006), '*Libido amandi* e *libido regnandi*, ovvero elegia e potere nel teatro senecano', *Dioniso* 5, 94–106.

Rose, A. R. (1985), 'Seneca's Dawn Song (*Hercules Furens*, 125–58) and the Imagery of Cosmic Disruption', *Latomus* 44, 101–23.

Runchina, G. (1960), *Tecnica drammatica e retorica nelle tragedie di Seneca*, Cagliari.

Sahin, S. (1975), 'Das Grabmal des Pantomimen Krispos in Herakleia Pontile', *ZPE* 18, 293–7.

Salvatore, A. (1981), 'La pars secreta di Diana nella *Fedra* di Seneca', *Orpheus* II, 29–57.

Sandy, G. N. (1969), 'Satire in the *Satyricon*', *AJPh* 90, 293–303.

Sandy, G. N. (1970), 'Petronius and the Tradition of the Interpolated Narrative', *TAPhA* 101, 463–76.

Sandys, J. F. (ed.) (1885), *M. Tulli Ciceronis ad M. Brutum Orator*, Cambridge.

Savarese, N. (2002–2003), 'L'orazione di Libanio in difesa della pantomima', *Dioniso* 2, 84–107.

Savarese, N. (ed.) (1996), *Teatri romani*, Bologna.

Schein, S. L. (1982), 'The Cassandra Scene in Aeschylus' *Agamemnon*', *G&R* 29, 11–16.

Schetter, W. (1965), 'Sulla struttura delle *Troiane* di Seneca', *RFIC* 93, 396–429.

Schmitt, J-C. (1989), 'The Ethics of Gesture' in M. Feher, R. Naddaff, and N. Tazi (eds), *Fragments for a History of the Human Body 2*, 129–47, New York.

Sear, F. (2006), *Roman Theatres: an Architectural Study*, Oxford.

Setaioli, A. (2003), 'Le due poesie in sotadei di Petronio (*Sat.* 23.3; 132.8)', *Cuadernos de Filología Clásica, Estudios Latinos* 23, 89–106.

Slater, N.W. (1987), '*Satyricon* 80.9: Petronius and Manuscript Illustrations', *CJ* 82, 216–17.

Slater, W. J. (1991), *Dining in a Classical Context*, Ann Arbor.

Slater, W. J. (1993), 'Three Problems in the History of Drama', *Phoenix* 47, 189–212.

Slater, W. J. (1994), 'Features: Beyond Spoken Drama', *Didaskalia* 1.2.

Slater, W. J. (ed.) (1996), *Roman Theater and Society*. Ann Arbor.

Solimano, G. (1980), 'Il mito di Orfeo-Ippolito in Seneca', *Sandalion* 3, 151–74.

Sonkowsky, R. P. (1959), 'An Aspect of Delivery in Ancient Rhetorical Theory', *TAPhA* 90, 256–74.

Stanford, W. B. (1983), *Greek Tragedy and the Emotions*, London.

Starks, J. H. (2008), 'Pantomime Actress in Latin Inscriptions', in E. Hall and R. Wyles (eds), *New Directions in Ancient Pantomime*, 110–45, Oxford.

Steinmetz, P. (1970), 'Ein metrisches Experiment Seneca's', *Museum Helveticum* 27, 97–103.

Stemplinger, E. (1918), 'Der Mimus in horazischen Lyrik', *Philologus* 75, 466–9.

Strong, E. and N. Jolliffe (1924), 'The Stuccoes of the Underground Basilica near the Porta Maggiore', *JHS* 44, 65–111.

Sullivan, J. P. (1968), 'Petronius, Seneca, and Lucan: a Neronian literary feud?', *TAPhA* 99, 453–67.

Sullivan, J. P. (1991), *Martial: the unexpected classic*, 56–77, Cambridge.

Sutton, D. F. (1984), 'Cicero on Minor Dramatic Forms', *SO* 59, 29–36.

Traversari, G. (1950), 'Tetimimo e Colimbétra: ultime manifestazioni del teatro antico', *Dioniso* 13, 18–34.

Trombino, R. (1988), '*Phaedra* on the Stage', *Dioniso* 58, 137–40.

Turner, E. G. (1963), 'Dramatic Representations in Graeco-Roman Egypt: how long do they continue?', *Antiquité Classique* 32, 120–8.

Ullman, B. L. (1914), 'Dramatic Satura', *CPh* 9, 1–23.

Vogt-Spira, G. (ed.) (1989), *Studien zur vorliterarischen Periode im frühen Rom*, Tübingen.

Welborn, L. L. (2002), 'Μωρὸς γένεσθω: Paul's Appropriation of the Role of the Fool in 1 Corinthians 1–4', *Biblical Interpretation* 10, 420–35.

Westermann, W. L. (1924), 'The Castanet Dancers of Arsinoe', *JEA* 10, 134–44.

Westermann, W. L. (1932), 'Entertainment in the Villages of Graeco-Roman Egypt', *JEA* 18, 16–27.

Wille, G. (1967), *Musica Romana*, Amsterdam.

Williams, G. (1992), 'Poet and Audience in Senecan Tragedy: *Phaedra* 358–430', in T. Woodman and J. Powell (eds), *Author and Audience in Latin Literature*, 138–49, Cambridge.

Winkler, J. J. (1991), *Auctor & Actor*, Berkley.

Wiseman, T. P. (1984), 'Cybele, Virgil and Augustus', in T. Woodman and D. West (eds), *Poetry and Politics in the Age of Augustus*, 117–28, Cambridge.

Wiseman, T. P. (1985), *Cinna and the Poet and Other Roman Essays*, 130–7, Leicester.

Wiseman, T. P. (1988), 'Satyrs in Rome? the background to Horace's *Ars Poetica*', *JRS* 78, 1–13.

Wiseman, T. P. (1998), *Roman Drama and Roman History*, Exeter.

Xanthakis-Karamanos, G. (1979), 'The Influence of Rhetoric on Fourth-Century Tragedy', *CQ* 29, 66–76.

Zerba, M. (2002), 'Love, Envy, and Pantomimic Morality in Cicero's *De oratore*', *CPh* 97, 299–321.

Zorzetti, N. (1991), 'Poetry and Ancient City: the Case of Rome', *CJ* 86, 311–29.

Zwierlein, O. (1969), 'Kritisches und exegetisches zu den Tragödien Senecas', *Philologus* 113, 256–67.

Zwierlein, O. (1977), 'Weiteres zum Seneca Tragicus (I)', *WJA* N. F. 3, 149–77.

Zwierlein, O. (1978), 'Weiteres zum Seneca Tragicus (II)', *WJA* N. F. 4, 143–61.

Zwierlein, O. (1979), 'Weiteres zum Seneca Tragicus (III)', *WJA* N. F. 5, 163–87.

Zwierlein, O. (1980), 'Weiteres zum Seneca Tragicus (IV)', *WJA* N. F. 6a, 181–95.

Zwierlein, O. (1984), *Prolegomena zu einer kritischen Ausgabe der Tragödien Senecas*, (Abh. Akad. Mainz, Geistes-und Sozialwiss. Klasse Jg.1983, Nr. 3), Wiesbaden.

Zwierlein, O. (1987), 'Seneca, *Medea* 616–621', *Hermes* 115, 382–4.

Index of Ancient Authors

Aeschylus: *Agamemnon* (530 ff.) 80; (636–80) 148, 193–4; (659) 251n. 129, 251n. 130; (660) 251n. 129, 251n. 130; (672) 251n. 129, 251n. 130; (673) 251n. 129, 251n. 130; (1085 ff.) 132; (1577 ff.) 80; *Persians* (619–84) 251n. 124; (694–6) 99; (700–2) 99

Apuleius: *Apologia* (78, 3 ff.) 13, 235n. 24; (10) 219n. 153; and Corinth 227n. 257; *Met.* (1, 15, 2) 40, 224n. 209; (6) 232n. 55; (9, 23, 26) 30; (10, 32) 9, 93, 212n. 54; (10, 2–12) 23–4, 46, 224n. 213; (10, 30–4) 46–51, 212n. 51, 213n. 76

Aristotle vii, 69, 137, 228n. 14

Arnobius: *Adv. Nat.* (VII, 33) 217n. 124

Athenaeus: *Deipnosophistae* (I, 20d) 3, 208n. 12; (I, 20d–e) 207n. 6; (I, 20–1) 5, 210n. 36, 219n. 143; (XIV, 62e) 218n. 134

Augustine: *De civitate dei* (6, 7) 37; (6, 10) 216n. 103; (6, 75) 225n. 220; (18, 10) 226n. 246; *De doctrina christiana* (2, 4, 5) 9, 212n. 54; *De magistro* (3, 5) 8, 211n. 47; *Sermones* (241, 5) 213n. 73, 234n. 8, 246n. 35; (311, VII, 7) 11, 212n. 60

Cassiodorus: *Variae* (4, 51, 9) 6, 211n. 42

Catullus 25–9; (63) 100; and galliambics 236n. 37; and *Garland* of Meleager 216n. 116, 217n. 117; genre of 216n. 111; on Lesbia/Clodia 219n. 153; and *Megalensia* 218n. 133; (63, 11–26) 28; (63, 73) 99; (68, 56) 114; *Phasma* (title of a mime) 224n. 211

Choricius of Gaza: adultery-mime (30) 46, 225n. 213; *Apologia mimorum* (mimic trial) 32; mimic *convivia* (110) 45, 232n. 52

Cicero: *Acad.* (2, 105) 196, 251n. 135; *Ad Att.* (I, 16, 13) 41, 224n. 211; in Jerome (*Ep.* 52, 8, 3) 44; *Brutus* (225) 214n. 87; (278) 214n. 82; *De orat.* (1, 151), (3, 188) 20, 29–31; (2, 193) 9, 212n. 53; (2, 239), (2, 251), (3, 214) 18; (3, 216), (3, 222) 17; (3, 220) 215n. 94; (3, 222) 17; *In Pisonem* (X, 22) 227n. 249, 232n. 57; *In Verrem* (III, 36, 83) 219n. 148; *Orat.* (57, 175, 229) 20, 29–31; (18, 59), 215n. 94; *Phil.* (II, 27, 65) 226n. 238, 232n. 58; *Pro Caelio* (1) 219n. 145; (18) 219n. 153; (63, 4), (65, 6), (67) 30; (65) 37–8, 223n. 190; (68) 219n. 150; *Pro Rabirio Postumo* (35) 208n. 18, 219n. 152; *Pro Sestio* (54, 116) 31

Claudian: *In Eutropium* (2, 402–5) 213n. 80, 233n. 67; *In Rufinum* (2, 355–7) 196, 251n. 136

Dio Cassius: *Historia Romana* (54, 17, 5) 4, 209n. 22, 210n. 37; (60, 35, 2 ff.) 224n. 207

Ennius: *Medea exul* (246 Vahlen) 219n. 153; (Var. 25–9 Vahlen) 218n. 135

Euripides vii: *Alcestis* (244–72) 132; *Bacchae* 99; (1122–3) 236n. 44; divinity in prologue 78; *Hecuba* 185, 251n. 124; (1109–30) 80; (523–79)

176, 177; (524) 248n. 91; (566–8)
186; (568–70) 186; 726ff. 243n. 36;
Heracles 70, 156; *Hippolytus* 247n.
55; (208–3) 132; (1173–248) 162, 163;
Medea (277–80) 243n. 36; (1173–4)
236n. 44; monologues 129; *Orestes*
(356 ff.) 80; (669 ff.) 243n. 36; (1554
ff.) 80; *Philoctetes* (572 ff.), 243n. 36;
Phoenician Women 73; (261–77) 80;
similes 130; *Suppliants* (1034 ff.) 80;
Trojan Women (153 ff.) 85, 86; (173)
101; (860 ff.) 80; (1117–24) 176, 177;
(1119–22) 180; (1133–5) 180; (1173–4)
182; (1176–7) 182

Fronto: *On Orations* (4) 9–10, 212n.
55

Gellius, Aulius: *Noctes Atticae* (1, 5, 2),
214n. 86; (1, 11, 12) 208n. 9; (10, 24,
10) 216n. 103; (16, 7, 10) 45, 226n.
234; (16, 7, 17) 249n. 105; (20, 6, 6)
249n. 105

Hephaestion: *Enchiridion* (12, 3) 25, 99,
216n. 113, 216n. 115, 236n. 36
Horace vii: *Carm.* (3, 6, 21–4) 207n. 5;
coram populo 137; *Epist.* (II, 2, 124–5)
3; *Serm.* (I, 2, 58–9) 219n. 148; (I, 2,
127–34) 32; (I, 5, 63) 22, 222n. 186,
248n. 80; (I, 10, 5–6) 22; (II, 7, 58–61)
32; (II, 7, 59) 30

Isidore of Seville: *Etymologiae* (18, 49)
8, 201, 211n. 48, 232n. 51, 232n. 52,
253n. 2

Jacob of Serugh: *Hom.* (5, F22vb) 221n.
168
Jerome: *Annotations to Eusebius'
Chronicon* (Ol. 180, 3) 3, 208n. 17; *Ep.*
(52, 8, 3) 44

Juvenal: *Sat.* (1, 36) 220n. 161; (6, 1–3)
218n. 140; (6, 41–4) 32, 33, 220n.
158; (6, 44) 30; (6, 63) 222n. 186, 227n.
251; (6, 63–6) 218n. 141; (6, 275–9)
221n. 163; (7, 86–7) 14, 213n. 74,
252n. 1

Laberius 3: *Anna Peranna* 45, 226n. 234;
(frag. 10) 37; *Belonistria* 23; *Cancer*
224n. 212; *Compitalia* (frag. 3) 29, 32;
(frag. 176) 36; Horace on 22; Laberius
and Clodius 31; *Necyomantia* 249n.
105; and *Lacus Avernus* 41; *Nuptiae*
43; *prologue* (155–61, 167–70) in
Macrobius, *Sat.* (II, 7, 1–9) 84
Libanius: *Oration* 64; (67) 16, 36, 238n.
67, 239n. 79; (68–9) 11; (70) 157; (80)
207n. 3; (103) 10, 175; (104) 10; (105)
10; (113) 7; (116) 7, 15, 150; (118) 11;
pantomimic themes 12
Livy (7, 2) 208n. 18
Lucan: *Phar.* (1, 543–4) 207n. 1, 248n.
83; (5, 446) 196, 251n. 135; *salticae
fabulae* x, 14, 201, 213n. 74, 252n. 1
Lucian: *De mercede conductis* (27) 207n.
5, 218n. 140; *De Saltatione* (2) 115; (9)
12; (11) 212n. 67; (19) 7, 199, 211n.
43, 211n. 45, 233n. 63, 245n. 21, 246n.
27; (26) 9; (29) 9; (31) 206n. 11; (32)
209n. 25; (34) 3, 208n. 16; (35) ix, 15,
19, 22; (36) 22; (37) 11, 221n. 175;
(37–61) 12; (38) 210n. 32, 212n. 67;
(39) 13, 211n. 43, 248n. 84; (40) 13,
235n. 24; (41) 4, 13, 103, 157, 211n.
43, 217n. 126, 239n. 73; (42) 237n. 50;
(43) 13, 240n. 90, 241n. 106, 248n.
83; (45) 226n. 246; (46) 194, 213n. 73,
217n. 126, 234n. 8; (48) 211n. 43; (50)
13, 36, 119; (51) 13, 248n. 84; (52–3)
235n. 24; (53) 13, 248n. 84; (57) 211n.
43; (60) 34, 157, 211n. 46; (61) 14, 90;
(63) 9, 10, 34; (63–4) 16; (64) 209n. 24;

(65) ix, 19; (66) 6; (67) 6, 12, 16, 234n. 13, 248n. 83; (68) 8, 9; (69) 10; (71) 10; (72) 9, 226n. 246; (75) 10; (80) 11, 13, 234n. 16, 248n. 84; (83) 8, 47, 231n. 50; (83–4) 13; *Rhetorum praeceptor* (15) 215n. 96

Lycophron: *Alexandra* (361–97) 194

Macrobius: *Sat.* (II, 6, 6) 31, 220n. 156; (II, 7) 209n. 22; (II, 7, 12) 3, 208n. 15, 240n. 90; (II, 7, 12 ff.), 118; (II, 7, 13–16) 6, 211n. 41; (II, 7, 16) 14, 103, 210n. 36, 237n. 50; (II, 7, 16–18) 4, 209n. 21; (II, 7, 18) 3, 208n. 14; (III, 14) 214n. 83; (III, 14, 5) 219n. 154; (III, 14, 12) 17, 214n. 84; (V, 17, 5) 115, 213n. 73, 234n. 8; (XIV) 218n. 139

Manilius: *Astronomica* (5, 483) 84, 232n. 57

Martial: *Ep.* (1, 4, 5–6) 220n. 161; (2, 86, 1–5) 27, 218n. 136; (3, 29) 218n. 135; (9, 2, 13) 218n. 138; (14, 203) 212n. 68

Minucius Felix: *Oct.* (23, 2) 36, 222n. 179; (37, 12) 220n. 158

Nonnus: *Dionysiaca* (1, 29–30) 252n. 147; (5, 104–7) 15, 212n. 54; (19, 226) 199, 252n. 146; (19, 288–95) 199, 211n. 44

Ovid: *A.A.* (3, 346) 221n. 172; (3, 605–8) 223n. 188; *Am.* (1, 7, 57–8) 114–15; (2, 4, 8) 135; (2, 4, 29–32) 13, 212n. 68, 227n. 251; (3, 4) 33, 34; *Fasti* (3, 535–8) 37; (3, 544–656), 45; *Her.* (4, 41–4) 242n. 13; (7) 221n. 173; (10) 221n. 173; (11, 75) 196; (15, 12) 134; language of the body 87, 234n. 70; *Med.* (frag.) 235n. 21; *Met.* (1, 3–4) 221n. 175; (1, 533–8) 138; (2, 161–2) 246n. 47; (2, 508 ff.) 228n. 11; (2, 760–96) 245n. 20;

(2, 852–3) 114–15; (3, 259 ff.) 228n. 11; (3, 683–6) 251n. 137; (4, 64) 114; (4, 420 ff.) 228n. 11; (4, 484–5) 245n. 20; (5, 164–7) 173; (7, 18–21) 242n. 11; (7, 19–21) 243n. 19; (7, 220–33) 241n. 99; (8, 465–6) 235n. 26; (8, 470–2) 243n. 20, 243n. 25; (8, 506–11) 242n. 11; (8, 799–822) 245n. 20; (11, 474–572) 194; (11, 490–1) 252n. 142; (11, 501–15) 197; (11, 507) 197; (11, 592–649) 245n. 20; (12, 39–63) 245n. 20; (13, 415–17) 249n. 94; (13, 449–82) 248n. 87; (13, 474–5) 249n. 96; (13, 476) 186; (13, 479–80) 186; (13, 547–9) 235n. 27; (13, 561–4) 118; (13, 867–9) 134; (15, 497–529) 162; (15, 508–11) 247n. 62; (15, 511–13) 166, 247n. 57; mime and pantomime in 34–8; *Polyxena* 185; *Rem.* (751–8) 12; (755) 222n. 186; (751–66) 226n. 245; *Tr.* (2, 497–500) 32; (2, 505–6) 32; (2, 515), 220n. 158; (2, 519) 90; (2, 519–20) 14; (5, 7) 205n. 2; (5, 25–8) 205n. 2; (14, 24) 196

Pacuvius: *Teucer* (the storm) 194
Paterculus, Velleius: *Historia Romana* (2, 83, 2) 211n. 44, 222n. 186
Paul (apostle): *Corinthians* (2) 50–1
Persius: *Satires* (1, 105) 210n. 32; (5, 122–3) 210n. 36
Petronius: *Sat.* ix–x, 25; (16–26) 42–6; (23, 3) 28, 218n. 135; (26–78) 42–6; (39, 12) 40, 224n. 209; (45) 221n. 163; (55) 29; (69) 221n. 163; (89) 162; (99–115) 42–6; (106–7) 224n. 213; (117) 42–6; (132, 8) 218n. 135; dance pattern 76; genre complexity 225n. 215, 225n. 221; Publilius in 219n. 149; reversal of fortune 232n. 58
Plautus: *Amph.* (168 ff.) 218n. 135; (551 ff.) 80; *Capt.* (3, 4) 226n. 231; *Cas.* (685 ff.) 243n. 36; *Curc.* (2, 3, 44) 226n.

231; *Mg* (667) 218n. 139; *Poen* (647 ff., 653 ff.) 243n. 36; (1317–20) 218n. 139; *Ps.* (1, 2, 33) 226n. 231; *Rud.* (160 ff.) 241n. 101; *Stich.* (58–67 ff.) 80; (68–74) 80; (75–85) 80; (769–70) 207n. 5; *Trinum.* (843 ff.) 80

Pliny the Elder: *Nat. Hist.* (VIII, 209) 44, 45

Pliny the Younger: *Epist.* (IX, 34) 215n. 95

Plutarch: *Cicero* (5) 214n. 83; *Quaest. Conv.* 5; (B IX, 15, 2) 7; (711e) 8, 47, 231n. 50

Propertius: *Eleg.* (2, 23, 9–10) 33; (2, 23, 19–20) 33; (3, 15) 33; (3, 15, 5–6) 221n. 165, 221n. 172; (4, 8) 33

Publilius Syrus: inclusion in tragedy ix; influence on Seneca 71; literary dimension 3; in Petronius *Sat.* (55) 29, 44, 219n. 149, 225n. 226; praised by Seneca 22, 206n. 15; *sententiae* 82, 84, 231n. 48; *Sumen* 45

Quintilian: *Inst. Orat.* (1, 11, 1) 18; (1, 11, 2) 214n. 88; (1, 11, 3) 214n. 89; (1, 11, 19) 214n. 93; (6, 3, 29) 214n. 85; (6, 3, 65) 8, 82, 212n. 49, 231n. 50; (9, 4, 142) 21; (11, 1, 55) 19; (11, 3, 57–60) 21; (11, 3, 66) 17; (11, 3, 75) 93; (11, 3, 88) 20; (11, 3, 88–9) 24, 216n. 109; (11, 3, 89) 214n. 93; (11, 3, 114), 241n. 97; (11, 3, 181) 214n. 93; (11, 3, 182) 227n. 250; (11, 3, 184) 19, 214n. 91

Seneca the Elder: *Controv.* (2, 4, 5) 220n. 158, 225n. 224; (3, *praef.* 10) 11, 212n. 59; (7, 3, 8), 231n. 48; *Suas.* (2, 19) 213n. 74, 252n. 1

Seneca the Younger: *Apoc.* 39–41; *De Brevitate Vitae* (12, 8) 232n. 58; *De Ira* (1, 1, 3–4) 235n. 22; (2, 2, 4–5) 45, 194; (2, 11, 3) 224n. 212, 234n. 14; *De Tranquillitate Animi* (11, 8) 22, 206n.

15; *Epist.* (8, 8) 22, 206n. 15; (15, 9) 40; (80, 1) ix; (108, 8) 82; (114, 6) 226n. 238; (121, 6) viii, 93; (122, 19) 242n. 17; *N.Q.* (7, 32, 2–3) 206n. 10, 211n. 39

Sidonius Apollinaris: *Carmina* (23, 272–3) 235n. 24; (23, 277–80) 248n. 83; (23, 277–99) 13

Silo: *salticae fabulae* 14, 201, 213n. 74, 252n. 1

Sophocles: *Ajax* 13; *Oedipus* 125, 186, 239n. 71, 249n. 104; *Oedipus at Colonus* 73; *Polyxena* 185; *Women of Trachis* 119

Statius: *Agave* 14, 201, 213n. 74, 252n. 1

Suetonius: *Augustus* (45, 4) 211n. 40; *Claudius* (2, 2; 3, 2; 15, 4; 38, 3) 224n. 205; *De Poetis* (frag. 3) 3, 208n. 13; *Gaius* (11) 210n. 30; (54) 210n. 30; (55) 210n. 30; (57) 226n. 236; *Nero* (6, 3) 210n. 32; (21) 118, 239n. 74; (21, 3) 210n. 32; (33, 1) 40; (54) 5, 210n. 33, 207n. 19; (54, 1) 213n. 73, 234n. 8; *Tiberius* (37, 2) 210n. 29; *Vesp.* (19) 223n. 200

Tacitus: *Ann.* (1, 54, 2) 210n. 37; (1, 54, 77) 209n. 25; (1, 77) 209n. 28, 210n. 29; (13, 3) ix; (14, 52) x, 207n. 18; *Dial.* (26, 2–3) 20, 215n. 95, 215n. 96; (26, 3) 238n. 66

Terentianus Maurus: *De Metris* (2899–900) 99, 236n. 33

Terentius: *Ad.* (548) 243n. 36

Tertullian: *Ad Nat.* (1, 10, 45), 36, 222n. 179; *Apol.* (15, 1) 220n. 158; (15, 2) 36, 222n. 179, 226n. 246; (15, 5) 217n. 124

Varro: *Antiquitates rerum divinarum* 36, 222n. 178, 209n. 18; *Eumenides* 99, 218n. 132; *Ling.* (7, 95) 248n. 81; poems in sotadeans 218n. 135; *Synephebus* (frag. 3) 4, 213n. 69

Virgil: *Aen.* (1, 37 ff.) 228n. 11; (1, 81–156) 194; (1, 82–3) 198; (1, 82–6) 252n. 142; (1, 90) 247n. 49; (1, 104–17) 197; (2) 162; (2, 206–8) 166; (3, 192–208) 194; (3, 626–7) 175; (3, 630–2) 175; (4) 134; (4, 1–5) 114, 242n. 16; (4, 2) 243n. 18; (4, 15–23) 242n. 11; (4, 65) 24; (4, 66–9) 114, 238n. 65; (4, 74–89) 114; (6, 46–51) 102; (6, 48) 252n. 139; (6, 49) 236n. 45; (6, 77) 101; (6, 86–7) 239n. 83; (6, 126–9), 158; (6, 237) 158; (6, 237–8) 249n. 107; (6, 243 ff.) 189; (6, 255–8) 191; (6, 274–7) 153, 160, 245n. 20; (6, 282–4) 249n. 108; (6, 298–301) 160; (6, 309–12) 250n. 116; (6, 557–8) 171; (7, 9) 196; (7, 293 ff.) 228n. 11; (7, 170–91), 247n. 68; (7, 569–70) 158; (12, 64–70) 242n. 2; (12, 665–71) 242n. 2; (12, 749–57) 138; *Egl.* (1, 24–5) 250n. 109; *Georg.* (1, 201–3) 135; (1, 356–9) 252n. 141; (3, 232–4) 166; (4, 471–4) 250n. 116; *katabasis* 246n. 35; Turnus x, 5; Virgilian cento 241n. 100

Xenophon: *Symp.* (9, 43) 2

Zosimus: *Historia Nova* (I, 6) 3, 208n. 16

General Index

abstractions, personification of 114,
130–2, 135, 136, 151, 153, 155, 159, 160,
192, 245n. 20, 250n. 114

adultery-mime 1, 3, 23, 30, 46, 119, 220n.
159, 223n. 188, 239n. 78; in the Elegiac
poets 32–4

Aeneas, pantomimic representation of:
descent to the Underworld 246n. 35;
wanderings 213n. 73, 234n. 8

Agamemnon, murder of: in pantomime
6, 13, 211n. 41, 240n. 90; in Seneca
120–3

alien technique, importation into drama
of 90

anapaests, colometry of 106–8, 141, 233n.
68, 237n. 56, 243n. 26

Ares and Aphrodite, love of in
pantomime 34, 221n. 169

asyndeton 97, 102, 120, 133, 145, 235n. 23

Attis 13, 25–9, 36, 100, 176, 210n. 32,
217n. 121, 218n. 136, 236n. 33, 236n.
40, 236n. 41

Augustus (Roman emperor) 3–6, 8, 34,
82, 209n. 21, 209n. 25, 210n. 34, 211n.
40

Bacchus 36, 84–5

Bathyllus (dancer) 3–6, 29, 210n. 36,
210n. 37, 218n. 141

bodily symptoms, portrayal of 93, 113,
116

Cadmus, metamorphosis of 211n. 43

Cassandra: clairvoyant vision of 72, 73,
74, 111, 112, 120–3, 205n. 3, 239n.

82, 239n. 83, 240n. 92; representation
of prophetic *furor* of 78, 89, 91, 93,
100–3, 205n. 3

Cerberus 151, 153, 155, 156, 157, 161,
162, 191, 247n. 51, 250n. 112

Charition-mime 22–3, 45, 216n. 106

Charon 151, 155, 159–60

cinaedus 27–8, 43, 207n. 5, 218n.
134, 218n. 136, 218n. 138, 218n.
139, 218n. 140, 225n. 223 *see also*
gallus

Claudius (Roman emperor) 5, 38–42, 50,
224n. 204, 224n. 205, 224n. 207

Clodia, presentation as *meretrix/mima*
29–31

Clytemnestra, self-analysis of 132, 133,
135–6, 144, 198–9, 243n. 25

declamation x, 19–20, 84, 206n. 16, 231n.
43

Deianira, representation of jealousy of:
in pantomime 13, 37, 119, 223n. 188,
239n. 79; in Seneca 118–20

Dido: influence on Seneca's Phaedra 114–
15, 134; pantomimic representation of
115, 213n. 73, 234n. 8

Dionysus, role in pantomime 210n. 36,
212n. 52

dismemberment/*sparagmos*: Astyanax
182; Hippolytus 168; in pantomime
13, 175–6, 248n. 83, 248n. 84; in
Seneca 164–5; Thyestes' sons 174–6

doubling of themes 73–4, 230n. 28

dramatic time, acceleration/suspension of
53, 73, 80, 89

ecphrasis topou 15, 48, 77, 149, 156–7, 158, 161, 164, 168, 169, 178, 180, 182, 188, 213n. 76

emotions: externalization of 93, 97, 116; representation of viii–ix, 6, 12, 13, 24, 70, 86, 92–4, 103, 113, 114, 115, 119, 141, 202, 206n. 10

emotionally charged themes, preference for 12, 73, 118

Eucharis (dancer) 31, 220n. 155

extispicium 169, 173

fluidity of setting 53, 76–7, 105, 126, 150, 187, 230n. 35, 230n. 37, 241n. 102

formulaic vocabulary 16, 87, 94, 96, 191

furor 12, 13, 89, 92, 100, 101, 113, 114, 116, 119, 120, 121, 131, 134–5, 137, 199, 217n. 121, 217n. 127, 220n. 158, 230n. 28, 235n. 22

galliambics 25–9, 95, 99–100, 218n. 132, 218n. 136, 236n. 33, 236n. 34, 236n. 37

gallus/galli/gallae 26–8, 99–100, 216n. 116, 217n. 124, 217n. 128, 218n. 137, 222n. 179, 236n. 33, 236n. 34

generic enrichment viii–x, 21–4, 201

gestural dialogue 82 *see also interpellator*

Greek tragedy, comparison with vii, 71, 80, 83, 89, 111, 121, 144, 147–8, 153, 205n. 4, 251n. 124

Hercules, representation of madness of: in pantomime 13, 14, 103, 209n. 21, 213n. 71, 210n. 32, 210n. 36, 217n. 126, 237n. 50; in Seneca 103–5

hybrid ix, 14, 15, 21, 23, 90, 213n. 75

Hylas (dancer) 4, 6, 118, 211n. 40, 211n. 41, 240n. 90

iactare manus/artus (*vox propria* for pantomime) 37, 115, 238n. 66

imagery, set repertoire of 94 *see also* maenad; wild animal

imaginary landscape 7, 149, 154, 159

incantation scene (*Medea*) 60, 73, 111, 123–5, 186, 190, 229n. 21, 241n. 99, 247n. 65

interpellator 8, 82, 212n. 49

Judgment of Paris, Apuleius' description of 46–51, 226n. 246

language of the body 87, 97, 118, 202, 239n. 71

Laius, necromancy of 125, 147, 149, 186–93, 229n. 21, 230n. 26, 249n. 104

libretti (*fabulae salticae*) x, 6, 9, 10, 14–17, 22, 38, 47, 48, 90, 93, 123, 129, 131, 150, 157, 168, 201, 210n. 32, 213n. 72, 213n. 74, 221n. 173, 226n. 244, 232n. 52, 234n. 6, 234n. 7, 244n. 12, 246n. 34, 252n. 1, 253n. 2

ludus talarius 2, 207n. 6

Maecenas 5, 209n. 25, 210n. 37

maenad, comparison with 94: Andromache 106; Cassandra 101–2; Deianira 120; Medea 96–8

Magna Mater (*Cybele*) 25–9, 36, 99–100, 217n. 117, 217n. 124, 218n. 132, 218n. 138, 222n. 179, 236n. 33, 236n. 36

Manto 64, 187

Mars and Venus, love of 34 *see also* Ares and Aphrodite

Medea, representation of *furor* of: in pantomime 13, 97, 235n. 24; in Seneca 95–7, 97–100

Megalesia/Ludi Megalenses 29, 216n. 11, 218n. 133, 236n. 36

mime, sister art of pantomime xi, 2, 84, 251n. 128

mimicum naufragium 45, 194, 199, 251n. 128

Mnester (dancer) 5, 40, 210n. 30, 210n. 31

monologues, prominence of in Seneca's tragedies 53, 77–81

musical accompaniment 3, 16, 44, 93, 103, 108, 154, 208n. 13, 208n. 14, 225n. 227

mute performance 6, 15, 91, 92: Astyanax 106; Cassandra 101; Hecuba 110; Polyxena 109

myth, climactic moment of 14, 16, 71

natural elements, animation of 151, 153–4, 158, 159, 168–70, 174, 188, 190–1, 196, 245n. 24

nautical imagery, recurrent use of 136, 138, 143, 198–9, 242n. 17, 243n. 34, 252n. 144, 252n. 145

Nero (Roman emperor) x, 5, 38, 40, 118, 207n. 18, 207n. 19, 210n. 32, 210n.33, 210n.34, 213n. 73, 223n. 194, 234n. 8, 239n. 74

Oedipus, representation of self-blinding of: in pantomime 6, 13, 118, 210n. 32, 211n. 41, 239n. 73, 239n.74; in Seneca 111, 115–18

pallium/palla (mantle) 9, 189, 196, 212n. 55, 250n. 111

pantomimic mask 4, 6, 7, 9, 16, 26, 47, 100, 209n. 26, 212n. 52, 226n. 244

pantomimic costume 9, 196, 212n. 55, 233n. 60 *see also pallium*

pantomimic orchestra 9 *see also* musical accompaniment

pantomimic thematic repertoire 1, 3, 4, 6, 12–14, 20, 26, 34, 36, 84–5, 118, 119, 149, 157, 175–6, 186, 194, 207n. 1, 212n. 65, 212n. 67, 213n. 69, 213n. 71, 213n. 73, 217n. 126, 222n. 182, 232n. 57, 237n. 50, 239n. 73, 239n. 74, 239n.

79, 240n. 90, 241n. 106, 246n. 35, 248n. 83, 248n. 84, 249n. 105, 251n. 128

paratactic style 27, 97, 102, 114, 133, 197

Paris (dancer) 5, 14, 34, 210 n. 33

passion-restraint scene 81–2, 134, 135, 230n. 32

Phaedra, representation as love-sick: in pantomime 115, 238n. 67; in Seneca 112–15, 133–5

plot development, lack of 69–73

post-classical drama viii, 80, 205n. 6

Proteus 153, 211n. 43

Pylades (dancer) 3–6, 22, 29, 118, 208n. 13, 208n. 15, 208n. 17, 209n. 21, 210n. 35, 210n. 36, 210n. 37, 211n. 41, 237n. 50, 240n. 90

recitation vii, 90, 92, 109

running commentaries, definition of 91

saltare (*vox propria* for pantomime) 37, 222n. 186

scabellum/scabella 9, 30, 223n. 190

secondary roles 8, 231n. 50

sexual roles, interchange of 26, 217n. 128

soliloquy 35, 70, 77, 79, 80, 141, 155, 228n. 12, 233n. 60

staccato mode 102, 114, 133

stichomythia 81, 82–3

stupidus (mimic role) 32, 39–40, 50–1

sub-literary genres ix, xi, 1, 21–5, 51, 201, 206n. 15, 222n. 180

Tiberius (Roman emperor) 4, 5, 210n. 29, 223n. 200

Tiresias 151–2, 186–90, 192, 230n. 26

tragoedia cantata viii

tragoedia rhetorica x, 206n.16

tragoedia saltata viii

Turnus, role in pantomime x, 5, 207n. 19, 213n. 73, 234n. 8

verbal scenery 48, 150, 244n. 11

violence, representation of 13, 20, 70, 119, 127, 172, 103, 148, 213n. 70

wild animal, comparison with 94: Agamemnon 122, 239n. 86; Astyanax 181; Atreus 172–3; Deianira 120; Medea 98; Oedipus 116

zelotipia 33, 37, 118–19, 221n. 163, 221n. 165, 223n. 188

Zeus, adulterous love of 34, 221n. 168

CPSIA information can be obtained at www.ICGtesting.com
Printed in the USA
LVOW04s1759300715

448266LV00003B/78/P